App Inventor 2

Create Your Own Android Apps

David Wolber, Hal Abelson, Ellen Spertus, and Liz Looney

Beijing • Cambridge • Farnham • Köln • Sebastopol • Tokyo O'REILLY®

App Inventor 2
by David Wolber, Hal Abelson, Ellen Spertus, and Liz Looney

Printed in the United States of America.

Published by O'Reilly Media, Inc., 1005 Gravenstein Highway North, Sebastopol, CA 95472.

O'Reilly books may be purchased for educational, business, or sales promotional use. Online editions are also available for most titles (*http://safaribooksonline.com*). For more information, contact our corporate/institutional sales department: 800-998-9938 or *corporate@oreilly.com*.

Editor: Rachel Roumeliotis
Production Editor: Kara Ebrahim
Copyeditor: Dianne Russell
Proofreader: Eliahu Sussman
Indexer: Wendy Catalano
Interior Designer: Monica Kamsvaag
Cover Designer: Ellie Volckhausen
Illustrator: Rebecca Demarest

April 2011: First Edition
October 2014: Second Edition

Revision History for the Second Edition
2014-10-03: First Release

See *http://oreilly.com/catalog/errata.csp?isbn=9781491906842* for release details.

978-1-491-90684-2

[LSI]

Table of Contents

Part II. Inventor's Manual

Foreword

Our consumer culture gives us all sorts of opportunities for entertainment, pleasure, and sometimes even learning. However, by and large, these are passive activities. That's OK—we all like to kick back sometimes and be entertained—but it shouldn't be the whole picture. In addition to the appeal of consuming, there's the satisfaction of producing—that is, of creating. It's the joy and pride that results when we draw a picture, build a model airplane, or bake some bread.

The high-tech objects (like cell phones, tablet computers, TVs, etc.) that we use today to consume entertainment and information are black boxes to most of us. Their workings are incomprehensible and, while there are capabilities in some of them that enable the user to draw pictures, make videos, etc., they are not, in and of themselves, creative media. In other words, most people can't create the apps that run on these gadgets.

What if we could change that? What if we could take creative control of our everyday gadgets, like cell phones? What if building an app for your cell phone was as easy as drawing a picture or baking a loaf of bread? What if we could close the gap between the objects of our consumer culture and the media of our creative lives?

For one, it could demystify those objects. Rather than being black boxes, impenetrable to our sight, they become objects that can be tinkered with. They become objects capable of our understanding. We gain a less passive and more creative relationship to them, and we get to play with these devices in a much deeper, more significant way when we can actually build things for them.

When Hal Abelson first spoke to me about the idea that became App Inventor, we talked about the unique motivating force that cell phones could have in education. He wondered if we could use that motivating force to help introduce students to concepts in computer science. As we built it and tried it in classes like Dave Wolber's, we started to realize that something even more powerful was happening: App Inventor was starting to turn students from consumers to creators. Students thought it was fun and exhilarating to build apps for their phones! When one of Dave's students built the simple but powerful No Texting While Driving app, we really started to imagine what would happen if anybody, not just professional software engineers, could build an app.

So, at Google, we worked hard to make App Inventor easier, more fun to use, and ever more powerful. Hal and his incredible team at MIT took over in 2012 and have continued to improve the experience for beginners and developers alike. The new version, described in this book and commonly called *App Inventor 2*, provides a fully in-browser experience that can turn you into an app creator within minutes!

The authors of this book are truly world-class educators and software engineers. I'd like to personally thank them for their work in building, testing, and documenting App Inventor and, of course, for writing this wonderful book.

Now go, unleash your creativity and build an app!

—Mark Friedman,
Tech Lead and Manager of the App Inventor for Android project, Google

Preface

You're on your regular running route, just jogging along, and an idea for the next killer mobile app hits you. All the way home, you don't even care what your time is, all you can think about is getting your idea out there. But how exactly do you do that? You're no programmer, and that would take years, and time is money, and...well, someone has probably done it already anyway. Just like that, your idea is dead in the water.

Now imagine a different world, where creating apps doesn't require years of programming experience, where artists, scientists, humanitarians, health-care workers, attorneys, firefighters, marathon runners, football coaches, and people from all walks of life can create apps. Imagine a world where you can transform ideas into prototypes without hiring programmers, where you can make apps that work specifically for you, where you can adapt mobile computing to fit your personal needs.

This is the world of App Inventor, a visual programming tool for building mobile apps. Based on a visual "blocks" programming method that's proven successful even with kids, App Inventor dramatically lowers the barriers to creating apps for Android phones and devices. How about a video game where the characters look like you and your friends? Or a "did you pick up the milk?" app that reminds you if it's after 3 p.m. and you're near the grocery store? Or a quiz app you give your significant other that's in fact a surprise marriage proposal? "Question 4: Will you marry me? Press the button to accept by sending a text message." Someone really created an App Inventor app to propose marriage like this, and she said yes!

A Blocks Language for Mobile Phones

App Inventor is a visual, drag-and-drop tool for building mobile apps on the Android platform. You design the user interface (the visual appearance) of an app using a web-based graphical user interface (GUI) builder, then you specify the app's behavior by piecing together "blocks" as if you were working on a puzzle.

Figure P-1 shows the blocks for an early version of an app created by Daniel Finnegan, a university student who had never programmed before. Can you tell what the app does?

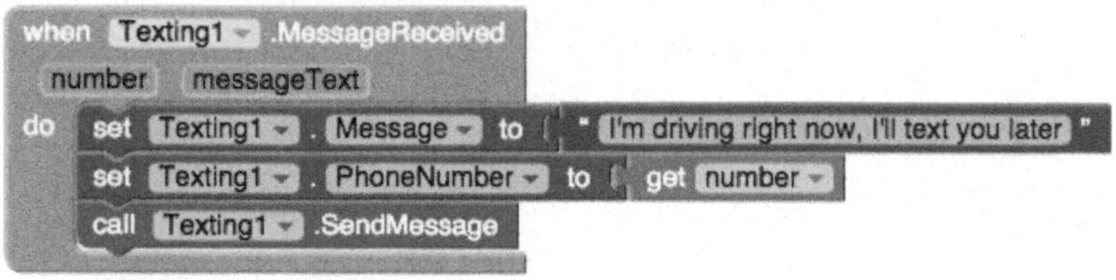

Figure P-1. An app that autoresponds to texts

The app is a text "answering machine." You launch it when you're driving and it autoresponds to the texts you receive.

Because the blocks are more understandable than traditional programming code, you're immediately drawn in, and the real-world utility gets you asking questions like: Can I make it so the received texts are spoken aloud? Can I make it so the response sent back could be customized? Can I write an app that lets people vote for something by text, like on *American Idol*? The answer to all these questions is "yes," and in this book, we'll show you how.

What Can You Do with App Inventor?

Lots of stuff!

Play
: Creating apps for your phone is fun, and App Inventor promotes exploration and discovery. Just open App Inventor in a web browser, connect your phone, and start putting together blocks like those in the app shown in Figure P-1. You can immediately see and interact with the app you're building on the phone. So you're programming, but you're also emailing your friend to send you a text to test your app, or you're controlling a LEGO NXT robot with the app you just built, or you're unplugging the phone and walking outside to see if your app is using the location sensor correctly.

Prototype
: Have an idea for an app? Instead of writing it down on a napkin or letting it float off into the ether, build a quick prototype. Prototypes are incomplete and unrefined working models of your idea. Expressing an idea in text is like writing a to a friend or loved one with prose; think of an App Inventor prototype as poetry to a venture capitalist. In this way, App Inventor can serve as an electronic napkin for mobile app development.

Build apps with personal utility
: In the current state of the mobile app world, we're stuck with the apps we're given. Who hasn't complained about an app and wished it could be personalized or adjusted in some way? With App Inventor, you can build an app exactly how you want it. In Chapter 3, you'll build a MoleMash game that lets you score points by touching a

randomly moving mole. But instead of using the image of the mole in the tutorial, you can customize it so that you mash a picture of your brother or sister—something that only you might want to do, but who cares? In Chapter 8, you'll write a quiz app that asks questions about US Presidents, but you can easily customize it to ask questions on any topic you want, from your favorite music to your family history.

Develop complete apps
: App Inventor is not just a prototyping system or an interface designer—you can build complete, general-purpose apps. The language provides all the fundamental programming building blocks like loops and conditionals, but in block form.

Teach and learn
: Whether you're at a middle school, high school, or university, App Inventor is a great teaching and learning tool. It's great for computer science, but is also a terrific tool for math, physics, entrepreneurship, and just about any other discipline. The key is that you learn by creating. Instead of memorizing formulas, you build an app to, say, find the closest hospital (or mall!). Instead of writing an essay on Black History, you create a multimedia quiz app with video and speeches from Martin Luther King, Jr., and Malcolm X. We think App Inventor, and this book, can be a great tool in classes throughout the curriculum.

Why App Inventor Works

Most people say that App Inventor is easy to use because of its visual, drag-and-drop interface. But what does this mean? Why is App Inventor so easy to use?

You don't have to remember and type instructions
: One of the biggest sources of frustration for beginning programmers comes from typing in code and having the computer spit back indecipherable error messages. This frustration discourages many beginners from programming before they even get to the more fun, logical problem solving.

You choose from a set of options
: With App Inventor, the components and blocks are organized into drawers that are readily available to you. You program by finding a block—which helps specify the functionality you want to build—and dragging it into the program. You don't have to remember what the instructions are or refer to a programming manual.

Only some blocks plug in to each other
: Instead of chastising programmers with cryptic error messages, App Inventor's blocks language restricts you from making many mistakes in the first place. For instance, if a function block expects a number, you can't plug in text. This doesn't eliminate all errors, but it sure helps.

You deal with events directly
: Traditional programming languages were designed when programming was like working with recipes, or sets of instructions. But with graphical interfaces, and

especially with mobile apps where events can happen at any time (for example, receiving a text message or phone call), most programs are not recipes, but are instead sets of event handlers. An event handler is a way of saying, "When this happens, the app does this." In a traditional language like Java, you have to understand classes, objects, and special objects called listeners to express a simple event. With App Inventor, you can say, "When a user clicks this button..." or "When a text is received..." by dragging out a "When" block.

What Kind of Apps Can You Build?

You can build many different types of apps with App Inventor. Use your imagination, and you can create all kinds of fun, useful apps.

Games
: People often begin by building games like MoleMash (Chapter 3) or apps that let you draw funny pictures on your friend's faces (Chapter 2). As you progress, you can build your own versions of more complex games like Pac-Man and Space Invaders. You can even use the phone's sensors and move characters by tilting the phone (Chapter 5).

Educational software
: App building is not limited to simple games. You can also build apps that inform and educate. You can create a quiz app (Chapter 8) to help you and your classmates study for a test, or even a create-a-quiz app (Chapter 10) that lets the users of your app create their own quizzes (think of all the parents that would love this one for those long road trips!).

Location-aware apps
: Because App Inventor provides access to a GPS-location sensor, you can build apps that know where you are. You can build an app to help you remember where you parked your car (Chapter 7), an app that shows the location of your friends or colleagues at a concert or conference, or your own custom tour app of your school, workplace, or a museum.

High-tech apps
: You can create apps that scan bar codes, talk, listen (recognize words), play music, make music (Chapter 9), play video, detect the phone's orientation and acceleration, take pictures, and make phone calls. Smartphones are like Swiss Army knives for technology, and App Inventor makes it easy to control that technology.

SMS Texting apps
: No Texting While Driving (Chapter 4) is just one example of the SMS processing apps you can build. You can also write an app that periodically texts "missing you" to your loved ones, or an app like Broadcast Hub (Chapter 11) that helps coordinate large events. Want an app that lets your friends vote for things by texting, like on *American Idol*? You can build it with App Inventor.

Apps that control robots

Chapter 12 shows how to create an app that acts as a controller for a LEGO robot. You can use the phone as a remote control, or you can program it to be a "brain" that the robot carries around with it. The robot and phone communicate via Bluetooth, and App Inventor's Bluetooth components let you create similar apps that control other Bluetooth devices.

Complex apps

App Inventor dramatically lowers the entrance barrier to programming and lets you build flashy, high-tech apps within hours. But the language also provides loops, conditionals, and other programming and logic constructs necessary to build apps with complex logic. You'll be surprised at how fun such logic problems can be when you're trying to build an app.

Web-enabled apps

App Inventor also provides a way for your apps to communicate with the Web. You can write apps that pull in data from Twitter or an RSS feed, or an Amazon Bookstore Browser that lets you check the online cost of a book by scanning its barcode.

Who Can Build Apps?

App Inventor is freely available for anyone to use. It runs online (instead of directly on your computer) and is accessible from any browser. You don't even need a phone to use it: you can test your apps on an included Android emulator. As of September 2014, there were 1.9 million registered App Inventor users from 195 countries. Together they have created nearly five million apps.

Who are these app builders? Were they already programmers when they started? Some of them were, but most were not.

One of the most telling experiences has been the courses that coauthor David Wolber teaches at the University of San Francisco. At USF, App Inventor is taught as part of a general education computer science course targeting primarily business and humanities students. Many students take the course because they are afraid of math, and the course fulfills the dreaded Math Core requirement. The vast majority have never even dreamed of writing a computer program.

Despite having no prior experience, the students have been successful in learning App Inventor and building great apps. An English major created the first No Texting While Driving app, two communications majors created Android, Where's My Car? (Chapter 7), and an International Studies major created the Broadcast Hub app (Chapter 11). When an art major knocked on Wolber's office door one night well after hours asking how to write a `while` loop, Wolber knew that App Inventor had dramatically changed the computer science education landscape.

The media grasped the significance as well. The *New York Times* called App Inventor "Do-It-Yourself App Creation Software." The *San Francisco Chronicle* reported on the

USF students' work in an article, "Google brings app making to the masses." *Wired* magazine featured Daniel Finnegan, the author of No Texting While Driving, and wrote that "Finnegan's story illustrates a powerful point: It's time for computer programming to be democratized."

The cat is, as they say, out of the bag (your first app will involve a kitty, by the way). App Inventor is now used in middle school and high school courses around the world; by over 2,500 girls in 28 countries who have participated in in the Technovation Challenge (*http://www.technovationchallenge.org/*), an after-school program for high school girls; in pilot courses for the new high school Computer Science Principles Advance Placement course (*http://mobile-csp.org*); and in new introductory courses at several universities. There are now thousands of hobbyists, businesspersons, marriage proposers, and tinkerers roaming the App Inventor site building apps. Want to get in on the action? No programming experience is required!

Conventions Used in This Book

The following typographical conventions are used in this book:

Italic
: Indicates new terms, URLs, email addresses, filenames, and file extensions.

`Constant width`
: Used for program listings, as well as within paragraphs to refer to program elements such as variable or function names, databases, data types, environment variables, statements, and keywords.

`Constant width bold`
: Shows commands or other text that should be typed literally by the user.

`Constant width italic`
: Shows text that should be replaced with user-supplied values or by values determined by context.

Tip This element signifies a tip or suggestion.

Note This element signifies instructions for testing the app you are building.

Using Code Examples

Supplemental material (code examples, exercises, etc.) is available for download at *https://appinventor.org/bookFiles*.

This book is here to help you get your job done. In general, if example code is offered with this book, you may use it in your programs and documentation. You do not need to contact us for permission unless you're reproducing a significant portion of the code. For example, writing a program that uses several chunks of code from this book does not require permission. Selling or distributing a CD-ROM of examples from O'Reilly books does require permission. Answering a question by citing this book and quoting example code does not require permission. Incorporating a significant amount of example code from this book into your product's documentation does require permission.

We appreciate, but do not require, attribution. An attribution usually includes the title, author, publisher, and ISBN. For example: "*App Inventor 2* by David Wolber, Hal Abelson, Ellen Spertus, and Liz Looney (O'Reilly). Copyright 2015 David Wolber, Hal Abelson, Ellen Spertus, and Liz Looney, 978-1-491-90684-2."

If you feel your use of code examples falls outside fair use or the permission given above, feel free to contact us at *permissions@oreilly.com*.

Safari® Books Online

Safari Books Online is an on-demand digital library that delivers expert content in both book and video form from the world's leading authors in technology and business.

Technology professionals, software developers, web designers, and business and creative professionals use Safari Books Online as their primary resource for research, problem solving, learning, and certification training.

Safari Books Online offers a range of plans and pricing for enterprise, government, education, and individuals.

Members have access to thousands of books, training videos, and prepublication manuscripts in one fully searchable database from publishers like O'Reilly Media, Prentice Hall Professional, Addison-Wesley Professional, Microsoft Press, Sams, Que,

Peachpit Press, Focal Press, Cisco Press, John Wiley & Sons, Syngress, Morgan Kaufmann, IBM Redbooks, Packt, Adobe Press, FT Press, Apress, Manning, New Riders, McGraw-Hill, Jones & Bartlett, Course Technology, and hundreds more. For more information about Safari Books Online, please visit us online.

How to Contact Us

Please address comments and questions concerning this book to the publisher:

O'Reilly Media, Inc.
1005 Gravenstein Highway North
Sebastopol, CA 95472
800-998-9938 (in the United States or Canada)
707-829-0515 (international or local)
707-829-0104 (fax)

We have a web page for this book, where we list errata, examples, and any additional information. You can access this page at *http://bit.ly/app-inventor2*.

To comment or ask technical questions about this book, send email to *bookquestions@oreilly.com*.

For more information about our books, courses, conferences, and news, see our website at *http://www.oreilly.com*.

Find us on Facebook: *http://facebook.com/oreilly*

Follow us on Twitter: *http://twitter.com/oreillymedia*

Watch us on YouTube: *http://www.youtube.com/oreillymedia*

Acknowledgments

The educational perspective that motivates App Inventor holds that computing can be a vehicle for engaging powerful ideas through active learning. As such, App Inventor is part of an ongoing movement in computers and education that began with the work of Seymour Papert and the MIT Logo Group in the 1960s, and whose influence persists today through many activities and programs designed to support computational thinking.

App Inventor's design draws upon prior research in educational computing and upon Google's work with online development environments. The visual programming framework is closely related to the MIT Scratch programming language. The specific implementation for App Inventor 2 is based on Blockly, which is developed at Google and led by Neil Fraser. The compiler that translates the visual blocks language for implementation on Android uses the Kawa Language Framework and

Kawa's dialect of the Scheme programming language, developed by Per Bothner and distributed as part of the GNU Operating System by the Free Software Foundation.

The authors would like to thank Google and the original App Inventor team for their support of our work and teaching efforts at USF, Mills College, and MIT. Special thanks go to App Inventor Technical Lead Mark Friedman, Project Manager Karen Parker, and engineers Sharon Perl and Debby Wallach.

We would also like to thank the MIT App Inventor team for their work and continued development of App Inventor. Special thanks go to Technical Lead Andrew Mckinney, all-around guru Jeff Schiller, education and outreach directors Shaileen Pokress and Josh Sheldon, unsung hero and engineer Jose Domínguez, and key "sabbatical" contributors Franklyn Turbak and Ralph Morelli.

We also owe a special thanks to University of San Francisco student Cayla Shaver for her extraordinary editing work and helping convert this book for App Inventor 2.

Finally, we'd like to acknowledge the support of our respective spouses: Ellen's husband, Keith Golden; Hal's wife, Lynn Abelson; Liz's husband, Kevin Looney; and David's wife, Minerva Novoa. New mother Ellen is also grateful for the help of nanny Neil Fullagar.

PART I
AI2 Tutorials

CHAPTER 1

HelloPurr

This chapter gets you started building apps. It presents the key elements of App Inventor, the Component Designer and the Blocks Editor, and leads you through the basic steps of creating your first app, HelloPurr. When you're finished, you'll be ready to build apps on your own.

A typical first program with a new computer system prints the message "Hello World" to show that everything is connected correctly. This tradition goes back to the 1970s and Brian Kernighan's work on the C programming language at Bell Labs. With App Inventor, even the simplest apps do more than just show messages: they play sounds and react when you touch the device. So, we're going to get started right away with something more exciting: your first app (as shown in Figure 1-1) will be "HelloPurr," a picture of a cat that meows when you touch it and purrs when you shake the device on which it's being viewed.

Figure 1-1. The HelloPurr app

What You'll Learn

The chapter covers the following topics:

- Building apps by selecting components and specifying their behavior.
- Using the Component Designer to select components. Some components are visible on the device's screen and some aren't.
- Adding media (sounds and images) to apps by uploading them from your computer.
- Using the Blocks Editor to assemble blocks that define the components' behavior.
- Testing apps with App Inventor's *live testing*. This lets you see how apps will look and behave on the device, step by step, even as you're building them.
- Packaging the apps you build and downloading them to a device.

The App Inventor Environment

You can begin programming with App Inventor by opening a browser to *ai2.appinventor.mit.edu*. This opens the newest version of App Inventor, which was released in December, 2013. Some people call it App Inventor 2, but it is formally just named *App Inventor*, and the previous version is called *App Inventor Classic*. In this book, you'll be using the new version.

The App Inventor programming environment has three key parts:

- The *Component Designer* (Figure 1-2). You use it to select components for your app and specify their properties.
- The *Blocks Editor* (Figure 1-3). You use it to specify how the components will behave (e.g., what happens when a user clicks a button).
- An Android device with which you can actually run and test your app as you are developing it. If you don't have an Android device handy, you can test the apps you build by using the Android emulator that comes with the system.

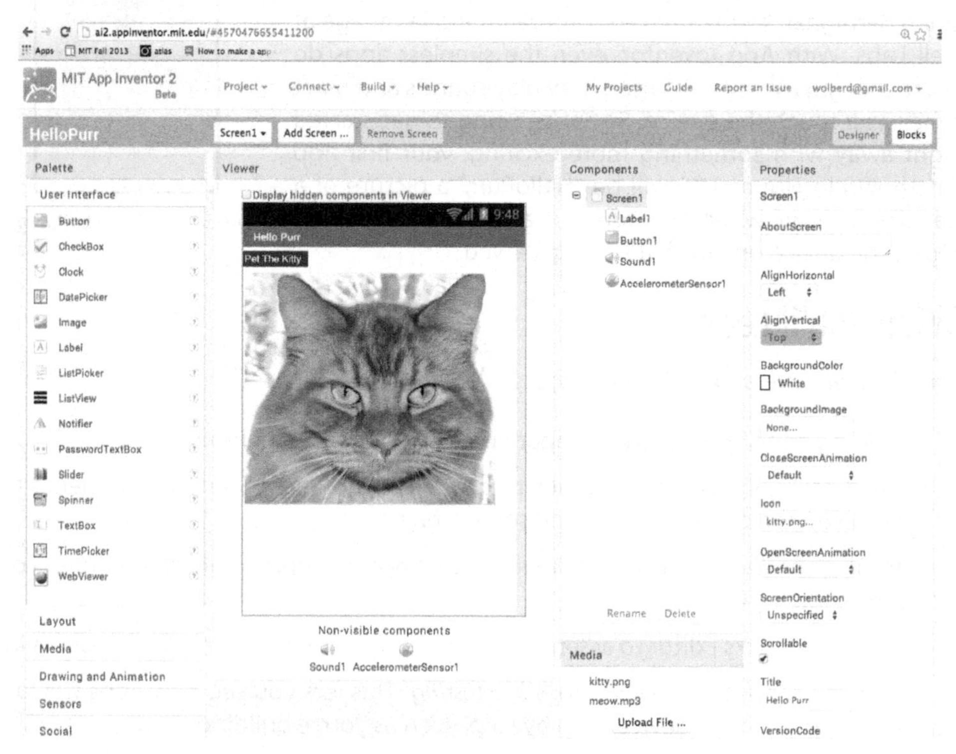

Figure 1-2. The Components Designer for specifying how the app will look

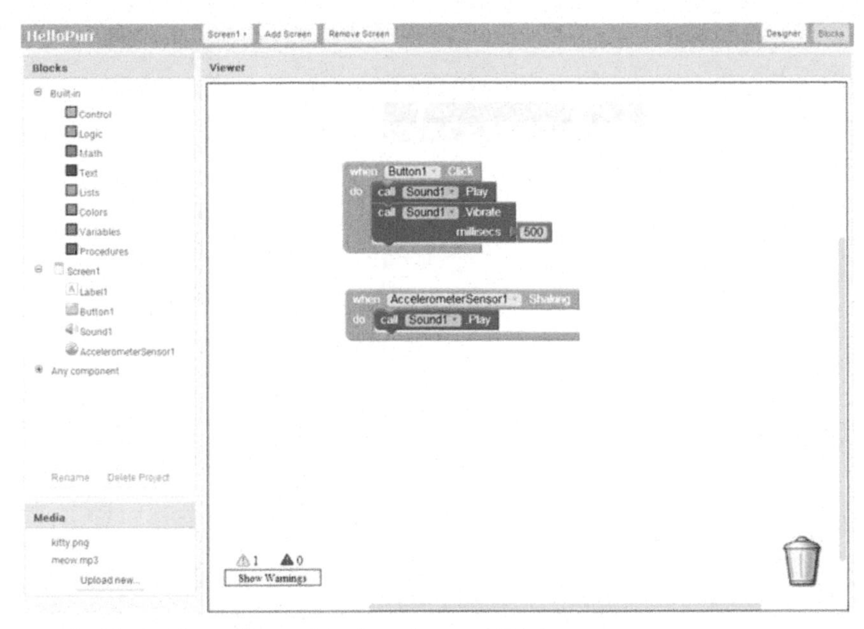

Figure 1-3. The Blocks Editor for specifying how the app will behave

The first time you browse to *ai2.appinventor.mit.edu,* you'll see the Projects page, which will be mostly blank because you haven't created any projects yet. To create a project, at the upper left of the page, click "New Project," enter the project name "HelloPurr" (one word with no spaces), and then click OK.

The first window that opens is the Component Designer. The Blocks Editor is available by clicking on the "Blocks" button in the upper-right corner of the window.

App Inventor is a *cloud computing* tool, meaning that your app is stored on an online server as you work. So if you close App Inventor, your app will be there when you return; you don't have to save anything on your computer as you would with, for example, a Microsoft Word file.

Designing the Components

The first tool you'll use is the Component Designer (or just Designer). Components are the elements you combine to create apps, like ingredients in a recipe. Some components are very simple, like a `Label` component, which shows text on the screen, or a `Button` component, which you tap to initiate an action. Other components are more elaborate: a drawing `Canvas` that can hold still images or animations; an *accelerometer*, which is a motion sensor that detects when you move or shake the device; or components that make or send text messages, play music, and video, get information from websites, and so on.

When you open the Designer, it will appear as shown in Figure 1-4.

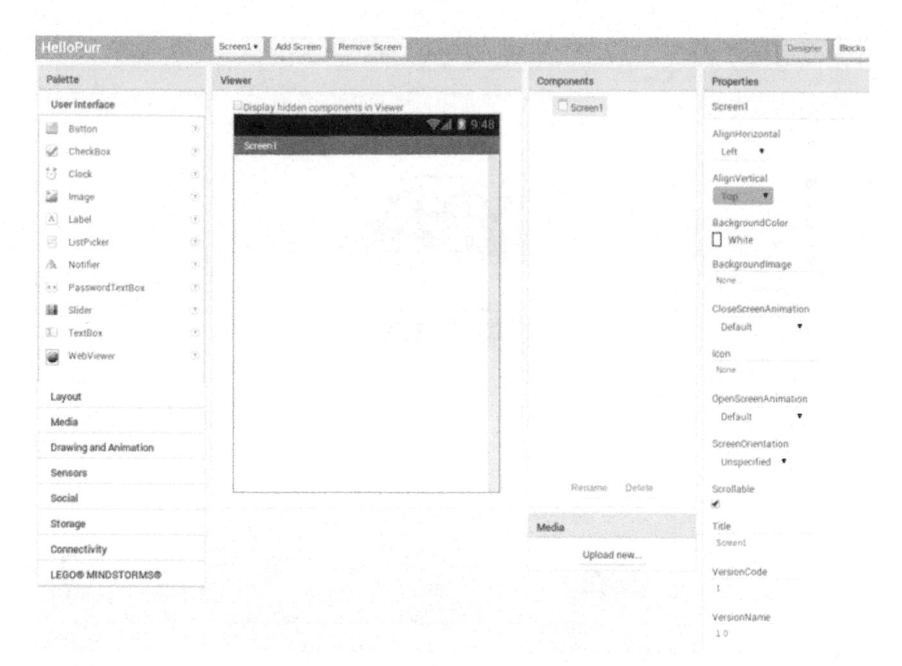

Figure 1-4. The App Inventor Component Designer

The Designer is divided into several areas:

- Toward the center is a white area called the *Viewer*. This is where you place components and arrange them to map out what you want your app to look like. The Viewer shows only a rough indication of how the app will look, so for example, a line of text might break at a different place on your device than on the Viewer. To see how your app will *really* appear, you'll need to test it on your device or the emulator (we'll show you how to do this shortly).
- To the left of the Viewer is the *Palette*, which is a list of components from which you can select. The Palette is divided into sections; at this point, only the User Interface components are visible, but you can see components in other sections of the Palette by clicking the headers labeled Layout, Media, and so on.
- To the right of the Viewer is the *Components* list, which lists the components in your project. Any component that you drag into the Viewer will also show up in this list. Currently, the project has only one component listed: `Screen1`, which represents the screen of the device itself.
- Under the Components list is an area that shows the *Media* (pictures and sound) in the project. This project doesn't have any media yet, but you'll be adding some soon.
- To the far right is a section that shows the Properties of components; when you click a component in the Viewer, you'll see its Properties listed here. Properties are details about each component that you can change. (For example, when clicking

on a `Label` component, you might see properties related to color, text, font, and so on.) Right now, it shows the properties of the screen (called `Screen1`), which include a background color, a background image, and a title.

For the HelloPurr app, you'll need two *visible* components (think of these as components that you can actually see in the app): the `Label` component reading "Pet the Kitty" and a `Button` component with an image of a cat in it. You'll also need a *non-visible* `Sound` component that knows how to play sounds, such as "meow," and an `Accelerometer` component for detecting when the device is being shaken. Don't worry—we'll walk you through each component, step by step.

Making a Label

The first component to add is a `Label`:

1. Go to the Palette, open the User Interface drawer if it is not open, click `Label` (which appears about six spots down in the list of components), and drag it to the Viewer. You'll see a rectangular shape appear on the Viewer, containing the words "Text for Label1."
2. Look at the Properties box on the right side of the Designer. It shows the properties of the label. About halfway down, there's a property called Text, with a box for the label's text. Change the text to "Pet the Kitty" and press Return. You'll see the text change in the Viewer.
3. Change the `BackgroundColor` of the label by clicking the box, which currently reads None, to select a color from the list that appears. Select Blue. Also change the `TextColor` of the label to Yellow. Finally, change the `FontSize` to 20.

The Designer should now appear as shown in Figure 1-5.

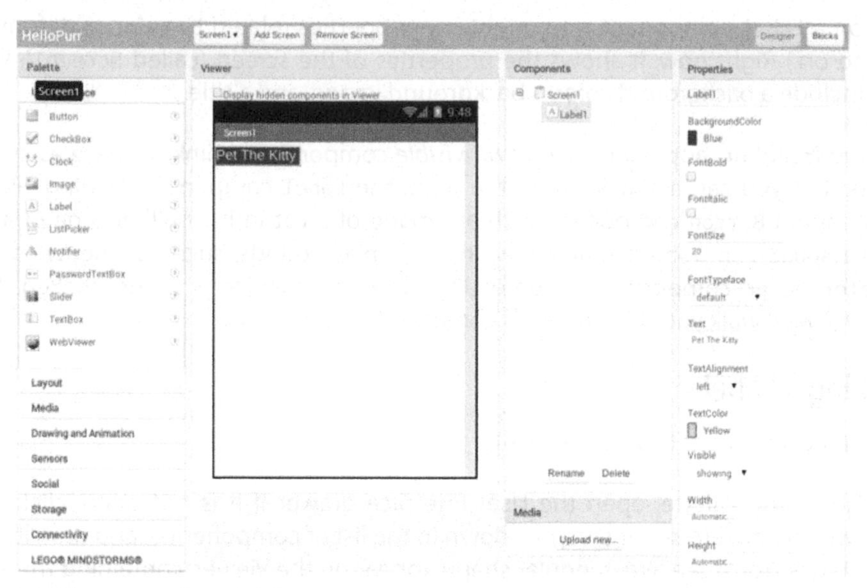

Figure 1-5. The app now has a label

Adding the Button

The kitty for HelloPurr is implemented as a `Button` component—you create a normal button and then change the button image to the kitty. To make the basic button first, go to the Palette in the Designer and click `Button` (at the top of the list of components). Drag it onto the Viewer, placing it below the label. You'll see a rectangular button appear on the Viewer.

Now you've got a button that you'll use to trigger the sound effect when someone taps it, but we really want it to look like the picture of the kitty, not a plain, old rectangle. To make the button look like the kitty:

1. First, you need to download a picture of the kitty and save it on your computer desktop. You can download it at *http://appinventor.org/bookFiles/HelloPurr/kitty.png*. The extension *.png* is a standard image format similar to *.jpg* and *.gif*; all of these file types will work in App Inventor, as will most standard sound files such as *.mpg* or *.mp3*. You can also download the sound file you'll need to make the kitty meow at *http://appinventor.org/bookFiles/HelloPurr/meow.mp3*.
2. The Properties box should display the properties of the button. If it doesn't, click the button in the Viewer to reveal the button's properties on the right. In the Properties box, click the area under Image (which currently reads "None...").
3. Click "Upload file." Then, click "Choose File" and browse to select the *kitty.png* file you downloaded to your computer earlier, and then click OK.
4. After the image uploads, *kitty.png* should be listed as an option for the image property of the button. Click OK to choose it. You'll also see the file listed in the

Media area of the Designer window, just below the Components list. And if you look at the button in the designer, you'll see the kitty picture displayed—the button now looks like a kitty.

5. You might have also noticed that the kitty picture still has the words "Text for Button 1" displayed on it. You probably don't want that in your app, so go ahead and blank out the `Text` property of `Button1`.

Now, the Designer should appear as shown in Figure 1-6.

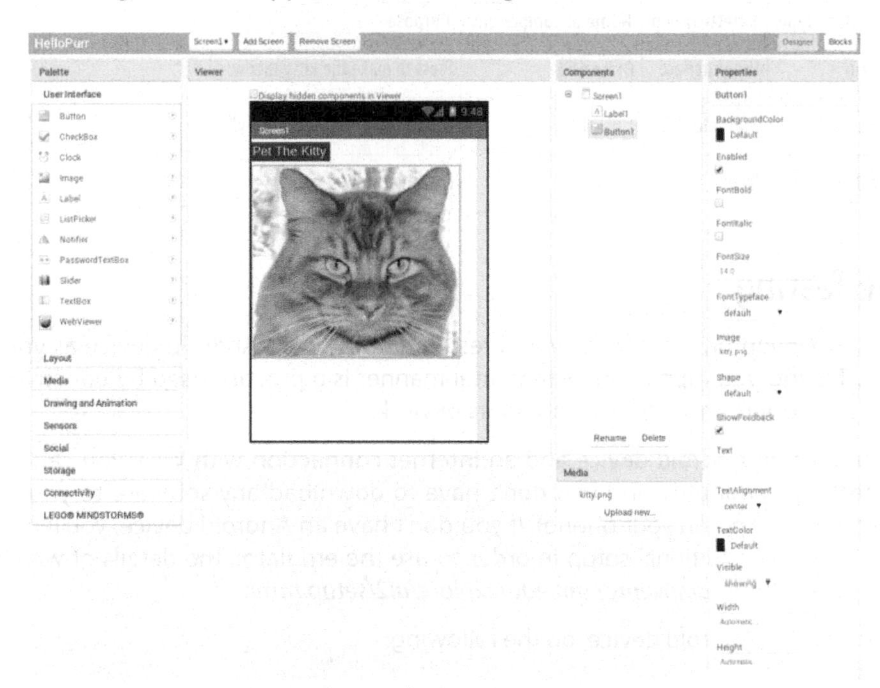

Figure 1-6. The app with a label and a button with an image on it

Adding the Meow Sound

In your app, you want the kitty to meow when you tap the button. For this, you'll need to add the meow sound and program the button behavior to play that sound when the button is clicked:

1. If you haven't downloaded the *meow.mp3* file to your computer's desktop, do so now by using this link: *http://appinventor.org/bookFiles/HelloPurr/meow.mp3*.

2. Go to the Palette at the left of the Designer window and click the header marked Media to expand the Media section. Drag out a `Sound` component and place it in the Viewer. No matter where you drop it, it will appear in the area at the bottom of the Viewer marked "Non-visible components." Non-visible components are objects that do things for the app but don't appear in the visual user interface.

3. Click `Sound1` to show its properties. Click the `Source` property and then go through the steps to upload and choose the *meow.mp3* file you downloaded earlier. When you're done, you should see both *kitty.png* and *meow.mp3* listed in the Media section of the Designer.

Table 1-1 lists the components that you've gathered for your app so far.

Table 1-1. The components you've added to the HelloPurr app

Component type	Palette group	Name of component	Purpose
`Button`	User Interface	`Button1`	Press to make the kitty meow.
`Label`	User Interface	`Label1`	Shows the text "Pet the Kitty."
`Sound`	Media	`Sound1`	Play the meow sound.

Live Testing

With App Inventor, you can view and test your app on an Android device as you create it. Testing your app in an incremental manner is a practice used by effective software developers and will save you hours of work.

If you have an Android device and an internet connection with WiFi, you can set up live testing in minutes, and you don't have to download any software to your computer (just an app on your phone). If you don't have an Android device, you'll need to perform some additional setup in order to use the emulator, the details of which are covered at *http://appinventor.mit.edu/explore/ai2/setup.html*.

If you have an Android device, do the following:

1. On your device, download and install the "MIT AI2 Companion" app from the Google Play Store. Launch the app when it's installed.
2. Connect both your computer and your device to the same WiFi connection.
3. In App Inventor (in the browser), from the top menu, select Connect and then choose AI Companion, as shown in Figure 1-7.

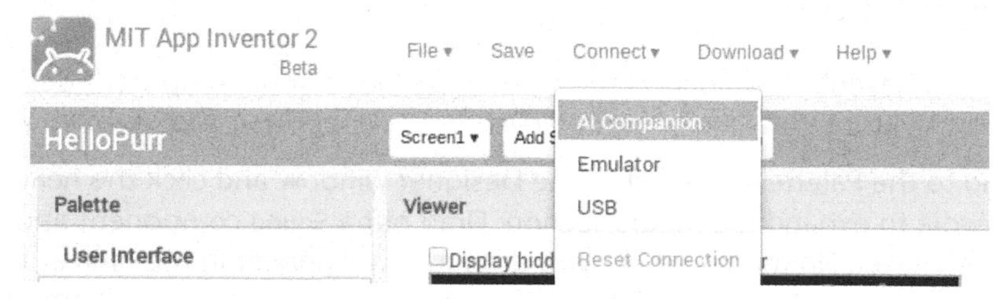

Figure 1-7. Click Connect and then select AI Companion

4. On your device, launch the app you installed, the MIT AI2 Companion, as shown in Figure 1-8. Select "Scan QR Code" and then hold your device up to the QR code on the computer screen to scan it.

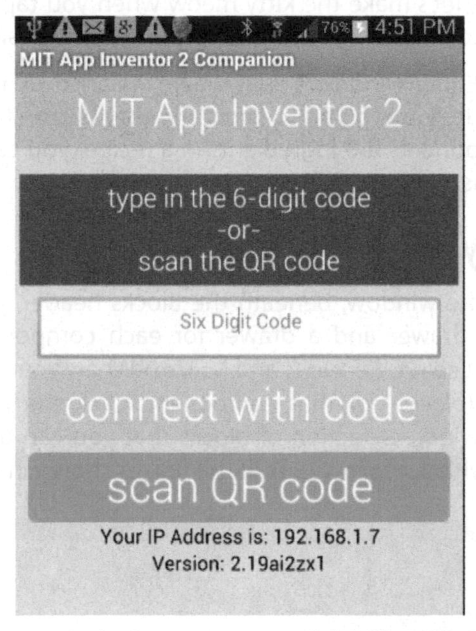

Figure 1-8. On your device, open the Companion app and click "Scan QR Code"

If all goes well, you should see the HelloPurr app running on your device, including all of the components you added. As you make changes in the App Inventor Designer or Blocks Editor, those changes will also appear on the device, as well.

Live testing setup If you have trouble setting up live testing, visit *http://appinventor.mit.edu/explore/ai2/setup.html.*

If your app does appear on the device, go ahead and tap the button. Do you think anything will happen? It won't, because you haven't instructed the button to do anything yet. This is the first important point to understand about App Inventor: for every component you add in the Designer, you have to move over to the Blocks Editor and create the code to make that component do whatever it is that you want it to do.

Adding Behaviors to the Components

You've just added `Button`, `Label`, and `Sound` components as the building blocks for your first app. Now, let's make the kitty meow when you tap the button. You do this with the Blocks Editor. In the top right of the Component Designer, click "Blocks."

Look at the Blocks Editor window. This is where you instruct the components what to do and when to do it. You're going to direct the kitty button to play a sound when the user taps it. If components are ingredients in a recipe, you can think of blocks as the cooking instructions.

Making the Kitty Meow

At the top left of the window, beneath the Blocks header, you'll see a column that includes a Built-in drawer and a drawer for each component you created in the Designer: `Button1`, `Label1`, `Screen1`, and `Sound1`. When you click a drawer, you get a bunch of options (*blocks*) for that component. Click the drawer for `Button1`. The drawer opens, showing a selection of blocks that you can use to build the button's behavior, starting with `Button1.Click` at the top, as shown in Figure 1-9.

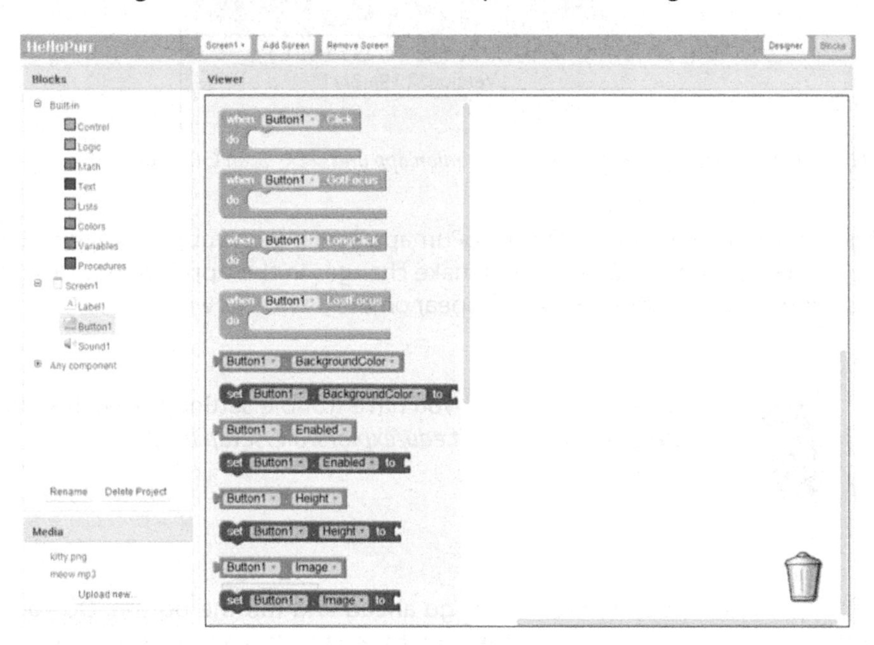

Figure 1-9. Clicking Button1 shows the component's blocks

Click the block labeled `Button1.Click` and drag it into the workspace. You'll notice that the word "when" is included on the `Button1.Click` block. Blocks including the word "when" are called *event handlers*; they specify what components should do *when* some particular event happens. In this case, the event we're interested in happens when the app user taps the image of the kitty (which is really a button), as shown in Figure 1-10. Next, you'll add some blocks to program what will happen in response to that event.

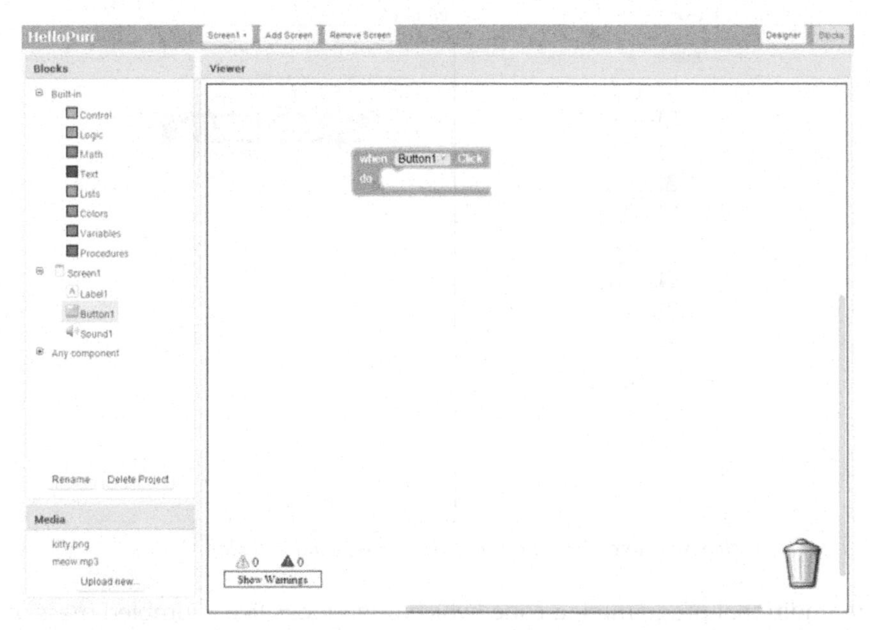

Figure 1-10. You'll specify a response to the user clicking within the Button.Click block

Click `Sound1` to open the drawer for the sound component, and then drag out the `call Sound1.Play` block. (Remember, earlier we set the property for `Sound1` to the meow sound file you downloaded to your computer.) At this point, you might have noticed that the `call Sound1.Play` block is shaped so that it can fit into a gap marked "do" in the `Button1.Click` block. App Inventor is set up so that only certain blocks fit together; this way, you always know you're connecting blocks that actually work together. In this case, blocks with the word "call" cause components to do things. The two blocks should snap together to form a unit, as shown in Figure 1-11, and you'll hear a snapping sound when they connect.

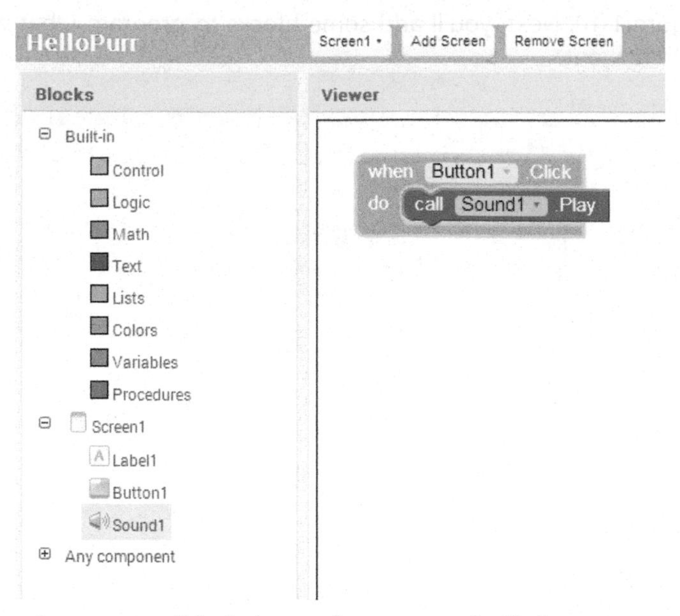

Figure 1-11. Now when someone clicks the button, the meow sound will play

Unlike traditional programming code (which often looks like a jumbled mess of gobbledygook "words"), the event-response blocks in App Inventor spell out the behaviors you're trying to create in a plain, understandable fashion. In this case, we're essentially saying, "Hey, App Inventor, when someone taps the kitty button, play the meow sound."

Test your app *Check to make sure everything is working properly—it's important to test your app each time you add something new. Tap the button on the device (or click it if you are using the emulator). You should hear the kitty meow. Congratulations, your first app is running!*

Adding a Purr

Now we're going to make the kitty purr *and* meow when you tap the button. We'll simulate the purr by making the device vibrate. That might sound hard, but in fact, it's easy to do because the `Sound` component we used to play the meow sound can make the device vibrate, as well. App Inventor helps you tap into this kind of core device functionality without having to deal with *how* the device actually vibrates. You don't need to do anything different in the Designer; you can just add a second function call block to the button click in the Blocks Editor:

1. Go to the Blocks Editor and click `Sound1` to open the drawer.

2. Select `call Sound1.Vibrate` and drag it under the `call Sound1.Play` block in the `Button1.Click` slot. The block should click into place, as shown in Figure 1-12. If it doesn't, try dragging it so that the little notch on the top edge of `call Sound1.Vibrate` touches the little bump on the bottom of `call Sound1.Play`.

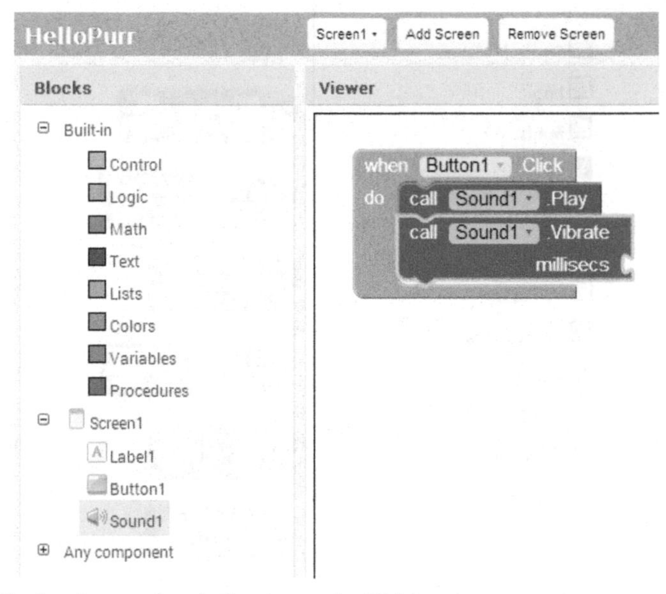

Figure 1-12. Playing the sound and vibrating on the Click event

3. You might have noticed that the `call Sound1.Vibrate` block includes the text "millisecs" at the lower right, and alongside it is an open socket protruding inward from the block's edge. An open socket in a block means that you need to plug something into it to specify more about how the behavior should work. In this case, you must tell the `Vibrate` block how long it should vibrate. You need to specify this time in thousandths of a second (milliseconds), which is pretty common for many programming languages. So, to make the device vibrate for half a second, you need to enter a value of 500 milliseconds. To do that, you need to grab a number block. Click the Math drawer and you'll see a list of blue blocks appear, as shown in Figure 1-13.

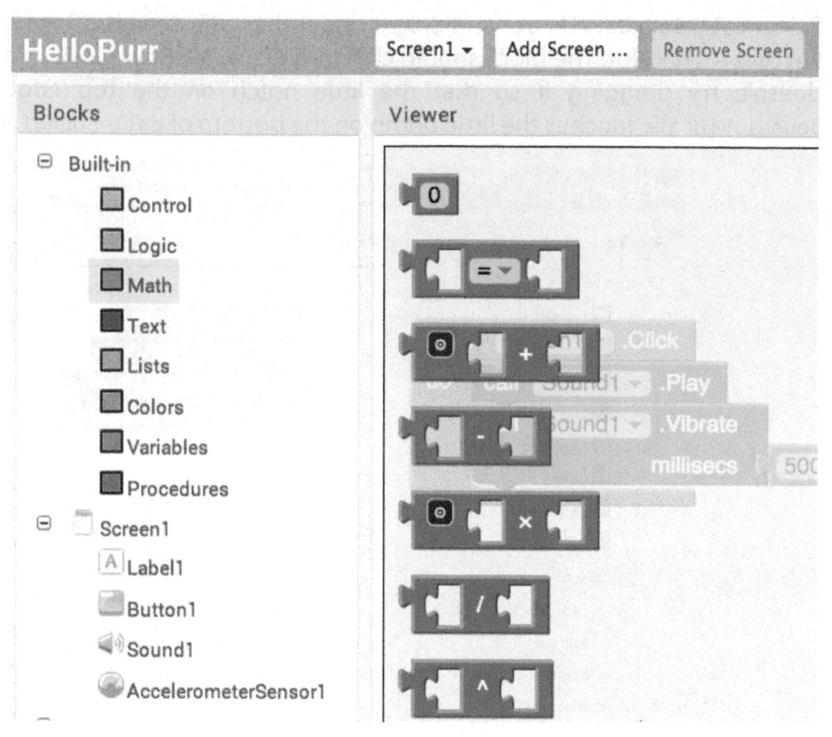

Figure 1-13. Opening the Math drawer

4. At the top of the list, you should see a block with a "0" in it. You can drag this block out and then change the 0 to any number you want. Go ahead and drag out the number block, as shown in Figure 1-14.

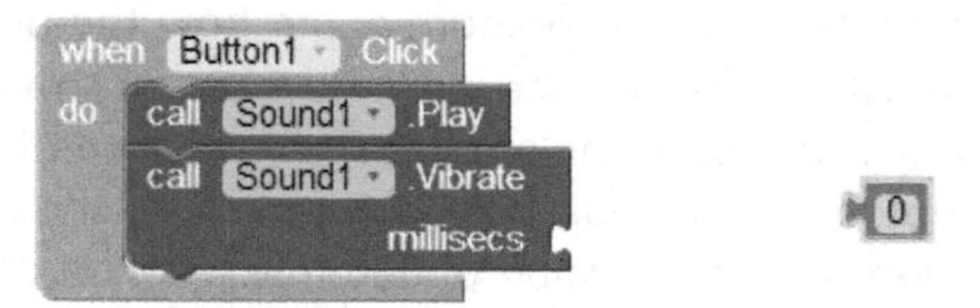

Figure 1-14. Choosing a number block (0 is the default value)

5. Click the 0 and type the new value, 500, as shown in Figure 1-15.

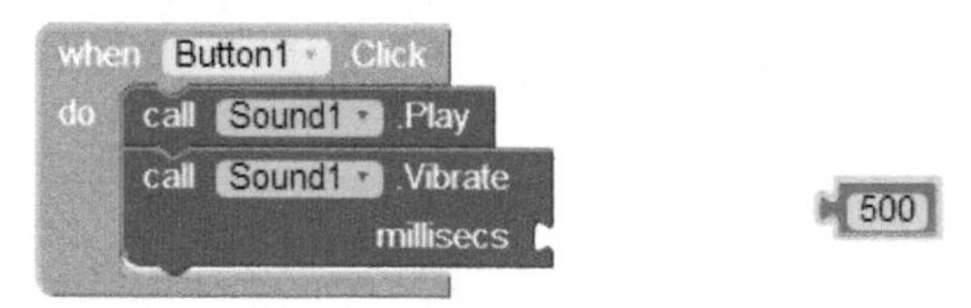

Figure 1-15. Changing the value to 500

6. Plug the 500 number block into the socket on the right side of `call Sound1.Vibrate`, as shown in Figure 1-16.

Figure 1-16. Plugging the value 500 into the millisecs socket

Test your app *Try it! Tap the button on the device, and you'll feel the purr for half a second.*

Shaking the Device

Now, let's add a final element that taps into another cool feature of Android: making the kitty meow when you shake the device. To do this, you'll use a component called `AccelerometerSensor` that can sense when you shake or move the device around.

1. In the Designer, in the Palette components list, expand the Sensors area and drag out an `AccelerometerSensor`. Don't worry about where you drag it. As with any non-visible component, no matter where you place it in the Viewer, it will move to the "Non-visible components" section at the bottom of the Viewer.
2. You'll want to treat someone shaking the device as a different, separate event from the button click. This means that you need a new event handler. Go to the Blocks Editor. There should be a new drawer for `AccelerometerSensor1`. Open it and drag out the `AccelerometerSensor1.Shaking` block. It should be the second block in the list.
3. Just as you did with the sound and the button click, drag out a `call Sound1.Play` block and fit it into the gap in `AccelerometerSensor1.Shaking`. Try it out by shaking the device.

Figure 1-17 shows the blocks for the completed HelloPurr app.

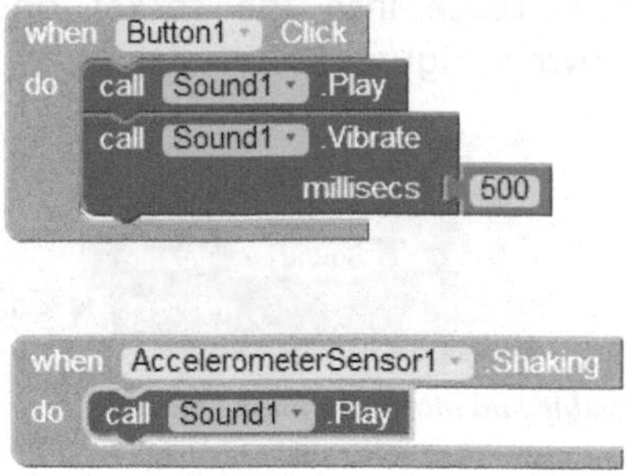

Figure 1-17. The blocks for HelloPurr

Downloading the App to Your Android Device

App Inventor's live testing feature allows you to easily test the app while connected to your device. The only problem is that if you disconnect your device from App Inventor, the app running on the device will stop, and you won't find the app anywhere on the device because it was never truly installed; it was just running within the App Inventor Companion app.

You can download and install the completed app so that it works on any device, even when it's not connected to the computer. To get ready for this, first set the app's icon so that when you install it on a device, it will appear with a distinguishing picture in the list of apps. You can do this in the Designer by selecting the `Screen` component, clicking its `Icon` property, and then uploading an image file as the icon (e.g., the picture of the kitty).

Next, ensure that your device allows apps to be downloaded from places other than the Android Market. For most Android devices, you do this by going to Settings→Applications, and then checking the box next to "Unknown sources."

Then, back in App Inventor, in the Designer, click Build, and select "App (provide QR code for .apk)." You should see a "Progress Bar" message in the window, a process that takes up to a minute. When the QR Code for the finished app is displayed, scan it onto your device with a Barcode Scanner app.[1] After scanning the QR Code, the device might prompt you to enter your password for your Google account. When you finish entering your password, your app will begin downloading to your device and you'll see a download icon in your device's notifications. Go to your notifications, wait until the download completes, and then choose the app to install it.

After you've installed it, look at the apps available on your device, and you'll now see HelloPurr, the app we just built. You run it just like any other app. (Make sure that you run your new app, not the App Inventor Companion application.) You can now stop

1 There are many QR Code scanners for Android. If you don't have one on your device, go to the Play Store and install one.

the Companion app or unplug your device from the computer, and your new packaged application will still be there.

It's important to understand that this means your packaged app is now separate from the project on App Inventor. You can do more work on the project in App Inventor by connecting the device with the AI Companion as before. But that won't change the packaged app that is now installed on your device. If you make further changes to your app in App Inventor, you'll want to package the result and download the new version to replace the old one on the device.

Sharing the App

You can share your app in a couple of ways. To share the executable app (the .apk file), first click Build and choose "Application (save to my computer)." This will create a file with a *.apk* extension on your computer. You can share this file with others by sending it to them as an email attachment, which they'll then open with their email app on their device. Or you can upload the .apk file somewhere on the Web (e.g., on Dropbox). Just be sure to let the people installing your app know that they need to allow "unknown sources" in their device's Application settings in order to install apps that aren't from the Android Market.

You can also create a QR code for the app so that people can scan it onto their device from the Web or even a physical poster. There are numerous tools that will generate a QR code from a URL (e.g., check out *qrcode.kaywa.com*). You can then cut and paste the QR code into a web page or document for printing and posting.

You can also share the *source code* (blocks) of your app with another App Inventor developer. To do this, click My Projects, check the app that you want to share (in this case, HelloPurr), and then select Project→Export Selected Project. The file created on your computer will have a *.aia* extension. You can send this file by email to someone, and they can open App Inventor, choose Project→Import project, and then select the *.aia* file. This will give the user a complete copy of your app, which can then be edited and customized without affecting your version.

App Inventor will soon have its own App gallery where you can share your apps and remix the apps from developers all over the world.

Variations

After you build the apps in this book, you'll likely think of ways to improve them. At the end of each chapter, we'll also suggest customization ideas for you to try. Customizing the apps will lead you to explore the available components and blocks, and learn to program on your own without the detailed instructions provided in the tutorials.

Here are a couple of things to try for HelloPurr:

- As you shake the device, the meows will sound strange, as if they are echoing. That's because the accelerometer sensor is triggering the shaking event many times a second in response to each individual up and down movement, so the meows are overlapping. If you look at the Sound component in the Designer, you'll see a property called `Minimum Interval`. This property determines how close together successive sounds can start. It's currently set at a little under half a second (400 milliseconds), which is less than the duration of a single meow. By adjusting the minimum interval, you can change how much the meows overlap.
- If you run the packaged app and walk around with the device in your pocket, your device will meow every time you move suddenly, something you might find embarrassing. Android apps are typically designed to keep running even when you're not looking at them; your app continues to communicate with the accelerometer and the meow just keeps going. To really quit the app, bring up HelloPurr and press the device's menu button. You'll be offered an option to stop the application. Select this to close the app completely.

Summary

Here are some of the concepts we covered in this chapter:

- You build apps by selecting components in the Designer, and then in the Blocks Editor, you tell the components what to do and when to do it.
- Some components are visible and some aren't. The visible ones appear in the user interface of the app. The non-visible ones do things such as play sounds.
- You define components' behavior by assembling blocks in the Blocks Editor. You first drag out an event handler, such as `Button1.Click`, and then place command blocks like `Sound.Play` within it. Any blocks within `Button1.Click` will be performed when the user taps the button.
- Some commands need extra information to make them work. An example is `Vibrate`, which needs to know how many milliseconds to vibrate for. These values are called *arguments* or *parameters*.
- Numbers are represented as number blocks. You can plug these into commands that take numbers as arguments.
- App Inventor has sensor components. The `AccelerometerSensor` can detect when the device is moved or shaken.
- You can package the apps you build and download them to the phone, where they run independently of App Inventor.

CHAPTER 2

PaintPot

This tutorial introduces the Canvas component for creating simple, two-dimensional (2D) graphics. You'll build PaintPot, an app that lets the user draw on the screen in different colors, and then update it so that the user can take a picture and draw on that instead. On a historical note, PaintPot was one of the first programs developed to demonstrate the potential of personal computers, as far back as the 1970s. Back then, making something like this simple drawing app was a very complex undertaking, and the results were pretty unpolished. But now, with App Inventor, anyone can quickly put together a fairly cool drawing app, which is a great starting point for building 2D games.

With the PaintPot app shown in Figure 2-1, you can:

Figure 2-1. The PaintPot app

- Dip your finger into a virtual paint pot to draw in that color.
- Drag your finger along the screen to draw a line.
- Poke the screen to make dots.
- Use the button at the bottom to wipe the screen clean.
- Change the dot size to large or small with the buttons at the bottom.
- Take a picture with the camera and then draw on that picture.

What You'll Learn

This tutorial introduces the following concepts:

- Using the `Canvas` component for drawing.
- Handling touch and drag events on the device surface.
- Controlling screen layout with arrangement components.
- Using event handlers that have arguments.
- Defining variables to remember things like the dot size the user has chosen for drawing.

Getting Started

Navigate to the App Inventor website (*http://ai2.appinventor.mit.edu*). Start a new project and name it "PaintPot". Click Connect and set up your device (or emulator) for live testing (see *http://appinventor.mit.edu/explore/ai2/setup* for help setting this up).

Next, on the right of the Designer, go to the Properties panel and change the screen title to "PaintPot". You should see this change on the device, with the new title displayed in the title bar of your app.

If you're concerned about confusing your project name and the screen name, don't worry! There are three key names in App Inventor:

- The name you choose for your project as you work on it. This will also be the name of the application when you package it for the device. Note that you can click Project and Save As in the Component Designer to start a new version or rename a project.
- The component name, Screen1, which you'll see in the Components panel. You can't change the name of this initial screen in the current version of App Inventor.
- The title of the screen, which is what you'll see in the app's title bar. This starts out being the same as the component name, Screen1, which is what you used in HelloPurr. But you can change it, as we just did for PaintPot.

Designing the Components

You'll use these components to make the app:

- Three `Button` components for selecting red, blue, or green paint, and a `HorizontalArrangement` component for organizing them.

- One `Button` component for wiping the drawing clean, two for changing the size of the dots that are drawn, and one for invoking the camera to take a picture.
- A `Canvas` component, which is the drawing surface. `Canvas` has a `BackgroundImage` property, which you'll set to the *kitty.png* file from the HelloPurr tutorial in Chapter 1. Later in this chapter, you'll modify the app so that the background can be set to a picture the user takes.

Creating the Color Buttons

First, create the three color buttons by following these instructions:

1. Drag a `Button` component onto the Viewer, change its `Text` attribute to "Red", and then make its `BackgroundColor` red.
2. In the Viewer, in the components list, click `Button1` to highlight it (it might already be highlighted) and click Rename to change its name from `Button1` to `RedButton`. Note that spaces aren't allowed in component names, so it's common to capitalize the first letter of each word in the name.
3. Similarly, make two more buttons for blue and green, named `BlueButton` and `GreenButton`, placing them under the red button vertically. Check your work up to this point against Figure 2-2.

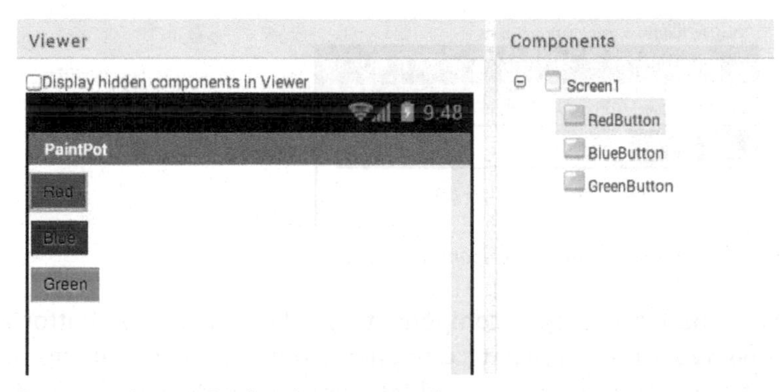

Figure 2-2. The Viewer showing the three buttons created

Note that in this project, you're changing the names of the components rather than leaving them as the default names, as you did with HelloPurr. Using more meaningful names makes your projects more readable, and it will really help when you move to the Blocks Editor and must refer to the components by name. In this book, we'll use the convention of having the component name end with its type (for example, `RedButton`).

Test your app *If you haven't clicked Connect and connected your device, do so now and check how your app looks on your device or in the emulator.*

Using Arrangements for Better Layouts

You should now have three buttons stacked one atop another. But for this app, you want them all lined up side by side, across the top of the screen, as shown in Figure 2-3. You do this using a `HorizontalArrangement` component:

1. From the Palette's Layout drawer, drag out a `HorizontalArrangement` component and place it under the buttons.
2. In the Properties panel, change the `Width` of the `HorizontalArrangement` to "Fill parent" so that it fills the entire width of the screen.
3. Move the three buttons one by one into the `HorizontalArrangement` component. *Hint*: You'll see a blue vertical line that shows where the piece you're dragging will go.

Figure 2-3. The three buttons within a horizontal arrangement

If you look in the list of project components, you'll see the three buttons indented under the `HorizontalArrangement` component. This indicates that the buttons are now subcomponents of the `HorizontalArrangement` component. Notice that all the components are indented under `Screen1`.

You can center the entire row of buttons on the screen by changing Screen1's Align-Horizontal property to "Center".

Test your app *On the device, you should see your three buttons lined up in a row at the top of the screen, although things might not look exactly as they do on the Designer. For example, the outline around* `HorizontalArrangement` *appears in the Viewer but not on the device.*

In general, you use screen arrangements to create simple vertical, horizontal, or tabular layouts. You can also create more complex layouts by inserting (or nesting) screen arrangement components within one another.

Adding the Canvas

The next step is to set up the canvas where the drawing will occur:

1. From the Palette's Drawing and Animation drawer, drag a `Canvas` component onto the Viewer. Change its name to `DrawingCanvas`. Set its `Width` to "Fill parent" so that it will span the entire width of the screen. Set its `Height` to 300 pixels, which will leave room for the two rows of buttons.
2. If you've completed the HelloPurr tutorial (Chapter 1), you have already downloaded the *kitty.png* file. If you haven't, you can download it at *http://appinventor.org/bookFiles/HelloPurr/kitty.png*.
3. Set the `BackgroundImage` of the `DrawingCanvas` to the *kitty.png* file. In the Properties section of the Components Designer, the `BackgroundImage` will be set to None. Click the field and upload the *kitty.png* file.
4. Set the `PaintColor` of the DrawingCanvas to red so that when the user starts the app but hasn't clicked on a button yet, his default color will be red. Check to see that what you've built looks like Figure 2-4.

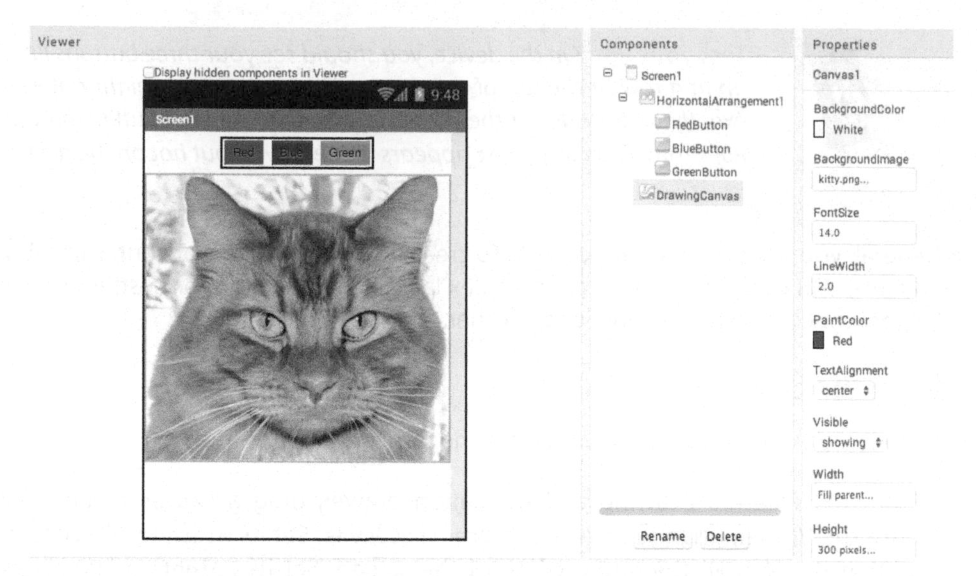

Figure 2-4. The DrawingCanvas component has a BackgroundImage of the kitty picture

Arranging the Bottom Buttons and the Camera Component

1. From the Palette, drag out a second `HorizontalArrangement` and place it under the canvas. Then, drag two more `Button` components onto the screen and place them in this bottom `HorizontalArrangement`. Change the name of the first button to `TakePictureButton` and its `Text` property to "Take Picture". Change the name of the second button to `WipeButton` and its `Text` property to "Wipe".
2. Drag two more `Button` components from the Palette into the `HorizontalArrangement`, placing them next to `WipeButton`.
3. Name the buttons `BigButton` and `SmallButton`, and set their `Text` to "Big Dots" and "Small Dots", respectively.
4. From the Media drawer, drag a `Camera` component into the Viewer. It will appear in the non-visible component area.

You've now completed the steps to set the appearance of your app, which should look like Figure 2-5.

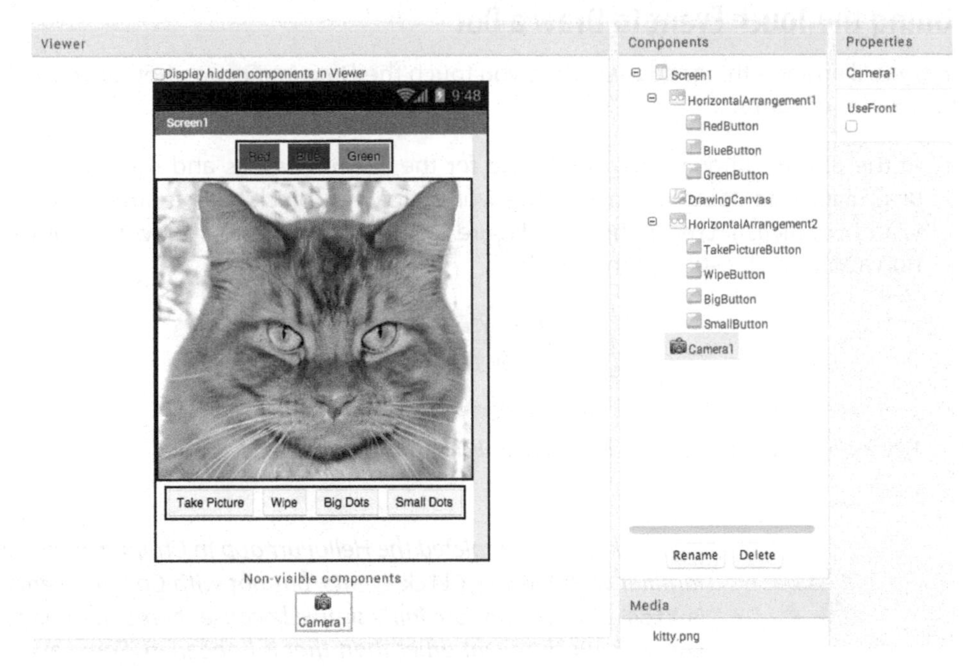

Figure 2-5. The complete user interface for PaintPot

Test your app *Check the app on the device. Does the kitty picture now appear under the top row of buttons? Is the bottom row of buttons in place below the picture?*

Adding Behaviors to the Components

The next step is to define how the components behave. Creating a painting program might seem overwhelming, but rest assured that App Inventor has done a lot of the heavy lifting for you: there are easy-to-use blocks for handling the user's touch and drag actions, and for drawing and taking pictures.

In the Designer, you added a `Canvas` component named `DrawingCanvas`. Like all Canvas components, `DrawingCanvas` has a `Touched` event and a `Dragged` event. You'll program the `DrawingCanvas.Touched` event so that a circle is drawn in response to the user touching her finger on the screen. You'll program the `DrawingCanvas.Dragged` event so that a line is drawn as the user drags her finger across the canvas. You'll then program the buttons to change the drawing color, clear the canvas, and change the canvas background to a picture taken with the camera.

Adding the Touch Event to Draw a Dot

First, you'll arrange things so that when you touch the *DrawingCanvas*, you draw a dot at the point of contact:

1. In the Blocks Editor, select the drawer for the `DrawingCanvas` and then drag the `DrawingCanvas.Touched` block to the workspace. The block has parameters for `x`, `y`, and `touchedSprite`, as shown in Figure 2-6. These parameters provide information about the location of the touch.

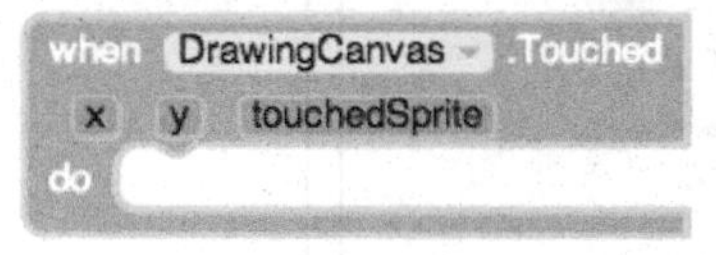
when DrawingCanvas .Touched
x y touchedSprite
do

Figure 2-6. The event comes with information about where the screen is touched

Note *If you've completed the HelloPurr app in Chapter 1, you're familiar with* `Button.Click` *events, but not with Canvas events.* `Button.Click` *events are fairly simple because there's nothing to know about the event other than that it happened. Some event handlers, however, come with information about the event called arguments. The* `DrawingCanvas.Touched` *event provides the x and y coordinates of the touch within the DrawingCanvas. It also lets you know if an object within the* `DrawingCanvas` *(in App Inventor, this is called a sprite) was touched, but we won't need that until Chapter 3. The x and y coordinates are the arguments we'll use to identify where the user touched the screen. We can then draw the dot at that position.*

2. From the DrawingCanvas drawer, drag out a `DrawingCanvas.DrawCircle` command and place it within the `DrawingCanvas.Touched` event handler, as shown in Figure 2-7.

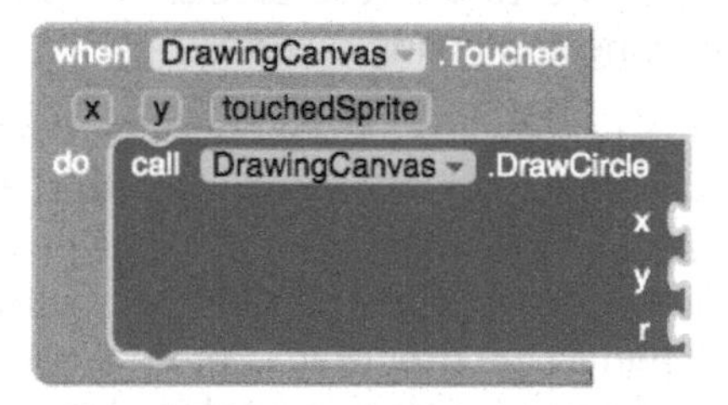
when DrawingCanvas .Touched
x y touchedSprite
do call DrawingCanvas .DrawCircle
x
y
r

Figure 2-7. When the user touches the canvas, the app draws a circle

On the right side of the `DrawingCanvas.DrawCircle` block, you'll see three sockets for the arguments we need to plug in: x, y, and r. The x and y arguments specify the location where the circle should be drawn, and r determines the radius (or size) of the circle. This event handler can be a bit confusing because the `DrawingCanvas.Touched` event also has an x and y; just keep in mind that the x and y for the `DrawingCanvas.Touched` event indicate where the user touched, whereas the x and y for the `DrawingCanvas.DrawCircle` event are open sockets for you to specify where the circle should be drawn. Because you want to draw the circle where the user touched, you'll plug in the x and y values from `DrawingCanvas.Touched` as the values to use for the x and y parameters in `DrawingCanvas.DrawCircle`.

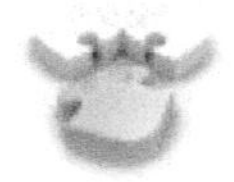

Note *You can access the event parameter values by mousing over them in the* `when` *block, as shown in Figure 2-8.*

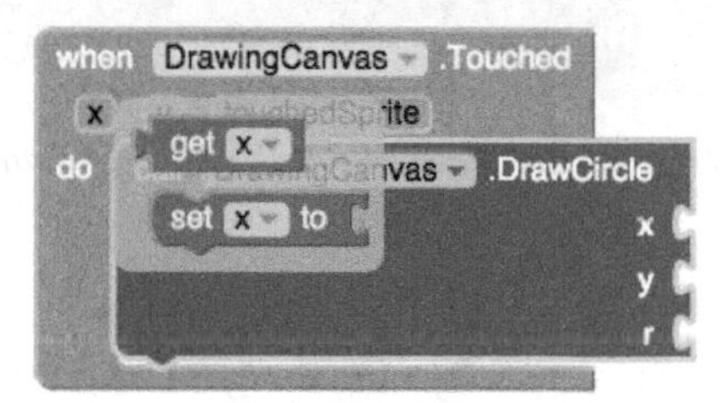

Figure 2-8. Mouse over an event parameter to drag out a get block for obtaining the value

3. Drag `get` blocks out for the x and y values and plug them into the sockets in the `DrawingCanvas.DrawCircle` block, as shown in Figure 2-9.

Figure 2-9. The app now knows where to draw (x,y), but we still need to specify how big the circle should be

4. Now, you'll need to specify the radius, r, of the circle to draw. The radius is measured in pixels, which is the tiniest dot that can be drawn on a device's screen. For now, set it to 5: click in a blank area of the screen, type 5 and then press Return

(this will create a number block automatically), and then plug that into the `r` socket. When you do, the yellow box in the bottom-left corner will return to 0 because all the sockets are now filled. Figure 2-10 illustrates how the final `Drawing Canvas.Touched` event handler should look.

Note *If you type a "5" in the Blocks Editor and press Return, a number block with a "5" in it will appear. This feature is called typeblocking: if you start typing, the Blocks Editor shows a list of blocks whose names match what you are typing; if you type a number, it creates a number block.*

Figure 2-10. When the user touches the DrawingCanvas, a circle of radius 5 is drawn at the location of the touch (x,y)

Test your app *Try out what you have so far on the device. When you touch the DrawingCanvas, your finger should leave a dot at each place you touch. The dots will be red if you set the* `DrawingCan vas.PaintColor` *property to red in the Component Designer (otherwise, it's black, as that's the default).*

Adding the Drag Event That Draws a Line

Next, you'll add the drag event handler. Here's the difference between a touch and a drag:

- A *touch* is when you place your finger on the DrawingCanvas and then lift it without moving it.
- A *drag* is when you place your finger on the DrawingCanvas and move it around while keeping it in contact with the screen.

In a paint program, dragging your finger in an arc across the screen appears to draw a curved line that follows your finger's path. What you're actually doing is drawing numerous tiny, straight lines; each time you move your finger, even a little bit, you draw the line from your finger's last position to its new position.

1. From the DrawingCanvas drawer, drag the `DrawingCanvas.Dragged` block to the workspace. You should see the event handler as it is shown in Figure 2-11. The `DrawingCanvas.Dragged` event comes with the following arguments:

   - `startX, startY`: the position of your finger at the point where the drag started.
   - `currentX, currentY`: the current position of your finger
   - `prevX, prevY`: the immediately previous position of your finger.
   - `draggedSprite`: a Boolean value, it will be true if the user drags directly on an image sprite. We won't use this argument in this tutorial.

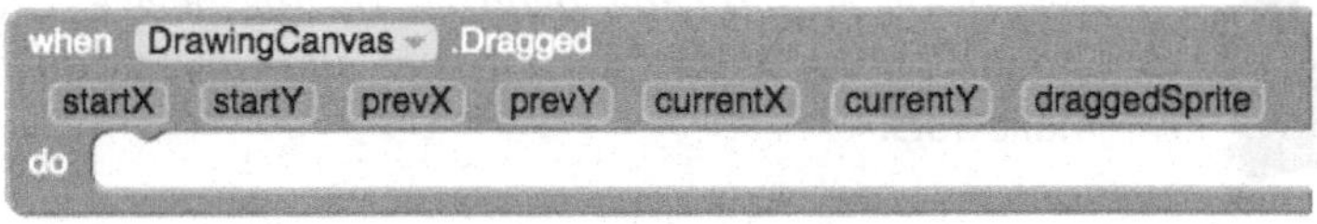

```
when DrawingCanvas .Dragged
 startX startY prevX prevY currentX currentY draggedSprite
do
```

Figure 2-11. A Dragged event has even more arguments than Touched

2. From the DrawingCanvas drawer, drag the `DrawingCanvas.DrawLine` block into the `DrawingCanvas.Dragged` block, as shown in Figure 2-12.

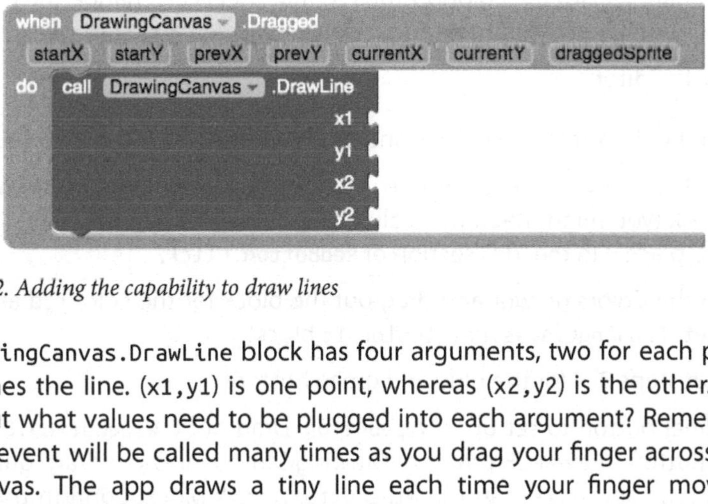

```
when DrawingCanvas .Dragged
 startX startY prevX prevY currentX currentY draggedSprite
do call DrawingCanvas .DrawLine
                            x1
                            y1
                            x2
                            y2
```

Figure 2-12. Adding the capability to draw lines

   The `DrawingCanvas.DrawLine` block has four arguments, two for each point that determines the line. (`x1,y1`) is one point, whereas (`x2,y2`) is the other. Can you figure out what values need to be plugged into each argument? Remember, the `Dragged` event will be called many times as you drag your finger across the DrawingCanvas. The app draws a tiny line each time your finger moves, from (`prevx,prevy`) to (`currentX,currentY`).

3. Drag out `get` blocks for the arguments you need. A `get prevX` and `get prevY` should be plugged into the `x1` and `y1` sockets, respectively. A `get currentX` and

`get currentY` should be plugged into the x2 and y2 sockets, respectively, as shown in Figure 2-13.

Figure 2-13. As the user drags, the app will draw a line from the previous spot to the current one

Test your app *Try this behavior on the device. Drag your finger around on the screen to draw lines and curves. Touch the screen to make dots.*

Changing the Color

The app you've built lets the user draw, but so far everything has been in red. Next, add event handlers for the color buttons so that users can change the paint color, and another for the WipeButton to let them clear the screen and start over.

In the Blocks Editor:

1. Open the drawer for `RedButton` and drag out the `RedButton.Click` block.
2. Open the DrawingCanvas drawer. Drag out the `set DrawingCanvas.PaintColor` to block (you might need to scroll through the list of blocks in the drawer to find it) and place it in the "do" section of `RedButton.Click`.
3. Open the Colors drawer and drag out the block for the color red and plug it into the `set DrawingCanvas.PaintColor to` block.
4. Repeat steps 2–4 for the blue and green buttons.
5. The final button to set up is `WipeButton`. Drag out a `WipeButton.Click` from the WipeButton drawer. From the DrawingCanvas drawer, drag out `DrawingCanvas.Clear` and place it in the `WipeButton.Click` block. Confirm that your blocks appear as they do in Figure 2-14.

Figure 2-14. Clicking the color buttons changes the DrawingCanvas's PaintColor; clicking Wipe clears the screen

Test your app *Try out the behaviors by clicking each of the color buttons and seeing if you can draw different colored circles. Then, click the Wipe button to see if the canvas is cleared.*

Letting the User Take a Picture

App Inventor apps can interact with the powerful features of an Android device, including the camera. To spice up the app, let the user set the background of the drawing by taking a picture with the camera.

The `Camera` component has two key blocks. The `Camera.TakePicture` block launches the camera application on the device. The event `Camera.AfterPicture` is triggered when the user has finished taking the picture. You'll add blocks in the `Camera.AfterPicture` event handler to set the `DrawingCanvas.BackgroundImage` to the image that the user just shot.

1. Open the TakePictureButton drawer and drag the `TakePictureButton.Click` event handler into the workspace.
2. From `Camera1`, drag out `Camera1.TakePicture` and place it in the `TakePictureButton.Click` event handler.
3. From `Camera1`, drag the `Camera1.AfterPicture` event handler into the workspace.
4. From `DrawingCanvas`, drag the `set DrawingCanvas.BackgroundImage to` block and place it in the `Camera1.AfterPicture` event handler.
5. `Camera1.AfterPicture` has an argument named `image`, which is the picture that was just taken. You can get a reference to it by using a `get` block from the `Camera1.AfterPicture` block, and then plug it into `DrawingCanvas.BackgroundImage`.

The blocks should look like Figure 2-15.

when Camera1 .AfterPicture
image
do set DrawingCanvas . BackgroundImage to get image

when TakePictureButton .Click
do call Camera1 .TakePicture

Figure 2-15. When the picture is taken, it's set as the background image for DrawingCanvas

Test your app *Try out this behavior by clicking Take Picture on your device and taking a picture. The image of the cat should change to the picture you just took, and then you can draw on that picture. (Drawing on Professor Wolber is a favorite pastime of his students, as exemplified in Figure 2-16.)*

Changing the Dot Size

The size of the dots drawn on the DrawingCanvas is determined in the call to `DrawingCanvas.DrawCircle`, where the radius argument r is set to 5. To change the size, you can put in a different value for r. To test this, try changing the 5 to a 10 and testing it out on the device to see how it looks.

The catch here is that the user is restricted to whatever size you set in the radius argument. What if the user wants to change the size of the dots? Let's modify the program so that the user, not just the programmer, can change the dot size. We'll program the button labeled "Big Dots" to change the dot size to 8, and program the button labeled "Small Dots" to adjust the size to 2.

To use different values for the radius argument, the app needs to know which one we want to apply. We have to instruct it to use a specific value, and it has to store (or remember) that value somehow so that it can keep using it. When your app needs to remember something that's not a property, you can define a *variable*. A variable is a *memory cell*; you can think of it like a bucket in which you can store data that can vary, which in this case is the current dot size (for more information about variables, see Chapter 16).

Figure 2-16. The PaintPot app with an "annotated" picture of Professor Wolber

Let's start by defining a variable named `dotSize`:

1. In the Blocks Editor, from the Variables drawer of the Built-in blocks, drag out an `initialize global name to` block. Within the initialize block, change the text "name" to "dotSize".

2. Notice that the `initialize global dotSize to` block has an open socket. This is where you can specify the initial value for the variable, or the value to which it defaults when the app begins. (This is often referred to as "initializing a variable" in programming terms.) For this app, initialize the `dotSize` to 2 by creating a number 2 block (use the typeblocking feature: type a "2" in the Blocks Editor and then press Return) and then plugging it into `initialize global dotSize to`, as shown in Figure 2-17.

Figure 2-17. Initializing the variable dotSize with a value of 2

Referencing the dotSize Variable in DrawCircle

Next, we want to change the argument of `DrawingCanvas.DrawCircle` in the `DrawingCanvas.Touched` event handler so that it uses the value of `dotSize` rather than always using a fixed number. (It might seem like we've "fixed" `dotSize` to the value 2 rather than made it variable because we initialized it that way, but you'll see in a minute how we can change the value of `dotSize` and, therefore, change the size of the dot that is drawn.)

1. Drag out a `get` block from the `initilize global dotsize to` block. You should see a `get global dotSize` block that provides the value of the variable.

2. Go to the `DrawingCanvas.DrawCircle` block, drag the number `5` block out of the r slot, and then place it into the trash. Then, replace it with the `get global dotSize`

block (see Figure 2-18). When the user touches the DrawingCanvas, the app will now determine the radius from the variable `dotSize`.

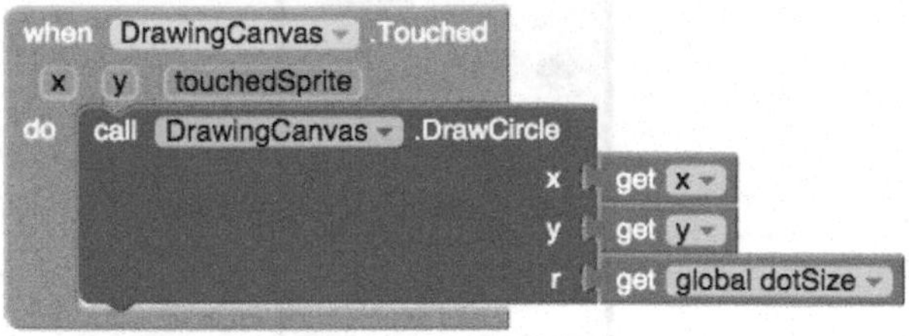

Figure 2-18. Now the size of each circle is dependent on what is stored in the variable dotSize

Changing the Value of dotSize

Your app will now draw circles that are sized based on the value in the variable `dot Size`, but you still need code so that `dotSize` changes (right now it stays as 2) according to what the user chooses. You'll implement this behavior by programming the `SmallButton.Click` and `BigButton.Click` event handlers:

1. Drag out a `SmallButton.Click` event handler from the SmallButton drawer. Next, mouse over the "dotsize" within the initialize global block and drag out the `set global dotSize to` block. Plug it into `SmallButton.Click`. Finally, create a `number` 2 block and plug it into the `set global dotSize to` block.
2. Make a similar event handler for `BigButton.Click`, but set `dotSize` to 8. Both event handlers should now show up in the Blocks Editor, as shown in Figure 2-19.

Note *The "global" in* `set global dotSize` *refers to the fact that the variable can be used in all the event handlers of the program (globally). In App Inventor, you can also define variables that are "local" to a particular part of the program (see Chapter 21 for details).*

Figure 2-19. Clicking the buttons changes the dotSize; touches thereafter will draw at that size

Test your app *Try clicking the size buttons and then touching the DrawingCanvas. Are the circles drawn with different sizes? Are the lines? The line size shouldn't change because you programmed dot-Size to only be used in the* `DrawingCanvas.DrawCircle` *block. Based on that, can you think of how you'd change your blocks so that users could change the line size, as well? (Hint: DrawingCanvas has a property named LineWidth.)*

The Complete App: PaintPot

Figure 2-20 illustrates our completed PaintPot app.

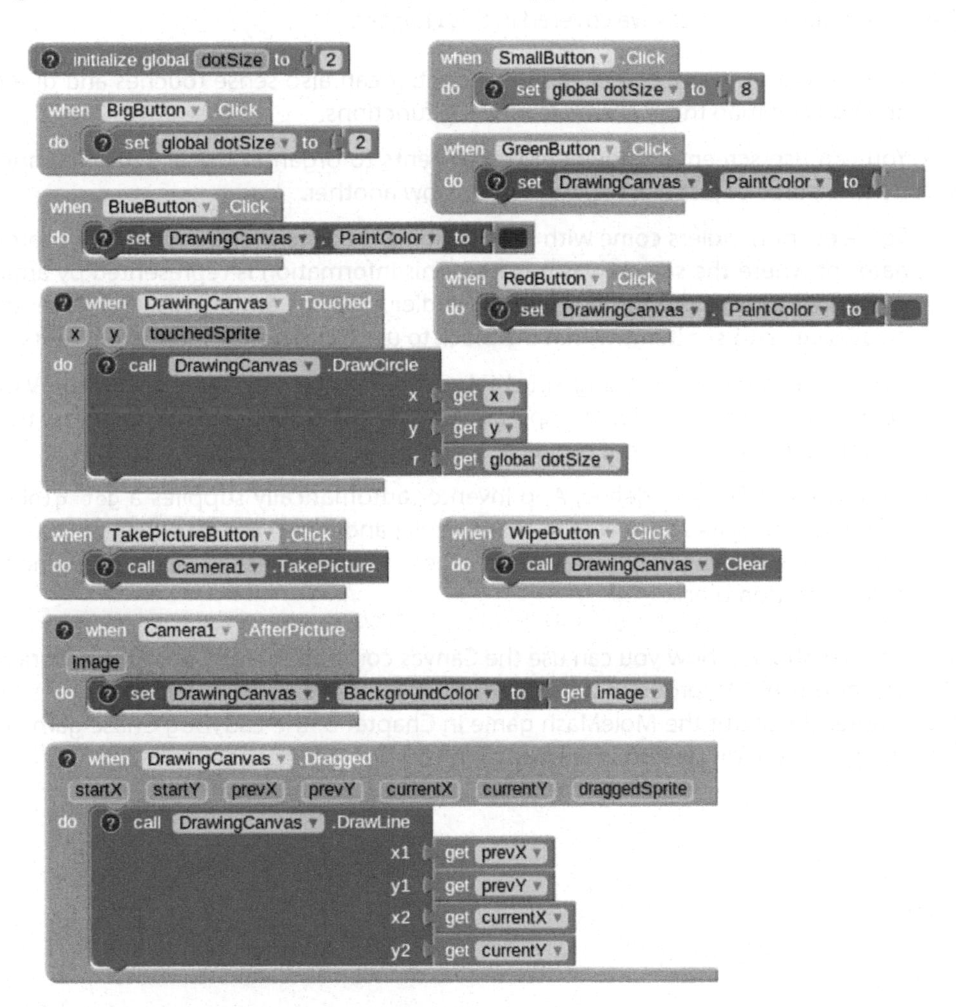

Figure 2-20. The final set of blocks for PaintPot

Variations

Here are some variations that you can explore:

- The app's user interface doesn't provide much information about the current settings (for example, the only way to know the current dot size or color is to draw something). Modify the app so that these settings are displayed to the user.
- Let the user specify values other than 2 and 8 for the dot size by using a Slider component.

Summary

Here are some of the ideas we covered in this chapter:

- The Canvas component lets you draw on it. It can also sense touches and drags, and you can map these events to drawing functions.
- You can use screen arrangement components to organize the layout of components instead of just placing them one below another.
- Some event handlers come with information about the event, such as the coordinates of where the screen was touched. This information is represented by arguments. When you drag out an event handler that has arguments, App Inventor creates `get` and `set` items within the block to use to reference these arguments.
- You create variables by using `initialize global name to` blocks from the Variables drawer. Variables let the app remember information, such as dot size, that isn't stored in a component property.
- For each variable you define, App Inventor automatically supplies a `get global` reference that gives the value of the variable, and a `set global` block for changing the value of the variable. To access these, mouse over the variable's name in its initialization block.

This chapter showed how you can use the Canvas component for a painting program. You can also use it to program animations, such as those you'd find in 2D games. To learn more, check out the MoleMash game in Chapter 3, the Ladybug Chase game in Chapter 5, and the discussion of animation in Chapter 17.

CHAPTER 3

MoleMash

This chapter shows you how to create MoleMash, a game inspired by the arcade classic Whac-A-Mole™, in which mechanical critters pop out of holes, and players score points when they successfully whack them with a mallet. MoleMash was created by a member of the App Inventor team, ostensibly to test the sprite functionality (which she implemented), but really because she's a fan of the game.

When Ellen Spertus joined the App Inventor team at Google, she was eager to add support for creating games, so she volunteered to implement sprites. The term, originally coined to describe mythological creatures such as fairies and pixies, was adopted by the computing community in the 1970s to refer to images capable of movement on a computer screen (for video games). Ellen first worked with sprites when she attended a computer camp in the early 1980s and programmed a TI 99/4. Her work on sprites and MoleMash was motivated by double nostalgia—for both the computers and games of her childhood.

What You'll Build

For the MoleMash app shown in Figure 3-1, you'll implement the following functionality:

Figure 3-1. The MoleMash user interface

- A mole pops up at random locations on the screen, moving once every second.
- Tapping the mole causes the device to vibrate, increment a display of "hits" (increasing it by one), and move the mole immediately to a new location.
- Tapping the screen but missing the mole increments a display of "misses."
- Pressing a Reset button resets the counts of hits and misses.

What You'll Learn

The tutorial covers the following components and concepts:

- The `ImageSprite` component for touch-sensitive movable images.
- The `Canvas` component, which acts as a surface on which to place the `Image Sprite`.
- The `Clock` component to move the sprite around once every second.
- The `Sound` component to produce a vibration when the mole is tapped.
- The `Button` component to start a new game.
- Procedures to implement repeated behavior, such as moving the mole.
- Generating random numbers.
- Using the addition (+) and subtraction (–) blocks.

Getting Started

Connect to the App Inventor website and start a new project. Name it "MoleMash" and also set the screen's title to "MoleMash". Click Connect and connect your device or emulator for live testing.

Download the picture of a mole from *http://appinventor.org/bookFiles/MoleMash/mole.png*. In the Component Designer, in the Media section, click "Upload File," browse to where the file is located on your computer, and then upload it to App Inventor.

Designing the Components

You'll use these components to make MoleMash:

- A `Canvas` that serves as a playing field.
- An `ImageSprite` that displays a picture of a mole and can move around and sense when the mole is touched.
- A `Sound` that vibrates when the mole is touched.
- `Labels` that display "Hits: ", "Misses: ", and the actual numbers of hits and misses.
- `HorizontalArrangements` to correctly position the `Labels`.
- A `Button` to reset the numbers of hits and misses to 0.
- A `Clock` to make the mole move once per second.

Table 3-1 shows all of the components you'll be using.

Table 3-1. The complete list of components for MoleMash

Component type	Palette group	What you'll name it	Purpose
Canvas	Drawing and Animation	Canvas1	The container for ImageSprite.
ImageSprite	Drawing and Animation	Mole	The user will try to touch this.
Button	User Interface	ResetButton	The user will press this to reset the score.
Clock	User Interface	Clock1	Control the mole's movement.
Sound	Media	Sound1	Vibrate when the mole is touched.
Label	User Interface	HitsLabel	Display "Hits: ".
Label	User Interface	HitsCountLabel	Display the number of hits.
HorizontalArrangement	Layout	Horizontal Arrangement1	Position HitsLabel next to HitsCountLabel.
Label	User Interface	MissesLabel	Display "Misses: ".
Label	User Interface	MissesCountLabel	Display the number of misses.
HorizontalArrangement	Layout	Horizontal Arrangement2	Position MissesLabel next to MissesCountLabel.

Placing the Action Components

In this section, you will place the components necessary for the game's action. In the next section, you will place the components for displaying the score.

1. From the Drawing and Animation drawer, drag in a Canvas component, leaving it with the default name Canvas1. Set its Width property to "Fill parent" so that it is as wide as the screen, and set its Height to 300 pixels.
2. Again from the Drawing and Animation drawer, drag in an ImageSprite component, placing it anywhere on Canvas1. At the bottom of the Components list, click Rename and change its name to "Mole". Set its Picture property to *mole.PNG*, which you uploaded earlier.
3. From the User Interface drawer, drag in a Button component, placing it beneath Canvas1. Rename it "ResetButton" and set its Text property to "Reset".
4. Also from the User Interface drawer, drag in a Clock component. It will appear at the bottom of the Viewer in the "Non-visible components" section.

5. From the Media drawer, drag in a `Sound` component. It, too, will appear in the "Non-visible components" section.

Your screen should now look something like Figure 3-2 (although your mole might be in a different position).

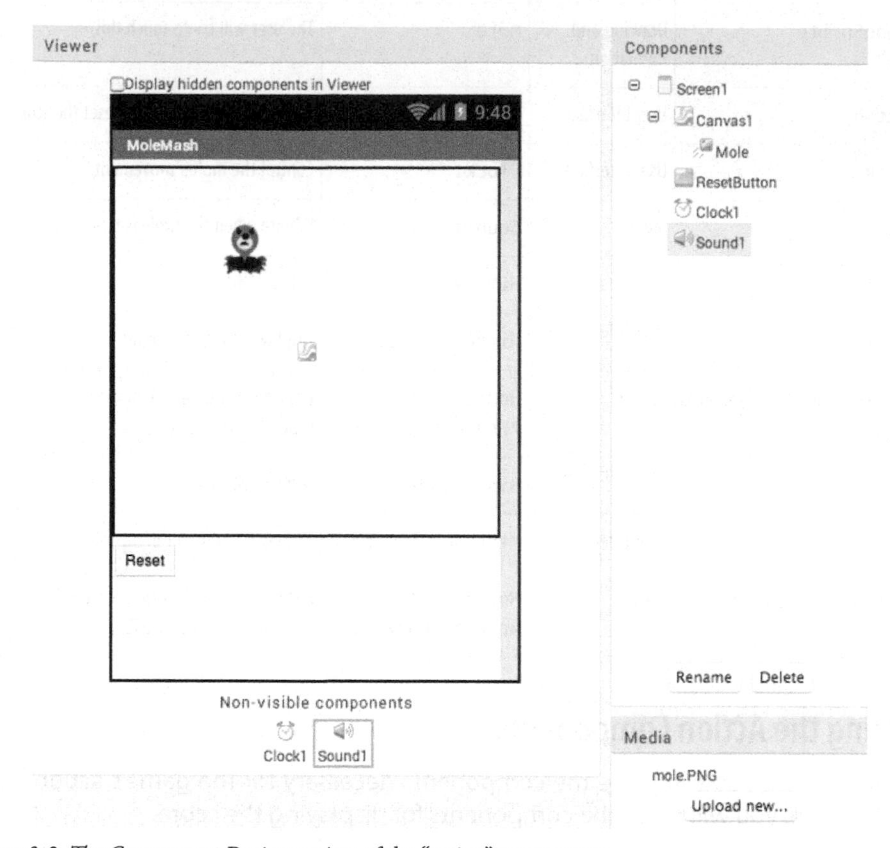

Figure 3-2. The Component Designer view of the "action" components

Placing the Label Components

You will now place components for displaying the user's score—specifically, the number of hits and misses.

1. From the Layout drawer, drag in a `HorizontalArrangement`, placing it beneath the `Button` and keeping the default name of `HorizontalArrangement1`.
2. From the User Interface drawer, drag two `Labels` into `HorizontalArrangement1`.
   - Rename the left `Label` "HitsLabel" and set its `Text` property to "Hits: " (making sure to include a space after the colon).

- Rename the right `Label` "HitsCountLabel" and set its `Text` property to the number 0.

3. Drag in a second `HorizontalArrangement`, placing it beneath `HorizontalArrangement1`.
4. Drag two Labels into `HorizontalArrangement2`.
   - Rename the left `Label` "MissesLabel" and set its `Text` property to "Misses: " (making sure to include a space after the colon).
   - Rename the right `Label` "MissesCountLabel" and set its `Text` property to the number 0.

Your screen should now look like something like Figure 3-3.

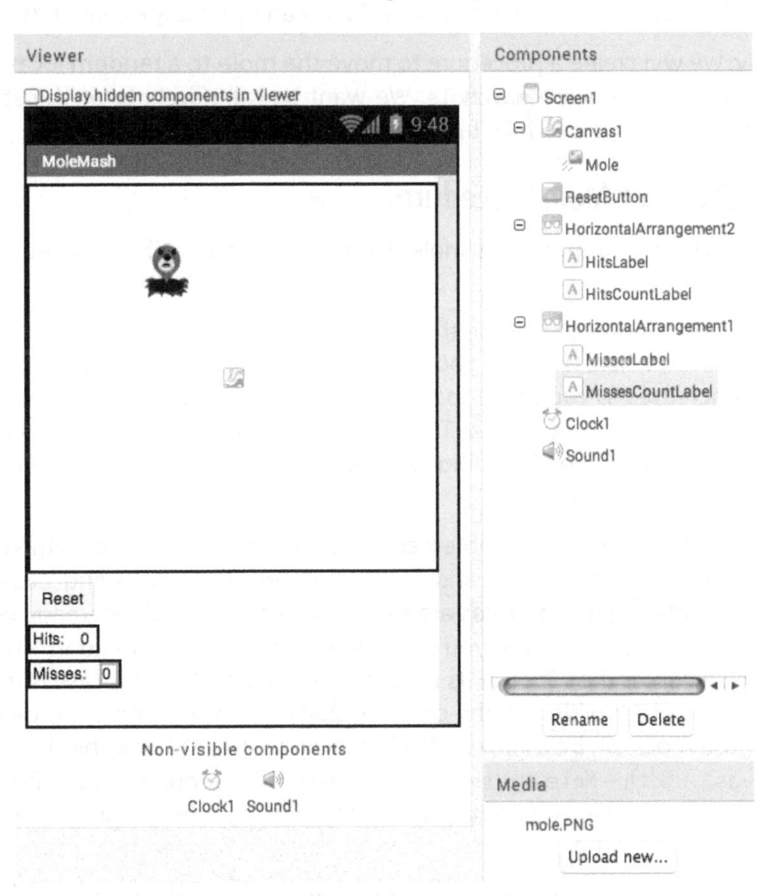

Figure 3-3. The Component Designer view of all the MoleMash components

Adding Behaviors to the Components

After creating the preceding components, let's move to the Blocks Editor to implement the program's behavior. Specifically, we want the mole to move to a random location on the canvas every second. The user's goal is to tap on the mole wherever it appears, and the app will display the number of times the user hits or misses the mole. (Note: We recommend using your finger, not a mallet!) Pressing the Reset button resets the number of hits and misses to 0.

Moving the Mole

In the programs you've written thus far, you've called built-in procedures such as `Vibrate` in HelloPurr. Wouldn't it be nice if App Inventor had a procedure that moved an `ImageSprite` to a random location on the screen? The bad news: it doesn't. The good news: you can create your own procedures! Just like the built-in procedures, your procedure will show up in a drawer and you can use it anywhere in the app.

Specifically, we will create a procedure to move the mole to a random location on the screen, which we will name `MoveMole`. We want to call `MoveMole` at the start of the game, when the user successfully taps the mole, and once per second.

Creating the MoveMole Procedure

To understand how to move the mole, we need to look at how Android graphics work.

The canvas (and the screen) can be thought of as a grid with *x* (horizontal) and *y* (vertical) coordinates, where the (x, y) coordinates of the upper-left corner are (0, 0). The *x* coordinate increases as you move to the right, and the *y* coordinate increases as you move down, as shown in Figure 3-4. The x and y properties of an `ImageSprite` indicate where its upper-left corner is positioned; thus, the mole in the upper-left corner in Figure 3-4 has x and y values of 0.

To determine the maximum available x and y values so that `Mole` fits on the screen, we need to make use of the `Width` and `Height` properties of `Mole` and `Canvas1`. (The mole's `Width` and `Height` properties are the same as the size of the image you uploaded. When you created `Canvas1`, you set its `Height` to 300 pixels and its `Width` to "Fill parent," which copies the width of its parent element, which in this case is the screen.) If the mole is 36 pixels wide and the canvas is 200 pixels wide, the x coordinate of the left side of the mole can be as low as 0 (all the way to the left) or as high as 164 (200 – 36, or `Canvas1.Width` – `Mole.Width`) without the mole extending off the right edge of the screen. Similarly, the y coordinate of the top of the mole can range from 0 to `Canvas1.Height` – `Mole.Height`.

Figure 3-5 shows the procedure you will create, annotated with descriptive comments (which you can optionally add to your procedure).

To randomly place the mole, we will want to select an x coordinate in the range from 0 to *Canvas1.Width – Mole.Width*. Similarly, we will want the y coordinate to be in the range from 0 to *Canvas1.Height – Mole.Height*. We can generate a random number through the built-in procedure *random integer*, which you can find in the Math drawer. You will need to change the default "from" parameter from 1 to 0 and replace the "to" parameters, as shown in Figure 3-5.

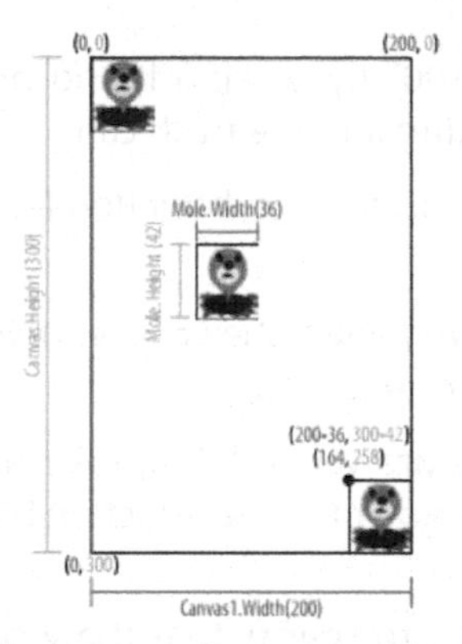

Figure 3-4. Positions of the mole on the screen, with coordinate, height, and width information; x coordinates and widths are shown in blue, while y coordinates and heights are in orange

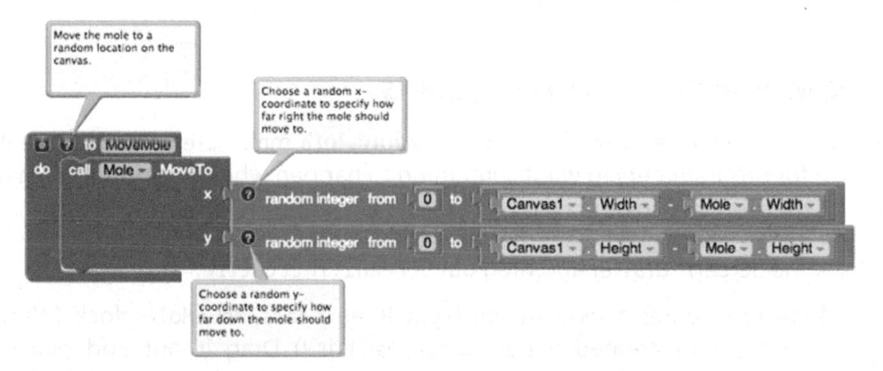

Figure 3-5. The MoveMole procedure, which places the mole in a random location

To create the procedure:

1. In the Blocks Editor, click the Procedure drawer.
2. Drag out the `to procedure` block (containing "do," not "result").
3. On the new block, click the text "procedure" and type "MoveMole" to set the name of the procedure.
4. Because we want to move the mole, click the Mole drawer, and drag `call Mole.MoveTo` into the procedure, to the right of "do." Note the open sockets on the right side which indicate that we need to provide x and y coordinates.

5. To specify that the new x coordinate for the mole should be between 0 and Canvas1.Width – Mole.Width, as discussed earlier, do the following:
   - From the Math drawer, drag in the random integer from block, putting the plug (protrusion) on its left side into the "x" socket on call Mole.MoveTo.
   - Change the number "1" block on the "from" socket by clicking it and then entering the number "0".
   - Discard the number "100" by clicking it and pressing your keyboard's Del or Delete key, or by dragging it to the trash can.
   - From the Math drawer, drag in a subtraction (–) block and place it into the "to" socket.
   - From the Canvas1 drawer, select the Canvas1.Width block and drag it to the left side of the subtraction operations.
   - Similarly, click the Mole drawer and drag Mole.Width into the workspace. Then, plug that into the right side of the subtraction block.

6. Follow a similar procedure to specify that the y coordinate should be a random integer in the range from 0 to Canvas1.Height – Mole.Height.
7. Check your results against Figure 3-5.

Calling MoveMole When the App Starts

Now that you've written the MoveMole procedure, let's make use of it. Because it's so common for programmers to want something to happen when an app starts, there's a block for that very purpose: Screen1.Initialize.

1. Click the Screen1 drawer and drag out Screen1.Initialize.
2. Click the Procedures drawer, in which you'll see a call MoveMole block. (It's pretty cool that you've created a new block, isn't it?!) Drag it out and place it in Screen1.Initialize, as shown in Figure 3-6.

Figure 3-6. Calling the MoveMole procedure when the application starts

Calling MoveMole every Second

Making the mole move every second will require the Clock component. We left the TimerInterval property for Clock1 at its default value of 1,000 (milliseconds), or 1 second. That means that every second, whatever is specified in a `Clock1.Timer` block will take place. Here's how to set that up:

1. Click the Clock1 drawer and drag out `Clock1.Timer`.
2. Click the Procedures drawer and drag a `call MoveMole` block into the `Clock1.Timer` block, as shown in Figure 3-7.

when Clock1 .Timer
do call MoveMole

Figure 3-7. Calling the MoveMole procedure when the timer goes off (every second)

If that's too fast or slow for you, you can change the `TimerInterval` property for `Clock1` in the Component Designer to make it move more or less frequently.

Keeping Score

As you might recall, you created two labels, `HitsCountsLabel` and `MissesCountsLabel`, which had initial values of 0. We'd like to increment the numbers in these labels whenever the user successfully taps the mole (a hit) or taps the screen without touching the mole (a miss). To do so, we will use the `Canvas1.Touched` block, which indicates that the canvas was touched, the x and y coordinates of where it was contacted (which we don't need to know), and whether a sprite was tapped (which we do need to know). Figure 3-8 shows the code you will create.

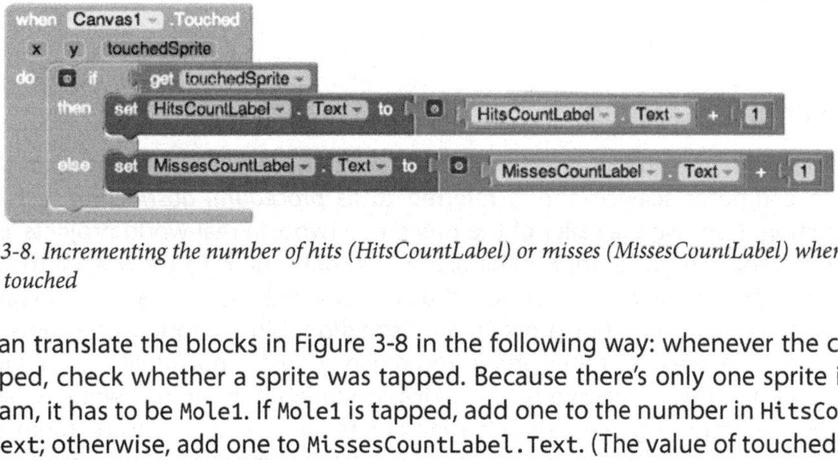

Figure 3-8. Incrementing the number of hits (HitsCountLabel) or misses (MissesCountLabel) when Canvas1 is touched

You can translate the blocks in Figure 3-8 in the following way: whenever the canvas is tapped, check whether a sprite was tapped. Because there's only one sprite in our program, it has to be `Mole1`. If `Mole1` is tapped, add one to the number in `HitsCountLabel.Text`; otherwise, add one to `MissesCountLabel.Text`. (The value of touchedSprite is false if no sprite was touched.)

Here's how to create the blocks:

1. Click the Canvas1 drawer and drag out `Canvas1.Touched`.

2. Click the Control drawer and drag out the `if-then` block. Click its blue icon and add an `else` branch. Then, place it within `Canvas1.Touched`.
3. Mouse over the `touchedSprite` event parameter on `Canvas1.Touched`, and then drag out the `get touchedSprite` block and place it in the test socket of `if-then-else`.
4. Because we want `HitsCountLabel.Text` to be incremented if the test succeeded (if the mole was touched), do the following:
   - From the HitsCountLabel drawer, drag out the `set HitsCountLabel.Text to` block, putting it to the right of "then."
   - Click the Math drawer and drag out a plus sign (+), placing it in the "to" socket.
   - Click the HitsCountLabel drawer and drag the `HitsCountLabel.Text` block to the left of the plus sign.
   - Click the Math drawer and drag a `0` block to the right of the plus sign. Click 0 and change it to 1.
5. Repeat step 4 for `MissesCountLabel` in the `else` section of the `ifelse` block.

Test your app *You can test this new code on your device by tapping the canvas, both on and off the mole, and watching the score change.*

Procedural Abstraction

The ability to name and later call a set of instructions like `MoveMole` is one of the key tools in computer science and is referred to as *procedural abstraction*. It is called "abstraction" because the caller of the procedure (who, in real-world projects, is likely to be different from the author of the procedure) only needs to know what the procedure does (moves the mole), not how it does it (by making two calls to the random-number generator). Without procedural abstraction, big computer programs would not be possible, because they contain too much code for individuals to hold in their head at a time. This is analogous to the division of labor in the real world, where, for example, different engineers design different parts of a car, none of them understanding all of the details, and the driver only has to understand the interface (e.g., pressing the brake pedal to stop the car), not the implementation.

Some advantages of procedural abstraction over copying and pasting code are:

- It is easier to test code if it is neatly segregated from the rest of the program.
- If there's a mistake in the code, it only needs to be fixed in one place.
- To change the implementation, such as ensuring that the mole doesn't move somewhere that it appeared recently, you only need to modify the code in one place.
- Procedures can be collected into a library and used in different programs. (Unfortunately, this functionality is not currently supported in App Inventor.)
- Breaking code into pieces helps you think about and implement the application ("divide and conquer").
- Choosing good names for procedures helps document the code, making it easier for someone else (or you, a month later) to read.

In later chapters, you will learn ways of making procedures even more powerful: adding arguments, providing return values, and having procedures call themselves. For an overview, see Chapter 21.

Resetting the Score

A friend who sees you playing MoleMash will probably want to give it a try, too, so it's good to have a way to reset the number of hits and misses to 0. Depending on which tutorials you've already worked through, you might be able to figure out how to do this without reading the following instructions. Consider giving it a try before reading ahead.

What we need is a `ResetButton.Click` block that sets the values of `HitsCountLabel.Text` and `MissesCountLabel.Text` to 0. Create the blocks shown in Figure 3-9.

```
when ResetButton .Click
do  set HitsCountLabel . Text to 0
    set MissesCountLabel . Text to 0
```

Figure 3-9. Resetting the number of hits (HitsCountLabel) and misses (MissesCountLabel) when the Reset button is pressed

At this point, you probably don't need step-by-step instructions for creating a button click event handler with text labels, but here's a tip to help speed up the process: instead of getting your number from the Math drawer, just type 0, and the block should be created for you. (These kinds of keyboard shortcuts exist for other blocks, too.)

Test your app *Try hitting and missing the mole and then pressing the Reset button.*

Vibrating When the Mole Is Touched

We said earlier that we want the device to vibrate when the user taps the mole, which we can do with the `Sound1.Vibrate` block, as shown in Figure 3-10.

Figure 3-10. Making the device vibrate briefly (for 100 milliseconds) when the mole is touched

Test your app See how the vibration works when you actually tap the mole. If the vibration is too long or too short for your taste, change the number of milliseconds in `Sound1.Vibrate` block.

The Complete App: MoleMash

Figure 3-11 illustrates the blocks for the complete MoleMash app.

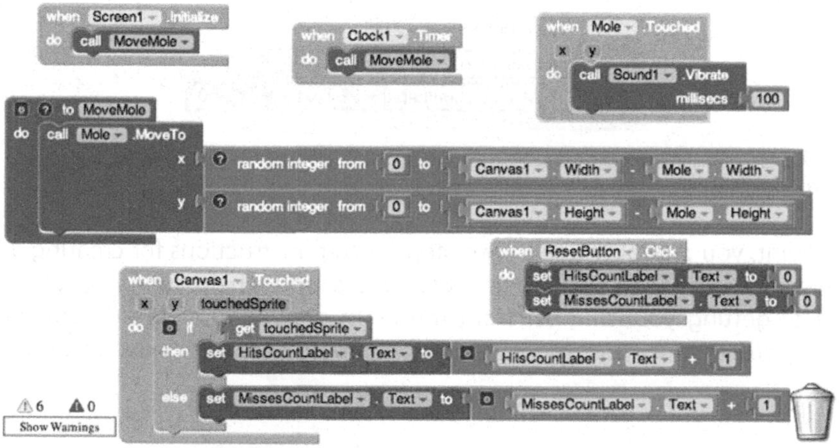

Figure 3-11. The complete MoleMash application

Variations

Here are some ideas for additions to MoleMash:

- Add buttons to let the user make the mole move faster or slower.
- Add a label to keep track of and display the number of times the mole has appeared (moved).
- Add a second `ImageSprite` with a picture of something that the user should *not* hit, such as a flower. If the user touches it, penalize him by reducing his score or ending the game.
- Instead of using a picture of a mole, let the user select a picture with the `Image Picker` component.

Summary

In this chapter, we covered a number of techniques that are useful for apps in general and games in particular:

- The `Canvas` component makes use of an x-y coordinate system, where x represents the horizontal direction (from 0 at the left to `Canvas.Width–1` at the right), and y the vertical direction (from 0 at the top to `Canvas.Height–1` at the bottom). The height and width of an `ImageSprite` can be subtracted from the height and width of a `Canvas` to make sure the sprite fits entirely on the `Canvas`.
- You can take advantage of the device's touchscreen through the `Canvas` and `ImageSprite` components' `Touched` methods.
- You can create real-time applications that react not just to user input but also in response to the device's internal timer. Specifically, the `Clock.Timer` block runs at the frequency specified in the *Clock.Interval* property and can be used to move `ImageSprite` (or other) components.
- You can use labels to display scores, which go up (or down) in response to the player's actions.
- You can provide tactile feedback to users through the `Sound.Vibrate` method, which makes the device vibrate for the specified number of milliseconds.
- Instead of just using the built-in methods, you can create procedures to name a set of blocks that can be called just like the built-in ones. This is called procedural abstraction and is a key concept in computer science, enabling code reuse and making complex applications possible.
- You can generate unpredictable behavior with the `random integer` block (in the Math drawer), making a game different every time it is played.

You'll learn more techniques for games, including detecting collisions between moving `ImageSprite` components, in Chapter 5.

CHAPTER 4

No Texting While Driving

This chapter walks you through the creation of No Texting While Driving, a "text answering machine" app that auto-responds to text messages you receive while you're driving (or in the office, etc.), speaks text messages aloud, and even sends location information as part of the automated text reply. The app demonstrates how you can control some of the great features of an Android phone, including SMS texting, text-to-speech, persistent data, and GPS location sensing.

In January 2010, the United States National Safety Council (NSC) announced the results of a study that found that at least 28 percent of all traffic accidents—close to 1.6 million crashes every year—are caused by drivers using cell phones, and at least 200,000 of those accidents occurred while drivers were texting.[1] As a result, many states have banned drivers from using cell phones altogether.

Daniel Finnegan, a student at the University of San Francisco taking an App Inventor programming class, came up with an app idea to help with the driving and texting epidemic. The app he created, which is shown in Figure 4-1, responds automatically (and hands-free) to any text with a message such as "I'm driving right now, I'll contact you shortly."

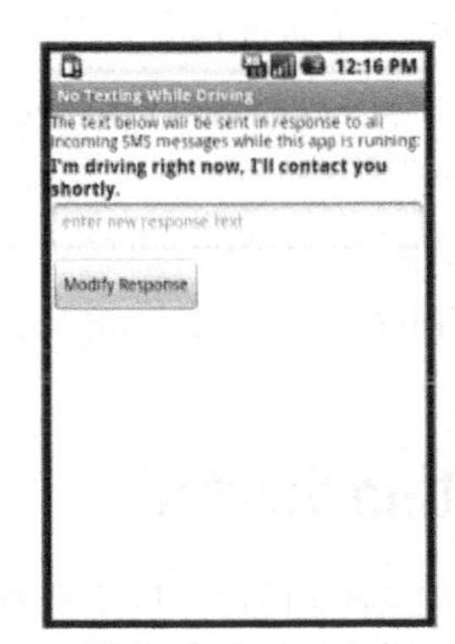

Figure 4-1. The No Texting While Driving app

The app was later extended so that it would speak the incoming texts aloud and add the driver's GPS location to the auto-response text, and it was turned into a tutorial for the App Inventor site.

Some weeks after the app was posted on the App Inventor site, State Farm Insurance created an Android app called On the Move, which had similar functionality to No Texting While Driving (*http://www.statefarm.com/aboutus/newsroom/20100819.asp*).

1 *http://bit.ly/1qiH7aZ*

We don't know if Daniel's app or the tutorial on the App Inventor site influenced On the Move, but it's interesting to consider the possibility that an app created in a beginning programming course (by a creative writing student, no less!) might have inspired this mass-produced piece of software, or at least contributed to the ecosystem that brought it about. It certainly demonstrated how App Inventor has lowered the barrier of entry so that anyone with a good idea can quickly and inexpensively turn his idea into a tangible, interactive app. Clive Thompson of *Wired* magazine picked up on the novelty and wrote this:

> Software, after all, affects almost everything we do. Pick any major problem—global warming, health care, or, in Finnegan's case, highway safety—and clever software is part of the solution. Yet only a tiny chunk of people ever consider learning to write code, which means we're not tapping the creativity of a big chunk of society.[2]

App Inventor is about tapping the creativity Thompson mentions, about opening up the world of software creation to everyone.

What You'll Learn

This is a more complex app than those in the previous chapters, so you'll build it one piece of functionality at a time, starting with the auto-response message. You'll learn about:

- The `Texting` component for sending texts and processing received texts.
- An input form for submitting the custom response message.
- The `TinyDB` database component for saving the customized message even after the app is closed.
- The `Screen.Initialize` event for loading the custom response when the app launches.
- The `TextToSpeech` component for speaking texts aloud.
- The `LocationSensor` component for reporting the driver's current location.

Getting Started

Open your brower to the App Inventor website and start a new project. Name it "NoTextingWhileDriving" (remember, project names can't have spaces) and set the screen's title to "No Texting While Driving". Then, click Connect and set up live testing on your device or the emulator.

---

2 Clive Thompson, "Clive Thompson on Coding for the Masses", *http://wrd.cm/1uT25O5*

Designing the Components

The user interface for the app is relatively simple: it has a label instructing the user how the app works, a label that displays the text that is to be automatically sent in response to incoming texts, a text box for changing the response, and a button for submitting the change. You'll also need to drag in a `Texting` component, a `TinyDB` component, a `TextToSpeech` component, and a `LocationSensor` component, all of which will appear in the "Non-visible components" area. You can see how this should look in the snapshot of the Component Designer in Figure 4-2.

Figure 4-2. The No Texting While Driving app in the Component Designer

You can build the user interface shown in Figure 4-2 by dragging out the components listed in Table 4-1.

Table 4-1. All of the components for the No Texting app

Component type	Palette group	What you'll name it	Purpose
`Label`	User Interface	`PromptLabel`	Let the user know how the app works.
`Label`	User Interface	`ResponseLabel`	The response that will be sent back to the sender.
`TextBox`	User Interface	`newResponseTextBox`	The user will enter the custom response here.
`Button`	User Interface	`SubmitResponseButton`	The user clicks this to submit response.
`Texting`	Social	`Texting1`	Process the texts.

Component type	Palette group	What you'll name it	Purpose
TinyDB	Storage	TinyDB1	Store the response in the database.
TextToSpeech	Media	TextToSpeech1	Speak the text aloud.
LocationSensor	Sensors	LocationSensor1	Sense where the device is.

Set the properties of the components in the following way:

- Set the `Text` of `PromptLabel` to "The text below will be sent in response to all SMS texts received while this app is running."
- Set the `Text` of `ResponseLabel` to "I'm driving right now, I'll contact you shortly." Check its `boldness` property.
- Set the `Text` of `NewResponseTextbox` to " ". (This leaves the text box blank for the user's input.)
- Set the `Hint` of `NewResponseTextbox` to "Enter new response text".
- Set the `Text` of `SubmitResponseButton` to "Modify Response".

Adding Behaviors to the Components

You'll start by programming the autoresponse behavior in which a text reply is sent to any incoming text. You'll then add blocks so that the user can specify a custom response and save that response persistently. Finally, you'll add blocks that read the incoming texts aloud and add location information to the auto-response texts.

Auto-Responding to a Text

For the auto-response behavior, you'll use App Inventor's `Texting` component. You can think of this component as a little person inside your phone who knows how to read and write texts. For reading texts, the component provides a `Texting.MessageReceived` event block. You can drag this block out and place blocks inside it to show what should happen when a text is received. In the case of this app, we want to automatically send back a text in response.

You can send a text with three blocks. First, you set the phone number to which the text should be sent, which is a property of the `Texting1` component. Next, you set the message to be sent, also a property of `Texting1`. Finally, you actually send the text with the `Texting1.SendMessage` block. Table 4-2 lists all the blocks you'll need for this auto-response behavior, and Figure 4-3 shows how they should look in the Blocks Editor.

Table 4-2. The blocks for sending an auto-response

Block type	Drawer	Purpose
`Texting1.MessageReceived`	Texting	The event handler that is triggered when the phone receives a text.
`set Texting1.PhoneNumber to`	Texting	Set the `PhoneNumber` property before sending.
`value number`	Drag from when block	The phone number of the person who sent the text.
`set Texting1.Message to`	Texting	Set the `Message` property before sending.
`ResponseLabel.Text`	ResponseLabel	The message the user has entered.
`Texting1.SendMessage`	Texting	Send the message.

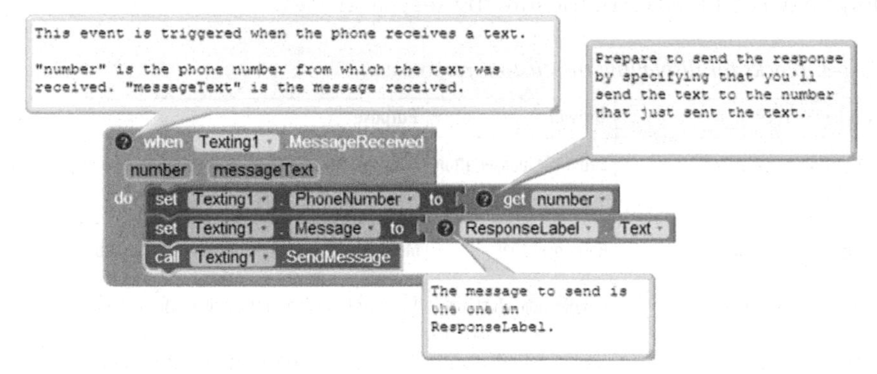

Figure 4-3. Responding to an incoming text

How the blocks work

When the phone receives a text message, the `Texting1.MessageReceived` event is triggered. The phone number of the sender is in the argument `number`, and the message received is in the argument `messageText`.

As the auto-response text should be sent back to the sender, `Texting. PhoneNumber` is set to `number`. `Texting.Message` is set to `ResponseLabel.Text`, which is what you typed while in the Designer: "I'm driving right now, I'll contact you shortly." When these are set, the app calls `Texting.SendMessage` to actually send the response.

Test your app *You'll need two phones to test this behavior, one to run the app and one to send the initial text. If you don't have a second phone handy, you can use Google Voice or a similar service on your computer and send texts from that service to the phone running the app. After you set things up, send a text to the phone running the app. Does the first phone receive the response text?*

Entering a Custom Response

Next, let's add blocks so the user can enter her own custom response. In the Component Designer, you added a `TextBox` component named `NewResponseTextbox`; this is where the user will type the custom response. When the user clicks on the `SubmitResponseButton`, you need to copy the entry (`NewResponseTextbox`) into the `ResponseLabel`, which is used to respond to texts. Table 4-3 lists the blocks you'll need for transferring a newly entered response into the `ResponseLabel`.

Table 4-3. Blocks for displaying the custom response

Block type	Drawer	Purpose
`SubmitResponseButton.Click`	SubmitResponseButton	The user clicks this button to submit a new response message.
`set ResponseLabel.Text to`	ResponseLabel	Move (set) the newly input value to this label.
`NewResponseTextbox.Text`	NewResponseTextbox	The user has entered the new response here.
`set NewResponseTextbox.Text to`	NewResponseTextbox	Blank out the text box after transferring information
`text` ("")	Text	The empty text.

How the blocks work

Think of how you interact with a typical input form: you first type something in a text box and then click a submit button to signal the system to process it. The input form for this app is no different. Figure 4-4 shows how the blocks are programmed so that when the user clicks the `SubmitResponseButton`, the `SubmitResponseButton.Click` event is triggered.

Put the user's entry into ResponseLabel.

when SubmitResponseButton .Click
do set ResponseLabel . Text to NewResponseTextBox . Text
set NewResponseTextBox . Text to " "

Blank out the entry after transferring to label.

Figure 4-4. Setting the response to the user's entry

The event handler in this case copies (or, in programming terms, *sets*) what the user has entered in `NewResponseTextbox` into the `ResponseLabel`. Recall that `ResponseLabel` holds the message that will be sent out in the auto-response, so you want to be sure to place the newly entered custom message there.

Test your app *Enter a custom response and submit it, and then use the second phone to send another text to the phone running the app. Was the custom response sent?*

Storing the Custom Response Persistently

Your user can now customize the auto-response, but there is one catch: if the user enters a custom response and then closes the app and relaunches it, the custom response will not appear (instead, the default response will). This behavior is not what your users will expect; they'll want to see the custom response they entered when they restart the app. To make this happen, you need to store that custom response *persistently*.

Placing data in the `ResponseLabel.Text` property is technically storing it, but the issue is that data stored in component properties is *transient* data. Transient data is like your short-term memory; the phone "forgets" it as soon as an app closes. If you want your app to remember something *persistently*, you have to transfer it from short-term memory (a component property or variable) to long-term memory (a database or file).

To store data persistently in App Inventor, you use the `TinyDB` component, which stores data in a file on the Android device. `TinyDB` provides two functions: `StoreValue` and `GetValue`. With the former, the app can store information in the device's database, whereas with the latter, the app can retrieve information that has already been stored.

For many apps, you'll use the following scheme:

1. Store data to the database each time the user submits a new value.

2. When the app launches, load the data from the database into a variable or property.

You'll start by modifying the `SubmitResponseButton.Click` event handler so that it stores the data persistently, using the blocks listed in Table 4-4.

Table 4-4. Blocks for storing the custom response with TinyDB

Block type	Drawer	Purpose
`TinyDB1.StoreValue`	TinyDB1	Store the custom message in the phone's database.
`text` ("responseMessage")	Text	Use this as the tag for the data.
`ResponseLabel.Text`	ResponseLabel	The response message is now here.

How the blocks work

This app uses `TinyDB` to take the text it just put in `ResponseLabel` and store it in the database. As shown in Figure 4-5, when you store something in the database, you provide a tag with it; in this case, the tag is "responseMessage." Think of the tag as the name for the data in the database; it uniquely identifies the data you are storing. As you'll see in the next section, you'll use the same tag ("responseMessage") when you load the data back in from the database.

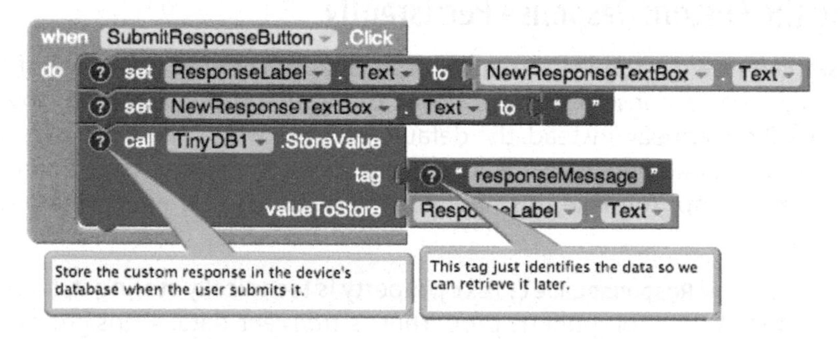

Figure 4-5. Storing the custom response persistently

Retrieving the Custom Response When the App Opens

The reason for storing the custom response in the database is so that it can be loaded back into the app the next time the user opens it. App Inventor provides a special event block that is triggered when the app opens: `Screen1.Initialize` (if you completed MoleMash in Chapter 3, you've seen this before). If you drag this event block out and place blocks in it, those blocks will be executed immediately when the app launches.

For this app, your `Screen1.Initialize` event handler will load the custom response from the database by using the `TinyDB.GetValue` function. The blocks you'll need for this are shown in Table 4-5.

Table 4-5. Blocks for loading the data back in when the app is opened

Block type	Drawer	Purpose
`Screen1.Initialize`	Screen1	This is triggered when the app begins.
`TinyDB1.GetValue`	TinyDB1	Get the stored response text from the database.
`text` ("responseMessage")	Text	Plug this into the `tag` socket of `TinyDB.GetValue`, making sure the text is the same as that used in `TinyDB.StoreValue` earlier.
`text` ("I'm driving right now, I'll contact you shortly")	Text	Plug this into the `valueIfTagNotThere` slot of `TinyDB.GetValue`. This is the default message that should be used if the user has not yet stored a custom response.
`set ResponseLabel.Text to`	ResponseLabel	Place the retrieved value in `ResponseLabel`.

How the blocks work

Figure 4-6 shows the blocks. To understand them, you must envision a user opening the app for the first time, entering a custom response, and opening the app subsequent times. The first time the user opens the app, there won't be any custom response in the database to load, so you want to leave the default response in the `ResponseLabel`. On successive launches, you want to load the previously stored custom response from the database and place it in the `ResponseLabel`.

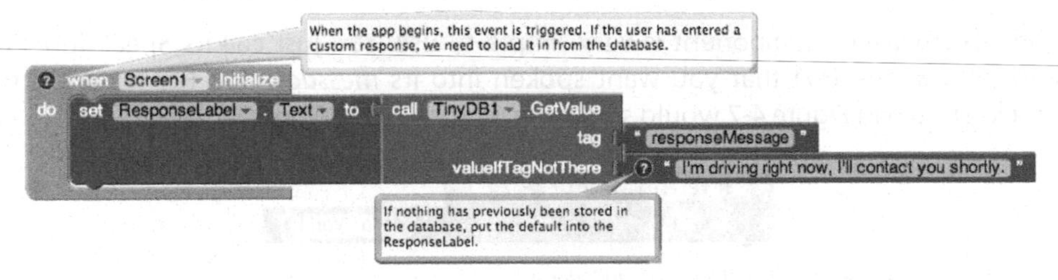

Figure 4-6. Loading the custom response from the database upon app initialization

When the app begins, the `Screen1.Initialize` event is triggered. The app calls the `TinyDB1.GetValue` with a tag of `responseMessage`, the same tag you used when you stored the user's custom response entry earlier. If there is data in the `TinyDB` with a tag of `responseMessage`, it is returned and placed in the `ResponseLabel`.

However, there won't be data the first time the app is launched; this will be the case until the user types a custom response. To handle such cases, `TinyDB1.GetValue` has a second parameter, `valueIfTagNotThere`. If no data is found, the value in `valueIfTag NotThere` is used instead. In this case, "I'm driving right now, I'll contact you shortly," the default value, is placed into `ResponseLabel`.

Test your app To test this behavior, you need to restart your app to see if the data is truly stored persistently and retrieved correctly. In live testing, you can restart the app by changing some component property in the designer, such as the font size of a Label. This will cause the app to reload and `Screen.Initialize` to be triggered. Of course, you can also test the app by actually building it and installing the .apk file on your phone. Once the app is on your phone, launch it, type a message for the custom response, close the app, and then reopen it. If the message you entered is still there, things are working correctly.

Speaking the Incoming Texts Aloud

In this section, you'll modify the app so that when you receive a text, the sender's phone number, along with the message, is spoken aloud. The idea here is that when you're driving and hear a text come in, you might be tempted to check the text even if you know the app is sending an auto-response. With text-to-speech, you can hear the incoming texts and keep your hands on the wheel.

Android devices provide text-to-speech capabilities, and App Inventor provides a component, `TextToSpeech`, that will speak any text you give it. Note that the "Text" in `TextToSpeech` refers to a sequence of letters, digits, and punctuation, not an SMS text.

The `TextToSpeech` component is very simple to use. You just call its Speak function and plug in the text that you want spoken into its *message* slot. For instance, the blocks shown in Figure 4-7 would speak the words, "Hello World."

call TextToSpeech1 .Speak
message " Hello World "

Figure 4-7. Blocks for speaking "Hello World" aloud

For the No Texting While Driving app, you'll need to provide a more complicated message to be spoken, one that includes both the text received and the phone number of the person who sent it. Instead of plugging in a static text object such as the "Hello World" text block, you'll plug in a `join` block. A commonly used function, `join`, makes it possible for you to combine separate pieces of text (or numbers and other characters) into a single text object.

You'll need to make the call to `TextToSpeech.Speak` within the `Texting.MessageReceived` event handler you programmed earlier. The blocks you programmed previously handle this event by setting the `PhoneNumber` and `Message` properties of the `Texting` component appropriately and then sending the response text. You'll extend that event handler by adding the blocks listed in Table 4-6.

Table 4-6. Blocks for speaking the incoming text aloud

Block type	Drawer	Purpose
`TextToSpeech1.Speak`	TextToSpeech1	Speak the message received aloud.
`join`	Text	Concatenate (join together) the words that will be spoken.
`text` ("SMS text received from")	Text	The first words spoken.
`get number`	Drag in from when block	The number from which the original text was received.
`text` (".The message is")	Text	Put a period in after the phone number and then say, "The message is."
`get messageText`	Drag in from when block	The original message received.

How the blocks work

After the response is sent, the `TextToSpeech1.Speak` function is called, as shown at the bottom of Figure 4-8. You can plug any text into the message socket of the `TextToSpeech1.Speak` function. In this case, `join` is used to build the words to be spoken—it *concatenates* (or joins) together the text "SMS text received from" and the phone number from which the message was received (`get number`), plus the text ".The message is," and finally the message received (`get messageText`). So, if the text "hello" was sent from the number "111-2222," the phone would say, "SMS text received from 111-2222. The message is hello."

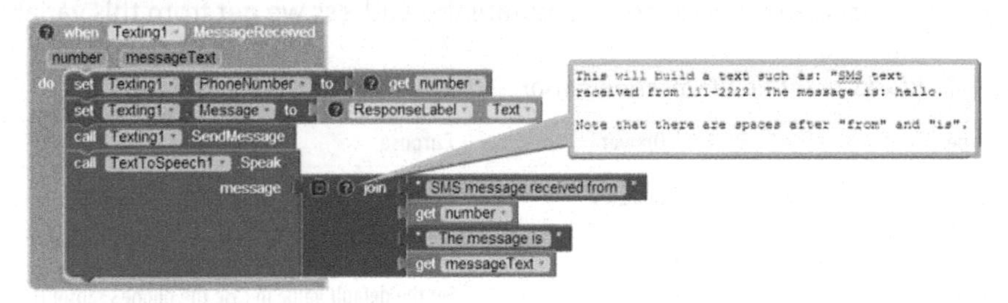

Figure 4-8. Speaking the incoming text aloud

Test your app *You'll need a second phone to test your app. From the second phone, send a text to the phone running the app. Does the phone running the app speak the text aloud? Does it still send an automated response?*

Adding Location Information to the Response

Check-In apps help people track one another's location. There are major privacy concerns with such apps, one reason being that location tracking kindles people's fear of a "Big Brother" apparatus that a totalitarian government might set up to track its citizens' whereabouts. But apps that use location information can be quite useful. Think of a lost child, or hikers who've gone off the trail in the woods.

In the No Texting While Driving app, you can use location tracking to convey a bit more information in the auto-response to incoming texts. Instead of just "I'm driving," the response message can be something like, "I'm driving and I'm currently at 3413 Cherry Avenue." For someone awaiting the arrival of a friend or family member, this extra information can be helpful.

App Inventor provides the `LocationSensor` component for interfacing with the phone's GPS (or *Global Positioning System*). Besides latitude and longitude information, the `LocationSensor` can also tap into Google Maps to provide the driver's current street address.

It's important to note that `LocationSensor` doesn't always have a reading. For this reason, you need to take care to use the component properly. Specifically, your app should respond to the `LocationSensor.LocationChanged` event handler. A `LocationChanged` event occurs when the phone's location sensor first gets a reading, and when the phone is moved to generate a new reading. Using the blocks listed in Table 4-7, our scheme, shown in Figure 4-9, will respond to the `LocationChanged` event by placing the current address in a variable we'll name `lastKnownLocation`. Later, we'll change the response message to incorporate the address we get from this variable.

Table 4-7. Blocks to set up the location sensor

Block type	Drawer	Purpose
`initialize global variable` ("lastKnownLocation")	Variables	Create a variable to hold the last read address.
`text` ("unknown")	Text	Set the default value in case the phone's sensor is not working.
`LocationSensor1.LocationChanged`	LocationSensor1	This is triggered on the first location reading and every location change.

Block type	Drawer	Purpose
`set global lastKnownLocation to`	Drag from initialize global block.	Set this variable to be used later.
`LocationSensor1.CurrentAddress`	LocationSensor1	This is a street address such as "2222 Willard Street, Atlanta, Georgia."

Figure 4-9. Recording the phone's location in a variable each time the GPS location is sensed

How the blocks work

The `LocationSensor1.LocationChanged` event is triggered the first time the sensor gets a location reading and then each time the device is moved so that a new reading is generated. The `LocationSensor1.CurrentAddress` function is called to get the current street address of the device and store it in the `lastKnownLocation` variable.

Note that with these blocks, you've finished only half of the job. The app still needs to incorporate the location information into the auto-response text that will be sent back to the sender. You'll do that next.

Sending the Location as Part of the Response

Using the variable `lastKnownLocation`, you can modify the `Texting1.MessageReceived` event handler to add location information to the response. Table 4-8 lists the blocks you'll need for this.

Table 4-8. Blocks to display location information in the auto-response

Block type	Drawer	Purpose
`join`	Text	concatenate some text together
`ResponseLabel.Text`	MessageTextBox	This is the (custom) message in the text box.
`text` ("My last known location is:")	Text	This will be spoken after the custom message (note the leading space).
`get global lastKnownLocation`	LocationSensor	This is an address such as "1600 Pennsylvania Ave NW, Washington, DC 20500."

How the blocks work

This behavior works in concert with the `LocationSensor1.LocationChanged` event and the variable `lastKnownLocation`. As you can see in Figure 4-10, instead of directly sending a message containing the text in `ResponseLabel.Text`, the app first builds a message by using `join`. It combines the response text in `ResponseLabel.Text` with the text "My last known location is:" followed by the variable `lastKnownLocation`.

Figure 4-10. Including location information in the response text

The default value of `lastKnownLocation` is "unknown," so if the location sensor hasn't yet generated a reading, the second part of the response message will contain the text, "My last known location is: unknown." If there has been a reading, the second part of the response will be something like, "My last known location is: 1600 Pennsylvania Ave NW, Washington, DC 20500."

Test your app *From the second phone, send a text to the phone running the app. Does the second phone receive the response text with the location information? If it doesn't, make sure you've turned GPS on in the Location settings of the phone running the app.*

The Complete App: No Texting While Driving

Figure 4-11 shows the final block configuration for No Texting While Driving.

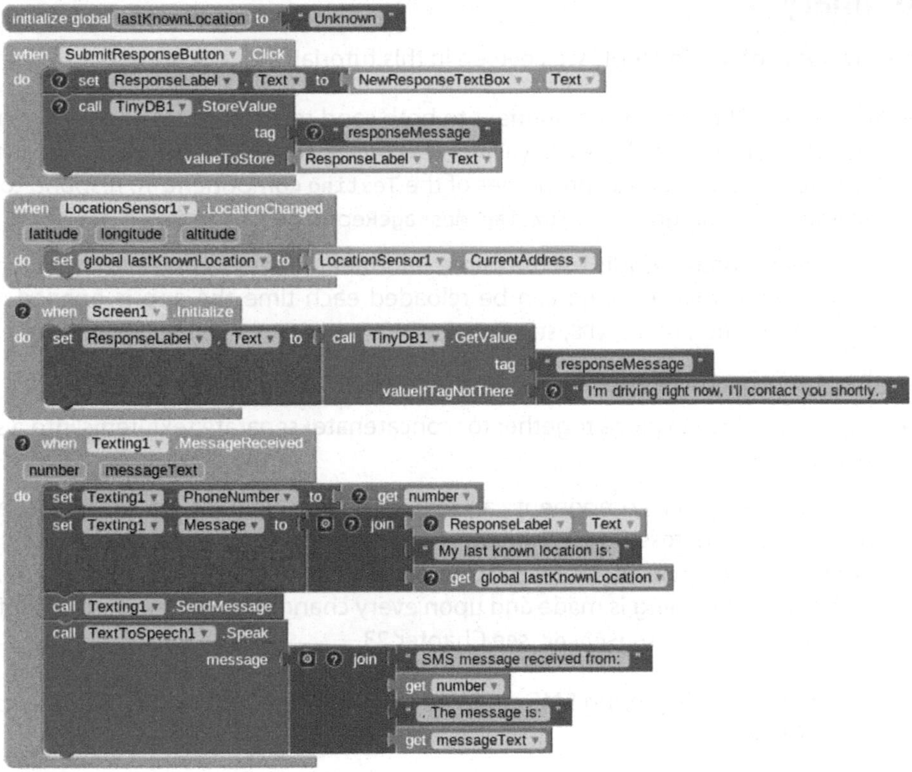

Figure 4-11. The complete No Texting While Driving app

Variations

Once you get the app working, you might want to explore some variations, such as the following:

- Write a version that lets the user define custom responses for particular incoming phone numbers. You'll need to add conditional (`if`) blocks that check for those numbers. For more information on conditional blocks, see Chapter 18.
- Write a version that sends custom responses based on whether the user is within certain latitude/longitude boundaries. So, if the app determines that you're in room 222, it will send back "Bob is in room 222 and can't text right now." For more information on the `LocationSensor` and determining boundaries, see Chapter 23.
- Write a version that sounds an alarm when a text is received from a number in a "notify" list. For help working with lists, see Chapter 19.

Summary

Here are some of the concepts we covered in this tutorial:

- You can use the `Texting` component to both send text messages and process the ones that are received. Before calling `Texting.SendMessage`, you should set the `PhoneNumber` and `Message` properties of the `Texting` component. To respond to an incoming text, program the `Texting.MessageReceived` handler.
- The `TinyDB` component is used to store information persistently—in the phone's database—so that the data can be reloaded each time the app is opened. For more information on `TinyDB`, see Chapter 22.
- The `TextToSpeech` component takes any text object and speaks it aloud.
- You can use `join` to piece together (or concatenate) separate text items into a single text object.
- The `LocationSensor` component can report the phone's latitude, longitude, and current street address. To ensure that it has a reading, you should access its data within the `LocationSensor.LocationChanged` event handler, which is triggered the first time a reading is made and upon every change thereafter. For more information on the `LocationSensor`, see Chapter 23.

If you're interested in exploring SMS-processing apps further, check out the Broadcast Hub app in Chapter 11.

CHAPTER 5

Ladybug Chase

Games are among the most exciting mobile device apps, both to play and to create. The recent smash hit Angry Birds was downloaded 50 million times in its first year and is played more than a million hours every day, according to Rovio, its developer. (There is even talk of making it into a feature film!) Although we can't guarantee that kind of success, we can help you create your own games with App Inventor, including this one involving a ladybug eating aphids while avoiding a frog.

What You'll Build

In this "first-person chewer" game, the user will be represented by a ladybug, whose movement will be controlled by the device's tilt. This brings the user into the game in a different way from MoleMash (Chapter 3), in which the user was outside the device, reaching in.

The Ladybug Chase app is shown in Figure 5-1. The user can:

- Control a ladybug by tilting the device.
- View an energy-level bar on the screen, which decreases over time, leading to the ladybug's starvation.
- Make the ladybug chase and eat aphids to gain energy and prevent starvation.
- Help the ladybug avoid a frog that wants to eat it.

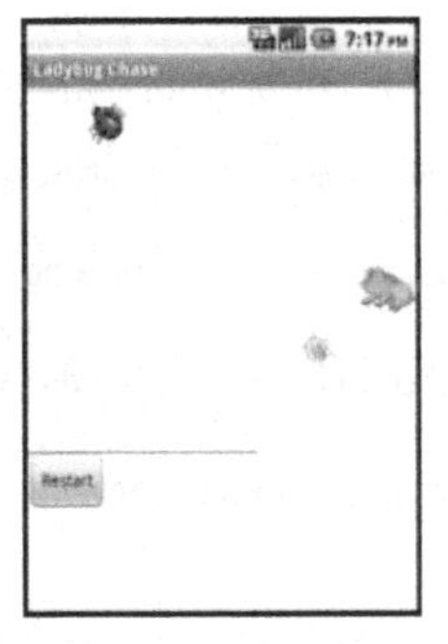

Figure 5-1. The Ladybug Chase game in the Designer

What You'll Learn

You should work through the MoleMash app in Chapter 3 before delving into this chapter, because it assumes you know about procedure creation, random-number generation, the `if-then-else` block, and the `ImageSprite`, `Canvas`, `Sound`, and `Clock` components.

In addition to reviewing material from MoleMash and other previous chapters, this chapter introduces:

- Using multiple `ImageSprite` components and detecting collisions between them.
- Detecting device tilts with an `OrientationSensor` component and using it to control an `ImageSprite`.
- Changing the picture displayed for an `ImageSprite`.
- Drawing lines on a `Canvas` component.
- Controlling multiple events with a `Clock` component.
- Using variables to keep track of numbers (the ladybug's energy level).
- Creating and using procedures with parameters.
- Using the and block.

Designing the Components

This application will have a `Canvas` that provides a playing field for three `ImageSprite` components: one for the ladybug, one for the aphid, and one for the frog, which will also require a `Sound` component for its "ribbit." The `OrientationSensor` will be used to measure the device's tilt to move the ladybug, and a `Clock` will be used to change the aphid's direction.

There will be a second `Canvas` that displays the ladybug's energy level. A Reset button will restart the game if the ladybug starves or is eaten. Table 5-1 provides a complete list of the components in this app.

Table 5-1. All of the components for the Ladybug Chase game

Component type	Palette group	What you'll name it	Purpose
`Canvas`	Drawing and Animation	`FieldCanvas`	Playing field.
`ImageSprite`	Drawing and Animation	`Ladybug`	User-controlled player.
`OrientationSensor`	Sensors	`OrientationSensor1`	Detect the phone's tilt to control the ladybug.
`Clock`	User Interface	`Clock1`	Determines when to change the `ImageSprites`' headings.
`ImageSprite`	Drawing and Animation	`Aphid`	The ladybug's prey.
`ImageSprite`	Drawing and Animation	`Frog`	The ladybug's predator.
`Canvas`	Drawing and Animation	`EnergyCanvas`	Display the ladybug's energy level.

Component type	Palette group	What you'll name it	Purpose
Button	User Interface	RestartButton	Restart the game.
Sound	Media	Sound1	"Ribbit" when the frog eats the ladybug.

Getting Started

Download the following files:

- *http://appinventor.org/bookFiles/LadybugChase/ladybug.png*
- *http://appinventor.org/bookFiles/LadybugChase/aphid.png*
- *http://appinventor.org/bookFiles/LadybugChase/dead_ladybug.png*
- *http://appinventor.org/bookFiles/LadybugChase/frog.png*
- *http://appinventor.org/bookFiles/LadybugChase/frog.wav*

These are images for the *ladybug*, *aphid*, *dead ladybug*, and *frog*, as well as a sound file for the frog's *ribbit*. After downloading them to your computer, add them to your app in the Media section of the Designer.

Connect to the App Inventor website and start a new project. Name it "Ladybug-Chase" and also set the screen's title to "Ladybug Chase". Open the Blocks Editor and connect to the device.

Placing the Initial Components

Although previous chapters have had you create all the components at once, that's not how developers typically work. Instead, it's more common to create one part of a program at a time, test it, and then move on to the next part of the program. In this section, we will create the ladybug and control its movement.

- In the Designer, create a `Canvas`, name it `FieldCanvas`, and set its `Width` to "Fill parent" and its `Height` to 300 pixels.
- Place an `ImageSprite` on the `Canvas`, renaming it `Ladybug` and setting its `Picture` property to the ladybug image. Don't worry about the values of the `X` and `Y` properties, because those will depend on where on the canvas you placed the `ImageSprite`.

As you might have noticed, `ImageSprites` also have `Interval`, `Heading`, and `Speed` properties, which you will use in this program:

- The `Interval` property, which you can set to 10 (milliseconds) for this game, specifies how often the `ImageSprite` should move itself (as opposed to being moved by the `MoveTo` procedure, which you used for MoleMash).

- The Heading property indicates the direction in which the ImageSprite should move, in degrees. For example, 0 means due right, 90 means straight up, 180 means due left, and so on. Leave the Heading as is right now; we will change it in the Blocks Editor.
- The Speed property specifies how many pixels the ImageSprite should move whenever its Interval (10 milliseconds) passes. We will also set the Speed property in the Blocks Editor.

The ladybug's movement will be controlled by an OrientationSensor, which detects how the device is tilted. We want to use the Clock component to check the device's orientation every 10 milliseconds (100 times per second) and change the ladybug's Heading (direction) accordingly. We will set this up in the Blocks Editor as follows:

1. Add an OrientationSensor, which will appear in the "Non-visible components" section.
2. Add a Clock, which will also appear in the "Non-visible components" section, and set its TimerInterval to 10 milliseconds. Check what you've added against Figure 5-2.

If you will be using a device other than the emulator, you'll need to disable autorotation for the screen, which changes the display direction when you turn the device. Select Screen1 and set its ScreenOrientation property to Portrait.

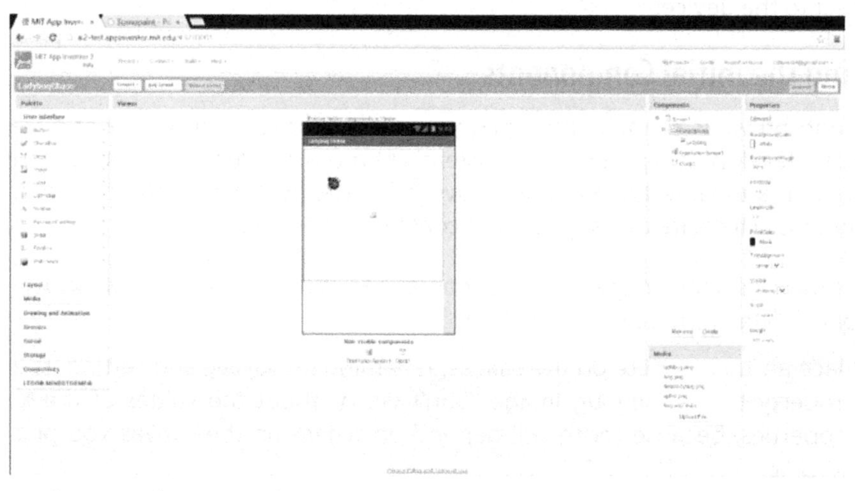

Figure 5-2. Setting up the user interface in the Component Designer for animating the ladybug

Adding Behaviors to the Components

Moving the Ladybug

Moving to the Blocks Editor, create the procedure `UpdateLadybug` and a `Clock1.Timer` block, as shown in Figure 5-3. Try typing the names of some of the blocks (such as "Clock1.Timer") instead of dragging them out of the drawers. (Note that the operation applied to the number 100 is multiplication, indicated by an asterisk, which might be hard to see in the figure.) You do not need to create the yellow comment callouts, although you can by right-clicking a block and selecting Add Comment.

The `UpdateLadybug` procedure makes use of two of the `OrientationSensor`'s most useful properties:

- `Angle`, which indicates the direction in which the device is tilted (in degrees).
- `Magnitude`, which indicates the amount of tilt, ranging from 0 (no tilt) to 1 (maximum tilt).

Multiplying the `Magnitude` by 100 tells the ladybug that it should move between 0 and 100 pixels in the specified `Heading` (direction) whenever its `TimerInterval`, which you previously set to 10 milliseconds in the Component Designer, passes.

Although you can try this out on the connected device, the ladybug's movement might be both slower and jerkier than if you package and download the app to the device. If, after doing that, you find the ladybug's movement too sluggish, increase the speed multiplier. If the ladybug seems too jerky, decrease it.

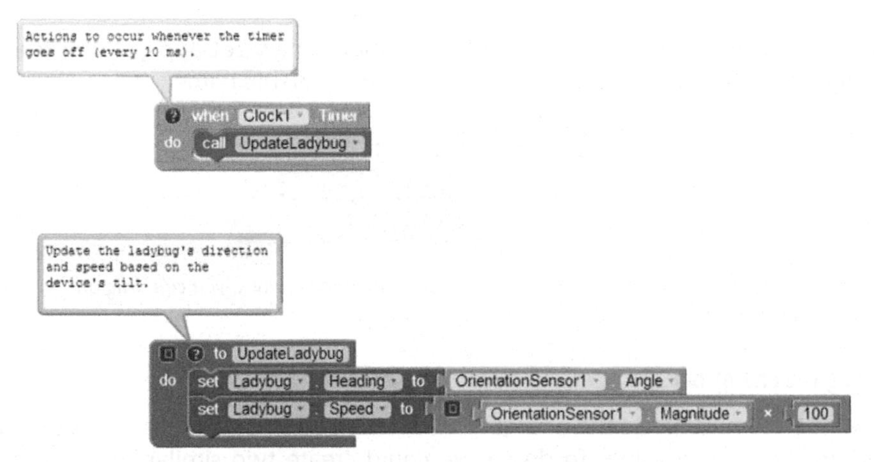

Figure 5-3. Changing the ladybug's heading and speed every 10 milliseconds

Displaying the Energy Level

We will display the ladybug's energy level via a red bar in a second canvas. The line will be 1 pixel high, and its width will be the same number of pixels as the ladybug's energy, which ranges from 200 (well fed) to 0 (dead).

Adding a component

In the Designer, create a new `Canvas`. Place it beneath `FieldCanvas` and name it `EnergyCanvas`. Set its `Width` property to "Fill parent" and its `Height` to 1 pixel.

Creating a variable: energy

In the Blocks Editor, you will need to create a variable `energy` with an initial value of 200 to keep track of the ladybug's energy level, as shown in Figure 5-4. (As you might recall, we first used a variable, `dotSize`, in the PaintPot app in Chapter 2.) Here's how to do it:

1. In the Blocks Editor, drag out an `initialize global name to` block. Change the text "name" to "energy".
2. Create a `number 200` block (by either starting to type the number 200 or dragging a `number` block from the Math drawer) and plug it into `global energy`, as shown in Figure 5-4.

Figure 5-4. Initializing the variable energy to 200

Figure 5-5 illustrates that when you define a variable, new `set` and `get` blocks are created for it that you can access by mousing over the variable name.

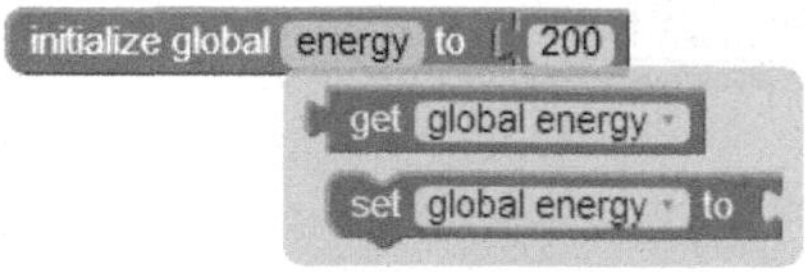

Figure 5-5. When you mouse over a variable in the initialize global block, you can drag out set and get blocks for the variable

Drawing the energy bar

We want to communicate the energy level with a red bar, which has a length in pixels equal to the energy value. To do so, we could create two similar sets of blocks as follows:

1. Draw a red line from (0, 0) to (`energy`, 0) in `FieldCanvas` to show the current energy level.

2. Draw a white line from (0, 0) to (`EnergyCanvas.Width`, 0) in `FieldCanvas` to erase the current energy level before drawing the new level.

However, a better alternative is to create a procedure that can draw a line of any length and of any color in `FieldCanvas`. To do this, we must specify two parameters, `length` and `color`, when our procedure is called, just as we needed to specify parameter values in MoleMash when we called the built-in `random integer` procedure. Here are the steps for creating a `DrawEnergyLine` procedure:

1. Go to the Procedures drawer and drag out a `to procedure do` block. Choose the version that contains "do" rather than "return" because our procedure will not return a value.
2. Click the procedure name ("procedure") and change it to "DrawEnergyLine".
3. At the upper left of the new block, click the little blue square. This opens the window shown on the left of Figure 5-6.
4. From the left side of this window, drag an input to the right side, changing its name from "x" to "length". This indicates that the procedure will have a parameter named "length".
5. Repeat for a second parameter named "color", which must go beneath the one named "length". This should look like the right side of Figure 5-6.
6. Click the blue icon again to close the inputs window.
7. Fill in the rest of the procedure as shown in Figure 5-7. You can find `get color` and `get length` by mousing over their names in the procedure definition.

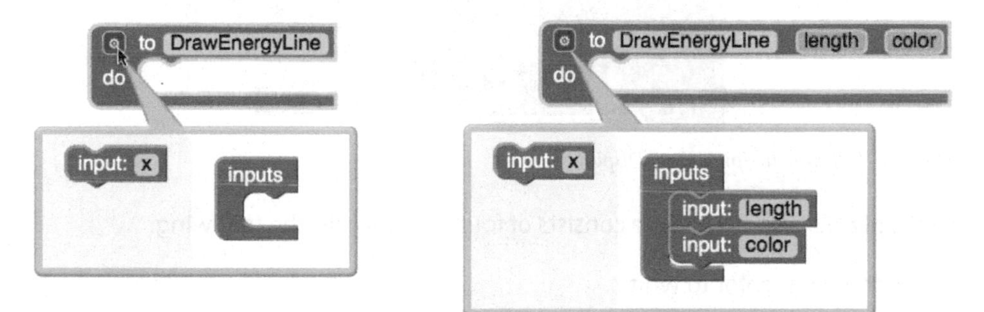

Figure 5-6. Adding inputs (parameters) to the procedure DrawEnergyLine

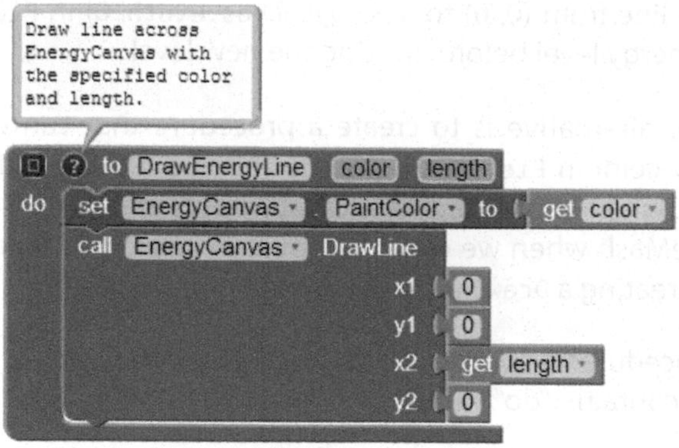

Figure 5-7. Defining the procedure DrawEnergyLine

Now that you're getting the hang of creating your own procedures, let's also write a `DisplayEnergy` procedure that calls `DrawEnergyLine` twice: once to erase the old line (by drawing a white line all the way across the canvas), and once to display the new line, as shown in Figure 5-8.

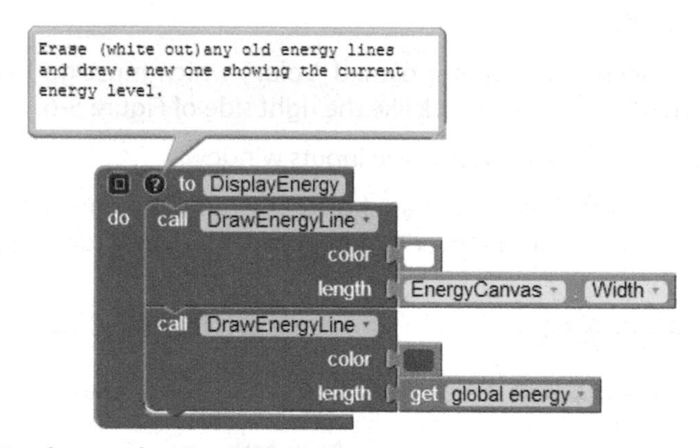

Figure 5-8. Defining the procedure DisplayEnergy

The `DisplayEnergy` procedure consists of four lines that do the following:

1. Set the paint color to white.
2. Draw a line all the way across `EnergyCanvas` (which is only 1 pixel high).
3. Set the paint color to red.
4. Draw a line whose length in pixels is the same as the energy value.

Note *The process of replacing common code with calls to a new procedure is called* refactoring, *a set of powerful techniques for making programs more maintainable and reliable. In this case, if we ever wanted to change the height or location of the energy line, we would just have to make a single change to* `DrawEnergyLine`, *rather than making changes to every call to it.*

Starvation

Unlike the apps in previous chapters, this game has a way to end: it's over if the ladybug fails to eat enough aphids or is herself eaten by the frog. In either of these cases, we want the ladybug to stop moving (which we can do by setting `Ladybug.Enabled` to false) and for the picture to change from a live ladybug to a dead one (which we can do by changing `Ladybug.Picture` to the name of the appropriate uploaded image). Create the `GameOver` procedure as shown in Figure 5-9.

```
to GameOver
do  set Ladybug . Enabled to false
    set Ladybug . Picture to " deadladybug.png "
```

Figure 5-9. Defining the procedure GameOver

Next, add the code outlined in red in Figure 5-10 to `UpdateLadybug` (which, as you might recall, is called by `Clock.Timer` every 10 milliseconds) to the following:

- Decrement its energy level.
- Display the new level.
- End the game if energy is 0.

```
Decrement and display the ladybug's energy
level, ending the game if it reaches zero.
Otherwise update the ladybug's direction and
speed based on the device's tilt.

to UpdateLadybug
do  set global energy to get global energy - 1
    call DisplayEnergy
    if   get global energy = 0
    then call GameOver
    set Ladybug . Heading to OrientationSensor1 . Angle
    set Ladybug . Speed to OrientationSensor1 . Magnitude × 100
```

Figure 5-10. Second version of the procedure UpdateLadybug

Test your app *On your device, verify that the energy level decreases over time, eventually causing the ladybug's demise.*

Adding an Aphid

The next step is to add an aphid. Specifically, an aphid should flit around `FieldCanvas`. If the ladybug runs into the aphid (thereby "eating" it), the ladybug's energy level should increase and the aphid should disappear, to be replaced by another one a little later. (From the user's point of view, it will be a different aphid, but it will really be the same `ImageSprite` component.)

Adding an ImageSprite

The first step you need to undertake to add an aphid is to go back to the Designer and create another `ImageSprite`, being sure not to place it on top of the ladybug. It should be renamed `Aphid` and its properties set as follows:

- Set its `Picture` property to the aphid image file you uploaded.
- Set its `Interval` property to 10, so, like the ladybug, it moves every 10 milliseconds.
- Set its Speed to 2, so it doesn't move too fast for the ladybug to catch it.

Don't worry about its `x` and `y` properties (as long as it's not on top of the ladybug) or its `Heading` property, which will be set in the Blocks Editor.

Controlling the aphid

By experimenting, we found that it worked best for the aphid to change directions approximately once every 50 milliseconds (5 "ticks" of `Clock1`). One approach to enabling this behavior would be to create a second clock with a `TimerInterval` of 50 milliseconds. However, we'd like you to try a different technique so that you can learn about the `random fraction` block, which returns a random number greater than or equal to 0 and less than 1 each time it is called. Create the `UpdateAphid` procedure shown in Figure 5-11 and add a call to it in `Clock1.Timer`.

How the blocks work

Whenever the timer goes off (100 times per second), both `UpdateLadybug` (like before) and `UpdateAphid` are called. The first thing that happens in `UpdateAphid` is that a random fraction between 0 and 1 is generated—for example, 0.15. If this number is less than 0.20 (which will happen 20% of the time), the aphid will change its direction to a random number of degrees between 0 and 360. If the number is not less than 0.20 (which will be the case the remaining 80% of the time), the aphid will stay the course.

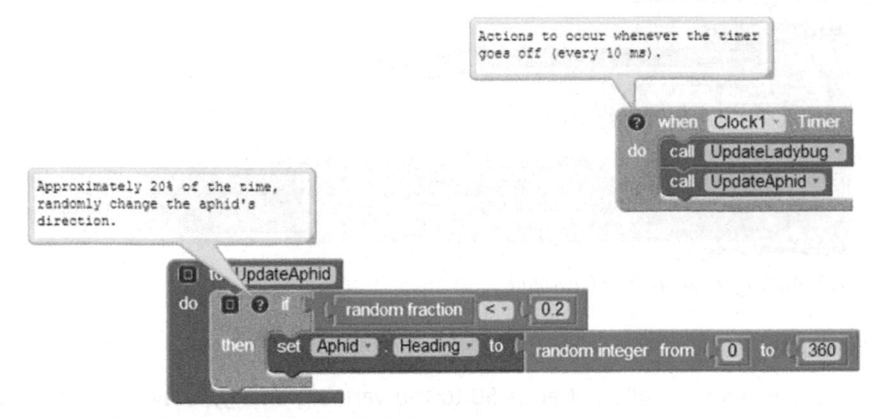

Figure 5-11. Adding the procedure UpdateAphid

Programming the Ladybug to Eat the Aphid

The next step is setting up the ladybug to "eat" the aphid when they collide. Fortunately, App Inventor provides blocks for detecting collisions between `ImageSprite` components, which raises the question: what should happen when the ladybug and the aphid collide? You might want to stop and think about this before reading on.

To handle what happens when the ladybug and aphid collide, let's create a procedure, `EatAphid`, that does the following:

- Increases the energy level by 50 to simulate eating the tasty treat.
- Causes the aphid to disappear (by setting its `Visible` property to false).
- Causes the aphid to stop moving (by setting its `Enabled` property to false).
- Causes the aphid to move to a random location on the screen. (This follows the same pattern as the code to move the mole in MoleMash).

Check that your blocks match Figure 5-12. If you had other ideas of what should happen, such as sound effects, you can add those, too.

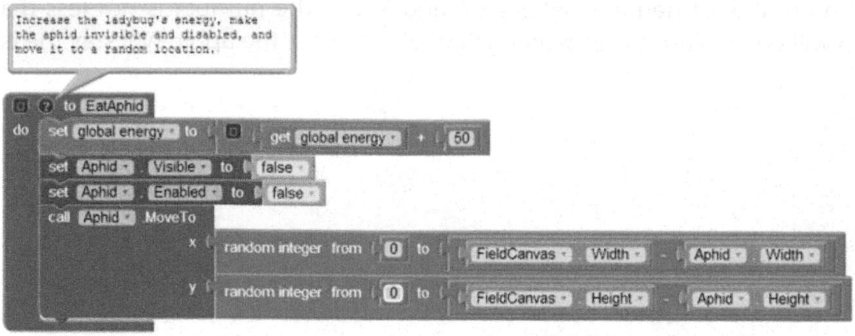

Figure 5-12. Adding the procedure EatAphid

How the blocks work

Whenever `EatAphid` is called, it adds 50 to the variable `energy`, staving off starvation for the ladybug. Next, the aphid's `Visible` and `Enabled` properties are set to false so it seems to disappear and stops moving, respectively. Finally, random x and y coordinates are generated for a call to `Aphid.MoveTo` so that, when the aphid reappears, it's in a new location (otherwise, it would be eaten as soon as it reemerges).

Detecting a Ladybug-Aphid Collision

Figure 5-13 shows the code to detect collisions between the ladybug and the aphid.

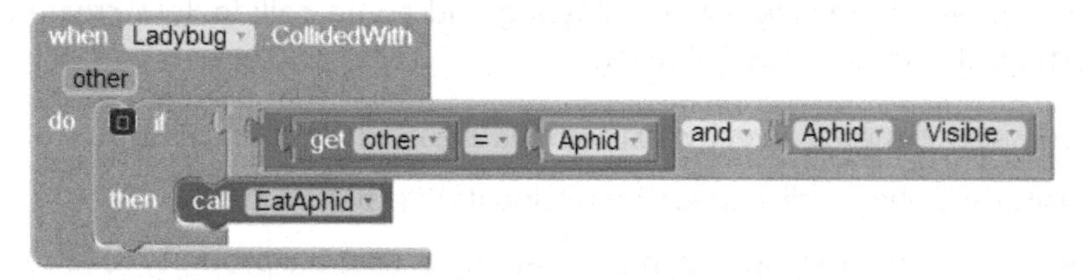

Figure 5-13. Detecting and acting on collisions between the ladybug and aphid

How the blocks work

When the ladybug collides with another `ImageSprite`, `Ladybug.CollidedWith` is called, with the parameter "other" bound to whatever the ladybug collided with. Right now, the only thing it can collide with is the aphid, but we'll be adding a frog later. We'll use *defensive programming* and explicitly check that the collision was with the aphid before calling `EatAphid`. There's also a check to confirm that the aphid is visible. Otherwise, after an aphid is eaten but before it reappears, it could collide with the ladybug again. Without the check, the invisible aphid would be eaten again, causing another jump in energy without the user understanding why.

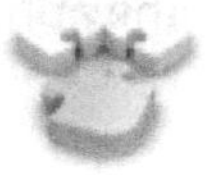

Note *Defensive programming is the practice of writing code in such a way that it is still likely to work even if the program is modified. In Figure 5-13, the test "other = Aphid" is not strictly necessary because the only thing the ladybug can currently collide with is the aphid, but having the check will prevent our program from malfunctioning if we add another* `ImageSprite` *and forget to change* `Ladybug.Collided With`. *Programmers generally spend more time fixing bugs (the software variety, not the aphid-eating sort) than writing new code, so it is well worth taking a little time to write code in a way that prevents problems in the first place.*

The Return of the Aphid

To make the aphid eventually reappear, you should modify `UpdateAphid` as shown in Figure 5-14 so that it changes the aphid's direction only if it is visible. (Changing it if it's invisible is a waste of time.) If the aphid is not visible (as in, it has been eaten recently), there is a 1 in 20 (5%) chance that it will be re-enabled—in other words, made eligible to be eaten again.

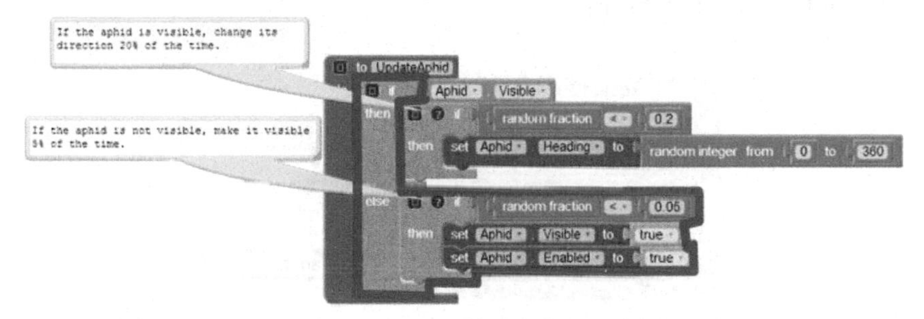

Figure 5-14. Modifying UpdateAphid to make invisible aphids come back to life

How the blocks work

`UpdateAphid` is getting pretty complex, so let's carefully step through its behavior:

- If the aphid is visible (which will be the case unless it was just eaten), `UpdateAphid` behaves as we first wrote it. Specifically, there is a 20% chance of its changing direction.
- If the aphid is not visible (i.e., it was recently eaten), then the `else` part of the `if else` block will run. A random number is then generated. If it is less than .05 (which it will be 5% of the time), the aphid becomes visible again and is enabled, making it eligible to be eaten again.

Because `UpdateAphid` is called by `Clock1.Timer`, which occurs every 10 milliseconds, and there is a 1 in 20 (5%) chance of the aphid becoming visible again, the aphid will take on average 200 milliseconds (1/5 of a second) to reappear.

Adding a Restart Button

As you might have noticed from testing the app with your new aphid-eating functionality, the game really needs a Restart button. (This is another reason why it's helpful to design and build your app in small chunks and then test it—you often discover things that you have overlooked, and it's easier to add them as you progress than to go back in and change them after the app is complete.) In the Component Designer, add a `Button` component underneath `EnergyCanvas`, rename it "RestartButton", and set its `Text` property to "Restart".

In the Blocks Editor, create the code shown in Figure 5-15 to do the following when the `RestartButton` is clicked:

1. Set the energy level back to 200.
2. Re-enable the aphid and make it visible.
3. Re-enable the ladybug and change its picture back to the live ladybug (unless you want zombie ladybugs!).

Figure 5-15. Restarting the game when RestartButton is pressed

Adding the Frog

Right now, keeping the ladybug alive isn't too hard. We need a predator. Specifically, we'll add a frog that moves directly toward the ladybug. If they collide, the ladybug becomes dinner, and the game ends.

Getting the frog to chase the ladybug

The first step to setting up the frog to chase the ladybug is returning to the Component Designer and adding a third `ImageSprite`—`Frog`—to `FieldCanvas`. Set its `Picture` property to the appropriate picture, its `Interval` to 10, and its `Speed` to 1, because it should be slower moving than the other creatures.

Figure 5-16 shows `UpdateFrog`, a new procedure you should create and call from `Clock1.Timer`.

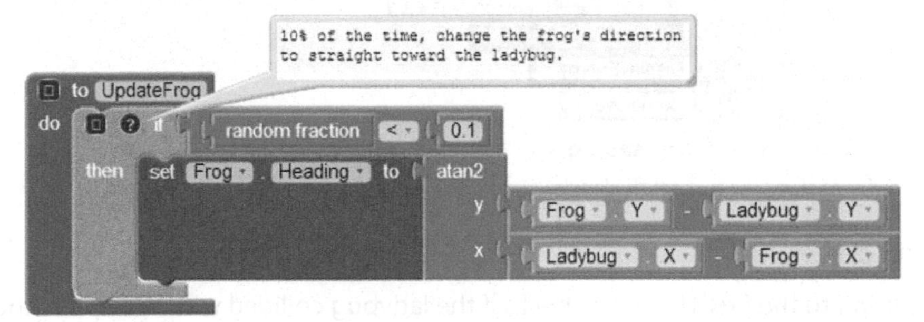

Figure 5-16. Making the frog move toward the ladybug

How the blocks work

By now, you should be familiar with the use of the `random fraction` block to make an event occur with a certain probability. In this case, there is a 10% chance that the frog's direction will be changed to head straight toward the ladybug. This requires trigonometry, but don't panic—you don't have to figure it out yourself. App Inventor handles a ton of math functions for you, even stuff like trigonometry. In this case, you want to use the `atan2` (arctangent) block, which returns the angle corresponding to a given set of x and y values. (For those of you familiar with trigonometry, the reason the y argument to `atan2` has the opposite sign of what you'd expect—the opposite order of arguments to subtract—is that the y coordinate increases in the downward direction on an Android Canvas, the opposite of what would occur in a standard x-y coordinate system.)

Setting up the frog to eat the ladybug

We now need to modify the collision code so that if the ladybug collides with the frog, the energy level and bar goes to 0 and the game ends, as shown in Figure 5-17.

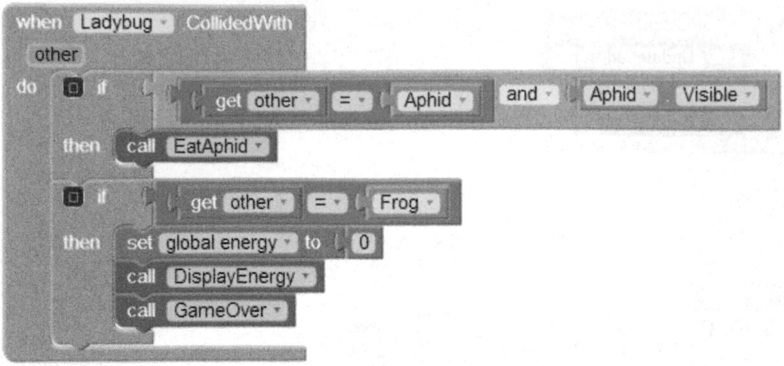

Figure 5-17. *Making the frog eat the ladybug*

How the blocks work

In addition to the first `if`, which checks if the ladybug collided with the aphid, there is now a second `if`, which checks if the ladybug has collided with the frog. If the ladybug and the frog collide, three things happen:

1. The variable energy goes down to 0, because the ladybug has lost its life force.
2. `DisplayEnergy` is called to erase the previous energy line (and draw the new, empty one).
3. The procedure you wrote earlier, `GameOver`, is called to stop the ladybug from moving and to change its picture to that of a dead ladybug.

The Return of the Ladybug

`RestartButton.Click` already has code to replace the picture of the dead ladybug with the one of the live ladybug. Now, you need to add code to move the live ladybug to a random location. (Think about what would happen if you didn't move the ladybug at the beginning of a new game. Where would it be in relation to the frog?) Figure 5-18 shows the blocks to move the ladybug when the game restarts.

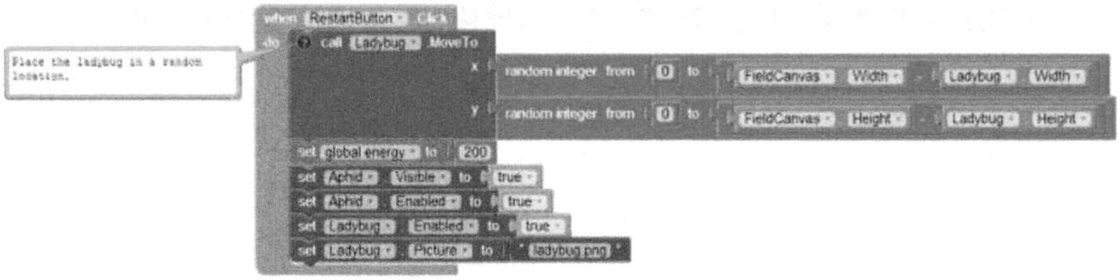

Figure 5-18. *The final version of RestartButton.Click*

How the blocks work

The only difference between this version of `RestartButton.Click` and the previous version is the `Ladybug.MoveTo` block and its arguments. The built-in function `random integer` is called twice: once to generate a legal x coordinate and once to generate a legal y coordinate. Even though there is nothing to prevent the ladybug from being placed on top of the aphid or the frog, the odds are against it.

Test your app *Restart the game and make sure the ladybug shows up in a new random location.*

Adding Sound Effects

When you tested the game, you might have noticed there isn't very good feedback when something is eaten. To add sound effects and tactile feedback, do the following:

1. In the Component Designer, add a `Sound` component. Set its `Source` to the sound file you uploaded.
2. Go to the Blocks Editor, where you will:
   - Make the device vibrate when an aphid is eaten by adding a `Sound1.Vibrate` block with an argument of 100 (milliseconds) in `EatAphid`.
   - Make the frog ribbit when it eats the ladybug by adding a call to `Sound1.Play` in `Ladybug.CollidedWith` just before the call to `GameOver`.

The Complete App: Ladybug Chase

Figure 5-19 shows the final block configuration for Ladybug Chase.

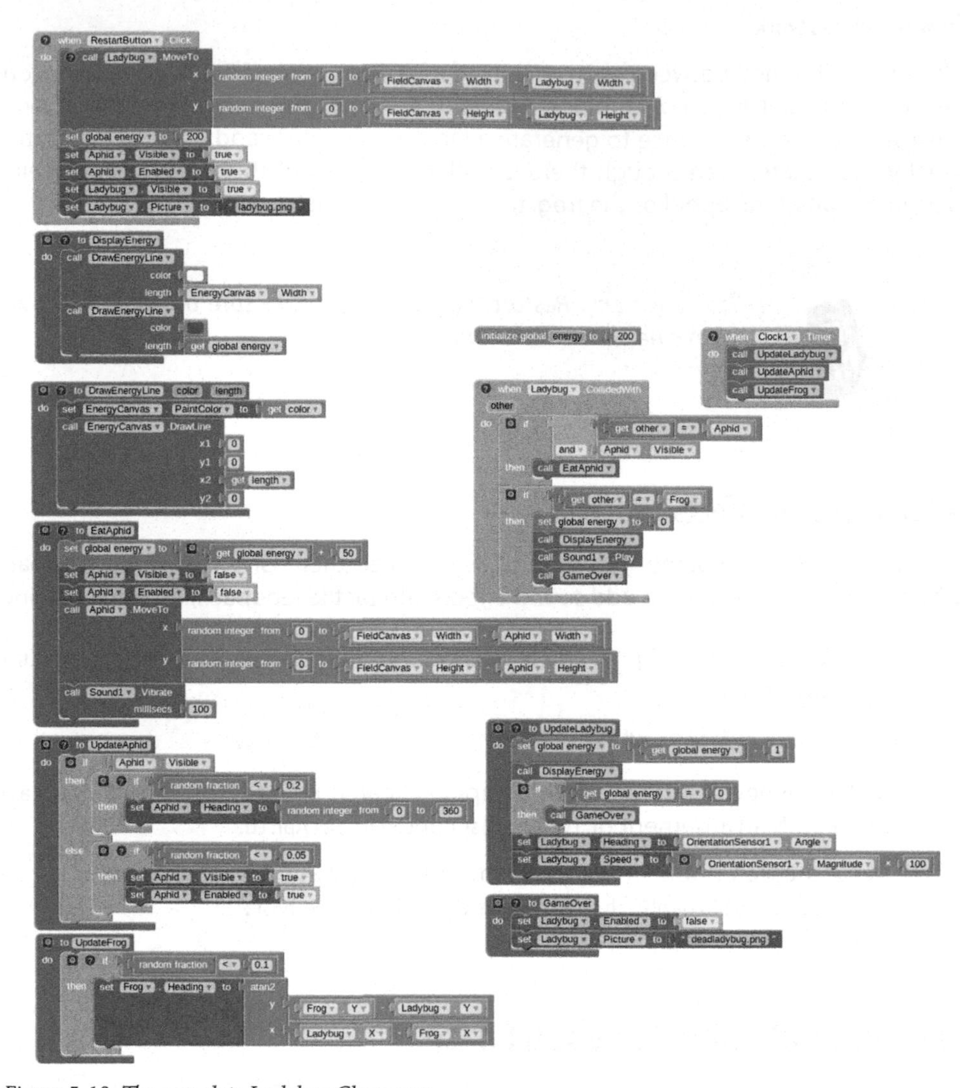

Figure 5-19. The complete Ladybug Chase app

Variations

Here are some ideas of how to improve or customize this game:

- Currently, the frog and aphid keep moving after the game has ended. Prevent this by setting their `Enabled` properties to false in `GameOver` and true in `RestartButton.Click`.
- Display a score indicating how long the ladybug has remained alive. You can do this by creating a label that you increment in `Clock1.Timer`.

- Make the energy bar more visible by increasing the `Height` of `EnergyCanvas` to 2 and drawing two lines, one above the other, in `DrawEnergyLine`. (This is another benefit of having a procedure rather than duplicated code to erase and redraw the energy line: you just need to make a change in one place to change the size —or color, or location—of the line.)
- Add ambiance with a background image and more sound effects, such as nature sounds or a warning when the ladybug's energy level becomes low.
- Have the game become harder over time, such as by increasing the frog's `Speed` property or decreasing its `Interval property`.
- Technically, the ladybug should disappear when it is eaten by the frog. Change the game so that the ladybug becomes invisible if eaten by the frog but not if it starves to death.
- Replace the ladybug, aphid, and frog pictures with ones more to your taste, such as a hobbit, orc, and evil wizard or a rebel starfighter, energy pod, and imperial starfighter.

Summary

With two games now under your belt (if you completed the MoleMash tutorial), you now know how to create your own games, which is the goal of many new programmers or wannabes! Specifically, you learned:

- You can have multiple `ImageSprite` components (the ladybug, the aphid, and the frog) and can detect collisions between them.
- The `OrientationSensor` can detect the tilt of the device and you can use that value to control the movement of a sprite (or anything else you can imagine).
- A single `Clock` component can control multiple events that occur at the same frequency (changes in the ladybug's and frog's directions), or at different frequencies, by using the `random fraction` block. For example, if you want an event to occur approximately one-fourth (25 percent) of the time, put it in the body of an `if` block that is only executed when the result of `random fraction` is less than .25.
- You can have multiple `Canvas` components in a single app, which we did to have a playing field and to display a variable graphically (instead of through a `Label`).
- You can define procedures with parameters (such as "color" and "length" in `DrawEnergyLine`) that control the behavior, greatly expanding the power of procedural abstraction.

Paris Map Tour

In this chapter, you'll build a tour guide app for a trip to Paris. Creating a fully functioning map app might seem really complicated, but App Inventor provides two high-level components to help: the `ActivityStarter`, which makes it possible for you to launch another app from your app, including Google Maps, and the `WebViewer`, which shows any web page you want within a subpanel of your app. You'll explore both of these components and build two different versions of a tour guide.

What You'll Learn

This chapter introduces the following App Inventor components and concepts:

- The `Activity Starter` component for launching other Android apps from your app.
- The `WebViewer` component for showing web pages within your app.
- How to use list variables to store information for your app.
- The `ListPicker` component to give the user the ability to choose from a list of locations.

- How to build a URL dynamically to show different maps.

Designing the Components

Create a new project in App Inventor and call it "ParisMapTour". The user interface for the app has an Image component with a picture of Paris, a Label component with some text, a ListPicker component that comes with an associated button, and in this first version, an ActivityStarter (non-visible) component. You can design the components using the snapshot in Figure 6-1.

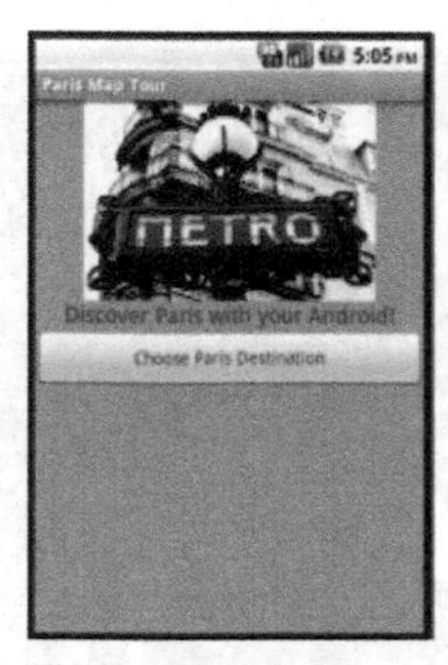

Figure 6-1. The Paris Map Tour app running in the emulator

You'll need the components listed in Table 6-1 to build this app. Drag each component from the Palette into the Viewer and name it as specified.

Table 6-1. Components for the Paris Map Tour

Component type	Palette group	What you'll name it	Purpose
Image	User Interface	Image1	Show a static image of Paris on screen.
Label	User Interface	Label1	Display the text "Discover Paris with your Android!"
ListPicker	User Interface	ListPicker1	When clicked, a list of destination choices will appear.
ActivityStarter	Connectivity	ActivityStarter1	Launch the Maps app when a destination is chosen.

Setting the Properties of ActivityStarter

ActivityStarter is a component with which you can launch any Android app, including Google Maps or another one of your own apps. You'll first build ParisMapTour so that the Maps application is launched to show particular maps based on the user's choice. The user can then tap the back button to return to your app and choose a different destination.

`ActivityStarter` is a relatively low-level component in that you'll need to set some properties with information that would be familiar to a Java Android SDK programmer, but completely foreign to the other 99.99% of the world. For this app, enter the properties as specified in Table 6-2, and *be careful*—they're case-sensitive, meaning that whether a letter is uppercase or lowercase is important.

Table 6-2. ActivityStarter properties for launching Google Maps

Property	Value
`Action`	android.intent.action.VIEW
`ActivityClass`	com.google.android.maps.MapsActivity
`ActivityPackage`	com.google.android.apps.maps

In the Blocks Editor, you'll set one more property, `DataUri`, which lets you provide a URL to launch a specific map in Google Maps. This property must be set in the Blocks Editor instead of the Component Designer because it needs to be dynamic: it will change based on whether the user chooses to visit the Eiffel Tower, the Louvre, or the Notre Dame Cathedral.

We'll get to the Blocks Editor in just a moment, but there are a couple more details to take care of before you can move on to programming the behavior for your components:

1. Download the file *metro.jpg* to load into your project. Then, set it as the `Picture` property of `Image1`.
2. The `ListPicker` component comes with a button; when the user clicks it, the choices are listed. Set the text of that button by changing the `Text` property of `ListPicker1` to "Choose Paris Destination".

Adding Behaviors to the Components

In the Blocks Editor, you'll need to define a list of destinations and two behaviors:

- When the app begins, the app loads the destinations into the `ListPicker` component so that the user can choose one.
- When the user chooses a destination from the ListPicker, the Maps application is launched and shows a map of that destination. In this first version of the app, you'll just open Maps and instruct it to run a search for the chosen destination.

Creating a List of Destinations

Open the Blocks Editor and create a variable with the list of Paris destinations by using the blocks listed in Table 6-3.

Table 6-3. Blocks for creating a destinations variable

Block type	Drawer	Purpose
`initialize global` ("Destinations")	Variables	Create a list of the destinations.
`make a list`	Lists	Add the items to the list.
`text` ("Tour Eiffel")	Text	The first destination.
`text` ("Musée du Louvre")	Text	The second destination.
`text` ("Cathédrale Notre Dame")	Text	The third destination.

When you drag the `make a list` block into your app, it will have only two available sockets. You can add another one by clicking the dark blue icon it and adding a third item.

After you've done that, just create the text blocks for each destination and place them in the three sockets of `make a list`, as shown in Figure 6-2.

Figure 6-2. A list of three items

Letting the User Choose a Destination

The list you just defined does not appear in the user interface—no variables do. You'll use a `ListPicker` component to display the list of items for the user to choose from. You preload the choices into the `ListPicker` by setting the property `Elements` to a list. For this app, you want to set the `Elements` property for `ListPicker` to the `destinations` list you just created. Because this only needs to be set once, you'll define this behavior in the `Screen1.Initialize` event. You'll need the blocks that are listed in Table 6-4.

Table 6-4. Blocks for launching the ListPicker when the app starts

Block type	Drawer	Purpose
`Screen1.Initialize`	Screen1	This event is triggered when the app starts.
`set ListPicker1.Elements to`	ListPicker1	Set this property to the list that you want to appear.
`get global destinations`	Drag out from variable initialization block	The list of destinations.

How the blocks work

`Screen1.Initialize` is triggered when the app begins. Figure 6-3 illustrates that the event handler sets the `Elements` property of `ListPicker` so that the three destinations will appear.

Figure 6-3. Initialize the ListPicker with the three choices when the app launches

Test your apps *Click Connect and set up live testing with your device or emulator. Then, click the button labeled "Choose Paris Destination." The list picker should appear with the three items. At this point, nothing should happen when you choose an item.*

Opening Maps with a Search URL

Next, you'll program the app so that when the user chooses one of the destinations, the `ActivityStarter` launches Google Maps and searches for the selected location.

First, consider the URL *http://maps.google.com?q=Paris*. When you type this URL into the address bar of a browser, it shows a map of Paris. The "?" is common to many URLS; it signifies that a parameter is coming. A parameter is the information the website needs to process the request. In this case, the parameter name is "q", short for "query", and its value is "Paris". It instructs Google Maps what map to display.

In this app, you'll build a URL dynamically, adding the parameter value based on which location the user chooses. This way you can show different maps based on the user's choices.

When the user chooses an item from the `ListPicker` component, the `ListPicker.AfterPicking` event is triggered. In the event handler for `AfterPicking`, you need to set the `DataUri` of the `ActivityStarter` component so that it knows which map to open, and then you need to launch Google Maps by using `ActivityStar ter.StartActivity`. The blocks for this functionality are listed in Table 6-5.

Table 6-5. Blocks to launch Google Maps with the Activity Starter

Block type	Drawer	Purpose
`ListPicker1.AfterPicking`	ListPicker1	This event is triggered when the user chooses from `List Picker`.
`set ActivityStarter1.DataUri to`	ActivityStarter1	The `DataUri` instructs Maps which map to open on launch.
`join`	Text	Build the `DataUri` from two pieces of text.
`text` ("http://maps.google.com?q=")	Text	The first part of the `DataUri` expected by Maps.
`ListPicker1.Selection`	ListPicker1	The item the user chose.
`ActivityStarter1.StartActivity`	ActivityStarter1	Launch Maps.

How the blocks work

When the user chooses from the `ListPicker`, the chosen item is stored in `List Picker.Selection` and the `AfterPicking` event is triggered. As shown in Figure 6-4, the `DataUri` property is set to a text object that combines "http://maps.google.com/?q" with the chosen item. So, if the user chose the first item, "Tour Eiffel," the `DataUri` would be set to "http://maps.google.com/?q= Tour Eiffel."

Figure 6-4. Setting the DataURI to launch the selected map

Because you already set the other properties of the `ActivityStarter` so that it knows to open Maps, the `ActivityStarter1.StartActivity` block launches the Maps app and invokes the search prescribed by the `DataUri`.

Test your app *Restart the app and click the "Choose Paris Destination" button again. When you choose one of the destinations, does a map of that destination appear? Can you get back to your app with the device's back button?*

The Complete App: Map Tour with Activity Starter

Figure 6-5 shows the final block configuration for version 1 of Paris Map Tour.

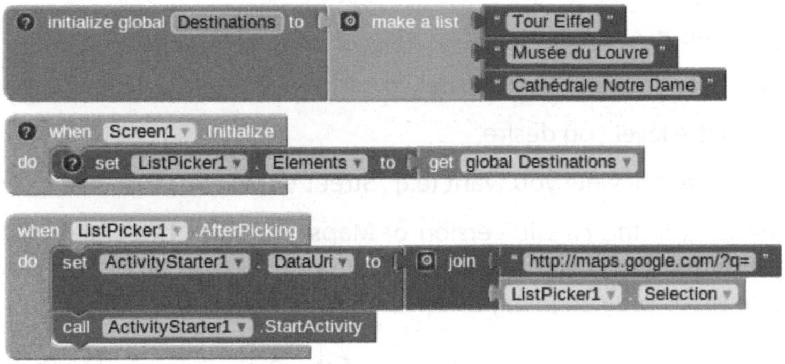

Figure 6-5. The complete Map Tour app (version 1)

A Virtual Tour with the Web Viewer

The `ActivityStarter` is an important component because it provides access to any other app on the device. But, there is another way to build a tour guide that uses a different component, instead; the `WebViewer`. `WebViewer` is a panel you place directly within your app that behaves like a browser. You can open any web page, including a Google Map, in the viewer, and you can programmatically change the page that appears. Unlike with an ActivityStarter, your user doesn't ever leave your app, so you don't have to count on them hitting the back button to get back.

In this second version of the app, you'll use the `WebViewer` and you'll also spice up the app so that it opens some zoomed-in and street views of the Paris monuments. You'll define a second list and use a more complicated scheme to decide which map to show. To begin, you'll first explore Google Maps to obtain the URLs of some specific maps. You'll still use the same Parisian landmarks for the destinations, but when the user chooses one, you'll use the *index* (the position in the list) of her choice to select and open a specific zoomed-in or street-view map.

Before going on, you might want to save your project (using Save As) so you have a copy of the `ActivityStarter` map tour you've created so far. That way, if you do anything that causes issues in your app, you can always go back to this working version and try again.

Add the Web Viewer

In the designer, delete the `ActivityStarter` component. Then, from the User Interface drawer, drag in a `WebViewer` component and place it below the other components. Uncheck the `Screen1.Scrollable` property so the `WebViewer` will display pages correctly.

Finding the URL for Specific Maps

The next step is to open Google Maps on your computer to find the specific maps you want to launch for each destination:

1. On your computer, browse to *http://maps.google.com*.
2. Search for a landmark (e.g., the Eiffel Tower).
3. Zoom in to the level you desire.
4. Choose the type of view you want (e.g., Street View).
5. Grab the URL. In the classic version of Maps, you click the Link button near the top right of the Maps window and copy the URL for the map. In the newer version of Google Maps you can just grab the URL from the address bar.

Use this scheme to create some cool maps of the Paris monuments and extract the URLs. Table 6-6 provides some samples if you'd rather use them (the URLs have been shortened with the bit.ly service).

Table 6-6. Virtual tour URLs for Google Maps

Landmark	Maps URL
Tour Eiffel	*http://bit.ly/1qiEy8B*
Musée du Louvre	*http://bit.ly/1qiEVQA*
Cathédrale Notre Dame (street view)	*http://bit.ly/1qiF1YD*

To view any of these maps in a browser, paste the URLs from Table 6-6 into the address bar.

Defining the URLs List

You'll need a list named `URLs`, containing a URL for each of the destinations. Create this list as shown in Figure 6-6 so that the items correspond to the items in the destinations list (i.e., the first `URL` should correspond to the first destination, the Eiffel Tower).

Figure 6-6. Copy and paste the URLs into the text blocks of the URLs list

Modifying the ListPicker.AfterPicking Behavior

In the first version of this app, the `ListPicker.AfterPicking` behavior set the `DataUri` to a combination of "http://maps.google.com/?q=" and the destination the user chose from the list (e.g., "Tour Eiffel"). In this second version, the `AfterPicking` behavior must be more sophisticated, because the user is choosing from one list (`destinations`), but the app is choosing from the `URLs list` for the URL. Specifically, when the user chooses an item from the `ListPicker`, you need to know the index of the choice so you can use it to select the correct URL from the list. We'll explain more about what an index is in a moment, but it helps to set up the blocks first to better illustrate the concept. There are quite a few blocks required for this functionality, all of which are listed in Table 6-7.

Table 6-7. Blocks for choosing a list item based on the user's selection

Block type	Drawer	Purpose
`ListPicker1.AfterPicking`	ListPicker1	This event is triggered when the user chooses an item.
`ListPicker1.SelectionIndex`	ListPicker1	The index (position) of the chosen item.
`select list item`	Lists	Select an item from the `URLs` list.
`get global URLs`	Drag it from the variable initializatlon	The list of `URLs`.
`WebViewer.GoToURL`	WebViewer	Load the URL in the viewer to show the map.

How the blocks work

When the user chooses an item from the `ListPicker`, the `AfterPicking` event is triggered, as shown in Figure 6-7. The chosen item—for example, "Tour Eiffel"—is in `ListPicker.Selection`. You used this property in the first version of this app. However, ListPicker also has a property `SelectionIndex`, which corresponds to the position of the chosen destination in the list. So, if "Tour Eiffel" is chosen, the `SelectionIndex` will be 1; if "Musée du Louvre" is chosen, it will be 2; and if "Cathédrale Notre Dame de Paris" is chosen, it will be 3.

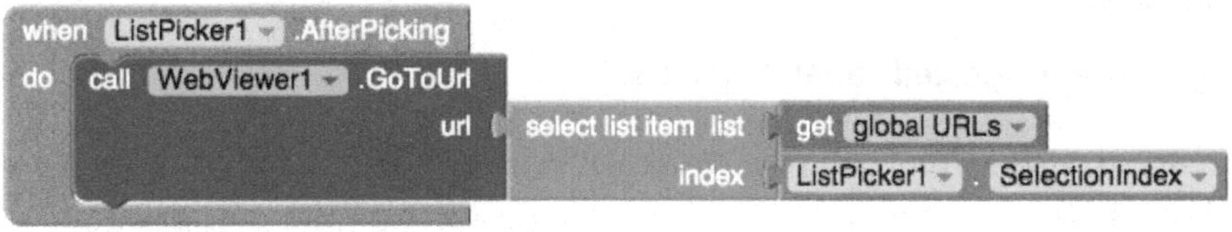

Figure 6-7. Open the selected URL in the WebViewer

You use `ListPicker.SelectionIndex` to select an item from the `URLs` list. This works because the items on the two lists, `destinations` and `URLs`, are in sync: the first destination corresponds to the first URL, the second to the second, and the third to the third. So, even though the user chooses an item from one list, you can use their choice (well, the index of their choice) to select the right URL to show.

Test your app *On the device, click the button labeled "Choose Paris Destination." The list should appear with the three items. Choose one of the items and see which map appears.*

The Complete App: Map Tour (Web Viewer)

Figure 6-8 shows the final block configuration for this second version of Paris Map Tour.

```
initialize global Destinations to make a list " Tour Eiffel "
                                              " Musée du Louvre "
                                              " Cathédrale Notre Dame "
initialize global URLs to make a list " http://bit.ly/1qiEy8B "
                                      " http://bit.ly/1qiEVQA "
                                      " http://bit.ly/1qiF1YD "
when Screen1 .Initialize
do set ListPicker1 . Elements to get global Destinations
when ListPicker1 .AfterPicking
do call WebViewer1 .GoToUrl
        url select list item list get global URLs
                             index ListPicker1 . SelectionIndex
```

Figure 6-8. The complete Map Tour App (WebViewer version)

Variations

Here are some suggested variations to try:

- Create a virtual tour of your workplace or school, or for your next vacation destination.
- Explore `ActivityStarter` and use it to send an email or launch an app such as YouTube (see *http://bit.ly/1qiFx8Z* for help).

- Difficult: Create a customizable Virtual Tour app that lets a user create a guide for a location of her choice by entering the name of each destination along with the URL of a corresponding map. You'll need to store the data in a `TinyWebDB` database and create a Virtual Tour app that works with the entered data. For an example of how to create a `TinyWebDB` database, see the MakeQuiz/TakeQuiz app.

Summary

Here are some of the ideas we covered in this chapter:

- You can use list variables to hold data such as map destinations and URLs.
- The `ListPicker` component lets the user choose from a list of items. The `ListPicker's` `Elements` property holds the list, the `Selection` property holds the selected item, the `SelectionIndex` holds the position of the selected item, and the `AfterPicking` event is triggered when the user chooses an item from the list.
- The `ActivityStarter` component makes it possible for your app to launch other apps. This chapter demonstrated its use with the Google Maps application, but you can launch a browser or any other Android app as well, even another one that you created yourself.
- You can use `ListPicker.SelectionIndex` to get the position of an item that a user chooses from a list. You can then use that index to select information from a different list (whose items are synchronized with the first list). For more information on `List` variables and the `ListPicker` component, see Chapter 19.

CHAPTER 7

Android, Where's My Car?

You parked as close to the stadium as you possibly could, but when the concert ends, you don't have a clue where your car is. Your friends are equally clueless. Fortunately, you haven't lost your Android phone, which never forgets anything, and you remember you have the hot new app, Android, Where's My Car? With this app, you click a button when you park your car, and the Android uses its location sensor to record the car's GPS coordinates and address. Later, when you reopen the app, it gives you directions from where you currently are to the saved location—problem solved!

What You'll Learn

This app covers the following concepts:

- Determining the location of the Android device by using the `LocationSensor` component.
- Persistently recording data in a database directly on the device by using `TinyDB`.
- Using the `WebViewer` component to open Google Maps from your app and show directions from one location to another.

Getting Started

Connect to the App Inventor website and start a new project. Since project names can't have spaces, name it "AndroidWhere". Set the screen's title to "Android, Where's My Car?" Connect your device or emulator for live testing.

Designing the Components

The user interface for Android, Where's My Car? consists of labels to show your current and remembered locations, and buttons to record a location and show directions to it. You'll need some labels that just show static text; for example, `GPSLabel` will provide the text "GPS:" that appears in the user interface. Other labels, such as `CurrentLatLabel`, will display data from the location sensor. For these labels, you'll provide a default value, (0,0), which will change as the GPS acquires location information.

You'll also need three non-visible components: a `LocationSensor` for obtaining the current location, a `TinyDB` for storing locations persistently, and a `WebViewer` for displaying Google Maps directions between the current and stored locations.

You can build the components from the snapshot of the Component Designer in Figure 7-1.

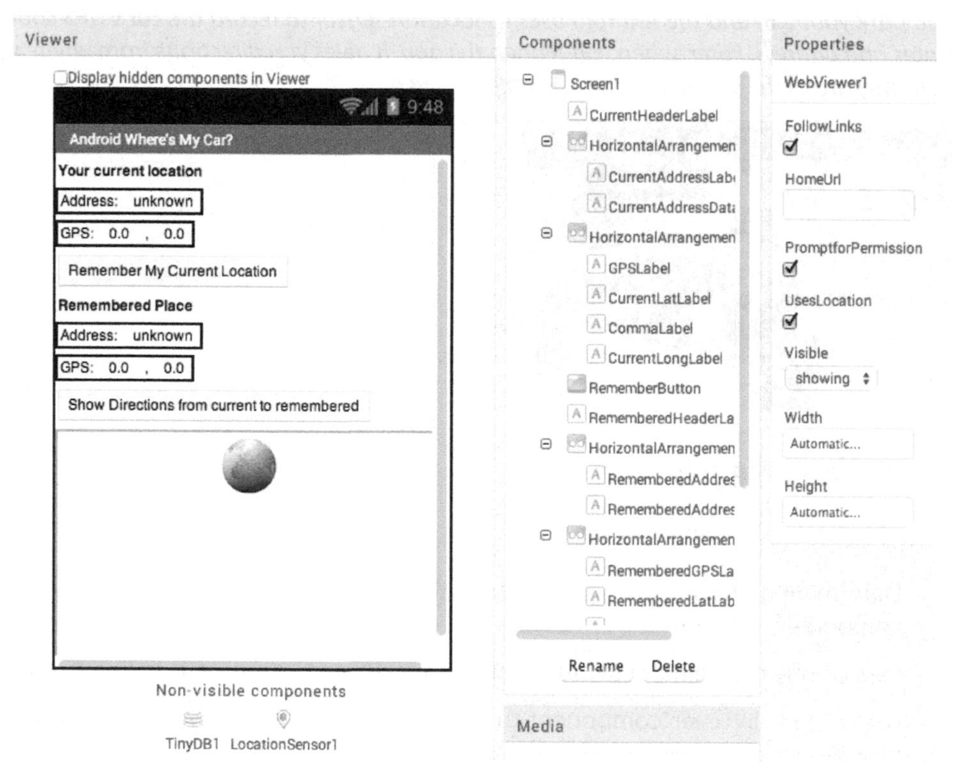

Figure 7-1. The Android, Where's My Car? app in the Component Designer

You'll need the components in Table 7-1.

Table 7-1. All of the components for the app

Component type	Palette group	What you'll name it	Purpose
Label	User Interface	CurrentHeaderLabel	Display the header "Your current location".
HorizontalArrangement	Layout	HorizontalArrangement1	Arrange the address info.
Label	User Interface	CurrentAddressLabel	Display the text "Address:".
Label	User Interface	CurrentAddressDataLabel	Display dynamic data: the current address.
HorizontalArrangement	Layout	HorizontalArrangement2	Arrange the GPS info.
Label	User Interface	GPSLabel	Display the text "GPS:".
Label	User Interface	CurrentLatLabel	Display dynamic data: the current latitude.
Label	User Interface	CommaLabel	Display ",".
Label	User Interface	CurrentLongLabel	Display dynamic data: the current longitude.
Button	User Interface	RememberButton	Click to record the current location.
Label	User Interface	HorizontalArrangement2	Arrange remembered address info.
Label	User Interface	RememberedAddressLabel	Display the text "Remembered Place".
Label	User Interface	RememberedAddressDataLabel	Display dynamic data: the remembered address.
Label	User Interface	RememberedGPSLabel	Display the text "GPS".
Label	User Interface	RememberedLatLabel	Display dynamic data: the remembered latitude.
Label	User Interface	Comma2Label	Display ",".
Label	User Interface	RememberedLongLabel	Display dynamic data: the remembered longitude.
Button	User Interface	DirectionsButton	Click to show the map.
LocationSensor	Sensors	LocationSensor1	Sense GPS info.
TinyDB	Storage	TinyDB1	Store the remembered location persistently.

Component type	Palette group	What you'll name it	Purpose
WebViewer	User Interface	WebViewer1	Show directions.

Set the properties of the components in the following way:

- Set the Text property for the labels with fixed text as specified in Table 7-1.
- Set the Text property of the labels for dynamic GPS data to "0.0".
- Set the Text property of the labels for dynamic addresses to "unknown".
- Uncheck the Enabled property of the RememberButton and DirectionsButton.
- Uncheck the Screen.Scrollable property so that the WebViewer will fit on the screen.

Adding Behaviors to the Components

You'll need the following behaviors for this app:

- When the LocationSensor gets a reading, place the current location data into the appropriate labels of the user interface. This will let the user know the sensor has read a location and is ready to remember it.
- When the user clicks the RememberButton, copy the current location data into the labels for the remembered location. You'll also need to store the remembered location data so that it will be there if the user closes and relaunches the app.
- When the user clicks the DirectionsButton, launch Google Maps in the WebViewer so that it shows directions to the remembered location.
- When the app is relaunched, load the remembered location from the database into the app.

Displaying the Current Location

The LocationSensor.LocationChanged event occurs not just when the device's location changes, but also when the sensor first gets a reading. Sometimes that first reading will take a few seconds, and sometimes you won't get a reading at all if the sight lines to GPS satellites are blocked (and depending on the device settings). For more information about GPS and LocationSensor, see Chapter 23.

When you do get a location reading, the app should place the data into the appropriate labels. Table 7-2 lists all the blocks you'll need to do this.

Table 7-2. Blocks for getting a location reading and displaying it in the app's UI

Block type	Drawer	Purpose
`LocationSensor1.LocationChanged`	LocationSensor1	This is the event handler that is triggered when the phone receives a new GPS reading.
`set CurrentAddressDataLabel.Text to`	CurrentAddressDataLabel	Place the new data into the label for the current address.
`LocationSensor1.CurrentAddress`	LocationSensor1	This property gives you a street address.
`set CurrentLatLabel.Text to`	CurrentLatLabel	Place the latitude into the appropriate label.
`get latitude`	Drag out from LocationChanged event	Plug into `set CurrentLatLabel.Text to`.
`set CurrentLongLabel.Text to`	CurrentLongLabel	Place the longitude into the appropriate label.
`value longitude`	Drag out from LocationChanged event	Plug into `set CurrentLongLabel.Text to`.
`set RememberButton.Enabled to`	RememberButton	Remember the reading for current location.
`true`	Logic	Plug into `set RememberButton.Enabled to`.

How the blocks work

Figure 7-2 illustrates that `latitude` and `longitude` are parameters of the `LocationChanged` event. You can grab `get` references to event parameters by mousing over them. `CurrentAddress` is not an argument; rather, it's a property of the `LocationSensor`, so you grab it from `LocationSensor`'s drawer. The `LocationSensor` does some additional work for you by calling Google Maps to get a street address corresponding to the GPS location.

This event handler also enables the `RememberButton`. We initialized it as disabled (unchecked) in the Component Designer because there is nothing for the user to remember until the sensor gets a reading, so now we'll program that behavior.

Figure 7-2. Using the LocationSensor to read the current location

Test your app *You probably want to walk around to test this app. So you'll need to build the the app and install it to your phone by selecting Build -> App (provide QR code for .apk). When you run the app, you should see some GPS data appear and the* `RememberButton` *enabled. If you don't get a reading, check your Android settings for Location & Security and try going outside. For more information, see Chapter 23.*

Recording the Current Location

When the user clicks the `RememberButton`, the most current location data should be placed into the labels for displaying the remembered data. Table 7-3 shows you which blocks you'll need for this functionality.

Table 7-3. Blocks for recording and displaying the current location

Block type	Drawer	Purpose
`RememberButton.Click`	RememberButton	Triggered when the user clicks "Remember."
`set RememberedAddressDataLabel.Text to`	RememberedAddressDataLabel	Place the sensor's address data into the label for the remembered address.
`LocationSensor1.CurrentAddress`	LocationSensor1	This property gives you a street address.
`set RememberedLatLabel.Text to`	RememberedLatLabel	Place the latitude sensed into the "remembered" label.
`LocationSensor.Latitude`	LocationSensor1	Plug into `set RememberedLatLabel.Text to`.

Block type	Drawer	Purpose
`set RememberedLongLabel.Text to`	RememberedLongLabel	Place the longitude sensed into the "remembered" label.
`LocationSensor.Longitude`	LocationSensor1	Plug into `set RememberedLongLabel.Text to`.
`set DirectionsButton.Enabled to`	DirectionsButton	Map the remembered place.
`true`	Logic	Plug into `set DirectionsButton.Enabled to`.

How the blocks work

When the user clicks the `RememberButton`, the current readings for the location sensor are inserted into the "remembered" labels, as shown in Figure 7-3.

Figure 7-3. Placing the current location information in the "remembered" labels

You'll also notice that the `DirectionsButton` is enabled. This could become tricky, because if the user clicks the `DirectionsButton` immediately, the remembered location will be the same as the current location, so the map that appears won't provide much in terms of directions. But that's not something anyone is likely to do; after the user moves (e.g., walks to the concert), the current location and remembered location will diverge.

Test your app *Download the new version of the app to your phone and test again. When you click the `RememberButton`, is the data from the current settings copied into the remembered settings?*

Displaying Directions to the Remembered Location

When the user clicks the `DirectionsButton`, you want the app to open Google Maps and then display the directions from the user's current location to the remembered location (e.g., where the car is parked).

The `WebViewer` component can display any web page, including Google Maps. You'll call `WebViewer.GoToURL` to open the map, but you want to open a URL that will show directions from the current location to the remembered location.

One way to show directions in Maps is with a URL of the following form:

http://maps.google.com/maps?
saddr=37.82557,-122.47898&daddr=37.81079,-122.47710

Type that URL into a browser—can you tell which famous landmark it directs you across?

For this app, you need to build the URL and set its source address (`saddr`) and destination address (`daddr`) parameters dynamically (in blocks). You've put text together before in earlier chapters using `join`; we'll do that here, as well, plugging in the GPS data for the remembered and current locations. You'll put the URL you build into the parameter slot of `WebViewer.GotToURL`. Table 7-4 lists all the blocks you'll need for this.

Table 7-4. Blocks for recording and displaying the current location

Block type	Drawer	Purpose
`DirectionsButton.Click`	DirectionsButton	Triggered when the user clicks "Directions."
`WebViewer1.GoToURL`	WebViewer1	Set the URL for the map that you want to bring up.
`join`	Text	Build a URL from multiple parts.
`text` ("http://maps.google.com/maps?saddr=")	Text	The fixed part of the URL, the source address.
`CurrentLatLabel.Text`	CurrentLatLabel	The current latitude.
`text` (",")	Text	Put a comma between the latitude and longitude values.
`CurrentLongLabel.Text`	CurrentLongLabel	The current longitude.
`text` ("&daddr=")	Text	The second parameter of the URL, the destination address.
`RememberedLatLabel.Text`	RememberedLatLabel	The remembered latitude.
`text` (",")	Text	Put a comma between the values for latitude and longitude.
`RememberedLongLabel.Text`	RememberedLongLabel	The remembered longitude.

How the blocks work

When the user clicks the `DirectionsButton`, the event handler builds a URL for a map and calls `WebViewer.GoToURL`to open the map, as shown in Figure 7-4. `join` is used to build the URL for the map.

The resulting URL consists of the Google Maps domain (*http://maps.google.com/maps*) along with two URL parameters, `saddr` and `daddr`, which specify the source and destination locations for the directions. For this app, the `saddr` is set to the latitude and longitude of the current location, and the `daddr` is set to the latitude and longitude of the location stored for the car.

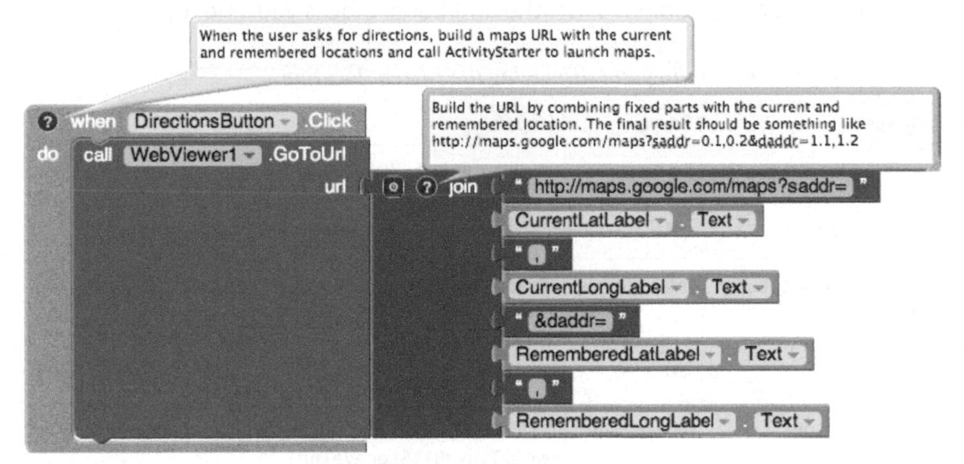

Figure 7-4. Building the URL to use for opening the map in the WebViewer

Test your app *Download the new version of the app to your phone and test again. When a reading comes in, click the `RememberButton` and then take a walk. When you click the `DirectionsButton`, does the map show you how to retrace your steps? After looking at the map, click the back button a few times. Do you get back to your app?*

Storing the Remembered Location Persistently

You now have a fully functioning app that remembers a start location and draws a map back to that location from wherever the user current location is. However, if the user "remembers" a location and then closes the app, the remembered data will not be available when the app is reopened. What you really want is for the user to be able to record the location of the car, close the app and go to some event, and then relaunch the app later on to get directions to the recorded location.

If you're already thinking back to the No Texting While Driving app (Chapter 4), you're on the right track. You need to store the data *persistently* in a database by using `TinyDB`. You'll use a scheme similar to the one you used in that app:

1. When the user clicks the `RememberButton`, store the location data to the database.
2. When the app launches, load the location data from the database into a variable or property.

You'll start by modifying the `RememberButton.Click` event handler so that it stores the remembered data. To store the latitude, longitude, and address, you'll need three calls to `TinyDB.StoreValue`. Table 7-5 lists the additional blocks you'll need.

Table 7-5. Blocks for recording and displaying the current location

Block type	Drawer	Purpose
`TinyDB1.StoreValue` (3)	TinyDB	Store the data in the device database.
`text` ("address")	Text	Plug this into the "tag" socket of `TinyDB1.StoreValue`.
`LocationSensor1.CurrentAddress`	LocationSensor1	The address to store persistently; plug this into the "value" socket of `TinyDB1.StoreValue`.
`text` ("lat")	Text	Plug this into the "tag" socket of the second `TinyDB1.StoreValue`.
`LocationSensor1.CurrentLatitude`	LocationSensor1	The latitude to store persistently; plug this into the "value" socket of the second `TinyDB1.StoreValue`.
`text` ("long")	Text	Plug this into the "tag" socket of the third `TinyDB1.StoreValue`.
`LocationSensor1.CurrentLongitude`	LocationSensor1	The longitude to store persistently; plug this into the "value" socket of the third `TinyDB1.StoreValue`.

How the blocks work

As shown in Figure 7-5, `TinyDB1.StoreValue` copies the location data from the `LocationSensor` properties into the database. As you might recall from No Texting While Driving, the `StoreValue` function has two arguments, the *tag* and the *value*. The tag identifies the data that you want to store, and the value is the actual data that you want saved—in this case, the `LocationSensor` data.

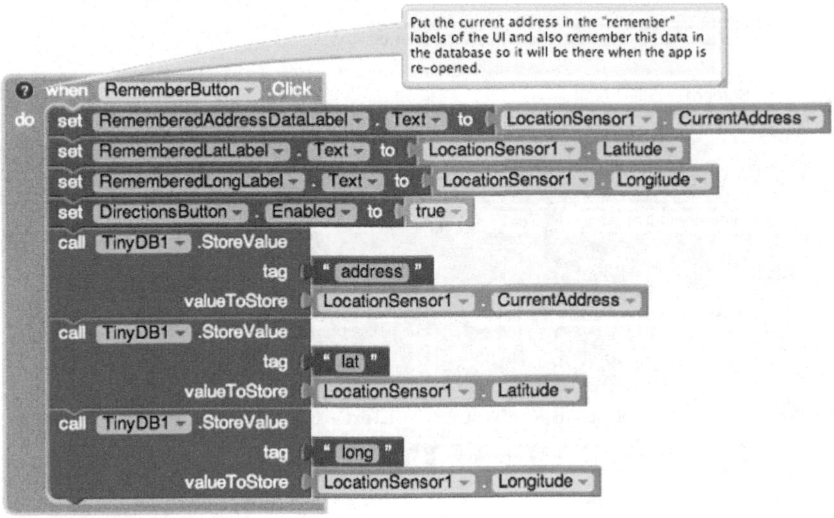

Figure 7-5. Storing the remembered location data in a database

Retrieving the Remembered Location When the App Launches

You store data in a database so that you can recall it later. In this app, if a user stores a location and then closes the app, you want to retrieve that information from the database and show it when the user relaunches the app.

As discussed in previous chapters, the `Screen.Initialize` event is triggered when your app launches. Retrieving data from a database is a very common thing to do on startup, and it's exactly what we want to do for this app.

You'll use the `TinyDB.GetValue` function to retrieve the stored GPS data. Because you need to retrieve the stored address, latitude, and longitude, you'll need three calls to `GetValue`. As with No Texting While Driving, you'll need to check if there is indeed data available (if it's the first time you're launching your app, `TinyDB.GetValue` will return an empty text).

As a challenge, see if you can create these blocks and then compare your creation to the blocks shown in Figure 7-6.

Figure 7-6. When the app launches, load in the remembered location from the database

How the blocks work

To understand these blocks, envision two use cases: a user opening the app the first time, and the user opening it later, after previously recording location data. The first time the user opens the app, there won't be any location data in the database to load. On successive launches, if there is data stored, you want to load the previously stored location data from the database.

The blocks call `TinyDB1.GetValue` three times, once for each of the data fields you stored previously: "address", "lat", and "long". The `valueIfTagNotThere` parameter is set to a default value for each so that if there isn't data yet in the database, the labels will be set to the default values (the same as they were set in the designer).

The `if` block is used to determine if the `DirectionsButton` should be enabled. It should be if data was indeed retrieved from the database. The test used is to compare the `RememberedAddressDataLabel` to its default value, `unknown`. If it is not `unknown`, it must have been replaced with some remembered address.

Test your app *Download the new version of the app to your phone and test again. Click the `RememberButton` and make sure the readings are recorded. Then close the app and reopen it. Does the remembered data appear?*

The Complete App: Android, Where's My Car?

Figure 7-7 shows the final blocks for the complete Android, Where's My Car? app.

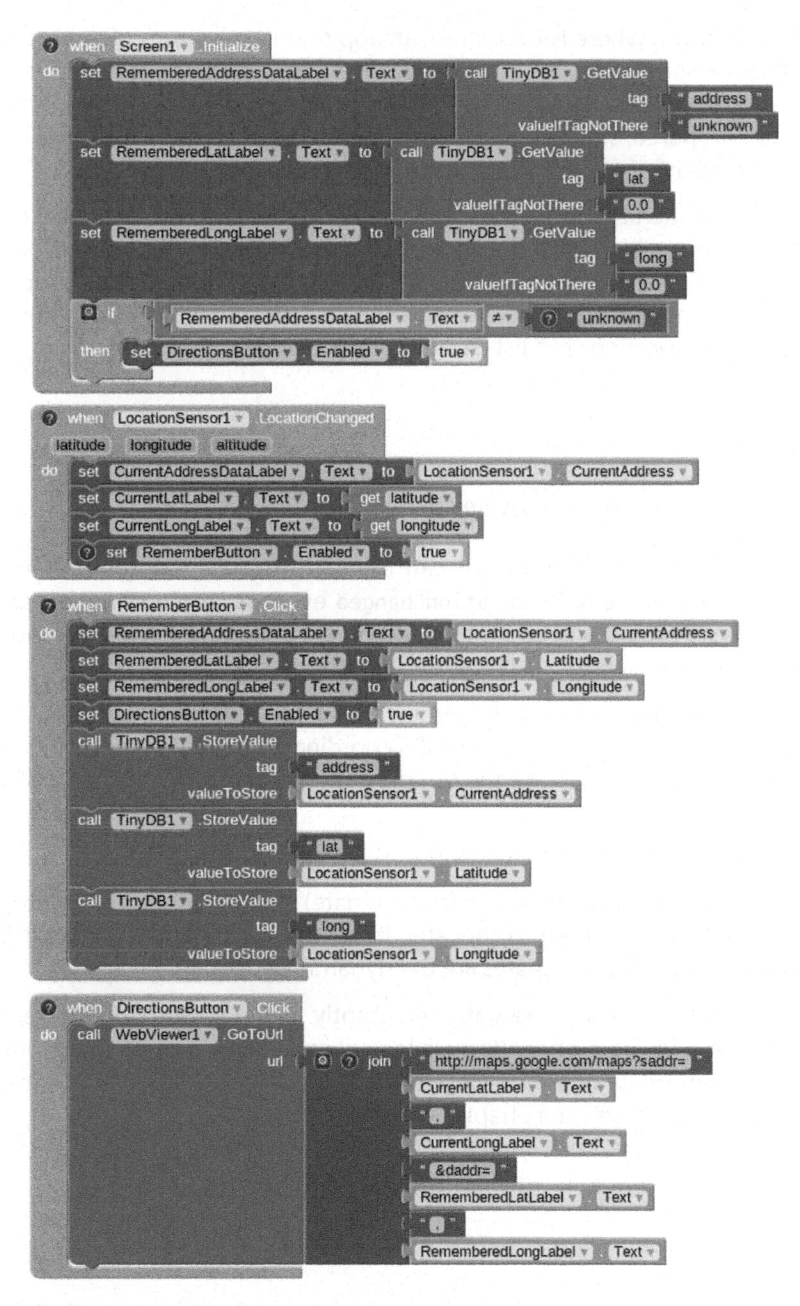
when Screen1 .Initialize
do set RememberedAddressDataLabel . Text to call TinyDB1 .GetValue
tag "address"
valueIfTagNotThere "unknown"
set RememberedLatLabel . Text to call TinyDB1 .GetValue
tag "lat"
valueIfTagNotThere "0.0"
set RememberedLongLabel . Text to call TinyDB1 .GetValue
tag "long"
valueIfTagNotThere "0.0"
if RememberedAddressDataLabel . Text ≠ "unknown"
then set DirectionsButton . Enabled to true
when LocationSensor1 .LocationChanged
latitude longitude altitude
do set CurrentAddressDataLabel . Text to LocationSensor1 . CurrentAddress
set CurrentLatLabel . Text to get latitude
set CurrentLongLabel . Text to get longitude
set RememberButton . Enabled to true
when RememberButton .Click
do set RememberedAddressDataLabel . Text to LocationSensor1 . CurrentAddress
set RememberedLatLabel . Text to LocationSensor1 . Latitude
set RememberedLongLabel . Text to LocationSensor1 . Longitude
set DirectionsButton . Enabled to true
call TinyDB1 .StoreValue
tag "address"
valueToStore LocationSensor1 . CurrentAddress
call TinyDB1 .StoreValue
tag "lat"
valueToStore LocationSensor1 . Latitude
call TinyDB1 .StoreValue
tag "long"
valueToStore LocationSensor1 . Longitude
when DirectionsButton .Click
do call WebViewer1 .GoToUrl
url join "http://maps.google.com/maps?saddr="
CurrentLatLabel . Text
","
CurrentLongLabel . Text
"&daddr="
RememberedLatLabel . Text
","
RememberedLongLabel . Text

Figure 7-7. The blocks for Android, Where's My Car?

Variations

Here are some variations you can experiment with:

- Create Android, Where Is Everyone?, an app that lets a group of people track one another's whereabouts. Whether you're hiking in the woods or become separated at the park, this app could help save time and possibly even lives. The data for this app is shared, so you'll need to use a web database and the `TinyWebDB` component instead of `TinyDB`. See Chapter 22 for more information.
- Create a Breadcrumb app that tracks your whereabouts by recording each location change in a list. You should only record a new breadcrumb if the location has changed by a certain amount, or a certain amount of time has elapsed, because even slight movement can generate a new location reading. You'll need to store the recorded locations in a list. See Chapter 19 for help.

Summary

Here are some of the ideas we covered in this tutorial:

- The `LocationSensor` component can report the user's latitude, longitude, and current street address. Its `LocationChanged` event is triggered when the sensor gets its first reading and when the reading changes (the device has moved). For more information on the `LocationSensor`, see Chapter 23.
- The `WebViewer` component displays any web page, including Google Maps. If you want to show directions between GPS coordinates, the URL will be in the following format, but you'd replace the sample data shown here with actual GPS coordinates:

  http://maps.google.com/maps/?saddr=0.1,0.1&daddr=0.2,0.2
- You use `join` to piece together (concatenate) separate text items into a single text object. You can use it to concatenate dynamic data with static text. With the Maps URL, the GPS coordinates are the dynamic data.
- Using `TinyDB`, you can store data persistently in the phone's database. Whereas the data in a variable or property is lost when an app closes, data stored in the database can be loaded each time the app is opened. For more information on `TinyDB` and databases, see Chapter 22.

CHAPTER 8

Presidents Quiz

The Presidents Quiz is a trivia game about former leaders of the United States. Though this quiz is about presidents, you can use it as a template to build quizzes or study guides on any topic.

In the previous chapters, you've been introduced to some fundamental programming concepts. Now, you're ready for something more challenging. You'll find that this chapter requires a conceptual leap in terms of programming skills and abstract thinking. In particular, you'll use two list variables to store the data—in this case, the quiz questions and answers—and you'll use an index variable to track where the user is in the quiz. When you finish, you'll be armed with the knowledge to create quiz apps and many other apps that require list processing.

This chapter assumes that you're familiar with the basics of App Inventor: using the Component Designer to build the user interface, and using the Blocks Editor to specify event handlers and program the component behavior. If you are not familiar with these fundamentals, be sure to review the previous chapters before continuing.

You'll design the quiz so that the user proceeds from question to question by clicking a Next button and receives feedback about the answers.

What You'll Learn

Figure 8-1. The Presidents Quiz in action

This app, shown in Figure 8-1, covers:

- Defining list variables for storing the questions and answers in lists.
- Sequencing through a list using an index; each time the user clicks Next, you'll display the next question.
- Using conditional (if) behaviors: performing certain operations only under specific conditions. You'll use an `if` block to handle the app's behavior when the user reaches the end of the quiz.

- Switching an image to show a different picture for each quiz question.

Getting Started

Navigate to the App Inventor website and start a new project. Give the project the name "PresidentsQuiz" and set the screen's title to "Presidents Quiz". Connect your device or emulator for live testing.

You'll need to download the following pictures for the quiz from the *appinventor.org* website onto your computer:

- *http://appinventor.org/bookFiles/PresidentsQuiz/roosChurch.gif*
- *http://appinventor.org/bookFiles/PresidentsQuiz/nixon.gif*
- *http://appinventor.org/bookFiles/PresidentsQuiz/carterChina.gif*
- *http://appinventor.org/bookFiles/PresidentsQuiz/atomic.gif*

You'll load these images into your project in the next section.

Designing the Components

The Presidents Quiz app has a simple interface for displaying the questions and allowing the user to answer. You can build the components from the snapshot of the Component Designer shown in Figure 8-2.

Figure 8-2. The Presidents Quiz in the Designer

To create this interface, first load the images you downloaded into the project. In the Media area, click Add and select one of the downloaded files (e.g., *roosChurch.gif*). Do the same for the other three images. Then, add the components listed in Table 8-1.

Table 8-1. Components for the Presidents Quiz app

Component type	Palette group	What you'll name it	Purpose
`Image`	User Interface	`Image1`	The picture displayed with the question.
`Label`	User Interface	`QuestionLabel`	Display the current question.
`HorizontalArrangement`	Layout	`HorizontalArrangement1`	Put the answer text and button in a row.
`TextBox`	User Interface	`AnswerText`	The user will enter his answer here.
`Button`	User Interface	`AnswerButton`	The user clicks this to submit an answer.
`Label`	User Interface	`RightWrongLabel`	Display "correct!" or "incorrect!"
`Button`	User Interface	`NextButton`	The user clicks this to proceed to the next question.

1. Set `Image1.Picture` to the image file *roosChurch.gif*, the first picture that should appear. Set its Width to "Fill parent" and its Height to 200.
2. Set `QuestionLabel.Text` to "Question..." (you'll input the first question in the Blocks Editor).
3. Set `AnswerText.Hint` to "Enter an answer". Set its `Text` property to blank. Move it into `HorizontalArrangement1`.
4. Change `AnswerButton.Text` to "Submit" and move it into `HorizontalArrange ment1`.
5. Change `NextButton.Text` to "Next".
6. Change `RightWrongLabel.Text` to blank.

Adding Behaviors to the Components

You'll need to program the following behaviors:

- When the app starts, the first question appears, including its corresponding image.
- When the user clicks the `NextButton`, the second question appears. When it's clicked again, the third question appears, and so on.

- When the user reaches the last question and clicks the NextButton, the first question should appear again.
- When the user answers a question, the app will report whether it is correct.

You'll code these behaviors one by one, testing as you go.

Defining the Question and Answer Lists

To begin, define two list variables based on the items in Table 8-2: QuestionList to hold the list of questions, and AnswerList to hold the list of corresponding answers. Figure 8-3 shows the two lists you'll create in the Blocks Editor.

Table 8-2. Variables for holding question and answer lists

Block type	Drawer	Purpose
initialize global to ("QuestionList")	Variables	Store the list of questions (rename it QuestionList).
initialize global to("AnswerList")	Variables	Store the list of answers (rename it AnswerList).
make a list	Lists	Insert the items of the QuestionList.
text (three of them)	Text	The questions.
make a list	Lists	Insert the items of the AnswerList.
text (three of them)	Text	The answers.

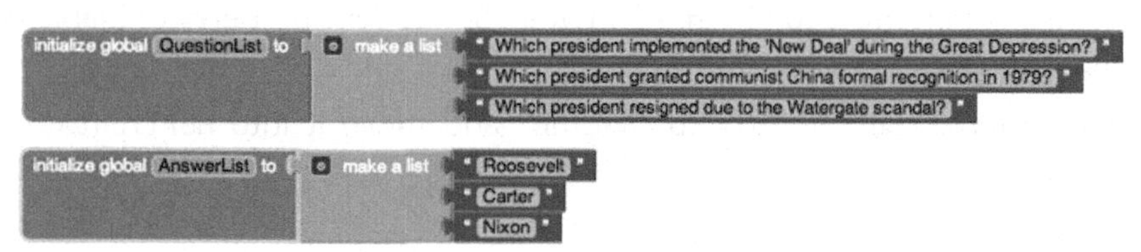

Figure 8-3. The lists for the quiz

Defining the Index Variable

The app needs to keep track of the current question as the user clicks the NextButton to proceed through the quiz. You'll define a variable named currentQuestionIndex for this, and the variable will serve as the index into both the QuestionList and AnswerList. Table 8-3 lists the blocks you'll need to do this, and Figure 8-4 shows what that variable will look like.

Table 8-3. Creating the index

Block type	Drawer	Purpose
`initialize global to` ("currentQuestionIndex")	Variables	Hold the index (position) of the current question/answer.
`number` (1)	Math	Set the initial value of `currentQuestionIndex` to 1 (the first question).

```
initialize global currentQuestionIndex to 1
```

Figure 8-4. Initiating the index variable with a value of 1

Displaying the First Question

Now that you've defined the variables you need, you can specify the app's interactive behavior. As with any app, it's important to work incrementally and define one behavior at a time. To begin, think only about the questions and, specifically, displaying the first question on the list when the app launches. We'll come back and deal with the images and answers a bit later.

You want your code blocks to work regardless of the specific questions that are on the list. That way, if you decide to change the questions or create a new quiz by copying and modifying this app, you'll only need to change the actual questions in the list definitions, and you won't need to change any event handlers.

So, for this first behavior, you don't want to refer directly to the first question, "Which president implemented the 'New Deal' during the Great Depression?" Instead, you want to refer, abstractly, to the first socket in the `QuestionList` (regardless of the specific question there). That way, the blocks will still work even if you modify the question in that first socket.

You select particular items in a list with the `select list item` block. The block asks you to specify the list and an index (a position in the list). If a list has three items, you can enter 1, 2, or 3 as the index.

For this first behavior, when the app launches, you want to select the first item in `QuestionList` and place it in the `QuestionLabel`. Recall from the Android, Where's My Car? app, if you want something to happen when your app launches, you program that behavior in the `Screen1.Initialize` event handler. You can use the blocks listed in Table 8-4.

Table 8-4. Blocks to load the initial question when the app starts

Block type	Drawer	Purpose
`Screen1.Initialize`	Screen1	Event handler triggered when the app begins.
`set QuestionLabel.Text to`	QuestionLabel	Put the first question in `QuestionLabel`.
`select list item`	Lists	Select the first question from `QuestionList`.
`get global QuestionList`	Variables	The list to select questions from.
`number` (1)	Math	Select the first question by using an index of 1.

How the blocks work

The `Screen1.Initialize` event is triggered when the app starts. As shown in Figure 8-5, the first item of the variable `QuestionList` is selected and placed into `QuestionLabel.Text`. So, when the app launches, the user will see the first question.

Figure 8-5. Selecting the first question

Test your app *Click Connect and connect to your device or the emulator for live testing. When your app loads, do you see the first item of* `QuestionList`, *"Which president implemented the 'New Deal' during the Great Depression?"*

Iterating Through the Questions

Now, program the behavior of the `NextButton`. You've already defined the `currentQuestionIndex` to remember the current question. When the user clicks the `NextButton`, the app needs to increment the `currentQuestionIndex` (i.e., change it from 1 to 2 or from 2 to 3, and so on). You'll then use the resulting value of `currentQuestionIndex` to select the new question to display. As a challenge, see if you can build these blocks on your own. When you're finished, compare your results against Figure 8-6.

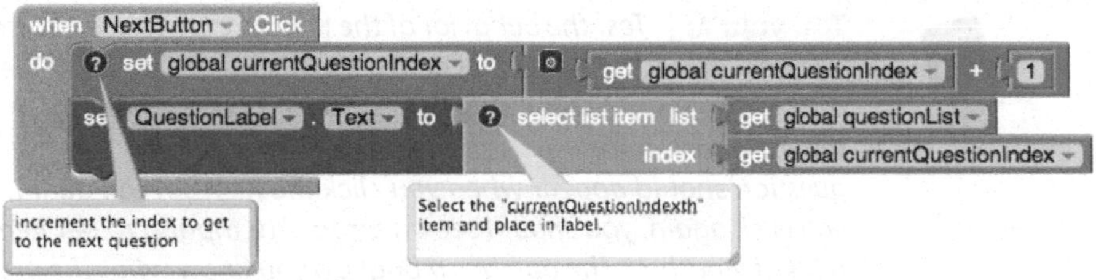

Figure 8-6. Moving to the next question

How the blocks work

The first row of blocks increments the variable `currentQuestionIndex`. If `currentQuestionIndex` has a 1 in it, it is changed to 2. If it has a 2, it is changed to 3, and so on. After the `currentQuestionIndex` variable has been changed, the app uses it to select the new question to display. When the user clicks `NextButton` for the first time, the increment blocks will change `currentQuestionIndex` from 1 to 2, so the app will select the second item from `QuestionList`, "Which president granted communist China formal recognition in 1979?" The second time `NextButton` is clicked, `currentQuestionIndex` will be set from 2 to 3, and the app will select the third question on the list, "Which president resigned due to the Watergate scandal?"

Note *Take a minute to compare the blocks of* `NextButton.Click` *to those in the* `Screen.Initialize` *event handler. In the* `Screen.Initialize` *blocks, the app used* `select list item` *with a concrete number (1) to select the list item. In these blocks, you're selecting the list item by using a variable as the index. The app doesn't choose the first item in the list, or the second, or the third; it chooses the* `currentQuestionIndexth` *item, and thus a different item will be selected each time the user clicks* `NextButton`. *This is a very common use for an index—incrementing its value to find and display or process items in a list.*

Test your app *Test the behavior of the* `NextButton` *to see if the app is working correctly. Click the* `NextButton` *on the phone. Does the phone display the second question, "Which president granted communist China formal recognition in 1979?" It should, and the third question should appear when you click the* `NextButton` *again. But if you click again, you should see an error: "Attempting to get item 4 of a list of length 3." The app has a bug! Do you know what the problem is? Try figuring it out before moving on.*

The problem with the code thus far is that it simply increments to the next question each time without any concern for the end of the quiz. When `currentQuestionIndex` is already 3 and the user clicks the`NextButton`, the app changes `currentQuestionIn dex` from 3 to 4. It then calls `select list item` to get the `currentQuestionIndexth` item—in this case, the fourth item. Because there are only three items in the variable `QuestionList`, the Android device doesn't know what to do. As a result, it displays an error and forces the app to quit. How can we let the app know that it has reached the end of the quiz?

The app needs to ask a question when the `NextButton` is clicked, and execute different blocks depending on the answer. Because you know your app contains three questions, one way to ask the question would be, "Is the variable `currentQuestionIn dex` greater than 3?" If the answer is yes, you should set `currentQuestionIndex` back to 1 and take the user back to the first question. The blocks you'll need for this are listed in Table 8-5.

Table 8-5. Blocks for checking the index value for the end of the list

Block type	Drawer	Purpose
`if`	Control	Figure out if the user is on the last question.
`>=`	Math	Test if `currentQuestionIndex` is greater than 3.
`get global current QuestionIndex`	Drag from initialize block	Put this into the left side of =.
`number 3`	Math	Put this into the right side of = because 3 is the number of items in the list.
`set global current QuestionIndex to`	Drag from initialize block	Set to 1 to revert to the first question.
`number 1`	Math	Set the index to 1.

The blocks should appear as illustrated in Figure 8-7.

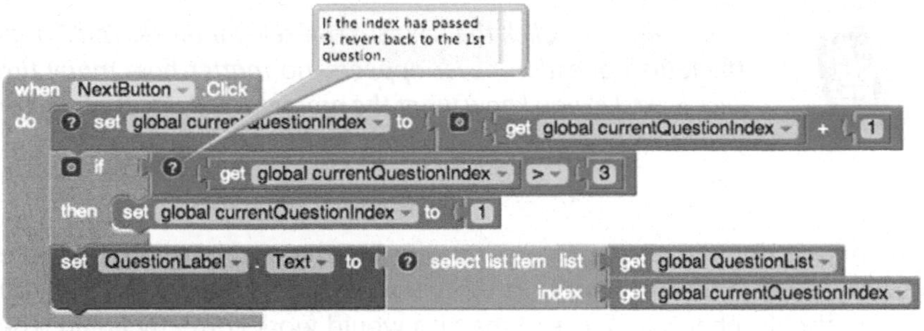

Figure 8-7. Checking if the index is past the last question

How the blocks work

When the user clicks the `NextButton`, the app increments the index as it did before. But then, as is shown in Figure 8-8, it checks to see if `currentQuestionIndex` is greater than 3, which is the number of questions. If it is greater than 3, `currentQuestionIndex` is set back to 1, and the first question is displayed. If it is 3 or less, the blocks within the `if` block are not performed, and the current question is displayed as usual.

Test your app *Pick up the phone and click the* `NextButton`*. The second question, "Which president granted communist China formal recognition in 1979?" should appear in the* `QuestionLabel` *on the phone, as before. When you click again, the third question should appear on the phone. Now, for the behavior you're really testing: if you click again, you should see the first question ("Which president implemented the 'New Deal' during the Great Depression?") appear on the phone.*

Making the Quiz Easy to Modify

If your blocks for the `NextButton` work, pat yourself on the back; you are on your way to becoming a programmer! But what if you added a new question (and answer) to the quiz? Would your blocks still work? To explore this, first add a fourth question to `QuestionList` and a fourth answer into `AnswerList`, as shown in Figure 8-8.

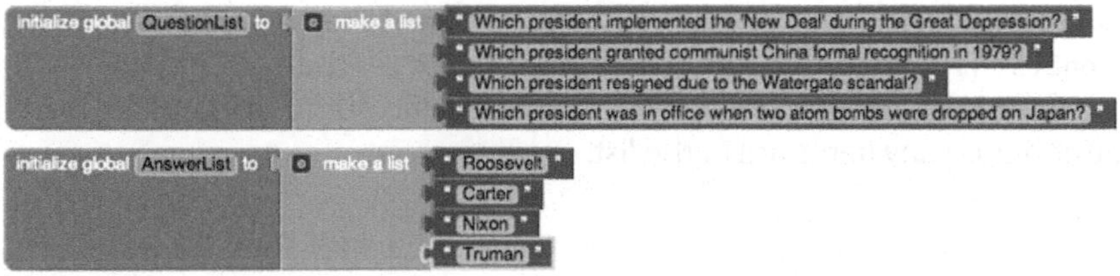

Figure 8-8. Adding an item to both lists

Test your app *Click the* `NextButton` *several times. You'll notice that the fourth question never appears, no matter how many times you click Next. Do you know what the problem is? Before reading on, see if you can fix the blocks so that the fourth question appears.*

The issue here is that the test to determine whether the user is on the last question is too specific; it asks if the `currentQuestionIndex` variable is greater than 3. You could just change the number 3 to a 4, and the app would work correctly again. The problem with that solution, however, is that each time you modify the questions and answer lists, you must also remember to make this change to the if-test.

Such dependencies in a computer program often lead to bugs, especially as an app grows in complexity. A much better strategy is to design the blocks so that they will work no matter how many questions there are. Such generality makes it easier if you, as a programmer, want to customize your quiz for some other topic. It is also essential if the list you are working with changes dynamically—for example, think of a quiz app that allows the user to add new questions (you'll build this in Chapter 10). For a program to be more general, it can't refer to concrete numbers such as 3, because that only works for quizzes of three questions.

So, instead of asking if the value of `currentQuestionIndex` is greater than the specific number 3, ask if it is greater than the number of items in `QuestionList`. If the app asks this more general question, it will work even when you add to or remove items from the `QuestionList`. Let's modify the `NextButton.Click` event handler to replace the previous test that referred directly to 3. You'll need the blocks listed in Table 8-6.

Table 8-6. Blocks to check the length of the list

Block type	Drawer	Purpose
`length of list`	Lists	Ask how many items are in `QuestionList`.
`get global QuestionList`	Drag in from initialization block	Put this into the "list" socket of `length of list`.

How the blocks work

The `if` test now compares the `currentQuestionIndex` to the length of the `QuestionList`, as shown in Figure 8-11. So, if `currentQuestionIndex` is 5, and the length of the `QuestionList` is 4, then the `currentQuestionIndex` will be set back to 1. Note that, because the blocks no longer refer to 3 or any specific number, the behavior will work no matter how many items are in the list.

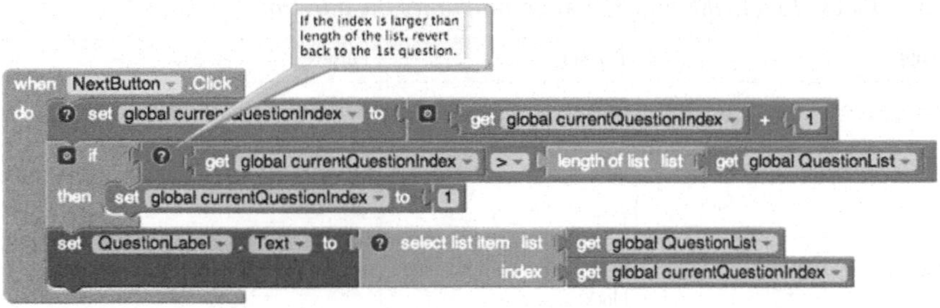

Figure 8-9. Checking if the index is larger than length of list (instead of 3)

Test your app When you click the `NextButton`, does the app now cycle through the four questions, moving to the first one after the fourth?

Switching the Image for Each Question

Now that you've programmed all the behaviors for moving through the questions (and you've made your code smarter and more flexible by making it more abstract), your next task is to get the images working properly, too. Right now, the app shows the same image no matter what question is being asked. You can change this so an image pertaining to each question appears when the user clicks the `NextButton`. Earlier, you added four pictures as media for the project. Now, you'll create a third list, `PictureList`, with the image filenames as its items. You'll also modify the `NextButton.Click` event handler to switch the picture each time, just as you switch the question text. (If you're already thinking about using the `currentQuestionIndex` here, you're on the right track!) First, create a `PictureList` and initialize it with the names of the image files. Be sure that the names are exactly the same as the filenames you loaded into the Media section of the project. Figure 8-10 shows how the blocks for the `PictureList` should look.

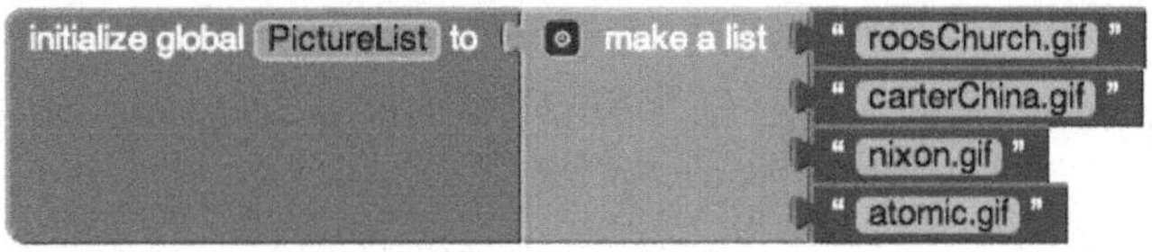

Figure 8-10. The PictureList with image filenames as items

Next, modify the `NextButton.Click` event handler so that it changes the picture that appears for each question. The `Image.Picture` property is used to change the picture displayed. To modify `NextButton.Click`, you'll need the blocks listed in Table 8-7.

Table 8-7. Blocks to add the image that accompanies the question

Block type	Drawer	Purpose
`set Image1.Picture to`	Image1	Set this to change the picture.
`select list item`	Lists	Select the picture corresponding to the current question.
`get global PictureList`	Drag out from initialization block	Select a filename from this list.
`get global currentQuestionIndex`	Drag out from initialization block	Select the `currentQuestionIndex` item.

How the blocks work

The `currentQuestionIndex` serves as the index for both the `QuestionList` and the `PictureList`. As long as you've set up your lists properly such that the first question corresponds to the first picture, the second to the second, and so on, the single index can serve both lists, as shown in Figure 8-11. For instance, the first picture, *roosChurch.gif*, is a picture of President Franklin Delano Roosevelt (sitting with British Prime Minister Winston Churchill), and "Roosevelt" is the answer to the first question.

Figure 8-11. Selecting the currentQuestionIndexth picture each time

Test your app *Click Next a few times. Does a different image appear each time you click the* `NextButton`?

Checking the User's Answers

Thus far, you've created an app that simply cycles through questions and answers (paired with an image of the answer). It's a great example of apps that use lists, but to be a true quiz app, it needs to give users feedback on whether their answers are correct. Let's add the blocks to do just that. Our interface is set up so that the user types an answer in `AnswerText` and then clicks the `AnswerButton`. The app must compare the user's entry with the answer to the current question, using an `if else` block to check. The `RightWrongLabel` should then be modified to report whether the answer is correct. There are quite a few blocks needed to program this behavior, all of which are listed in Table 8-8.

Table 8-8. Blocks for indicating whether an answer is correct

Block type	Drawer	Purpose
`AnswerButton.Click`	AnswerButton	Triggered when the user clicks the `AnswerButton`.
`ifelse`	Control	If the answer is correct, do one thing; otherwise, do another.
=	Math	Ask if the answer is correct.
`AnswerText.Text`	AnswerText	Contains the user's answer.
`select list item`	Lists	Select the current answer from `AnswerList`.
`get global AnswerList`	Drag out from initialization block	The list to select from.
`get global currentQuestionIndex`	Drag out from initialization block	The current question (and answer) number.
`set RightWrongLabel.Text to`	RightWrongLabel	Report the answer here.
`text` ("correct!")	Text	Display this if the answer is right.
`set RightWrongLabel.Text to`	RightWrongLabel	Report the answer here.
`text` ("incorrect!")	Text	Display this if the answer is wrong.

How the blocks work

Figure 8-12 demonstrates how the `if else` test asks whether the answer the user provided (`AnswerText.Text`) is equal to the `currentQuestionIndexth` item in the `AnswerList`. If `currentQuestionIndex` is 1, the app will compare the user's answer with the first item in `AnswerList`, "Roosevelt." If `currentQuestionIndex` is 2, the app will compare the user's answer with the second answer in the list, "Carter," and so on. If the test result is positive, the `then` branch is executed and the `RightWrongLabel` is set to "correct!" If the test is false, the `else` branch is executed and the `RightWrongLabel` is set to "incorrect!"

Figure 8-12. Checking the answer

Test your app *Try answering one of the questions. It should report whether you answered the question exactly as specified in the* `AnswerList`*. Test with both a correct and incorrect answer. You'll likely notice that for an answer to be marked as correct, it has to be an exact match and case-specific to what you entered in the* `AnswerList`*. Be sure to also test that things work on successive questions.*

The app should work, but you might notice that when you click the `NextButton`, the "correct!" or "incorrect!" text and the previous answer are still there, as shown in Figure 8-13, even though you're looking at the next question. It's fairly innocuous, but your app users will definitely notice such user interface issues. To blank out the `RightWrongLabel` and the `AnswerText`, you'll put the blocks listed in Table 8-9 within the `NextButton.Click` event handler.

Figure 8-13. The quiz in action with the previous answer appearing when it shouldn't

Table 8-9. Blocks to clear the RightWrongLabel

Block type	Drawer	Purpose
`set RightWrongLabel.Text to`	RightWrongLabel	This is the label to blank out.
`text ("")`	Text	When the user clicks `NextButton`, clear the previous answer's feedback.
`set AnswerText.Text to`	AnswerText	The user's answer from the previous question.
`text ("")`	Text	When the user clicks the `NextButton`, clear the previous answer.

How the blocks work

As shown in Figure 8-14, by clicking the `NextButton`, the user moves on to the next question, so the top two rows of the event handler clear out the `RightWrongLabel` and the `AnswerText`.

Figure 8-14. The PictureList with image filenames as items

Test your app *Answer a question and click Submit, then click the* `NextButton`. *Did your previous answer and its feedback disappear?*

The Complete App: The Presidents Quiz

Figure 8-15 shows the final block configuration for the Presidents Quiz.

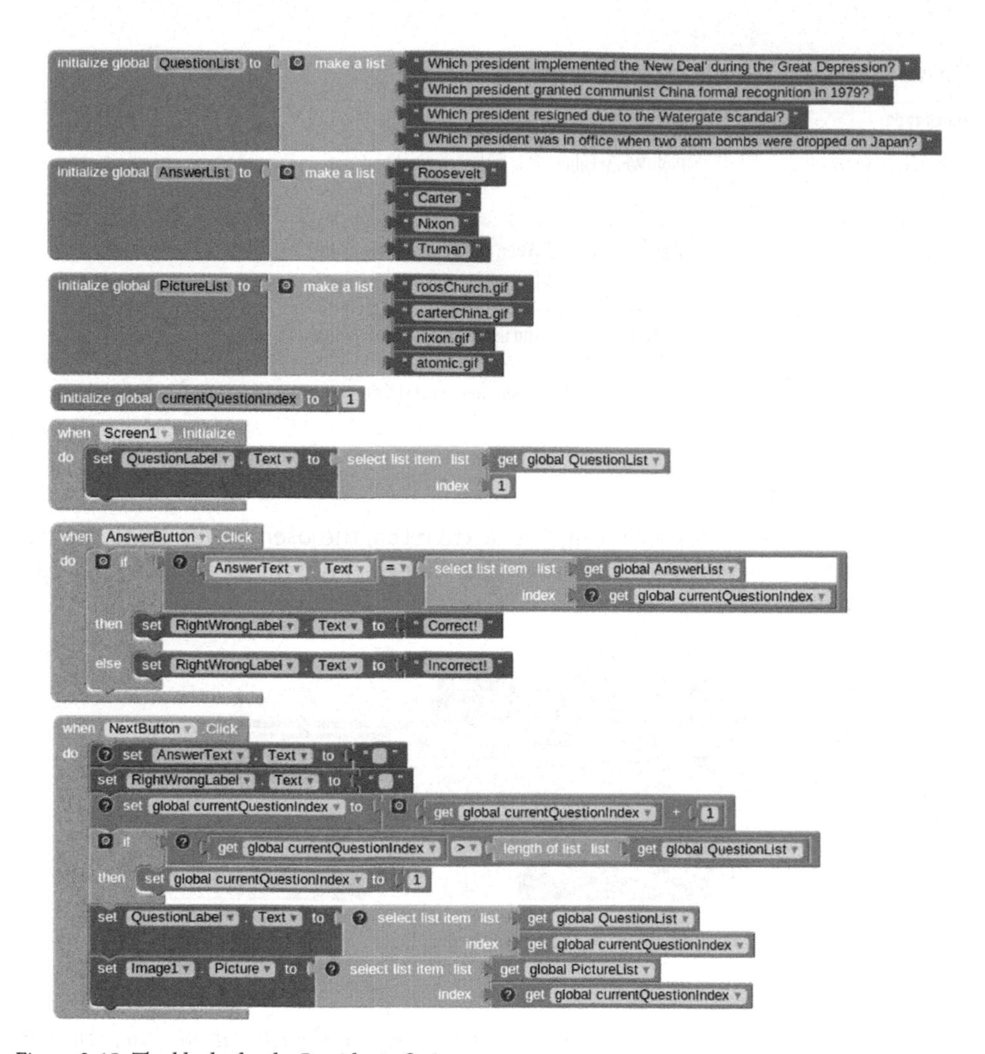
initialize global QuestionList to make a list
Which president implemented the 'New Deal' during the Great Depression?
Which president granted communist China formal recognition in 1979?
Which president resigned due to the Watergate scandal?
Which president was in office when two atom bombs were dropped on Japan?
initialize global AnswerList to make a list
Roosevelt
Carter
Nixon
Truman
initialize global PictureList to make a list
roosChurch.gif
carterChina.gif
nixon.gif
atomic.gif
initialize global currentQuestionIndex to 1
when Screen1 .Initialize
do set QuestionLabel . Text to select list item list get global QuestionList
index 1
when AnswerButton .Click
do if AnswerText . Text = select list item list get global AnswerList
index get global currentQuestionIndex
then set RightWrongLabel . Text to Correct!
else set RightWrongLabel . Text to Incorrect!
when NextButton .Click
do set AnswerText . Text to
set RightWrongLabel . Text to
set global currentQuestionIndex to get global currentQuestionIndex + 1
if get global currentQuestionIndex > length of list list get global QuestionList
then set global currentQuestionIndex to 1
set QuestionLabel . Text to select list item list get global QuestionList
index get global currentQuestionIndex
set Image1 . Picture to select list item list get global PictureList
index get global currentQuestionIndex

Figure 8-15. The blocks for the Presidents Quiz

Variations

When you get this quiz working, you might want to explore some variations, such as the following:

- Instead of just showing images for each question, try playing a sound clip or a short video. With sound, you can turn your quiz into a Name That Tune app.
- The quiz is very rigid in terms of what it accepts as a valid answer. There are a number of ways to improve this, taking advantage of text processing blocks in the text drawer. One way is to use the upcase block in the Text drawer to convert the user's answer and actual answer to all upper case before comparing. Another

is to use the `text.contains` block to see if the user's answer is contained in the actual answer. Another option is to provide multiple answers for each question and check by iterating (`foreach`) through them to see if any match.

- Another way to improve the answer checking is to transform the quiz so that it is multiple choice. You'll need an additional list to hold the answer choices for each question. The possible answers will be a list of lists, with each sublist holding the answer choices for a particular question. Use the `ListPicker` component to give the user the ability to choose an answer. You can read more about lists in Chapter 19.

Summary

Here are some of the ideas we covered in this tutorial:

- Most fairly sophisticated apps have data (often stored in lists) and behavior—its event handlers.
- Use an `ifelse` block to check conditions. For more information on conditionals, see Chapter 18.
- The blocks in event handlers should refer only abstractly to list items and list size so that the app will work even if the data in the list is changed.
- Index variables track the current position of an item within a list. When you increment them, use an `if` block to handle the app's behavior when the user reaches the end of the list.

CHAPTER 9

Xylophone

It's hard to believe that using technology to record and play back music only dates back to 1878, when Edison patented the phonograph. We've come so far since then—with music synthesizers, CDs, sampling and remixing, phones that play music, and even long-distance jamming over the Internet. In this chapter, you'll take part in this tradition by building a Xylophone app that records and plays music.

What You'll Build

With the app shown in Figure 9-1 (originally created by Liz Looney of the App Inventor team), you can:

- Play eight different notes by touching colored buttons on the screen.
- Press a Play button to replay the notes you played earlier.
- Press a Reset button to make the app clear any notes you played earlier so that you can enter a new song.

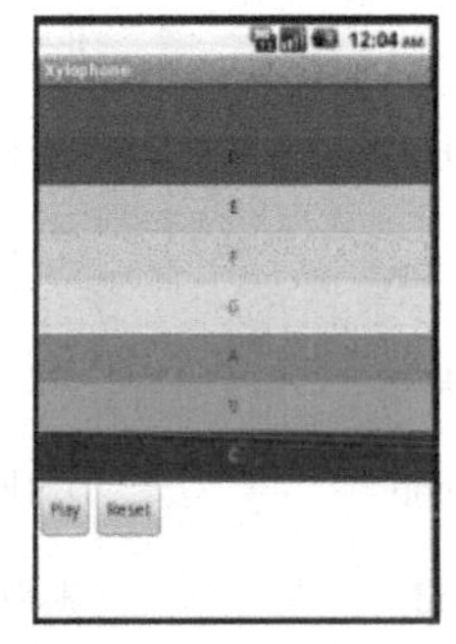

Figure 9-1. The Xylophone app user interface

What You'll Learn

This tutorial covers the following concepts:

- Using a single Sound component to play different audio files.
- Using the Clock component to measure and enforce delays between actions.
- Deciding when to create a procedure.
- Creating a procedure that calls itself.
- Advanced use of lists, including adding items, accessing them, and clearing the list.

Getting Started

Connect to the App Inventor website and start a new project. Name it "Xylophone", and also set the screen's title to "Xylophone". Connect your app to your device or emulator.

Designing the Components

This app has 13 different components (8 of which comprise the keyboard), which are listed in Table 9-1. Because there are so many, it would get pretty boring to create all of them before starting to write our program, so we'll break down the app into its functional parts and build them sequentially by going back and forth between the Designer and the Blocks Editor, as we did with the Ladybug Chase app in Chapter 5.

Table 9-1. All of the components for the Xylophone app

Component type	Palette group	What you'll name it	Purpose
Button	User Interface	Button1	Play Low C key.
Button	User Interface	Button2	Play D key.
Button	User Interface	Button3	Play E key.
Button	User Interface	Button4	Play F key.
Button	User Interface	Button5	Play G key.
Button	User Interface	Button6	Play A key.
Button	User Interface	Button7	Play B key.
Button	User Interface	Button8	Play High C key.
Sound	Media	Sound1	Play the notes.
Button	User Interface	PlayButton	Play back the song.
Button	User Interface	ResetButton	Reset the song memory.
HorizontalArrangement	Layout	HorizontalArrangement1	Place the Play and Reset buttons next to each other.
Clock	User Interface	Clock1	Keep track of delays between notes.

Creating the Keyboard

Our user interface will include an eight-note keyboard for a pentatonic (seven-note) major scale ranging from Low C to High C. We will create this musical keyboard in this section.

Creating the First Note Buttons

Start by creating the first two xylophone keys, which we will implement as buttons.

1. From the User Interface category, drag a `Button` onto the screen. Leave its name as `Button1`. We want it to be a long magenta bar, like that on a xylophone, so set its properties as follows:

    - Change the `BackgroundColor` property to Magenta.
    - Change the `Text` property to "C".
    - Set the `Width` property to "Fill parent" so that it spans all the way across the screen.
    - Set the `Height` property to 40 pixels.

2. Repeat for a second `Button`, named `Button2`, placing it below `Button1`. Use the same `Width` and `Height` property values, but set its `BackgroundColor` property to Red and its `Text` property to "D".

(Later, we will repeat step 2 for six more note buttons.)

The view in the Component Designer should look something like Figure 9-2.

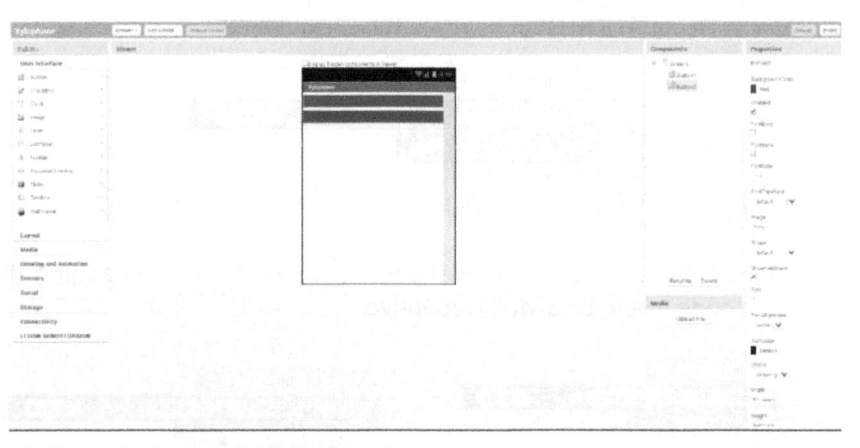

Figure 9-2. Placing buttons to create a keyboard

The display on your phone should look similar, although there will not be any empty space between the two colored buttons.

Adding the Sound Component

We can't have a xylophone without sounds, so drag in a `Sound` component, leaving its name as `Sound1`. Change the `MinimumInterval` property from its default value of 500 milliseconds to 0. This allows us to play the sound as often as we want, instead of having to wait half a second (500 milliseconds) between plays. Don't set its `Source` property, which we will set in the Blocks Editor.

Download the sound files: *http://appinventor.org/bookFiles/Xylophone/1.wav* and *http://appinventor.org/bookFiles/Xylophone/2.wav*. Unlike in previous chapters, where it was okay to change the names of media files, it is important to use these exact names for reasons that will soon become clear. You can upload the remaining six sound files when directed to later.

Connecting the Sounds to the Buttons

The behavior we need to program is for a sound file to play when the corresponding button is clicked. Specifically, if `Button1` is clicked, we'd like to play *1.wav*; if `Button2` is clicked, we'd like to play *2.wav*; and so on. We can set this up in the Blocks Editor, as shown in Figure 9-3, by doing the following:

1. From the Button1 drawer, drag out the `Button1.Click` block.
2. From the Sound1 drawer, drag out the set `Sound1.Source` block, placing it in the `Button1.Click` block.
3. Type "text" to create a text block. (This is quicker than going to the Built-In tab and then the Text drawer, although that would work, too.) Set its `text` value to "1.wav" and place it in the `Sound1.Source` block.
4. Add a `Sound1.Play` block.

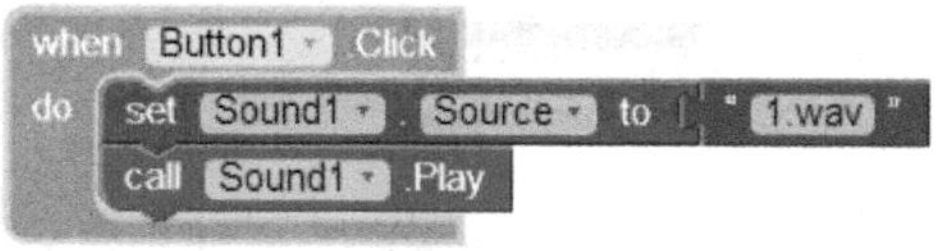

Figure 9-3. Playing a sound when a button is clicked

We could do the same for `Button2`, as shown in Figure 9-4 (just changing the text value), but the code would be awfully repetitive.

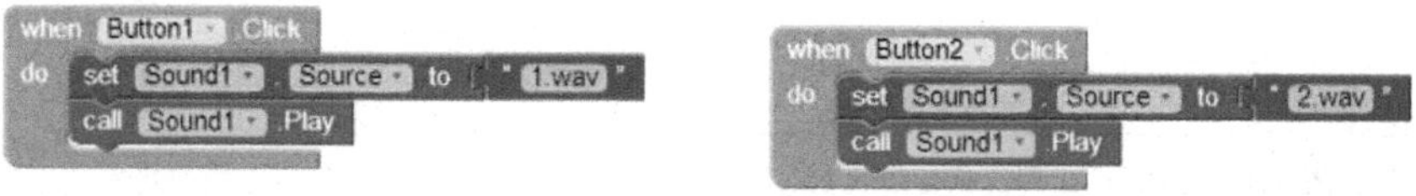

Figure 9-4. Adding more sounds

Repeated code is a good sign that you should create a procedure, which you've already done in the MoleMash game in Chapter 3 and the Ladybug Chase game in Chapter 5. Specifically, we'll create a procedure that takes a number as a parameter, sets `Sound1`'s `Source` to the appropriate file, and plays the sound. This is another example of *refactoring*—improving a program's implementation without changing its behavior, a concept introduced in the MoleMash tutorial. We can use the Text drawer's `join` block to combine the number (e.g., 1) and the text ".wav" to create the proper filename (e.g., "1.wav"). Here are the steps for creating the procedure we need:

1. Under the Built-In tab, go to the Procedures drawer and drag out the `to procedure do` block. (Unless otherwise specified, you should choose the version with "do", not "result".)
2. Add the parameter by clicking on the little blue icon on the `to procedure do` block, dragging over an input, and changing its name from "x" to "number". You might want to review Figure 5-6 from Chapter 5.
3. Click the name of the procedure, which by default is "procedure" and set it to "PlayNote".
4. Drag the `Sound1.Source` block from `Button1.Click` into `PlayNote` to the right of the word "do". Move the `Sound1.Play` block into PlayNote as well.
5. Drag the `1.wav` block into the trash can.
6. From the Text drawer, drag the `join` block into `Sound1.Source`'s socket.
7. Type "number" and move it to the top socket of the `join` block (if it is not already there).
8. From the Text drawer, drag the `text` block into the second socket of the `join` block.
9. Change the text value to ".wav". (Remember not to type the quotation marks.)
10. From the Procedures drawer, drag out a `call PlayNote` block and place into the empty body of `Button1.Click`.
11. Type "1" and put it in the "number" socket.

Now, when `Button1` is clicked, the procedure `PlayNote` will be called, with its number parameter having the value 1. It should set `Sound1.Source` to "1.wav" and play the sound.

Create a similar `Button2.Click` block with a call to `PlayNote` with a parameter of 2. (You can copy the existing `call PlayNote` block and move it into the body of `Button2.Click`, making sure to change the parameter.) Your program should look like Figure 9-5.

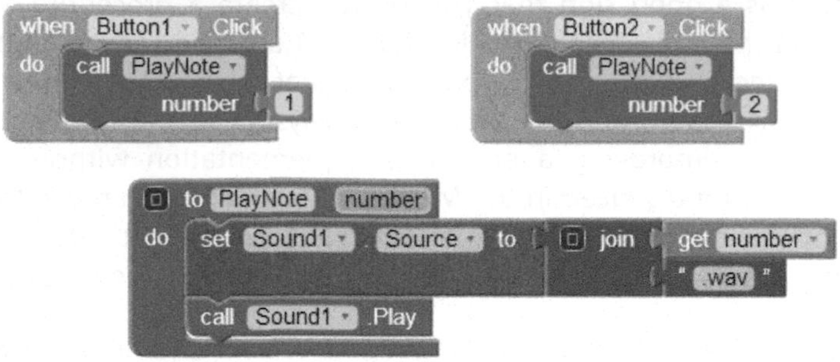

Figure 9-5. Creating a procedure to play a note

Instructing Android to Load the Sounds

If you tried out the preceding calls to `PlayNote`, you might have been disappointed by not hearing the sound you expected or by experiencing an error or unexpected delay. That's because Android needs to load sounds at runtime, which entails some lag before they can be played. This issue didn't come up earlier because filenames placed in a `Sound` component's `Source` property in the Designer are automatically loaded when the program starts. Because we don't set `Sound1.Source` until *after* the program has started, that initialization process does not take place. We have to explicitly load the sounds when the program starts up, as shown in Figure 9-6.

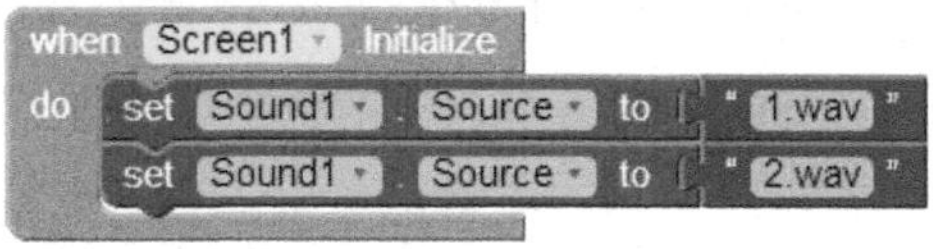

Figure 9-6. Loading sounds when the app launches

Test your app *Touch the buttons and check if the notes play without delay. (If you don't hear anything, make sure that the media volume on your phone is not set to mute.)*

Implementing the Remaining Notes

Now that we have the first two buttons and notes implemented and working, add the remaining six notes by going back to the Designer and downloading the sound files:

- *http://appinventor.org/bookFiles/Xylophone/3.wav*
- *http://appinventor.org/bookFiles/Xylophone/4.wav*
- *http://appinventor.org/bookFiles/Xylophone/5.wav*

- *http://appinventor.org/bookFiles/Xylophone/6.wav*
- *http://appinventor.org/bookFiles/Xylophone/7.wav*
- *http://appinventor.org/bookFiles/Xylophone/8.wav*

Then, create six new buttons, following the same steps as you did for the previous two but setting their `Text` and `BackgroundColor` properties as follows:

- Button3 ("E", Pink)
- Button4 ("F", Orange)
- Button5 ("G", Yellow)
- Button6 ("A", Green)
- Button7 ("B", Cyan)
- Button8 ("C", Blue)

You might also want to change `Button8`'s `TextColor` property to White, as shown in Figure 9-7, so it is more legible.

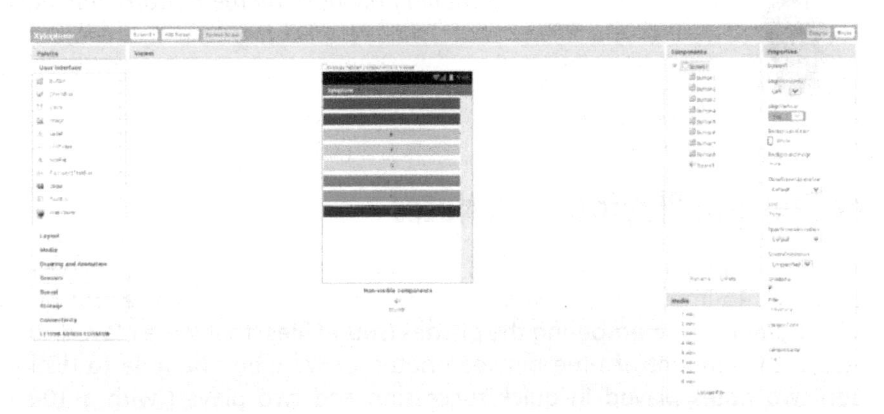

Figure 9-7. Putting the remaining buttons and sounds in the Component Designer

Back in the Blocks Editor, create `Click` blocks for each of the new buttons with appropriate calls to `PlayNote`. Similarly, add each new sound file to `Screen.Initialize`, as shown in Figure 9-8.

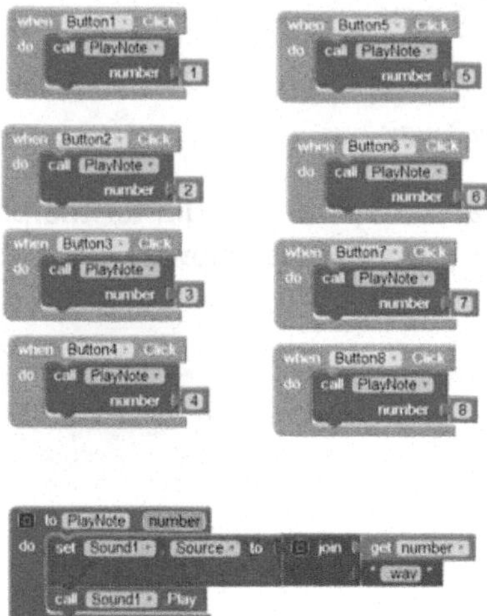

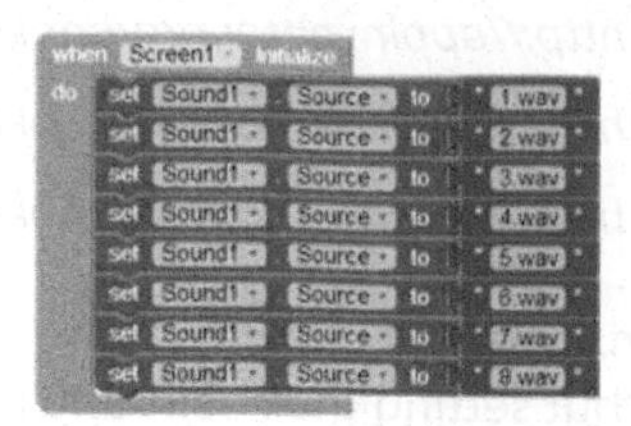

Figure 9-8. Programming the button click events to correspond to all the keyboard keys

Test your app *You should now have all the buttons, and each one will play a different note when you click it.*

Recording and Playing Back Notes

Playing notes by pressing buttons is fun, but being able to record and play back songs is even better. To implement playback, we will need to maintain a record of played notes. In addition to remembering the pitches (sound files) that were played, we must also record the amount of time between notes, or we won't be able to distinguish between two notes played in quick succession and two played with a 10-second silence between them.

Our app will maintain two lists, each of which will have one entry for each note that has been played:

- `notes`, which will contain the names of the sound files in the order in which they were played.
- `times`, which will record the points in time at which the notes were played.

Note *Before continuing, you might want to review lists, which are covered in the Presidents Quiz in Chapter 8 and in Chapter 19.*

We can get the timing information from a `Clock` component, which we will also use to properly time the notes for playback.

Adding the Components

In the Designer, you will need to add a `Clock` component and Play and Reset buttons, which you will put in a `HorizontalArrangement`:

1. From the Sensors drawer, drag in a `Clock` component. It will appear in the "Non-visible components" section. Uncheck its `TimerEnabled` property because we don't want its timer to go off until we tell it to during playback.
2. Go to the Layout drawer and drag a `HorizontalArrangement` component beneath the existing button. Set its `Width` property to "Fill parent."
3. From the User Interface drawer, drag in a `Button`. Rename it `"PlayButton"` and set its `Text` property to "Play".
4. Drag in another `Button`, placing it to the right of `PlayButton`. Rename the new `Button` `"ResetButton"` and set its `Text` property to "Reset".

The Designer view should look like Figure 9-9.

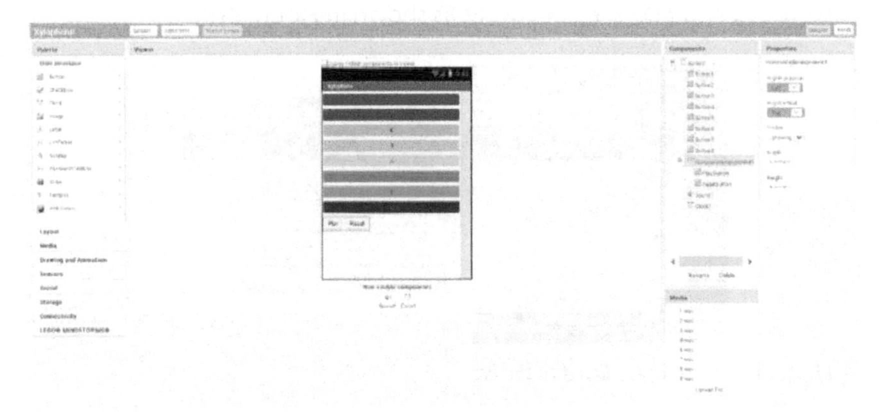

Figure 9-9. Adding components for recording and playing back sounds

Recording Notes and Times

We now need to add the correct behavior in the Blocks Editor. We will need to maintain lists of notes and times and add to the lists whenever the user presses a button.

1. Create a new variable by going to the Variables drawer and dragging out an `initialize global to` block from the Definition drawer.
2. Change the name of the variable to "notes".
3. Open the Lists drawer and drag a `create empty list` block out, placing it in the socket of the `initialize global to` block.

This defines a new variable named "notes" to be an empty list. Repeat the steps for another variable, which you should name "times". These new blocks should look like those in Figure 9-10.

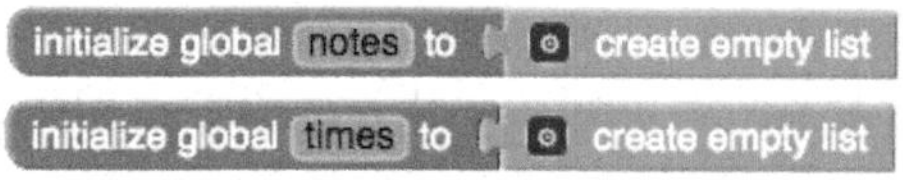

Figure 9-10. Initialize two variables to store the notes and the timing information

How the blocks work

Whenever a note is played, we need to save both the name of the sound file (to the list `notes`) and the instant in time at which it was played (to the list `times`). To record the instant in time, we will use the `Clock1.Now` block, which returns the current instant in time (e.g., March 12, 2011, 8:33:14 AM), to the nearest millisecond. These values, obtained through the `Sound1.Source` and `Clock1.Now` blocks, should be added to the lists `notes` and `times`, respectively, as shown in Figure 9-11.

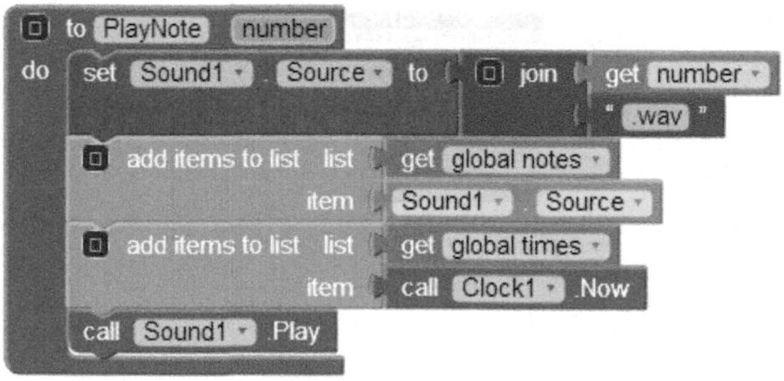

Figure 9-11. Adding the sounds played to the list

For example, if you play "Row, Row, Row Your Boat" [C C C D E], your lists would end up having five entries, which might appear as follows:

- `notes`: 1.wav, 1.wav, 1.wav, 2.wav, 3.wav
- `times` [dates omitted]: 12:00:01, 12:00:02, 12:00:03, 12:00:03.5, 12:00:04

When the user presses the Reset button, we want the two lists to go back to their original, empty states. Because the user won't see any change, it's nice to add a small `Sound1.Vibrate` block to indicate that the key click was registered. Figure 9-12 shows the blocks for this behavior.

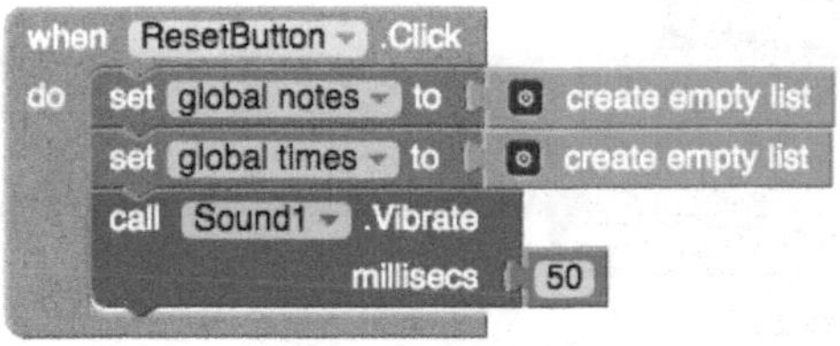

```
when ResetButton .Click
do  set global notes to  create empty list
    set global times to  create empty list
    call Sound1 .Vibrate
                 millisecs 50
```

Figure 9-12. Providing feedback when the user resets the app

Playing Back Notes

As a thought experiment, let's first look at how to implement note playback without worrying about timing. We could (but won't) do this by creating these blocks as shown in Figure 9-13:

- A variable `count` to keep track of which note we're on.
- A new procedure, `PlayBackNote`, which plays that note and moves on to the next one.
- Code to run when `PlayButton` is pressed that sets the count to 1 and calls `PlayBackNote` unless there are no saved notes.

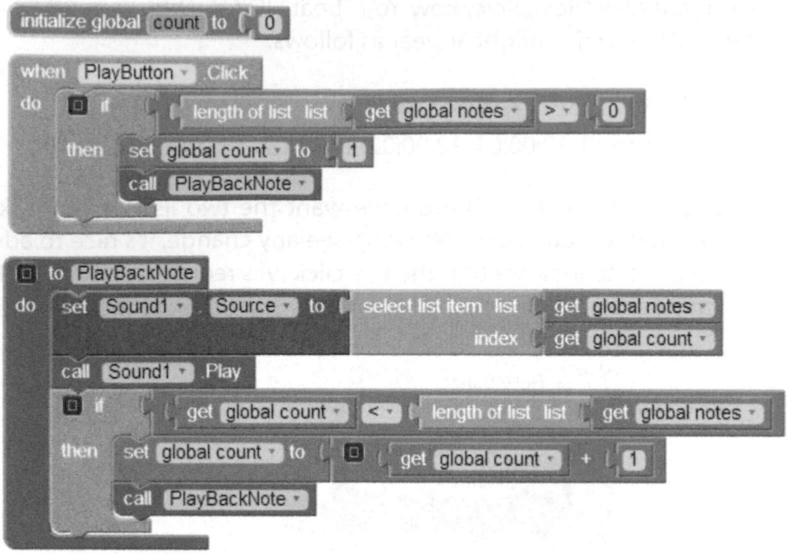

Figure 9-13. Playing back the recorded notes

How the blocks work

This might be the first time you've seen a procedure make a call to itself. Even though at first glance this might seem bogus, it is in fact an important and powerful computer science concept called *recursion*.

To get a better idea of how recursion works, let's step through what happens if a user plays/records three notes (*1.wav*, *3.wav*, and *6.wav*) and then presses the Play button. First, `PlayButton.Click` starts running. Because the length of the list `notes` is 3, which is greater than 0, `count` is set to 1, and `PlayBackNote` is called:

1. The first time `PlayBackNote` is called, `count` = 1:

   - `Sound1.Source` is set to the first item in `notes`, which is *1.wav*.
   - `Sound1.Play` is called, playing this note.
   - Because count (1) is less than the length of notes (3), `count` is incremented to 2, and `PlayBackNote` is called again.

2. The second time `PlayBackNote` is called, `count` = 2:

   - `Sound1.Source` is set to the second item in `notes`, which is *3.wav*.
   - `Sound1.Play` is called, playing this note.
   - Because `count` (2) is less than the length of `notes` (3), `count` is incremented to 3, and `PlayBackNote` is called again.

3. The third time `PlayBackNote` is called, `count` = 3:

   - `Sound1.Source` is set to the third item in notes, which is 6.wav.
   - `Sound1.Play` is called, playing this note.
   - Because `count` (3) is *not* less than the length of `notes` (3), nothing else happens, and playback is complete.

Note *Although recursion is powerful, it can also be dangerous. As a thought experiment, ask yourself what would have happened if the programmer forgot to insert the blocks in* `PlayBackNote` *that incremented* `count`.

Although the recursion is correct, there is a different problem with the preceding example: almost no time passes between one call to `Sound1.Play` and the next, so each note is interrupted by the next note, except for the last one. No note (except for the last) is allowed to complete before `Sound1`'s source is changed and `Sound1.Play` is called again. To achieve the correct behavior, we need to implement a delay between calls to `PlayBackNote`.

Playing Back Notes with Proper Delays

We will implement the delay by setting the timer on the clock to the amount of time between the current note and the next note. For example, if the next note is played 3,000 milliseconds (3 seconds) after the current note, we will set `Clock1.TimerInterval` to 3,000, after which `PlayBackNote` should be called again. Make the changes shown in Figure 9-14 to the body of the `if` block in `PlayBackNote` and create and fill in the `Clock1.Timer` event handler, which specifies what should happen when the timer goes off.

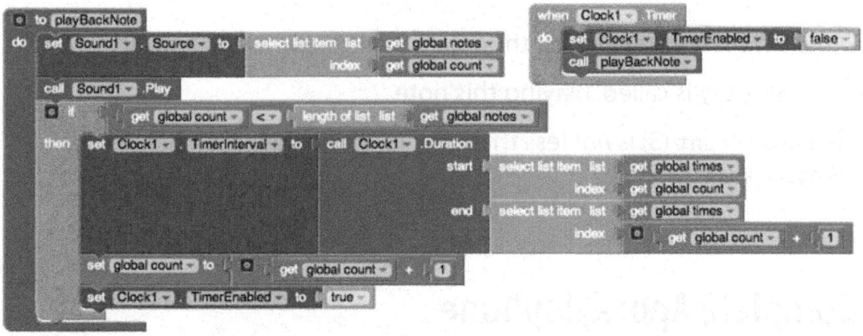

Figure 9-14. Adding delays between the notes

How the blocks work

Let's assume the following contents for the two lists:

- `notes`: *1.wav, 3.wav, 6.wav*
- `times`: 12:00:00, 12:00:01, 12:00:04

As Figure 9-14 shows, `PlayButton.Click` sets `count` to 1 and calls `PlayBackNote`.

1. The first time `PlayBackNote` is called, `count` = 1:

   - `Sound1.Source` is set to the first item in `notes`, which is "1.wav".
   - `Sound1.Play` is called, playing this note.
   - Because `count` (1) less than the length of `notes` (3), `Clock1.TimerInterval` is set to the amount of time between the first (12:00:00) and second items in `times` (12:00:01): 1 second. `count` is incremented to 2. `Clock1.Timer` is enabled and starts counting down.

   Nothing else happens for 1 second, at which time `Clock1.Timer` runs, temporarily disabling the timer and calling `PlayBackNote`.

2. The second time `PlayBackNote` is called, `count` = 2:

   - `Sound1.Source` is set to the second item in `notes`, which is "3.wav".
   - `Sound1.Play` is called, playing this note.
   - Because `count` (2) less than the length of `notes` (3), `Clock1.TimerInterval` is set to the amount of time between the second (12:00:01) and third items in `times` (12:00:04): 3 seconds. `count` is incremented to 3. `Clock1.Timer` is enabled and starts counting down.

   Nothing else happens for 3 seconds, at which time `Clock1.Timer` runs, temporarily disabling the timer and calling `PlayBackNote`.

3. The third time `PlayBackNote` is called, `count` = 3:

   - `Sound1.Source` is set to the third item in `notes`, which is "6.wav".
   - `Sound1.Play` is called, playing this note.
   - Because `count` (3) is *not* less than the length of `notes` (3), nothing else happens. Playback is complete.

The Complete App: Xylophone

Figure 9-15 shows the final block configuration for the Xylophone app.

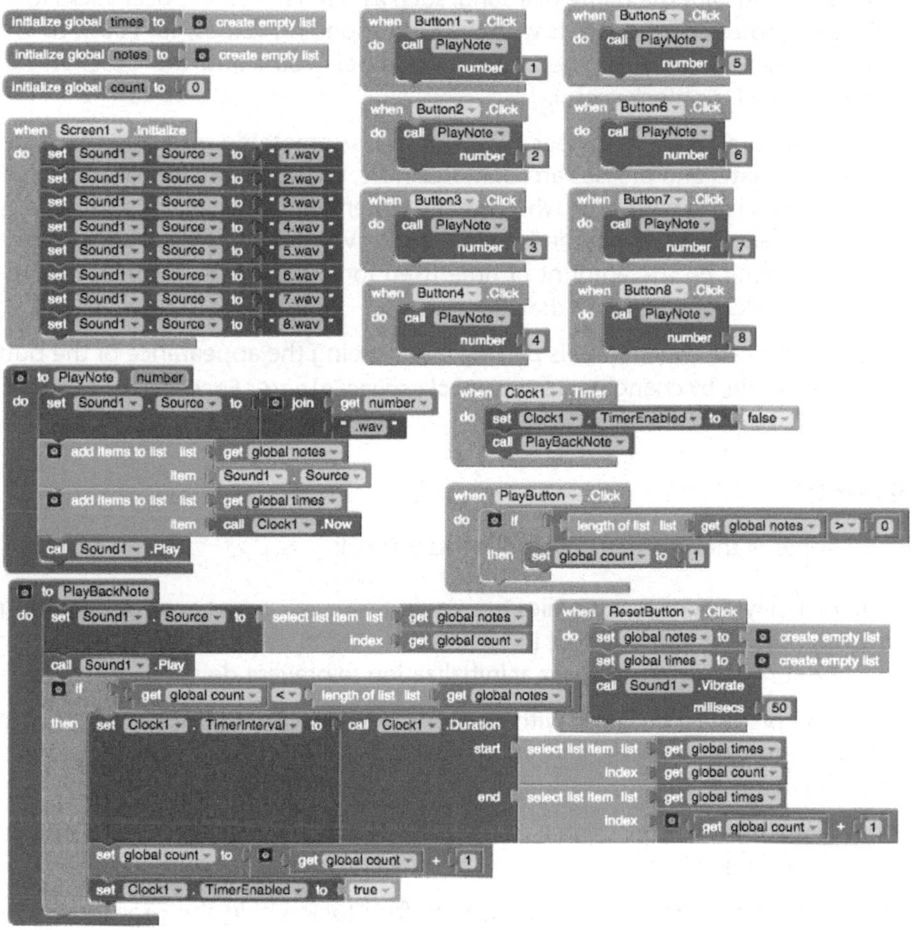

Figure 9-15. The blocks for Xylophone

Variations

Here are some alternative scenarios to explore:

- Currently, there's nothing to stop a user from clicking `ResetButton` during playback, which will cause the program to crash. (Can you figure out why?) Modify `PlayButton.Click` so it disables `ResetButton`. To re-enable it when the song is complete, change the `if` block in `PlayButton.Click` into an `if else` block, and re-enable `ResetButton` in the `else` portion.
- Similarly, the user can currently click `PlayButton` while a song is already playing. (Can you figure out what will happen?) Make it so `PlayButton.Click` disables `PlayButton` and changes its text to "Playing..." You can re-enable it and reset the text in an `ifelse` block, as described in the previous bullet.

- Add a button with the name of a song, such as "Für Elise". If the user clicks it, populate the notes and times lists with the corresponding values, set count to 1, and call `PlayBackNote`. To set the appropriate times, you'll find the `Clock1.MakeInstantFromMillis` block useful.
- If the user presses a note, goes away and does something else, and then comes back hours later and presses an additional note, the notes will be part of the same song, which is probably not what the user intended. Improve the program by 1) stopping recording after some reasonable interval of time, such as a minute; or, 2) putting a limit on the amount of time used for `Clock1.TimerInterval` by using the `max` block from the Math drawer.
- Visually indicate which note is playing by changing the appearance of the button —for example, by changing its `Text`, `BackgroundColor`, or `ForegroundColor`.

Summary

Here are some of the ideas we covered in this tutorial:

- You can play different audio files from a single `Sound` component by changing its `Source` property. This enabled us to have one `Sound` component instead of eight. Just be sure to load the sounds at initialization to prevent delays (Figure 9-6).
- Lists can provide a program with memory, with a record of user actions stored in the list and later retrieved and reprocessed. We used this functionality to record and play back a song.
- You can use the `Clock` component to determine the current time. Subtracting two time values gives us the amount of time between two events.
- You can set the `TimerInterval` property for `Clock` within the program, such as how we set it to the duration of time between the starts of two notes.
- It is not only possible but sometimes desirable for a procedure to make a call to itself. This is a powerful technique called *recursion*. When writing a recursive procedure, make sure that there is a base case in which the procedure ends, rather than calling itself, or the program will loop infinitely.

CHAPTER 10

MakeQuiz and TakeQuiz

You can customize the Presidents Quiz app in Chapter 8 to build any quiz, but it is only the programmer who can modify the questions and answers. There is no way for parents, teachers, or other app users to create their own quizzes or change the quiz questions (unless they too want to learn how to use App Inventor!).

In this chapter, you'll build a MakeQuiz app that lets a "teacher" create quizzes using an input form. The quiz questions and answers will be stored in a web database so that "students" can access a separate TakeQuiz app and take the test. While building these two apps, you'll make yet another significant conceptual leap: learning how to create apps with *user-generated* data that is shared across apps and users.

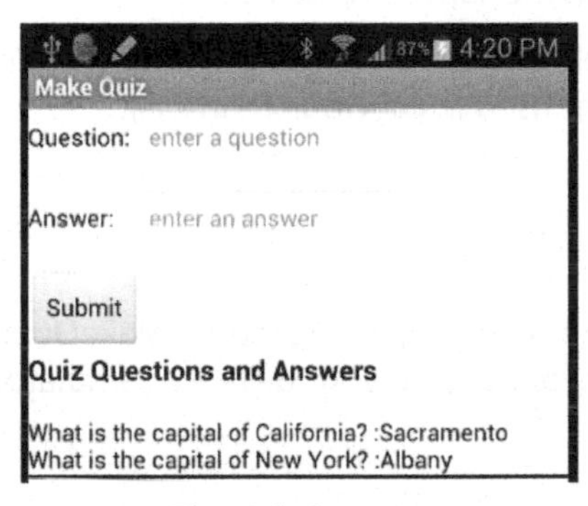

Figure 10-1. The MakeQuiz app in action

Parents can create fun trivia apps for their children during a long road trip, grade-school teachers can build "Math Blaster" quizzes, and college students can build quizzes to help their study groups prepare for a final. This chapter builds on the Presidents Quiz in Chapter 8, so if you haven't completed that app, you should do so before continuing on here.

You'll design two apps, MakeQuiz for the teacher (see Figure 10-1) and TakeQuiz for the student, which will appear similar to the Presidents Quiz.

Here are the behaviors you'll code for the first app, MakeQuiz:

- The user types questions and answers in an input form.
- The question-answer pairs are displayed.
- The quiz questions and answers are stored in a web database.

The second app you'll create, TakeQuiz, will work similarly to the Presidents Quiz app you've already built. In fact, you'll use the Presidents Quiz app as a starting point. TakeQuiz will differ in that the questions asked will be those that were entered into the database via MakeQuiz.

What You'll Learn

The Presidents Quiz was an example of an app with static data: no matter how many times you take the quiz, the questions are always the same because they are *hard-coded* into the app; that is, the questions and answers are part of the blocks. News apps, blogs, and social networking apps such as Facebook and Twitter work with *dynamic* data, meaning the data can change over time. Often, this dynamic information is user generated—the app allows users to enter, modify, and share information. With MakeQuiz and TakeQuiz, you'll learn how to build an app that handles shared, user-generated data.

If you completed the Xylophone app (Chapter 9), you've already been introduced to dynamic lists; in that app, the musical notes the user plays are recorded in lists. Apps with such user-generated data are more complex, and the blocks are more abstract because they don't rely on predefined, static data. You define list variables, but you define them without specific items. As you program your app, you need to envision the lists being populated with data provided by the end user.

This tutorial covers the following App Inventor concepts:

- Input forms for allowing the user to enter information.
- Using an indexed list along with `for each` to display items from multiple lists.
- Persistent list data—MakeQuiz will save the quiz questions and answers in a web database, and TakeQuiz will load them in from the same database.
- Data sharing—you'll store the data in a web database by using the `TinyWebDB` component (instead of the `TinyDB` component used in previous chapters).

Getting Started

Connect to the App Inventor website and start a new project. Name it "MakeQuiz" and set the screen's title to "Make Quiz". Connect your app to your device or emulator for live testing.

Designing the Components

Use the Component Designer to create the interface for MakeQuiz. When you finish, it should look something like Figure 10-2 (there are also more detailed instructions after the snapshot).

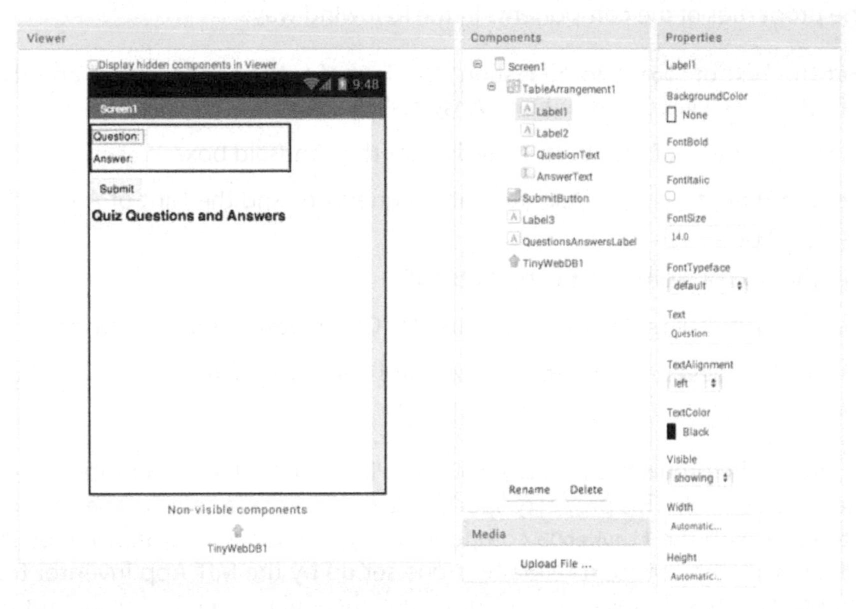

Figure 10-2. MakeQuiz in the Component Designer

You can build the user interface shown in Figure 10-2 by dragging out the components listed in Table 10-1. Drag each component from the Palette into the Viewer and name it as specified in the table. Note that you can leave the header label names (Label1 – Label4) as their defaults (you won't use them in the Blocks Editor anyway).

Table 10-1. All the components for the MakeQuiz app

Component type	Palette group	What you'll name it	Purpose
`TableArrangement`	Layout	`TableArrangement1`	Format the form, including the question and answer.
`Label`	User Interface	`Label1`	The "Question:" prompt.
`TextBox`	User Interface	`QuestionText`	The user enters questions here.
`Label`	User Interface	`Label2`	The "Answer:" prompt.
`TextBox`	User Interface	`AnswerText`	The user enters answers here.
`Button`	User Interface	`SubmitButton`	The user clicks this to submit a QA pair.
`Label`	User Interface	`Label3`	Display "Quiz Questions and Answers."
`Label`	User Interface	`QuestionsAnswersLabel`	Display previously entered QA pairs.
`TinyWebDB`	Storage	`TinyWebDB1`	Web storage for QA pairs.

Set the properties of the components in the following way:

1. Set the Text of `Label1` to "Question", the Text of `Label2` to "Answer", and the text of `Label3` to "Quiz Questions and Answers".
2. Set the FontSize of `Label3` to 18 and check the FontBold box.
3. Set the Hint of `QuestionText` to "Enter a question" and the Hint of AnswerText to "Enter an answer".
4. Set the Text of `SubmitButton` to "Submit".
5. Set the Text of `QuestionsAnswersLabel` to "Quiz Questions and Answers".
6. Move the `QuestionText`, `AnswerText`, and their associated labels into `TableArrangement1`.

If you look at the properties for `TinyWebDB`, you'll notice that it has a property `ServiceURL` (see Figure 10-3). This property specifies a web database service, specially configured to work with the `TinyWebDB` component, where your shared data will be stored. By default, the web service it refers to is one set up by the MIT App Inventor team at *http://appinvtinywebdb.appspot.com*. You'll use this default service in this tutorial as you work; however, it is important to know that anyone using App Inventor will be storing information to this same web service, and that the data your app puts there will be seen by all, and might even be overwritten by someone.

The default service is for testing only. It is fairly easy (and free!) to configure your own such service, which you'll want to do if you build an app that will be deployed with real users. For now, continue on and complete this tutorial, but when you're ready the instructions for setting up your own web service are at "TinyWebDB and TinyWebDB-Compliant APIs" on page 324.

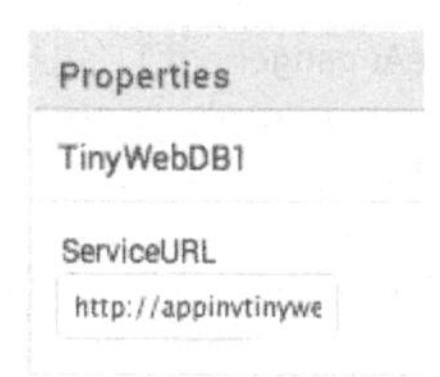

Figure 10-3. With TinyWebDB.ServiceURL, you can specify the URL of a web database you set up

Adding Behaviors to the Components

As with the Presidents Quiz app, you'll first define some global variables for the QuestionList and AnswerList, but this time you won't provide fixed questions and answers.

Creating Empty Question and Answer Lists

The blocks for the lists should look as shown in Figure 10-4.

Figure 10-4. The lists for MakeQuiz begin empty

The lists are defined with the `create empty list` block, instead of the `make a list` block. This is because with the MakeQuiz and TakeQuiz apps, all data will be created by the app user (it is dynamic, user-generated data).

Recording the User's Entries

The first behavior you'll build is for handling the user's input. Specifically, when the user enters a question and answer and clicks Submit, you'll use `add items to list` blocks to update the `QuestionList` and `AnswerList`. The blocks should appear as illustrated in Figure 10-5.

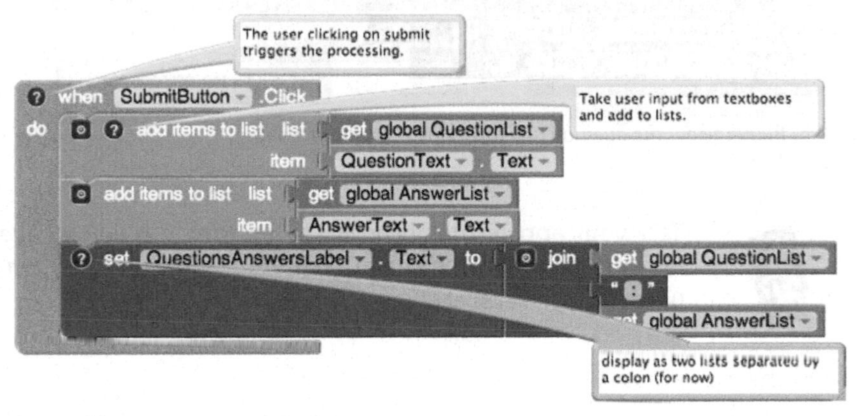

Figure 10-5. Adding new entries to the lists

How the blocks work

The `add items to list` block appends each item to the end of a list. As shown in Figure 10-5, the app takes the text the user has entered in the `QuestionText` and `AnswerText` text boxes and appends each to the corresponding list.

The `add items to list` blocks update the `QuestionList` and `AnswerList` variables, but these changes are not yet shown to the user. The third row of blocks displays these lists by concatenating them (joining them) with a colon inserted between. By default, App Inventor displays lists with surrounding parentheses and spaces between items: for example, "(item1 item2 item3)." Of course, this is not the ideal way to display the lists, but it will allow you to test the app's behavior for now. Later, you'll create a more sophisticated method of displaying the lists that shows each question-answer pair on a separate line.

Blanking Out the Question and Answer

Recall from the Presidents Quiz app that when you moved on to the next question in the list, you needed to blank out the user's answer from the previous question. In this app, when a user submits a question-answer pair, you'll want to clear the `QuestionText` and `AnswerText` text boxes so that they're ready for a new entry instead of showing the previous one. The blocks should appear as those shown in Figure 10-6.

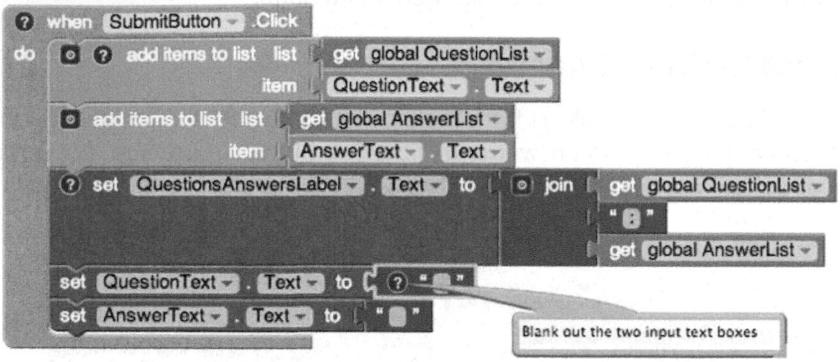

Figure 10-6. Blanking out the question and answer text boxes after submission

Test your app *Test the behavior by entering a couple of question-answer pairs. As you add them, do they appear below the form in the* `QuestionsAnswersLabel`*?*

How the blocks work

When the user submits a new question and answer, they are added to their respective lists and displayed. At that point, the text in the `QuestionText` and `AnswerText` is blanked out with empty text blocks.

Displaying Question-Answer Pairs on Multiple Lines

In the app you've built so far, the question and answer lists are displayed separately and using the default list display format for App Inventor. So if you were making a quiz on state capitals and had entered two pairs of questions and answers, it might appear as:

> (What is the capital of California? What is the capital of New York?: Sacramento Albany)

This is obviously not an ideal user interface for the quiz designer. A better display would show each question along with its corresponding answer, with one question-answer pair per line, like this:

What is the capital of California?: Sacramento
What is the capital of New York?: Albany

The technique for displaying a single list with each item on a separate line is described in Chapter 20—you might want to read that chapter before going on.

The task here is a bit more complicated because you're dealing with two lists. Because of its complexity, you'll put the blocks for displaying the data in a procedure named `displayQAs`, and call that procedure from the `SubmitButton.Click` event handler.

To display question-answer pairs on separate lines, you'll need to do the following:

- Use a `for each` block to iterate through each question in the `QuestionList`.
- Use a variable `answerIndex` so that you can grab each answer as you iterate through the questions.
- Use `join` to build a text object with each question and answer pair, and a newline character (\n) separating each pair.

The blocks should appear as illustrated in Figure 10-7.

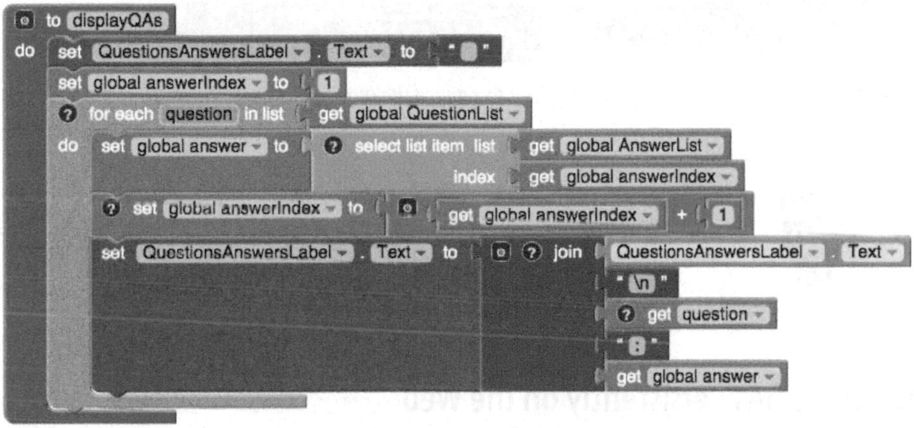

Figure 10-7. The displayQAs procedure

How the blocks work

The `displayQAs` procedure encapsulates all of the blocks for displaying the data.

By using a procedure, you won't have to copy the blocks needed to display the list more than once in the app—you can just call `displayQAs` when you need to display the lists.

The `for each` only allows you to iterate through a single list. In this case, there are two lists, `QuestionList` and `AnswerList`. The `for each` is used to iterate through the `QuestionList`, but you need to select an answer, as well, as you proceed through the questions. To accomplish this, you use an index variable, as was done with the `currentQues` `tionIndex` in the Presidents Quiz tutorial in Chapter 8. In this case, the index variable, `answerIndex`, is used to track the position in the `AnswerList` as the `for each` goes through the `QuestionList`.

`answerIndex` is set to 1 before the `for each` begins. Within the `for each`, `answerIndex` is used to select the current answer from the `AnswerList`, and then it is incremented. On each iteration of the `for each`, the current question and answer are concatenated to the end of the `QuestionsAnswersLabel.Text` property, with a colon between them.

Calling the displayQAs Procedure

You now have a procedure for displaying the question-answer pairs, but it won't help unless you call it when you need it. Modify the `SubmitButton.Click` event handler by calling `displayQAs` instead of displaying the lists, as was done previously. The updated blocks should appear as shown in Figure 10-8.

Figure 10-8. Calling the displayQAs procedure to replace the blocks shown to the right

Test your app *Test the behavior by entering a couple of question-answer pairs. As you add them, do they appear on separate lines in the* `QuestionsAnswersLabel`*?*

Saving the QAs Persistently on the Web

So far, you've created an app that places the entered questions and answers into a list. But what happens if the quiz maker closes the app? If you've completed the No Texting While Driving app (Chapter 4) or the Android, Where's My Car? app (Chapter 7), you know that if you don't store the data in a database, it won't be there when the user exits and restarts the app. Storing the data persistently will allow the quiz maker to view or edit the latest update of the quiz each time the app is started. Persistent storage is also necessary because the TakeQuiz app needs access to the data, as well.

You're already familiar with using the `TinyDB` component to store and retrieve data in a database. But in this case, you'll use the `TinyWebDB` component, instead. Whereas TinyDB stores information directly on a phone, `TinyWebDB` stores data in databases that reside on the Web.

What about your app design would merit using an online database instead of one stored on a person's phone? The key issue here is that you're building two apps that both need access to the same data—if the quiz maker stores the questions and answers on her phone, the quiz takers won't have any way of getting to the data for their quiz! Because `TinyWebDB` stores data on the Web, the quiz taker can access the quiz questions and answers on a different device than the quiz maker's. (Online data storage is often referred to as *the cloud*.)

Here's the general scheme for making list data (such as the questions and answers for our app) persistent:

- Store a list to the database each time a new item is added to it.
- When the app launches, load the list from the database into a variable.

Start by storing the `QuestionList` and `AnswerList` in the database each time the user enters a new pair.

How the blocks work

The `TinyWebDB1.StoreValue` blocks store data in a web database. `StoreValue` has two arguments: the tag that identifies the data, and the value that is the actual data you want to store. Figure 10-9 shows that the `QuestionList` is stored with a tag of "questions," whereas the `AnswerList` is stored with a tag of "answers."

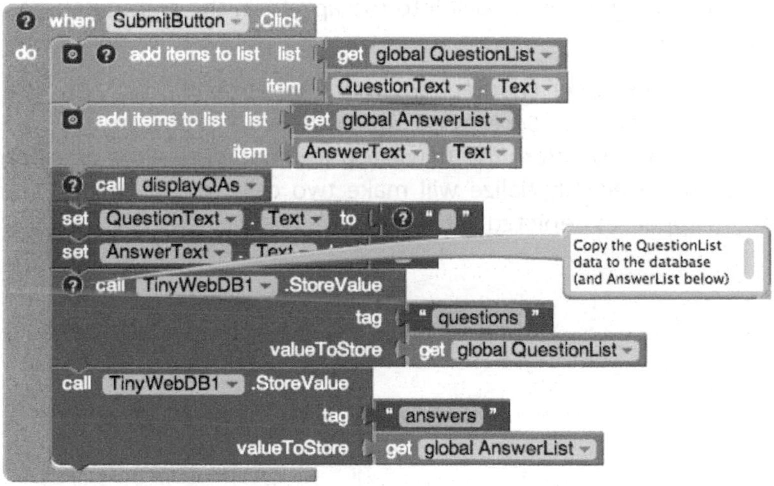

Figure 10-9. Storing the questions and answers in the database

For your app, you should use tags that are more distinctive than "questions" and "answers" (e.g., "DavesQuestions" and "DavesAnswers"). This is important because, at least initially, you're using the default web database service for App Inventor, which means that others can overwrite your questions and answers, including other people following this tutorial.

Test your app *Testing this part of the app is different from tests you've performed previously because your app is now affecting another entity, the default* `TinyDBWeb` *service. Run the app, enter a question and answer, and then open a browser window to the default web service at* http://appinvtinywebdb.appspot.com. *Then click "get_value" and enter one of your tags (in this sample, "questions" or "answers"). If things are working correctly, your question and answer lists should appear.*

As mentioned earlier, the default web service is shared among programmers and apps, so it is intended only for testing. When you're ready to deploy your app with real users, you'll want to set up your own private database service. Fortunately, doing so is straightforward and requires no programming (see "TinyWebDB and TinyWebDB-Compliant APIs" on page 324).

Loading Data from the Database

One reason we need to store the questions and answers in a database is to make it possible for the person creating the quiz to close the app and relaunch it at a later time without losing the questions and answers previously typed. (We also do it so that the quiz taker can access the questions, but we'll cover that later.) Let's program the blocks for loading the lists back into the app from the web database each time the app is restarted.

As we've covered in earlier chapters, to specify what should happen when an app launches, you program the `Screen.Initialize` event handler. In this case, the app needs to request two lists from the `TinyWebDB` web database—the questions and the answers—so the Screen1.Initialize will make two calls to `TinyWebDB.GetValue`. The blocks should appear as depicted in Figure 10-10.

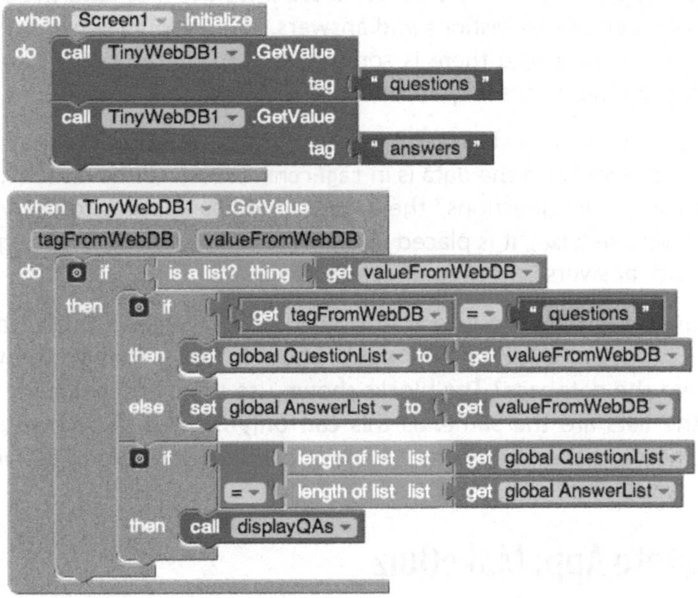

Figure 10-10. Requesting the lists from the database when the app opens and processing when lists arrive

How the blocks work

The `TinyWebDB.GetValue` blocks in Figure 10-10 work differently than `TinyDB.GetValue`, which returns a value immediately. `TinyWebDB.GetValue` only requests the data from the web database; it doesn't immediately receive a value. Instead, when the data arrives from the web database, a `TinyWebDB.GotValue` event is triggered. You must also program that event handler to process the data that is returned.

When the `TinyWebDB.GotValue` event occurs, the data requested is contained in an argument named `valueFromWebDB`. The tag you requested is contained in the argument `tagFromWebDB`.

In this app, because two different requests are made for the questions and answers, `GotValue` will be triggered twice. To avoid putting questions in your `AnswerList`, or vice versa, your app needs to check the tag to see which request has arrived and then put the value returned from the database into the corresponding list (`QuestionList` or `AnswerList`).

In `Screen.Initialize`, the app calls `TinyWebDB1.GetValue` twice: once to request the stored `QuestionList`, and once to request the stored `AnswerList`. When the data arrives from the web database from either request, the `TinyWebDB1.GotValue` event is triggered.

The `valueFromWebDB` argument of `GotValue` holds the data returned from the database request. You need the outer `if` block in the event handler because the database will return an empty text ("") in `valueFromWebDB` if it's the first time the app has been used and there aren't yet questions and answers. By asking if the `valueFromWebDB is a list?`, you're making sure there is some data actually returned. If there isn't any data, you'll bypass the blocks for processing it.

If data is returned (`is a list?` is true), the blocks go on to check which request has arrived. The tag identifying the data is in `tagFromWebDB`: it will be either "questions" or "answers." If the tag is "questions," the `valueFromWebDB` is put into the variable `QuestionList`. Otherwise (else), it is placed in the `AnswerList`. (If you used tags other than "questions" and "answers," check for those, instead.)

You only want to display the lists after both have arrived (`GotValue` has been triggered twice). Can you think of how you'd know for sure that you have both lists loaded in from the database? The blocks shown use an `if` test to check whether the lengths of the lists are the same, as this can only be true if both lists have been returned. If they are, the handy `displayQAs` procedure you wrote earlier is called to display the loaded data.

The Complete App: MakeQuiz

Figure 10-11 shows the blocks for the entire MakeQuiz app.

TakeQuiz: An App for Taking the Quiz in the Database

You now have a MakeQuiz app that will store a quiz in a web database. Building Take-Quiz, the app that dynamically loads the quiz, is simpler. You can build it with a few modifications to the Presidents Quiz you completed in Chapter 8 (if you have not completed that tutorial, do so now before continuing).

Begin by opening your Presidents Quiz app in App Inventor, choosing Save As, and naming the new project "TakeQuiz". This will leave your Presidents Quiz app unmodified but now you can use its blocks as the basis for TakeQuiz.

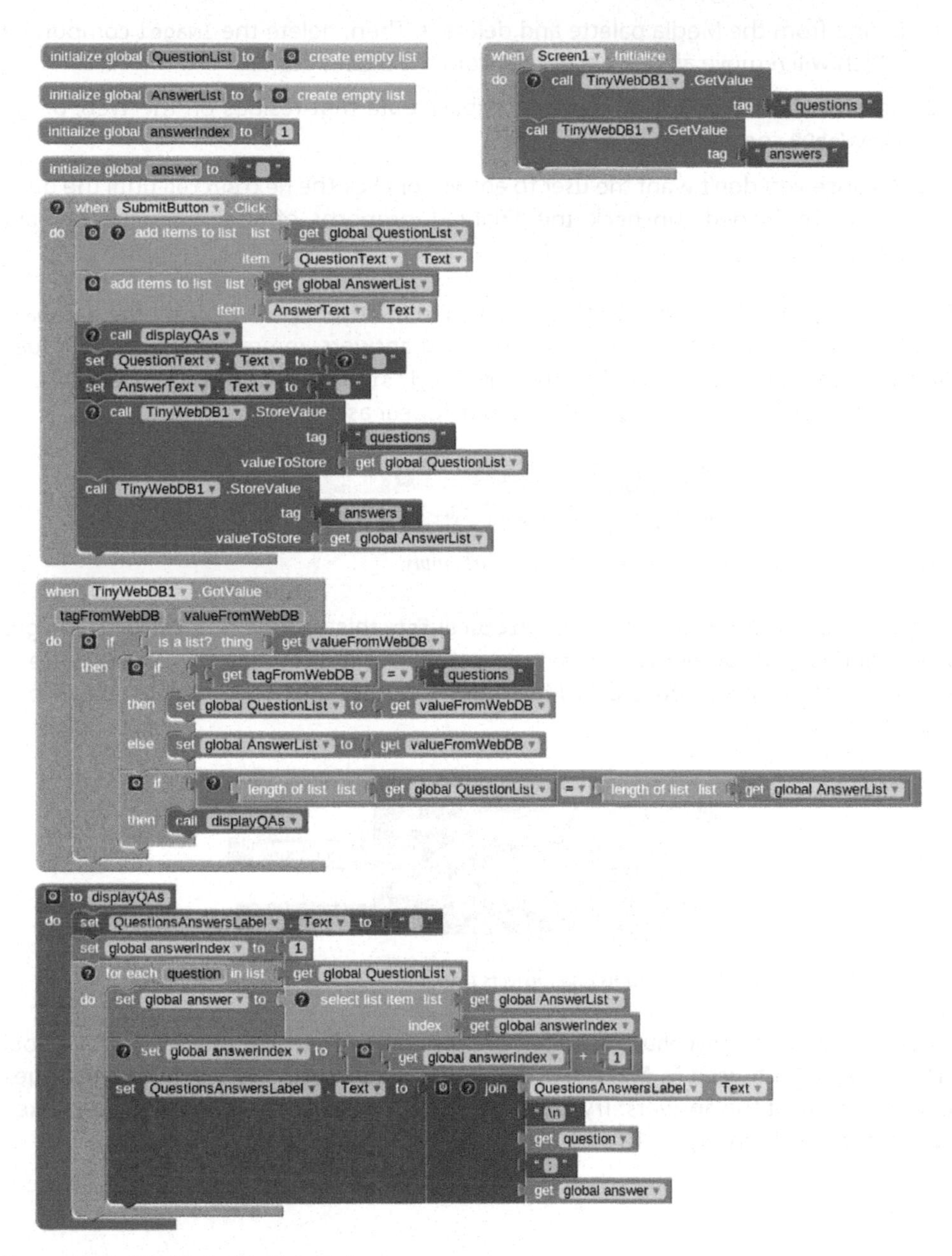

Figure 10-11. The blocks for MakeQuiz

Next, make the following changes in the Designer:

1. This version will not display images with each question, so first remove the references to images from the TakeQuiz app. In the Component Designer, choose each

image from the Media palette and delete it. Then, delete the `Image1` component, which will remove all references to it from the Blocks Editor.

2. Because TakeQuiz will work with database data that resides on the Web, drag a `TinyWebDB` component into the app.
3. Because you don't want the user to answer or click the `NextButton` until the questions are loaded, uncheck the Enabled property of the `AnswerButton` and `NextButton`.

Now, modify the blocks so that the quiz given to the user is loaded from the database. First, because there are no fixed questions and answers, remove all the actual question and answer text blocks from the `make a list` blocks within the `QuestionList` and `AnswerList`. The resulting blocks should appear as shown in Figure 10-12.

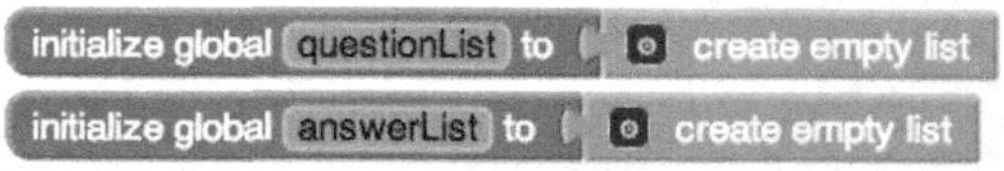

Figure 10-12. The question and answer lists now start empty

You can also completely delete the `PictureList`; this app won't deal with images. Now, modify your `Screen1.Initialize` so that it calls `TinyWebDB.GetValue` twice to load the lists, just as you did in MakeQuiz. The blocks should look as they do in Figure 10-13.

Figure 10-13. Requesting the questions and answers from the web database

Finally, drag out a `TinyWebDB.GotValue` event handler. This event handler should look similar to the one used in MakeQuiz, but here you want to show only the first question and none of the answers. Try making these changes yourself first, and then take a look at the blocks in Figure 10-14 to see if they match your solution.

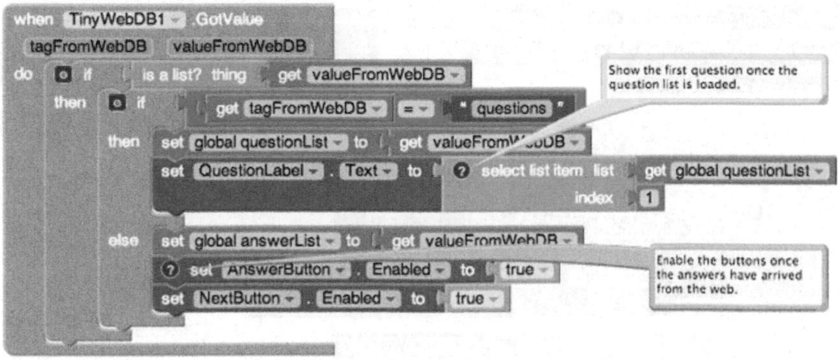

Figure 10-14. GotValue handles the data that arrives from the Web

How the Blocks Work

When the app starts, `Screen1.Initialize` is triggered and the app requests the questions and answers from the web database. When each request arrives, the `TinyWebDB.GotValue` event handler is triggered. The app first checks if there is indeed data in `valueFromWebDB` using `is a list?` If it finds data, the app asks which request has come in, using `tagFromWebDB`, and places the `valueFromWebDB` into the appropriate list. If the `QuestionList` is being loaded, the first question is selected from `QuestionList` and displayed. If the AnswerList is being loaded, the `AnswerButton` and `NextButton` are enabled so that the user can begin taking the test.

These are all the changes you need for TakeQuiz. If you've added some questions and answers with MakeQuiz and you run TakeQuiz, the questions that appear should be the ones you input.

The Complete App: TakeQuiz

Figure 10-15 shows the blocks for the entire TakeQuiz app.

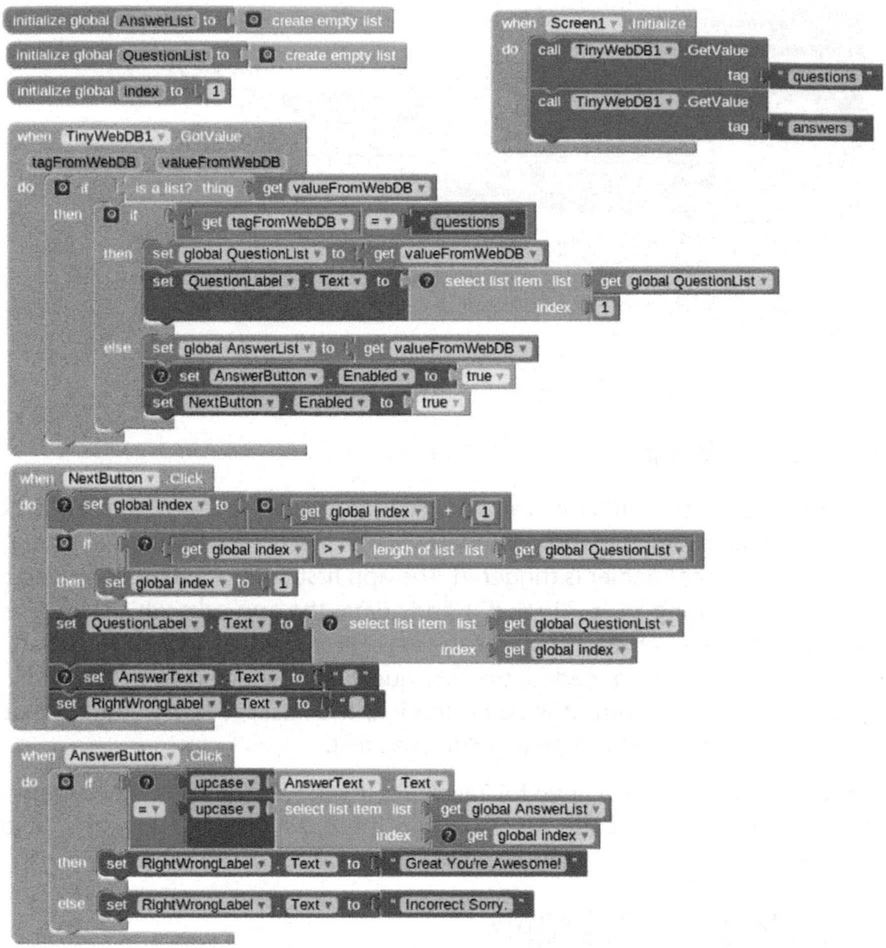

Figure 10-15. *The final blocks for TakeQuiz*

Variations

After you get MakeQuiz and TakeQuiz working, you might want to explore some of the following variations:

- Allow the quiz maker to specify an image for each question. This is a little complicated because `TinyWebDB` doesn't allow you to store images. Therefore, the images will need to be URLs to pictures on the Web, and the quiz maker will need to enter these URLs as a third item in the MakeQuiz form. Note that you can set the Picture property of an `Image` component to a URL.
- Allow the quiz maker to delete items from the questions and answers. You can let the user choose a question by using the `ListPicker` component, and you can remove an item with the `remove list item` block (remember to remove from

both lists and update the database). For help with `ListPicker` and list deletion, see Chapter 19.

- Let the quiz maker name the quiz. You'll need to store the quiz name under a different tag in the database, and you'll need to load the name along with the quiz in TakeQuiz. After you've loaded the name, use it to set the `Screen.Title` property so that it appears when the user takes a quiz.
- Allow multiple named quizzes to be created. You'll need a list of quizzes, and you can use each quiz name as (part of) the tag for storing its questions and answers.

Summary

Here are some of the concepts we covered in this chapter:

- Dynamic data is information input by the app's user or loaded in from a database. A program that works with dynamic data is more abstract. For more information, see Chapter 19.
- You can store data persistently in a web database with the `TinyWebDB` component.
- You retrieve data from a `TinyWebDB` database by requesting it with `TinyWebDB.GetValue`. When the web database returns the data, the `TinyWebDB.GotValue` event is triggered. In the `TinyWebDB.GotValue` event handler, you can put the data in a list or process it in some way.
- `TinyWebDB` data can be shared among multiple phones and apps. For more information on (web) databases, see Chapter 22.

CHAPTER 11

Broadcast Hub

FrontlineSMS (http://www.frontlinesms.com) is a software tool used in developing countries to monitor elections, broadcast weather changes, and connect people who don't have access to the Web but do have phones and mobile connectivity. It is the brainchild of Ken Banks, a pioneer in using mobile technology to help people in need.

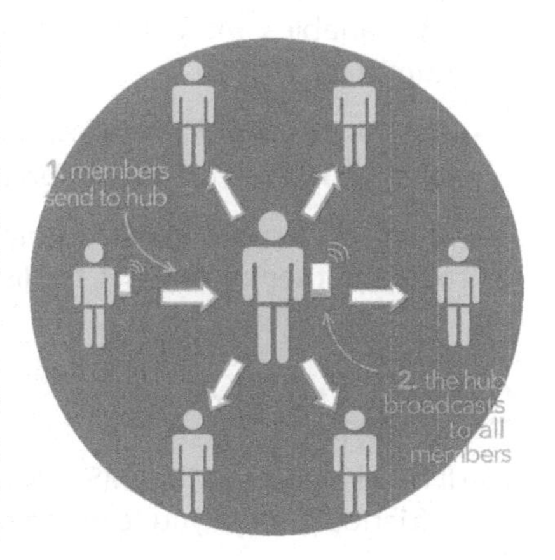

The software serves as a hub for SMS text communication within a group. People send in a special code to join the group, after which they receive broadcast messages from the hub. For places with no Internet access, the broadcast hub can serve as a vital connection to the outside world.

In this chapter, you'll create a broadcast hub app that works similarly to FrontlineSMS but runs on an Android phone. Having the hub itself on a mobile device means that the administrator can be on the move, something that is especially important in controversial situations, such as election monitoring and healthcare negotiations.

In this chapter, you'll build a broadcast hub app for the fictitious FlashMob Dance Team (FMDT), a group that uses the hub to organize flash mob dances anywhere, anytime. People will register with the group by texting "joinFMDT" to the hub, and anyone who is registered can broadcast messages to everyone else in the group.

Your app will process received text messages in the following manner:

1. If the text message is sent from someone not yet in the broadcast list, the app responds with a text that invites the person to join the broadcast list.
2. If the text message with the special code "joinFMDT" is received, the app adds the sender to the broadcast list.
3. If the text message is sent from a number already in the broadcast list, the message is broadcast to all numbers in the list.

This app is more complicated than the No Text While Driving app in Chapter 4, but you'll build it one piece of functionality at a time, starting with the first auto-response message that invites people to join. By the time you complete this, you'll have a pretty good idea of how to write apps utilizing SMS text as the user interface. Do you want to write a vote-by-text app such as those used on television talent shows, or the next great group texting app? You'll learn how here!

What You'll Learn

The tutorial covers the following App Inventor concepts, some of which you're likely familiar with by now:

- The `Texting` component for sending texts and processing received texts.
- List variables and dynamic data—in this case, to keep track of the list of phone numbers.
- The `for each` block to allow an app to repeat operations on a list of data. In this case, you'll use `for each` to broadcast messages to the list of phone numbers.
- The `TinyDB` component to store data persistently. This means that if you close the app and then relaunch it, the list of phone numbers will still be there.

Getting Started

You'll need a phone with SMS service to test or run this app. You'll also need to recruit some friends to send you texts in order to fully test the app.

Connect to the App Inventor website and start a new project. Name it "BroadcastHub", and also set the screen's title to "Broadcast Hub". Then, connect your device or emulator for live testing.

Designing the Components

Broadcast Hub facilitates communication between mobile phones. Those phones do not need to have the app installed, or even be smartphones; they'll communicate by text with your app. So, in this case, the user interface for your app is just for the group administrator.

The user interface for the administrator is simple: it displays the current *broadcast list*; that is, the list of phone numbers that have registered for the service, and all of the texts it receives and broadcasts.

To build the interface, add the components listed in Table 11-1.

Table 11-1. User interface components for Broadcast Hub

Component type	Palette group	What you'll name it	Purpose
`Label`	User Interface	`Label1`	This is the header "Registered Phone Numbers" above the list of phone numbers.
`Label`	User Interface	`BroadcastListLabel`	Display the phone numbers that are registered.
`Label`	User Interface	`Label2`	This is the header "Activity Log" above the log information.
`Label`	User Interface	`LogLabel`	Display a log of the texts received and broadcast.
`Texting`	Social	`Texting1`	Process the texts.
`TinyDB`	User Interface	`TinyDB1`	Store the list of registered phone numbers.

As you add the components, set the following properties:

1. Set the `Width` of each label to "Fill parent" so that it spans the phone horizontally.
2. Set the `FontSize` of the header labels (`Label1` and `Label2`) to 18 and check their FontBold boxes.
3. Set the `Height` of `BroadcastListLabel` and `LogLabel` to 200 pixels. They'll show multiple lines.
4. Set the `Text` property of `BroadcastListLabel` to "Broadcast List...".
5. Set the `Text` property of `LogLabel` to blank.
6. Set the `Text` property of `Label1` to "Registered Phone Numbers".
7. Set the `Text` property of `Label2` to "Activity Log".

Figure 11-1 shows the app layout in the Component Designer.

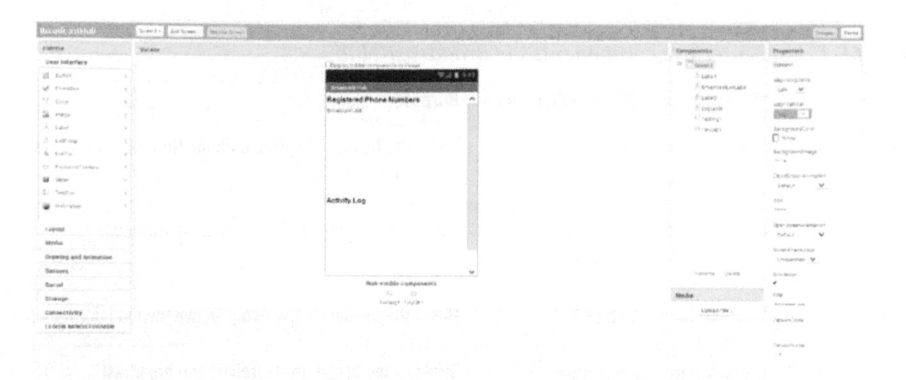

Figure 11-1. Broadcast Hub in the Components Designer

Adding Behaviors to the Components

The activity for Broadcast Hub is not triggered by the user typing information or clicking a button; rather, it's texts coming in from other phones. To process these texts and store the phone numbers that sent them in a list, you'll need the following behaviors:

- When the text message is sent from someone not already in the broadcast list, the app responds with a text that invites the sender to join.
- When the text message "joinFMDT" is received, register the sender as part of the broadcast list.
- When the text message is sent from a number already in the broadcast list, the message is broadcast to all numbers in the list.

Responding to Incoming Texts

You'll start by creating the first behavior: when you receive a text, send a message back to the sender inviting her to register by texting "joinFMDT" back to you. You'll need the blocks listed in Table 11-2.

Table 11-2. Blocks for adding the functionality to invite people to the group via text

Block type	Drawer	Purpose
`Texting1.MessageReceived`	Texting1	Triggered when the phone receives a text.
`set Texting1.PhoneNumber to`	Texting1	Set the number for the return text.
`get number`	Drag from MessageReceived event handler	The argument of `MessageReceived`. This is the phone number of the sender.

Block type	Drawer	Purpose
`set Texting1.Message`	Texting1	Set the invite message to send.
`text` ("To join this broadcast list, text 'joinFMDT' to this number")	Text	The invite message.
`Texting1.SendMessage`	Texting1	Send it!

How the blocks work

If you completed the No Texting While Driving app in Chapter 4, these blocks should look familiar. `Texting1.MessageReceived` is triggered when the phone receives any text message. Figure 11-2 shows how the blocks within the event handler set the `PhoneNumber` and `Message` of the `Texting1` component and then send the message.

Figure 11-2. Sending the invite message back after receiving a text

Test your app *You'll need a second phone to test this behavior; you don't want to text yourself, because it could loop forever! If you don't have another phone, you can register with Google Voice or a similar service and send SMS texts from that service to your phone. From the second phone, send the text "hello" to the phone running the app. The second phone should then receive a text that invites it to join the group.*

Adding Numbers to the Broadcast List

It's time to create the blocks for the second behavior: when the text message "joinFMDT" is received, the sender is added to the broadcast list. First, you'll need to define a list variable, `BroadcastList`, to store the phone numbers that register. From the Variables drawer, drag out an `initialize global` block and name it "BroadcastList". Initialize it to an empty list by using a `create a list` block from the Lists drawer, as shown in Figure 11-3 (we'll add the functionality to build this list shortly).

initialize global BroadcastList to create empty list

Figure 11-3. The BroadcastList variable for storing the list of registered numbers

Next, modify the `Texting1.MessageReceived` event handler so that it adds the sender's phone number to the `BroadcastList` if the message received is "joinFMDT." You'll need an `if else` block to check the message, and an `add item to list` block to add the new number to the list. The full set of blocks you'll need is listed in Table 11-3. After you add the number to the list, display the new list in the `BroadcastListLabel`.

Table 11-3. Blocks for checking a text message and adding the sender to the broadcast list

Block type	Drawer	Purpose
`if else`	Control	Depending on the message received, do different things.
=	Math	Determine whether `messageText` is equal to "joinFMDT."
`get messageText`	Drag out from MessageReceived event handler	Plug this into the = block.
`text` ("joinFMDT")	Text	Plug this into the = block.
`add items to list`	Lists	Add the sender's number to `BroadcastList`.
`get global Broadcast List`	Drag out from variable initialization block.	The list.
`get number`	Drag out from MessageReceived event handler	Plug this in as an item of `add items to list`.
`set BroadcastListLa bel.Text to`	BroadcastListLabel	Display the new list.
`global BroadcastList`	Drag out from variable initialization block	Plug this in to set the `BroadcastListLabel.Text to` block.
`set Texting1.Mes sage to`	Texting1	Prepare `Texting` to send a message back to the sender.
`text` ("Congrats, you...")	Text	Congratulate the sender for joining the group.

How the blocks work

The first row of blocks shown in Figure 11-4 sets `Texting1.PhoneNumber` to the phone number of the message that was just received; we know we're going to respond to the sender, so this sets that up. The app then asks if the `messageText` was the special code, "joinFMDT." If so, the sender's phone number is added to the `BroadcastList`, and a congratulations message is sent. If the `messageText` is something other than "joinFMDT," the reply message repeats the invitation message. After the `if else` block, the reply message is sent (bottom row of the blocks).

Figure 11-4. If the incoming message is "joinFMDT," add the sender to BroadcastList

Test your app *From a phone not running the app, send the text message "joinFMDT" to the phone running the app. You should see the phone number listed in the user interface under "Registered Phone Numbers." The "sending" phone should also receive the Congrats message as a text in reply. Try sending a message other than "joinFMDT," as well, to check if the invite message is still sent correctly.*

Broadcasting the Messages

Next, you'll add the behavior so that the app broadcasts received messages to the numbers in `BroadcastList`, but only if the message arrives from a number already stored in that list. This additional complexity will require more control blocks, including another `if else` and a `for each`. You'll need an additional `if else` block to check if the number is in the list, and a `for each` block to broadcast the message to each number in the list. You'll also need to move the `if else` blocks from the previous behavior and socket them into the `else` part of the new `if else`. All the additional blocks you'll need are listed in Table 11-4.

Table 11-4. Blocks for checking if the sender is in the group already

Block type	Drawer	Purpose
`if else`	Control	Depending on whether the sender is already in the list, do different things.
`is in list?`	Lists	Check to see if something is in a list.

Block type	Drawer	Purpose
`get global BroadcastList`	Drag out from variable initialization block	Plug this into the "list" socket of `is in list?`
`get number`	Drag out from MessageReceived event handler	Plug this into the "thing" socket of `is in list?`
`for each`	Control	Repeatedly send out a message to all members in the list.
`get global BroadcastList`	Drag out from variable initialization block	Plug this into the "list" socket of `for each`.
`set Texting1.Message to`	Texting1	Set the message.
`get messageText`	Drag out from the MessageReceived event	The message that was received and will be broadcast.
`set Texting1.PhoneNumber to`	Texting1	Set the phone number.
`get item`	Drag out from for each block	Hold the current item of the `BroadcastList`; it's a (phone) number.

How the blocks work

The app has become complex enough that it requires a *nested* `if else` block, which you can see in Figure 11-5. A nested `if else` block is one that is plugged into the socket of the `if` or `else` part of another, outer `if else`. In this case, the outer `if else` branch checks whether the phone number of the received message is already in the list. If it is, the message is relayed to everyone in the list. If the number is not in the list, the *nested* test is performed: the blocks check if the `messageText` is equal to "joinFMDT" and branch one of two ways based on the answer.

Figure 11-5. The blocks check if the sender is already in the group and broadcast the message if so

In general, `if` and `if else` blocks can be nested to arbitrary levels, giving you the power to program increasingly complex behaviors (see Chapter 18 for more information on conditional blocks).

The message is broadcast by using a `for each` (within the outer `then` clause). The `for each` iterates through the `BroadcastList` and sends the message to each item. As the `for each` repeats, each succeeding phone number from the `BroadcastList` is stored in `item` (`item` is a variable placeholder for the current item being processed in the `for each`). The blocks within the `for each` set `Texting.PhoneNumber` to the current item and then send the message. For more information on how `for each` works, see Chapter 20.

Test your app *First, have two different phones register by texting "joinFMDT" to the phone running the app. Then, text another message from one of the phones. Both phones should receive the text (including the one that sent it).*

Beautifying the List Display

The app can now broadcast messages, but the user interface for the app administrator needs some work. First, the list of phone numbers is displayed in an inelegant way. Specifically, when you place a list variable into a label, it displays the list with spaces between the items, fitting as much as possible on each line. So, the `BroadcastListLabel` might show the `BroadcastList` like this:

(+1415111-1111 +1415222-2222 +1415333-3333 +1415444-4444)

To improve this formatting, create a procedure named `displayBroadcastList` by using the blocks listed in Table 11-5. This procedure displays the list with each phone number on a separate line. Be sure to call the procedure from below the `add items to list` block so that the updated list is displayed.

Table 11-5. Blocks to clean up the display of phone numbers in your list

Block type	Drawer	Purpose
`to procedure` ("displayBroadcastList")	Procedures	Create the procedure (do not choose `to procedure result`).
`set BroadcastListLabel.Text to`	BroadcastListLabel	Display the list here.
`text` ("")	Text	Click `text` and then click Delete to create an empty text object.
`for each`	Control	Iterate through the numbers.
`get global BroadcastList`	Drag out from variable initialization block	Plug this into the "in list" socket of `for each`.
`set BroadcastListLabel.Text to`	BroadcastListLabel	Modify this with each of the numbers.
`join text`	Text	Build a text object from multiple parts.
`BroadcastListLabel.Text`	BroadcastListLabel	Add this to the label on each iteration of `for each`.
`text` ("\n")	Text	Add a newline character so that the next number is on the next line.
`get item`	Drag out from `for each` block.	The current number from the list.

How the blocks work

The `for each` in `displayBroadcastList` successively adds a phone number to the end of the label, as shown in Figure 11-6, placing a newline character (\n) between each item in order to display each number on a new line.

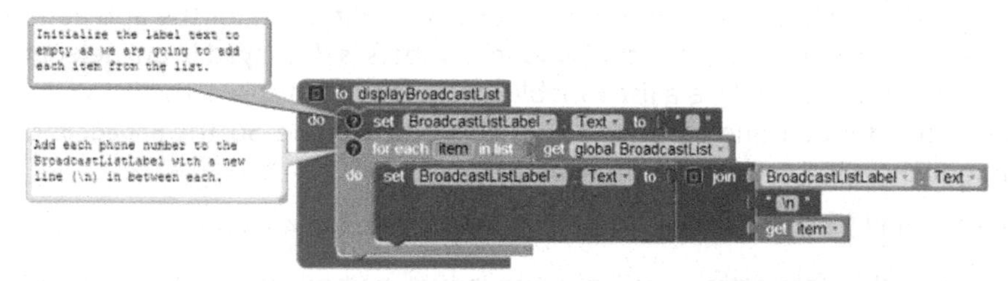

Figure 11-6. Displaying the phone numbers with a newline character between each

Of course, this displayBroadcastList procedure will not do anything unless you call it. Place a call to it in the Texting1.MessageReceived event handler, right below the call to add item to list. The call should replace the blocks that simply set the BroadcastListLabel.Text to BroadcastList. You can find the call displayBroadcastList block in the Procedures drawer.

Figure 11-7 shows how the relevant blocks within the Texting1.MessageReceived event handler should look.

Figure 11-7. Calling the displayBroadcastList procedure

For more information on using for each to display a list, see Chapter 20. For more information about creating and calling procedures, see Chapter 21.

Test your app *Restart the app to clear the list and then have at least two different phones register (again). Do the phone numbers appear on separate lines?*

Logging the Broadcasted Texts

When a text is received and broadcast to the other phones, the app should log that occurrence so that the administrator can monitor the activity. In the Component Designer, you added the label LogLabel to the user interface for this purpose. Now, you'll code some blocks that change LogLabel each time a new text arrives.

You need to build a text that says something like "message from +1415111-2222 was broadcast." The number +1415111-2222 is not fixed data; instead, it is the value of the argument number that comes with the MessageReceived event. So to build the text, you'll concatenate the first part, "message from," with a get number block and finally with the last part of the message, the text "broadcast."

As you've done in previous chapters, use join to concatenate the parts by using the blocks listed in Table 11-6.

Table 11-6. Blocks to build your log of broadcasted messages

Block type	Drawer	Purpose
`set LogLabel.Text to`	LogLabel	Display the log here.
`join`	Text	Build a text object out of multiple parts.
`text` ("message from")	Text	This is the report message.
`get number`	Drag out from MessageReceived event handler	The sender's phone number.
`text` ("broadcast\n")	Text	Add the last part of "message from 111–2222 broadcast" and include newline.
`LogLabel.Text`	LogLabel	Add a new log to the previous ones.

How the blocks work

After broadcasting the received message to all of the numbers in `BroadcastList`, the app now modifies the `LogLabel` to add a report of the just-broadcasted text, as shown in Figure 11-8. Note that the message is added to the beginning of the list instead of the end. This way, the most recent message sent to the group shows up at the top.

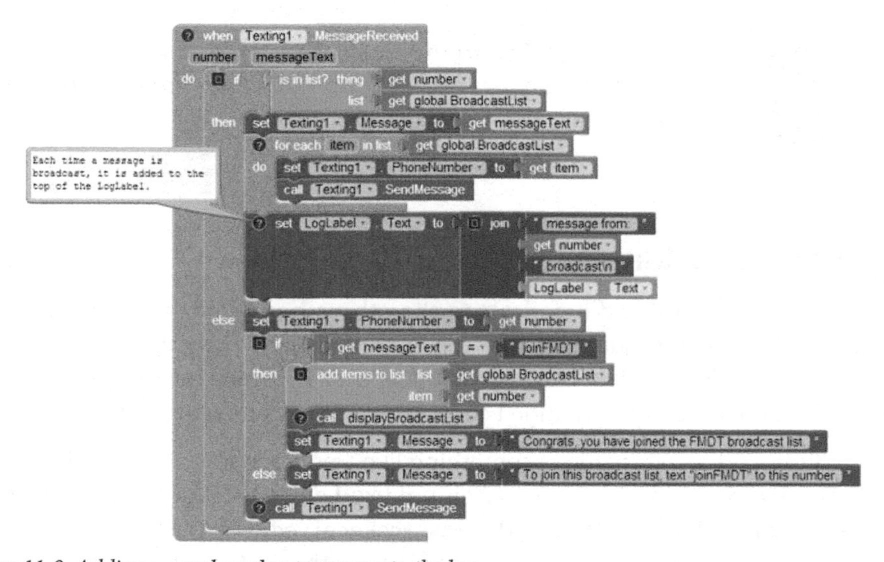

Figure 11-8. Adding a new broadcast message to the log

The `join` block creates new entries of the form:

> message from: 111-2222 broadcast

Each time a text is broadcast, the log entry is *prepended* (added to the front) to the `LogLabel.Text` so that the most recent entries will appear on top. The way you organize the `join` block determines the ordering of the entries. In this case, the new message is added with the top three sockets of `join`, and `LogLabel.Text`—which holds the existing entries—is plugged into the last socket.

The "\n" in the text "broadcast\n" is the newline character that causes each log entry to display on a separate line:

message from: 1112222 broadcast
message from: 555-6666 broadcast

For more information about using `for each` to display a list, see Chapter 20.

Storing the BroadcastList in a Database

Your app sort of works, but if you've completed some of the earlier tutorials, you've probably guessed that there's a problem: if the administrator closes the app and relaunches it, the broadcast list will be lost and everyone will have to register again. To fix this, you'll use the `TinyDB` component to store and retrieve the `BroadcastList` to and from a database.

You'll use a similar scheme to that which you used in the MakeQuiz app (Chapter 10):

- Store the list to the database each time a new item is added.
- When the app launches, load the list from the database into a variable.

Start by coding the blocks listed in Table 11-7 to store the list in the database. With the `TinyDB` component, a tag is used to identify the data and distinguish it from other data stored in the database. In this case, you can tag the data as "broadcastList." You'll add the blocks in the `Texting1.MessageReceived` event, under the `add items to list` block.

Table 11-7. Blocks to store the list with TinyDB

Block type	Drawer	Purpose
`TinyDB1.StoreValue`	TinyDB1	Store the data in the database.
`text` ("broadcastList")	Text	Plug this into the "tag" slot of `StoreValue`.
`get global BroadcastList`	Drag out from variable initialization block	Plug this into the "value" slot of `StoreValue`.

How the blocks work

When a "joinFMDT" text comes in and the new member's phone number is added to the list, `TinyDB1.StoreValue` is called to store the `BroadcastList` to the database. The tag (a text object named `broadcastList`) is used so that you can later retrieve the data. Figure 11-9 illustrates that the value that is called by `StoreValue` is the variable `BroadcastList`.

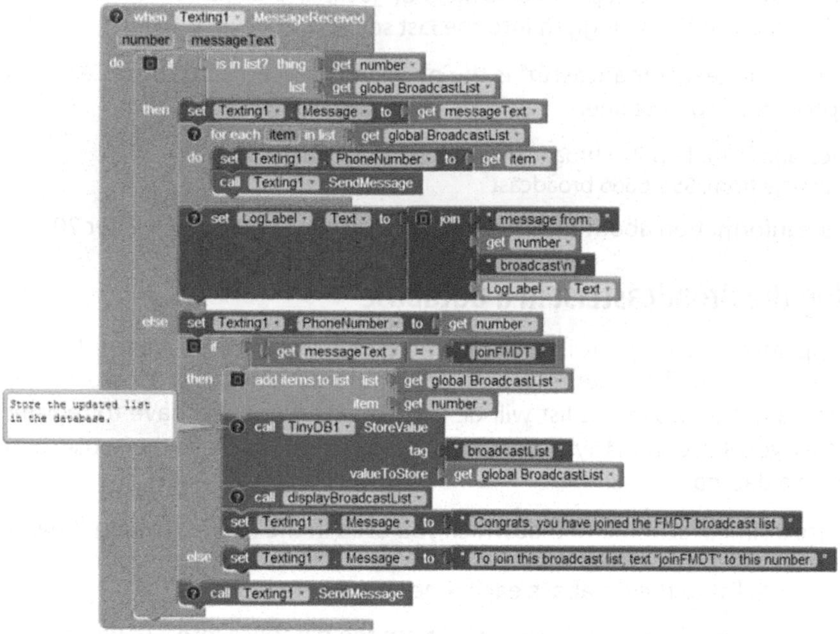

Figure 11-9. Calling TinyDB to store the BroadcastList

Loading the BroadcastList from a Database

Add the blocks listed in Table 11-8 for loading the list back in each time the app launches.

Table 11-8. Blocks to load the broadcast list back into the app when it launches

Block type	Drawer	Purpose
`Screen1.Initialize`	Screen1	Triggered when the app launches.
`TinyDB1.GetValue`	TinyDB1	Request the data from the database.
`text` ("broadcastList")	Text	Plug this into the "tag" socket of `GetValue`.
`call displayBroadcastList`	Procedures	After loading data, display it.

When the app begins, the `Screen1.Initialize` event is triggered, so your blocks will go in that event handler.

How the blocks work

When the app begins, the `Screen1.Initialize` event is triggered. The blocks shown in Figure 11-10 request the data from the database with `TinyDB1.GetValue`.

Figure 11-10. Loading the BroadcastList from the database

You call `TinyDB.GetValue` by using the same tag you used to store the list (`broadcast List`). In the general case, the previously stored list of phone numbers will be returned and placed in the variable `BroadcastList`. But `TinyDB.GetValue` provides a socket, `valueIfTagNotThere`, for specifying what the block should return if there is not yet data in the database for that tag, as will happen the first time this app is run. In this case, an empty list is returned.

Test your app *You can use live testing for apps that modify the database, but do it carefully. In this case, text the app with another phone to add numbers to the BroadcastList, and then restart the app. You can restart in live testing mode by switching to the designer and modifying some property, even something such as changing the font of a label. Note that to fully test database apps you need to package and truly download the app to a phone (choose "Build > App (save apk to my computer"). After you've downloaded your app, use your other phones to send a text to join the group and then close the app. If the numbers are still listed when you relaunch the app, the database part is working.*

The Complete App: Broadcast Hub

Figure 11-11 illustrates the blocks in the completed Broadcast Hub app.

```
initialize global BroadcastList to  create empty list

to displayBroadcastList
do  set BroadcastListLabel . Text to " "
    for each item in list  get global BroadcastList
    do  set BroadcastListLabel . Text to  join  BroadcastListLabel . Text
                                              " \n "
                                              get item

when Screen1 .Initialize
do  set global BroadcastList to  call TinyDB1 .GetValue
                                      tag  " broadcastList "
                                      valueIfTagNotThere  create empty list
    call displayBroadcastList

when Texting1 .MessageReceived
number  messageText
do  if  is in list?  thing  get number
                     list   get global BroadcastList
    then  set Texting1 . Message to  get messageText
          for each item in list  get global BroadcastList
          do  set Texting1 . PhoneNumber to  get item
              call Texting1 .SendMessage
          set LogLabel . Text to  join  " message from: "
                                        get number
                                        " broadcast \n "
                                        LogLabel . Text
    else  set Texting1 . PhoneNumber to  get number
          if  get messageText  =  " joinFMDT "
          then  add items to list  list  get global BroadcastList
                                   item  get number
                call TinyDB1 .StoreValue
                     tag  " broadcastList "
                     valueToStore  get global BroadcastList
                call displayBroadcastList
                set Texting1 . Message to " Congrats, you have joined the FMDT broadcast list. "
          else  set Texting1 . Message to " To join this broadcast list, text "joinFMDT" to this number. "
          call Texting1 .SendMessage
```

Figure 11-11. The complete Broadcast Hub app

Variations

After you've celebrated building such a complex app, you might want to explore some of the following variations:

- The app broadcasts each message to everyone, including the phone that sent the message. Modify this so that the message is broadcast to everyone but the sender.
- Allow client phones to remove themselves from the list by texting "quit" to the app. You'll need a `remove from list` block.
- Give the hub administrator the ability to add and remove numbers from the broadcast list through the user interface.
- Let the hub administrator specify numbers that should not be allowed into the list.
- Customize the app so that anyone can join to receive messages, but only the administrator can broadcast messages.
- Customize the app so that anyone can join to receive messages, but only a fixed list of phone numbers can broadcast messages to the group.

Summary

Here are some of the concepts we covered in this tutorial:

- Apps can react to events that are not initiated by the app user, such as a text being received. This means that you can build apps in which your "users" are on a different phone.
- You can use nested `if else` and `for each` blocks to code complex behaviors. For more information on conditionals and `for each` iteration, see Chapter 18 and Chapter 20, respectively.
- You can use the `join` block to build a text object out of multiple parts.
- You can use `TinyDB` to store and retrieve data from a database. A general scheme is to call `StoreValue` to update the database whenever the data changes and call `GetValue` to retrieve the database data when the app starts.

CHAPTER 12

Robot Remote

In this chapter, you'll create an app that turns your Android phone into a remote control for a LEGO MINDSTORMS NXT robot. The app will have buttons for driving the robot forward and backward, turning left and right, and stopping. You'll program it so that the robot automatically stops if it detects an obstacle. The app will use the Bluetooth capabilities of the phone to communicate with the robot.

LEGO MINDSTORMS robots are fun to play with, but they are also educational. Afterschool programs use robots to teach elementary- and middle-school children problem-solving skills and introduce them to engineering and computer programming. NXT robots are also used by kids aged 9–14 in FIRST Lego League robotics competitions.

The NXT programmable robotics kit includes a main unit called the NXT Intelligent Brick. It can control three motors and four input sensors. You can assemble a robot from LEGO building elements, gears, wheels, motors, and sensors. The kit comes with its own software to program the robot, but now you can use App Inventor to create Android applications to control an NXT via Bluetooth connectivity.

The application in this chapter is designed to work with a robot that has wheels and an ultrasonic sensor, such as the Shooterbot robot pictured here. The Shooterbot is often the first robot that people build with the LEGO MINDSTORMS NXT 2.0 set. It has left wheels connected to output port C, right wheels connected to output port B, a color sensor connected to input port 3, and an ultrasonic sensor connected to input port 4.

What You'll Learn

This chapter uses the following components and concepts:

- The `BluetoothClient` component for connecting to the NXT
- The `ListPicker` component to provide a user interface for connecting to the NXT
- The `NxtDrive` component for driving the robot's wheels
- The `NxtUltrasonicSensor` component for using the robot's ultrasonic sensor to detect obstacles

- The `Notifier` component for displaying error messages

Getting Started

You'll need Android version 2.0 or higher to use the application in this chapter. Also, for security reasons, Bluetooth devices must be paired before they can connect to each other. Before you get started building the app, you'll need to pair your Android with your NXT by following these steps:

1. On the NXT, click the right arrow until it says Bluetooth and then press the orange square.
2. Click the right arrow until the word Visibility appears and then press the orange square.
3. If the Visibility value is already Visible, continue to step 4. If not, click the left or right arrow to set the value to Visible.
4. On the Android, go to Settings.

   Steps 5–7 might vary slightly depending on your Android device.
5. Ensure that Bluetooth is ON.
6. Click "Bluetooth" and then "Search for devices."
7. Under "Available devices," look for a device named "NXT." If you've ever changed your robot's name, look for a device name that matches your robot's name instead of "NXT."
8. Click "NXT" or your robot's name.
9. On the NXT, you should see a prompt for a passkey. Press the orange square to accept 1234.
10. On the Android, you should see a prompt for the PIN. Type 1234 and then press OK.
11. Your robot and your Android are now paired.

Connect to the App Inventor website at *ai2.appinventor.mit.edu*. Start a new project and name it "NXTRemoteControl", and set the screen's title to "NXT Remote Control". Click Connect and set up your device (or emulator) for live testing (see *http://appinventor.mit.edu/explore/ai2/setup* for help setting this up).

Designing the Components

For this app, we'll need to create and define behaviors for both non-visible and visible components.

Non-Visible Components

Before creating the user interface components, you'll create some non-visible components, listed in Table 12-1 and illustrated in Figure 12-1, to control the NXT.

Table 12-1. Non-visible components for the Robot NXT controller app

Component type	Palette group	What you'll name it	Purpose
`BluetoothClient`	Connectivity	`BluetoothClient1`	Connect to the NXT.
`NxtDrive`	LEGO® MINDSTORMS®	`NxtDrive1`	Drive the robot's wheels.
`NxtUltrasonicSensor`	LEGO® MINDSTORMS®	`NxtUltrasonicSensor1`	Detect obstacles.
`Notifier`	User Interface	`Notifier1`	Display error messages.

Figure 12-1. The non-visible components displayed at the bottom of the Component Designer

Set the properties of the components in the following way:

1. Set the `BluetoothClient` property of `NxtDrive1` and `NxtUltrasonicSensor1` to "BluetoothClient1".
2. Check `BelowRangeEventEnabled` on `NxtUltrasonicSensor1`.
3. Set the `DriveMotors` property of `NxtDrive1`:
   - If your robot has the left wheel's motor connected to output port C and the right wheel's motor connected to output port B, the default setting of "CB" doesn't need to be changed.
   - If your robot is configured differently, set the `DriveMotors` property to a two-letter text value, where the first letter is the output port connected to the left wheel's motor and the second letter is the output port connected to the right wheel's motor.
4. Set the `SensorPort` property of `NxtUltrasonicSensor1`.
   - If your robot's ultrasonic sensor is connected to input port 4, the default setting of "4" doesn't need to be changed.
   - If your robot is configured differently, set the `SensorPort` property to the input port connected to the ultrasonic sensor.

Visible Components

Next, let's create the user interface components shown in Figure 12-2.

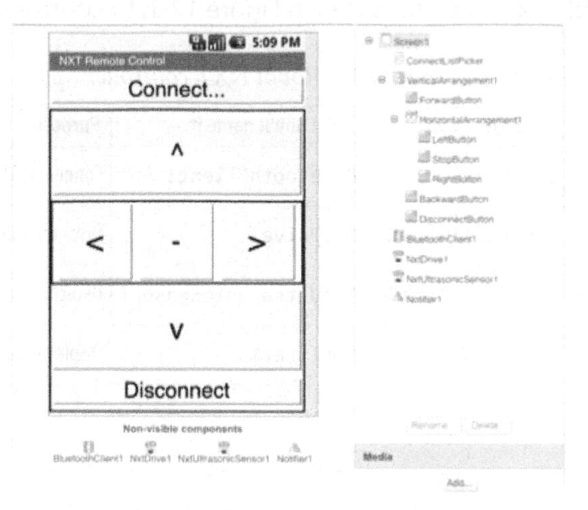

Figure 12-2. The app in the Component Designer

To make the Bluetooth connection, you'll need the unique Bluetooth address of the NXT. Unfortunately, Bluetooth addresses consist of eight two-digit hexadecimal numbers (a way of representing binary values) separated by colons, making them very cumbersome to type. You won't want to type in the address on your phone every time you run the app. So, to avoid that, you'll use a `ListPicker` that displays a list of the robots that have been paired with your phone and lets you choose one. You'll use buttons for driving forward and backward, turning left and right, stopping, and disconnecting. You can use a `VerticalArrangement` to lay out everything except for the `ListPicker`, and a `HorizontalArrangement` to contain the buttons for turning left, stopping, and turning right.

You can build the interface shown in Figure 12-2 by dragging out the components listed in Table 12-2.

Table 12-2. Visible components for the Robot NXT controller app

Component type	Palette group	What you'll name it	Purpose
`ListPicker`	User Interface	`ConnectListPicker`	Choose the robot to connect to.
`VerticalArrangement`	Layout	`VerticalArrangement1`	A visual container.
`Button`	User Interface	`ForwardButton`	Drive forward.
`HorizonalArrangement`	Layout	`HorizonalArrangement1`	A visual container.
`Button`	User Interface	`LeftButton`	Turn left.

Component type	Palette group	What you'll name it	Purpose
Button	User Interface	StopButton	Stop.
Button	User Interface	RightButton	Turn right.
Button	User Interface	BackwardButton	Drive backward.
Button	User Interface	DisconnectButton	Disconnect from the NXT.

To arrange the visual layout as shown in Figure 12-2, place LeftButton, StopButton, and RightButton inside HorizontalArrangement1, and place ForwardButton, HorizontalArrangement1, BackwardButton, and DisconnectButton inside VerticalArrangement1.

Set the properties of the components as follows:

1. Uncheck Scrollable on Screen1.
2. Set the Width of ConnectListPicker and DisconnectButton to "Fill parent."
3. Set the Width and Height of VerticalArrangement1, ForwardButton, HorizontalArrangement1, LeftButton, StopButton, RightButton, and BackwardButton to "Fill parent."
4. Set the Text of ConnectListPicker to "Connect...".
5. Set the Text of ForwardButton to "^".
6. Set the Text of LeftButton to "<".
7. Set the Text of StopButton to "-".
8. Set the Text of RightButton to ">".
9. Set the Text of BackwardButton to "v".
10. Set the Text of DisconnectButton to "Disconnect".
11. Set the FontSize of ConnectListPicker and DisconnectButton to 30.
12. Set the FontSize of ForwardButton, LeftButton, StopButton, RightButton, and BackwardButton to 40.

In this application, it makes sense to hide most of the user interface until the Bluetooth is connected to the NXT. To accomplish this, set the Visible property of VerticalArrangement1 to hidden. Don't worry—in a moment, we'll make the application reveal the user interface after it connects to the NXT.

Adding Behaviors to the Components

In this section, you'll program the behavior of the app, including:

- Letting the user connect the app to a robot by choosing it from a list.
- Letting the user disconnect the app from a robot.
- Letting the user drive the robot by using the control buttons.
- Forcing the robot to stop when it senses an obstacle.

Connecting to the NXT

The first behavior you'll add is connecting to the NXT. When you click `ConnectList Picker`, it will show a list of the paired robots. When you choose a robot, the app will make a Bluetooth connection to that robot.

Displaying the List of Robots

To display the list of robots, you'll use `ConnectListPicker`. A `ListPicker` looks like a button, but when it's clicked, it displays a list of items from which you can choose one. You'll use the `BluetoothClient1.AddressesAndNames` block to provide a list of the addresses and names of Bluetooth devices that have been paired with the Android. Because `BluetoothClient1` is used with NXT components, it automatically limits the devices included in the `AddressesAndNames` property to those that are robots, so you won't see other kinds of Bluetooth devices (such as headsets) in the list. Table 12-3 lists the blocks you'll need for this step.

Table 12-3. Blocks to add a ListPicker to the app

Block type	Drawer	Purpose
`ConnectListPicker.BeforePicking`	ConnectListPicker	Triggered when `ConnectListPicker` is clicked.
`set ConnectListPicker.Elements to`	ConnectListPicker	Set the choices that will appear.
`BluetoothClient1.AddressesAndNames`	BluetoothClient1	The addresses and names of robots that have been paired with the Android.

How the blocks work

When `ConnectListPicker` is clicked, the `ConnectListPicker.BeforePicking` event is triggered before the list of choices is displayed, as shown in Figure 12-3. To specify the items that will be listed, set the `ConnectListPicker.Elements` property to the `BluetoothClient1.AddressesAndNames` block. `ConnectListPicker` will list the robots that have been paired with the Android.

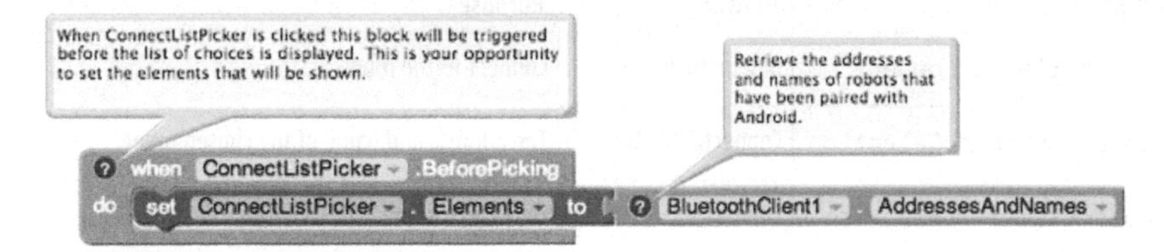

Figure 12-3. Displaying the list of robots

Test your app *On your phone, click "Connect..." and see what happens. You should see a list of all the robots your phone has been paired with. If you just see a black screen, your phone hasn't been paired with any robots. If you see addresses and names of other Bluetooth devices, such as a Bluetooth headset, the* `BluetoothClient` *property of* `NxtDrive1` *and* `NxtUltrasonicSensor1` *has not been set properly.*

Making the Bluetooth Connection

After you choose a robot from the list, the app will connect to that robot via Bluetooth. If the connection is successful, the user interface will change. `ConnectListPicker` will be hidden, and the rest of the user interface components will appear. If the robot is not turned on, the connection will fail and an error message will pop up. You'll use the `BluetoothClient1.Connect` block to make the connection. The `ConnectListPicker.Selection` property provides the address and name of the chosen robot. You'll use an `if then` block to test whether the connection was successful. We'll add `else` to the `if then` block, so it will have three different areas where blocks are connected: `if`, `then`, and `else`. The `if` area will contain the `BluetoothClient1.Connect` block. The `then` area will contain the blocks to be executed if the connection is successful. The `else` area will contain the blocks to be executed if the connection fails.

If the connection is successful, you will use the `Visible` property to hide `ConnectListPicker` and show `VerticalArrangement1`, which contains the rest of the user interface components. If the connection fails, you will use the `Notifier1.ShowAlert` block to display an error message. Table 12-4 lists the blocks you'll need for this behavior.

Table 12-4. Blocks for using Bluetooth to connect with the robot

Block type	Drawer	Purpose
`ConnectListPicker.AfterPicking`	ConnectListPicker	Triggered when a robot is chosen from `ConnectListPicker`.
`if then`	Control	Test whether the Bluetooth connection is successful.

Block type	Drawer	Purpose
`BluetoothClient1.Connect`	BluetoothClient1	Connect to the robot.
`ConnectListPicker.Selection`	ConnectListPicker	The address and name of the chosen robot.
`set ConnectListPicker.Visible to`	ConnectListPicker	Hide `ConnectListPicker`.
`false`	Logic	Plug into `set ConnectListPicker.Visible to`.
`set VerticalArrangement1.Visible to`	VerticalArrangement1	Show the rest of the user interface.
`true`	Logic	Plug into `set VerticalArrangement1.Visible to`.
`Notifier1.ShowAlert`	Notifier1	Show an error message.
`text` "Unable to make a Bluetooth connection."	Text	The error message.

How the blocks work

After a robot is picked, the `ConnectListPicker.AfterPicking` event is triggered, as shown in Figure 12-4. The `BluetoothClient1.Connect` block makes the Bluetooth connection to the selected robot. If the connection is successful, the then blocks are executed: the `ConnectListPicker.Visible` property is set to false to hide `ConnectListPicker`, and the `VerticalArrangement1.Visible` property is set to true to show `VerticalArrangement1`, which contains the remote control buttons. If the connection fails, the `else` blocks are executed: the `Notifier1.ShowAlert` block displays an error message.

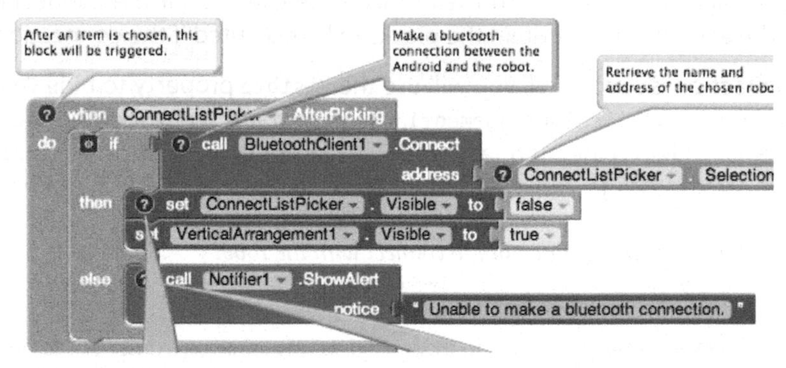

Figure 12-4. Making the Bluetooth connection

Disconnecting from the NXT

You're probably excited about connecting your Android to your NXT, but before you do that, let's do one more thing: add the behavior for disconnecting. That way, you'll be able to test both connecting and disconnecting. When `DisconnectButton` is clicked, the app will close the Bluetooth connection and the user interface will change. `ConnectListPicker` will reappear and the rest of the user interface components will be hidden. Use the blocks listed in Table 12-5 to build the `BluetoothClient1.Disconnect` block that closes the Bluetooth connection. You will use the `Visible` property to show `ConnectListPicker` and hide `VerticalArrangement1`, which contains the rest of the user interface components.

Table 12-5. Blocks for disconnecting from the robot

Block type	Drawer	Purpose
`DisconnectButton.Click`	DisconnectButton	Triggered when `DisconnectButton` is clicked.
`BluetoothClient1.Disconnect`	BluetoothClient1	Disconnect from the robot.
`set ConnectListPicker.Visible to`	ConnectListPicker	Show `ConnectListPicker`.
`true`	Logic	Plug into `set ConnectListPicker.Visible to`.
`set VerticalArrangement1.Visible to`	VerticalArrangement1	Hide the rest of the user interface.
`false`	Logic	Plug into `set VerticalArrangement1.Visible to`.

When `DisconnectButton` is clicked, the `DisconnectButton.Clicked` event is triggered, as shown in Figure 12-5. The `BluetoothClient1.Disconnect` block closes the Bluetooth connection. The `ConnectListPicker.Visible` property is set to true to show `ConnectListPicker`, and the `VerticalArrangement1.Visible` property is set to false to hide `VerticalArrangement1`, which contains the remote control buttons.

When DisconnectButton is clicked, this block will be triggered.

Close the bluetooth connection.

Show ConnectListPicker and hide the rest of the user interface components.

when DisconnectButton .Click
do call BluetoothClient1 .Disconnect
set ConnectListPicker . Visible to true
set DisconnectButton . Visible to false

Figure 12-5. Disconnecting from the robot

Test your app *Make sure that your robot is turned on and then, on your phone, click "Connect..." and choose the robot you want to connect to. It will take a moment to make the Bluetooth connection. After the robot connects, you should see the buttons for controlling the robot, as well as the Disconnect button. Click the Disconnect button. The buttons for controlling the robot should disappear, and the Connect button should reappear.*

Driving the NXT

Let's get to the really fun part: adding behavior for driving forward and backward, turning left and right, and stopping. Don't forget about stopping—if you do, you'll have an out-of-control robot on your hands! The `NxtDrive` component provides five blocks for driving the robot's motors:

- `MoveForwardIndefinitely` drives both motors forward.
- `MoveBackwardIndefinitely` drives both motors backward.
- `TurnCounterClockwiseIndefinitely` turns the robot to the left by driving the right motor forward and the left motor backward.
- `TurnClockwiseIndefinitely` turns the robot to the right by `driving` the left motor forward and the right motor backward.
- `Stop` stops both motors.

The `Move...` and `Turn...` blocks each have a parameter called `Power`. You'll use a number block, along with all the other items listed in Table 12-6, to specify the amount of power the robot should use to turn the motors. The value can range from 0 to 100. However, if you specify too little power, the motors will make a whining sound but not turn. In this application, you'll use 90 (percent).

Table 12-6. Blocks for controlling the robot

Block type	Drawer	Purpose
`ForwardButton.Click`	ForwardButton	Triggered when `ForwardButton` is clicked.
`NxtDrive1.MoveForwardIndefinitely`	NxtDrive1	Drive the robot forward.
`number` (90)	Math	The amount of power.
`BackwardButton.Click`	BackwardButton	Triggered when `BackwardButton` is clicked.
`NxtDrive1.MoveBackwardIndefinitely`	NxtDrive1	Drive the robot backward.
`number` (90)	Math	The amount of power.
`LeftButton.Click`	LeftButton	Triggered when `LeftButton` is clicked.
`NxtDrive1.TurnCounterClockwise Indefinitely`	NxtDrive1	Turn the robot counterclockwise.
`number` (90)	Math	The amount of power.
`RightButton.Click`	RightButton	Triggered when `RightButton` is clicked.
`NxtDrive1.TurnClockwiseIndefinitely`	NxtDrive1	Turn the robot clockwise.
`number` (90)	Math	The amount of power.
`StopButton.Click`	StopButton	Triggered when `StopButton` is clicked.
`NxtDrive1.Stop`	NxtDrive1	Stop the robot.

How the blocks work

When `ForwardButton` is clicked, the `ForwardButton.Clicked` event is triggered. The `NxtDrive1.MoveForwardIndefinitely` block shown in Figure 12-6 is used to move the robot forward at 90% power. The remaining events function similarly for the other buttons, each powering the robot backward, left, and right.

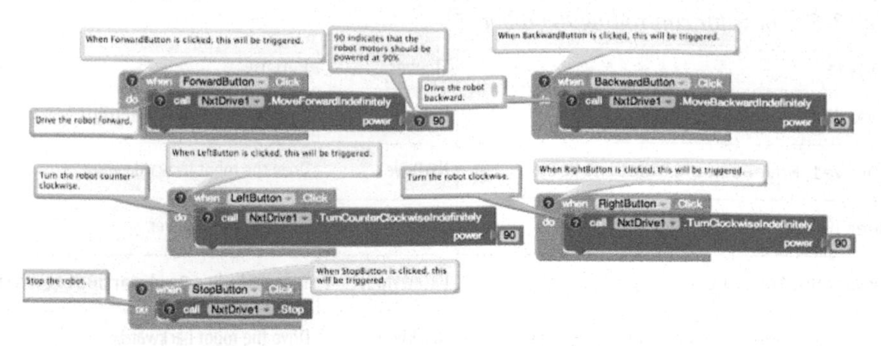

Figure 12-6. Driving the robot

When `StopButton` is clicked, the `StopButton.Clicked` event is triggered. The `NxtDrive1.Stop` block is used to stop the robot. Test your app. Follow the instructions in the previous "Test your app" section to connect to the NXT. Make sure the robot is not on a table where it could fall, and then test its behavior as follows:

1. Click the forward button. The robot should move forward.
2. Click the backward button. The robot should move backward.
3. Click the left button. The robot should turn counterclockwise.
4. Click the right button. The robot should turn clockwise.
5. Click the stop button. The robot should stop.

If your robot doesn't move, but you can hear a whining sound, you might need to increase the power. You can use 100 for maximum power.

Using the Ultrasonic Sensor to Detect Obstacles

Using the ultrasonic sensor, the robot will stop if it encounters an obstacle within 30 centimeters, such as the obstruction shown in Figure 12-7.

You can use the `NxtUltrasonicSensor` component to detect obstacles. It has two properties named `BottomOfRange` and `TopOfRange` that define the detection range in centimeters. By default, the `BottomOfRange` property is set to 30 centimeters and `TopO fRange` is set to 90 centimeters.

Figure 12-7. A common household obstacle for your NXT robot

The NxtUltrasonicSensor component also has three events called BelowRange, WithinRange, and AboveRange. The BelowRange event will be triggered when an obstacle is detected at a distance below BottomOfRange. The WithinRange event will be triggered when an obstacle is detected at a distance between BottomOfRange and TopOfRange. The AboveRange event will be triggered when an obstacle is detected at a distance above TopOfRange.

You'll use the NxtUltrasonicSensor1.BelowRange event block, shown in Table 12-7, to detect an obstacle within 30 centimeters. If you want to detect an obstacle within a different distance, you can adjust the BottomOfRange property. You'll use the NxtDrive1.Stop block to stop the robot.

Table 12-7. Blocks for using the NxtUltrasonicSensor

Block type	Drawer	Purpose
NxtUltrasonicSensor1.BelowRange	NxtUltrasonicSensor1	Triggered when the ultrasonic sensor detects an obstacle at a distance below 30 centimeters.
NxtDrive1.Stop	NxtDrive1	Stop the robot.

How the blocks work

When the robot's ultrasonic sensor detects an obstacle at a distance below 30 centimeters, the NxtUltrasonicSensor1.BelowRange event is triggered, as shown in Figure 12-8. The NxtDrive1.Stop block stops the robot.

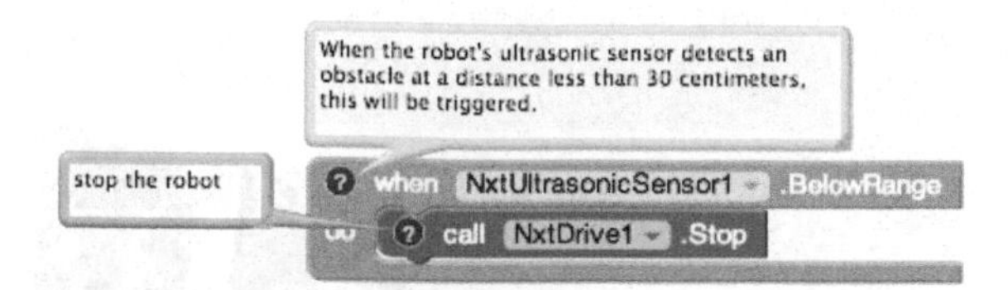

Figure 12-8. Detecting an obstacle and stopping the robot

Test your app *Follow the instructions in the previous "Test your app" section to connect to the NXT. Using the navigation buttons, drive your robot toward an obstacle, such as a cat. The robot should stop when it approaches within 30 centimeters of the cat.*

If the robot doesn't stop, the cat might have moved away from the robot before it drew within 30 centimeters. You might need to test your app with an inanimate obstacle.

Variations

After you get this application working—and you've spent enough time actually playing with your NXT robot—you might want to try the following:

- Vary the amount of power when driving the robot.
  - You can do this by changing the numeric value that you plug into the `MoveForwardIndefinitely`, `MoveBackwardIndefinitely`, `TurnCounterclockwiseIndefinitely`, and `TurnClockwiseIndefinitely` blocks.
- Use the `NxtColorSensor` to shine a red light when an obstacle is detected.
  - You can use an `NxtColorSensor` component and its `GenerateColor` property.
  - You'll need to set the `DetectColor` property to false (or uncheck it in the Component Designer) because the color sensor cannot detect and generate color at the same time.
- Use an `OrientationSensor` to control the robot.
- Use LEGO building elements to physically attach your phone to the robot. Create applications that make the robot autonomous.

Summary

Here are some of the concepts we covered in this tutorial:

- You can use the `ListPicker` component to choose from a list of paired robots.
- The `BluetoothClient` component makes the connection to the robot.
- The `Notifier` component displays an error message.
- You can use the `Visible` property to hide or show user interface components.
- The `NxtDrive` component can drive, turn, and stop the robot.
- You can use the `NxtUltrasonicSensor` component to detect obstacles.

Summary

CHAPTER 13

Amazon at the Bookstore

Suppose that you're browsing books at your favorite bookstore and want to know how much a book costs on Amazon.com. With the Amazon at the Bookstore app, you can scan a book or enter an ISBN, and the app will tell you the current lowest price of the book at Amazon.com. You can also search for books on a particular topic.

Amazon at the Bookstore demonstrates how you can use App Inventor to create apps that talk to web services (aka, application programming interfaces, or APIs). This app will get data from a web service created by one of the authors of this book. By the end of this chapter, you'll be able to create your own custom app for talking to Amazon. The application has a simple user interface with which the user can enter keywords or a book's ISBN (international standard book number—a 10- or 13-digit code that uniquely identifies a book) and then lists the title, ISBN, and lowest price for a new copy at Amazon. It also uses the `BarcodeScanner` component so that the user can scan a book to trigger a search instead of entering text (technically, the scanner just inputs the book's ISBN for you).

What You'll Learn

In this app (shown in Figure 13-1), you'll learn:

- How to use a barcode scanner within an app.
- How to access a web information source (Amazon's API) through the `TinyWebDB` component.
- How to process complex data returned from that web information source. In particular, you'll learn how to process a list of books in which each book is itself a list of three items (title, price, and ISBN).

Figure 13-1. Amazon at the Bookstore running in the emulator

You'll also be introduced to source code that you can use to create your own web service API with the Python programming language and Google's App Engine.

What is an API?

Before you start designing your components and programming the app, let's take a closer look at what an application programmer interface (API) is and how it works. An API is like a website, but instead of communicating with humans, it communicates with other computer programs. APIs are often called "server" programs because they typically serve information to "client" programs that actually interface with humans—such as an App Inventor app. If you've ever used a Facebook app on your phone, you're using a client program that communicates with the Facebook API server app.

In this chapter, you'll create an Android client app that communicates with an Amazon API. Your app will request book and ISBN information from the Amazon API, and the API will return up-to-date listings to your app. The app will then present the book data to the user.

The Amazon API you'll use is specially configured for use with App Inventor. We won't get into the gory details here, but it's useful to know that as a result of this configuration, you can use the `TinyWebDB` component to communicate with Amazon. The good news is you already know how to do that! You'll call `TinyWebDB.GetValue` to request information and then process the information returned in the `TinyWebDB.GotValue` event handler, just as you do when you use a web database. (You can go back to the MakeQuiz and TakeQuiz apps in Chapter 10 to refresh your memory, if needed.)

Before creating the app, you'll need to understand the Amazon API's protocol, which specifies the format for your request and the format of the data returned. Just as different human cultures have different protocols (when you meet someone, do you shake hands, bow, or nod your head?), computers talking to one another have protocols, as well. The Amazon API you'll be using here provides a web interface for exploring how the API works before you start using it. Although the API is designed to talk to other computers, this web interface makes it possible for you to see just how that communication will happen. Following these steps, you can try out what particular `GetValue` calls will return via the website, and know that the API interface will behave exactly the same when you ask it for data via the `TinyWebDB` component in App Inventor. Let's get underway:

1. Open a browser and go to *http://aiamazonapi.appspot.com/*. You'll see the website shown in Figure 13-2.

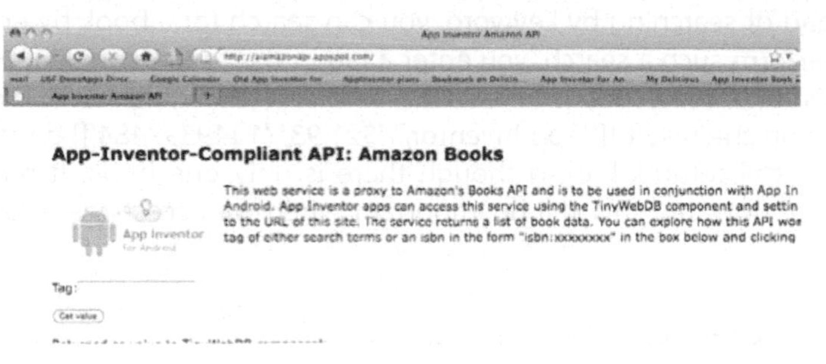

Figure 13-2. The web interface for the App Inventor Amazon API

2. On this web page, you can try the one function you can call with this API: get-value. Enter a term (e.g., "baseball") in the Tag field and then click "Get value." The web page will display a listing of the top five books returned from Amazon, as shown in Figure 13-3.

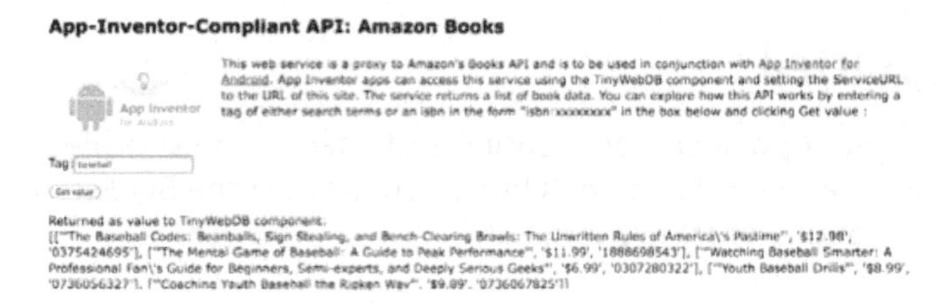

Figure 13-3. Making a call to the Amazon API to search for books related to the tag (or keyword) "baseball"

The value returned is a list of books, each one enclosed in brackets [like this] and providing the title, cost, and ISBN.

If you look closely, you'll see that each book is in fact represented as a sublist of another main list. The main list (about baseball) is enclosed in brackets, and each sublist (or book) is enclosed in its own set of brackets within the main brackets. So, the return value from this API is actually a list of lists, with each sublist providing the information for one book. Let's look at this a bit more closely. Each left bracket ([) in the data denotes the beginning of a list. The first left bracket of the result denotes the beginning of the outer list (the list of books). To its immediate right is the beginning of the first sublist, the first book, as demonstrated here:

["The Baseball Codes: Beanballs, Sign Stealing, and Bench-Clearing Brawls: The Unwritten Rules of America's Pastime," '$12.98,' '0375424695']

The sublist has three parts: a title, the lowest current price for the book at Amazon, and the book's ISBN. When you get this information into your App Inventor app, you'll be able to access each part by using `select list item`, with index 1 for the title, index 2 for the price, and index 3 for the ISBN. (To refresh your memory on working with an index and lists, revisit the MakeQuiz app in Chapter 10.)

3. Instead of searching by keyword, you can search for a book by entering an ISBN. To perform such a search, you enter a tag in the form "isbn:00000000000," where the list of 0s represent an actual ISBN number (see Figure 13-4). The double brackets ([[) in the result [["'App Inventor,"' '$21.93,' '1449397484']] denote that a list of lists is still returned, even though there is only one book. It might seem a bit strange now, but this will be important when we access the information for our app.

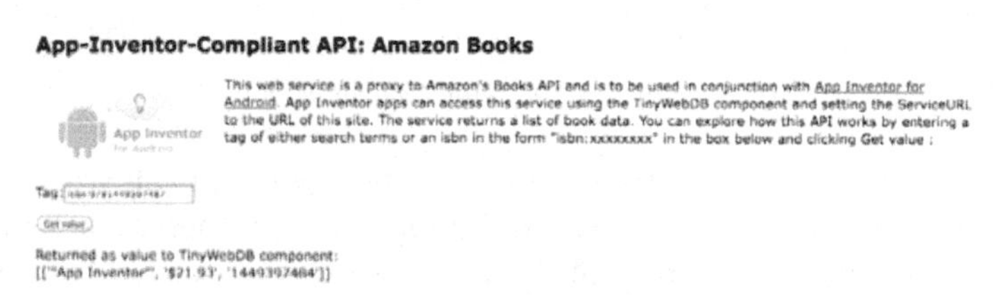

Figure 13-4. Querying the Amazon API by ISBN instead of keyword

Getting Started

Connect to the App Inventor website and start a new project. Then name it "AmazonBooks", and set the screen's title to "Amazon at the Bookstore". Then, connect your device or emulator for live testing.

Designing the Components

The user interface for the Amazon book app is relatively simple: give it a `Textbox` for entering keywords or ISBNs, two buttons for starting the two types of searches (keyword or ISBN), and a third button for letting the user scan a book (we'll get to that in a bit). Then, add a heading label and another label for listing the results that the Amazon API returns, and finally two non-visible components: `TinyWebDB` and a `BarcodeScanner`. Check your results against Figure 13-5.

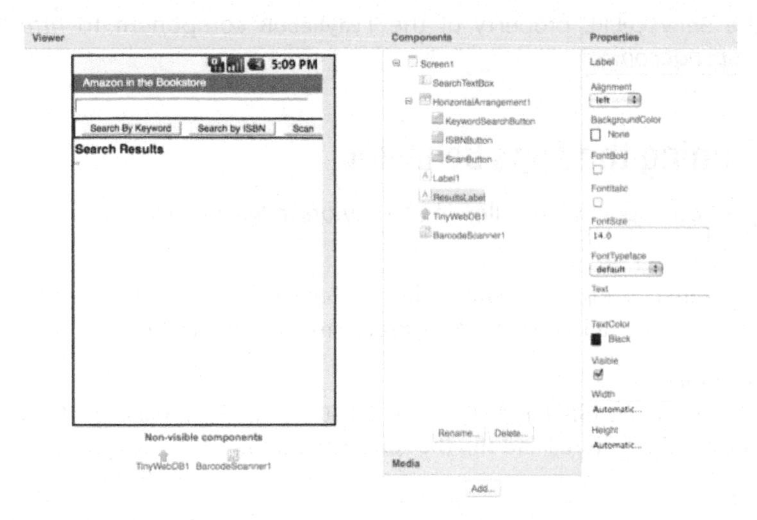

Figure 13-5. The Amazon at the Bookstore user interface shown in the Designer

Table 13-1 lists all the components you'll need to build the UI shown in Figure 13-5.

Table 13-1. Component list for the Amazon at the Bookstore app

Component type	Palette group	What you'll name it	Purpose
`Textbox`	User Interface	`SearchTextBox`	The user enters keywords or ISBN here.
`HorizontalArrangement`	Layout	`HorizontalArrangement1`	Arrange the buttons in a line.
`Button`	User Interface	`KeywordSearchButton`	Click to search by keyword.
`Button`	User Interface	`ISBNButton`	Click to search by ISBN.
`Button`	User Interface	`ScanButton`	Click to scan an ISBN from a book.
`Label`	User Interface	`Label1`	The header "Search Results."
`Label`	User Interface	`ResultsLabel`	Where you'll display the results.
`TinyWebDB`	Storage	`TinyWebDB1`	Talk to Amazon.com.
`BarcodeScanner`	Sensors	`BarcodeScanner1`	Scan barcodes.

Set the properties of the components in the following way:

1. Set the `Hint` of the `SearchTextBox` to "Enter keywords or ISBN".
2. Set the properties of the buttons and labels so that they appear as shown in Figure 13-5.

3. Set the `ServiceURL` property of the `TinyWebDB` component to *http://aiamazonapi.appspot.com/*.

Programming the App's Behavior

For this app, you'll specify the following behaviors in the Blocks Editor:

Searching by keyword
: The user enters some terms and clicks the KeywordSearchButton to invoke an Amazon search. You'll call `TinyWebDB1.GetValue` to make it happen.

Searching by ISBN
: The user enters an ISBN and clicks the `ISBNButton`. You'll package the prefix "isbn:" with the number entered and run the Amazon search.

Barcode scanning
: The user clicks a button and the scanner is launched. When the user scans an ISBN from a book, your app will launch a search by ISBN.

Processing the list of books
: At first, your app will display the data returned from Amazon in a rudimentary way. Later, you'll modify the blocks so that the app extracts the title, price, and ISBN from each book returned and displays them in an organized way.

Searching by Keyword

When the user clicks the `KeywordSearchButton`, you want to grab the text from the `SearchTextBox` and send it as the tag in your request to the Amazon API. You'll use the `TinyWebDB.GetValue` block to request the Amazon search. When the results come back from Amazon, the `TinyWebDB.GotValue` event handler will be triggered. For now, just display the result that is returned directly into the `ResultsLabel`, as shown in Figure 13-6. Later, after you see that the data is indeed being retrieved, you can display the data in a more sophisticated fashion.

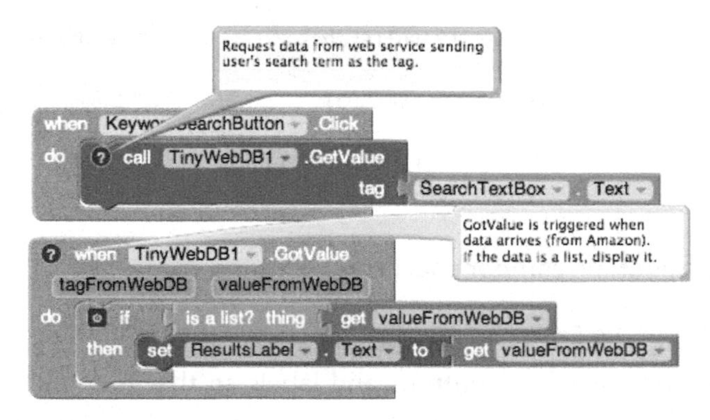

Figure 13-6. Send the search request to the API and put results in the ResultsLabel

How the blocks work

When the user clicks the `KeywordSearchButton`, the `TinyWebDB1.GetValue` request is made. The tag sent with the request is the information the user entered in the `Search TextBox`. If you completed the MakeQuiz app (Chapter 10), you know that `TinyWebDB1.GetValue` requests are not answered immediately. Instead, when the data arrives from the API, `TinyWebDB1.GotValue` is triggered. In `GotValue`, the blocks check the value returned to see if it's a list (it won't be if the Amazon API is offline or there is no data for the keywords). If it is a list, the data is placed into the `ResultsLabel`.

Test your app *Enter a term in the search box and click Search By Keyword. You should get a listing similar to what is shown in Figure 13-7. (It's not terribly nice-looking, but we'll deal with that shortly.)*

Figure 13-7. Keyword search result for "dogs"

Searching by ISBN

The code for searching by ISBN is similar, but in this case the Amazon API expects the tag to be in the form "isbn:xxxxxxxxxxxxx" (this is the protocol the API expects for searching by ISBN). You don't want to force the user to know this protocol; the user should just be able to enter the ISBN in the text box and click Search by ISBN, and the app should add the "isbn:" prefix behind the scenes with `make text`. Figure 13-8 shows the blocks to do that.

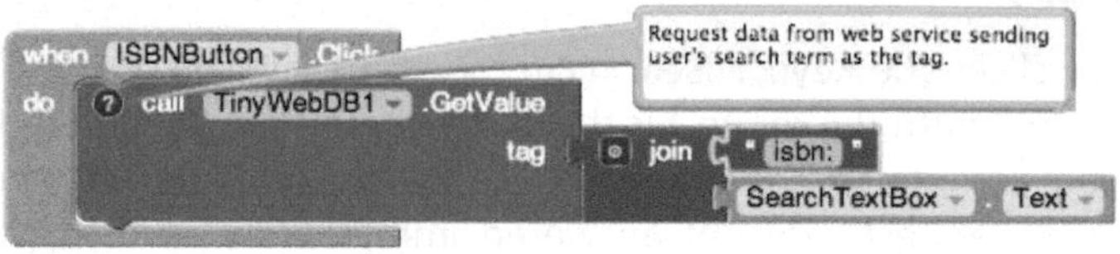

Figure 13-8. The app prefixes "isbn:" to the search so it will look up a particular book

How the blocks work

The `join` block concatenates the "isbn:" prefix with the information the user has input in the `SearchTextBox` and sends the result as the tag to `TinyWebDB1.GetValue`.

Just as with keyword search, the API sends back a list result for an ISBN search—in this case, a list of just the one item whose ISBN matches the user's input exactly. Because the `TinyWebDB.GotValue` event handler is already set up to process a list of books (even a list with only one item), you won't have to change your event handler to make this work.

Test your app *Enter an ISBN (e.g., 9781449397487) in the `SearchTextBox` and click the `ISBNButton`. Does the book information appear?*

Don't Leave Your Users Hanging

When you call a web service (API) with `TinyWebDB1.GetValue`, there can be a delay before the data arrives and `TinyWebDB1.GotValue` is triggered. It is generally a good idea to let users know the request is being processed to reassure them that the app hasn't hung. For this app, you can place a message in the `ResultsLabel` each time you make the call to `TinyWebDB1.GetValue`, as shown in Figure 13-9.

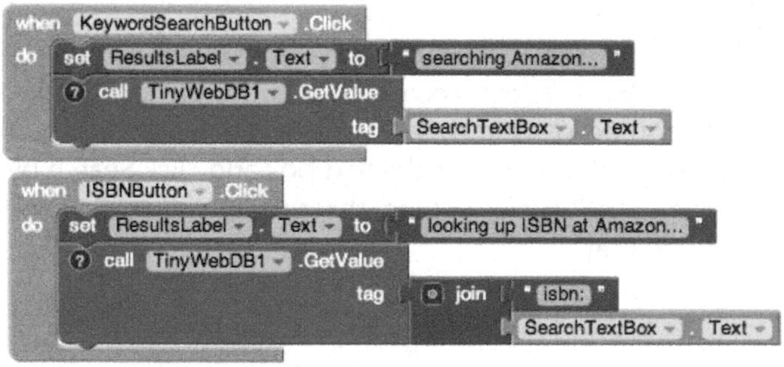

Figure 13-9. Adding a message to let the user know what is happening

How the blocks work

For both the keyword and ISBN searches, a "Searching Amazon..." message is placed in `ResultsLabel` when the data is requested. Note that when `GotValue` is triggered, this message is overwritten with the actual results from Amazon.

Scanning a Book

Let's face it: typing on a cell phone isn't always the easiest thing, and you tend to make a mistake here and there. It would certainly be easier (and result in fewer mistakes) if a user could just launch your app and scan the barcode of the book. This is another great built-in Android phone feature that you can tap into easily with App Inventor.

The function `BarcodeScanner.DoScan` starts up the scanner. You'll want to call this when the `ScanButton` is clicked. The event handler `BarcodeScanner.AfterScan` is triggered as soon as something has been scanned. It has one argument, `result`, which contains the information that was scanned. In this case, you want to initiate an ISBN search using that result, as shown in Figure 13-10.

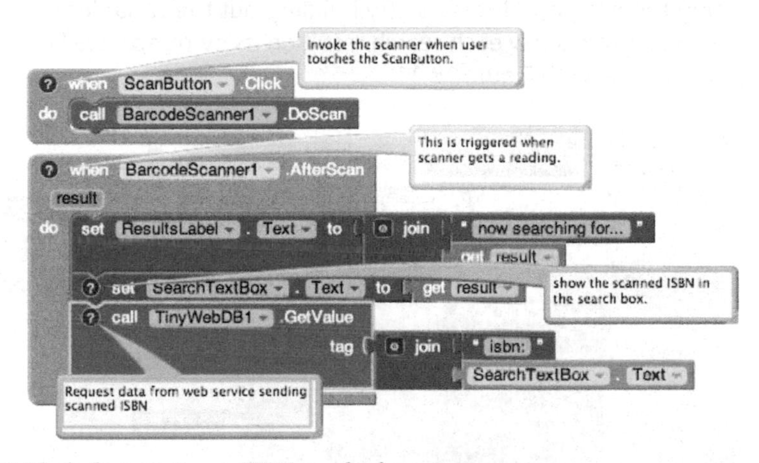

Figure 13-10. Blocks for initiating an ISBN search after a user scans

How the blocks work

When the user clicks the `ScanButton`, `DoScan` launches the scanner. When something has been scanned, `AfterScan` is triggered. The argument result holds the result of the scan—in this case, a book's ISBN. The user is notified that a request has been made, the result (the scanned ISBN number) is placed in the `SearchTextBox`, and `TinyWebDB1.GetValue` is called to initiate the search. Again, the `TinyWebDB1.GotValue` event handler will process the book information returned.

Test your app *Click the ScanButton and scan the barcode of a book. Does the app display the book information?*

Improving the Display

A client app like the one you're creating can do whatever it wants with the data it receives—you could compare the price information with that of other online stores, or use the title information to search for similar books from another library. Almost always, you'll want to get the API information loaded into variables that you can then process further. In the `TinyWebDB.GotValue` event handler you have so far, you just place all the information returned from Amazon into the `ResultsLabel`. Instead, let's process the data by 1) putting the title, price, and ISBN of each book returned into separate variables, and 2) displaying those items in an orderly fashion. If you've completed some of the earlier chapters, you're probably getting the hang of defining variables and using them in your display, so try building out the variables you think you'll need and the blocks to display each search result on its own separate line. Then, compare what you've done with Figure 13-11.

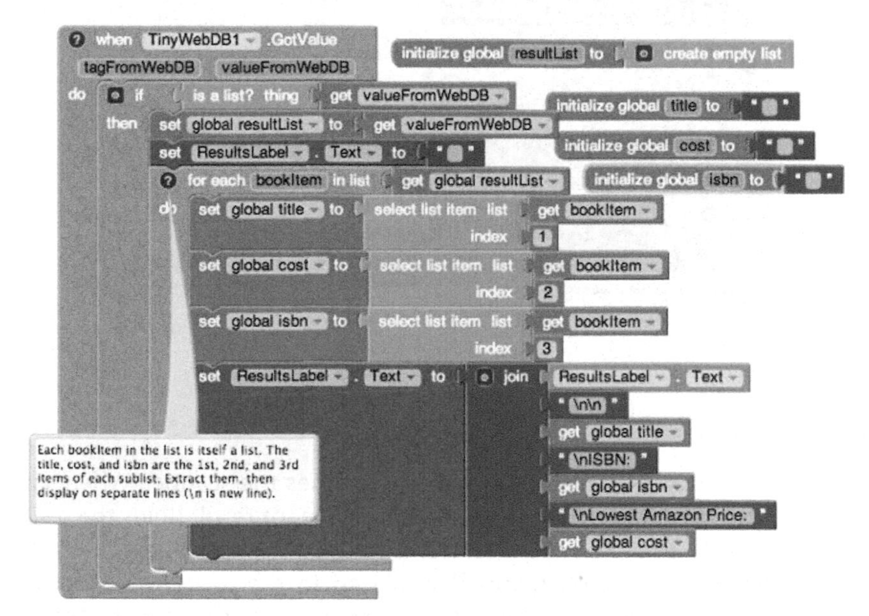

Figure 13-11. Extracting the title, cost, and ISBN of each book, and then displaying them on separate lines

How the blocks work

Four variables—`resultList`, `title`, `cost`, and `isbn`—are defined to hold each piece of data as it is returned from the API. The result from the API, `valueFromWebDB`, is placed into the variable `resultList`. This app could have processed the argument `valueFromWebDB` directly, but in general, you'll put it in a variable in case you want to process the data outside the event handler. (Event arguments like `valueFromWebDB` hold their value only within the event handler.)

A `for each` loop is used to iterate through each item of the result. Recall that the data returned from Amazon is a list of lists, with each sublist representing the information for a book. So, the placeholder of the `for each` is renamed `bookitem`, and it holds the current book information (a list) on each iteration.

Now we have to deal with the fact that the variable `bookitem` is a list—the first item is the title; the second, the price; and the third, the ISBN. Thus, we use `select list item` blocks to extract these items and place them into their respective variables (`title`, `price`, and `isbn`).

After the data has been organized into variables, you can process it however you'd like. This app just uses the variables as part of a `join` block that displays the title, price, and ISBN on separate lines.

Test your app *Try another search and check out how the book information is displayed. It should look similar to Figure 13-12.*

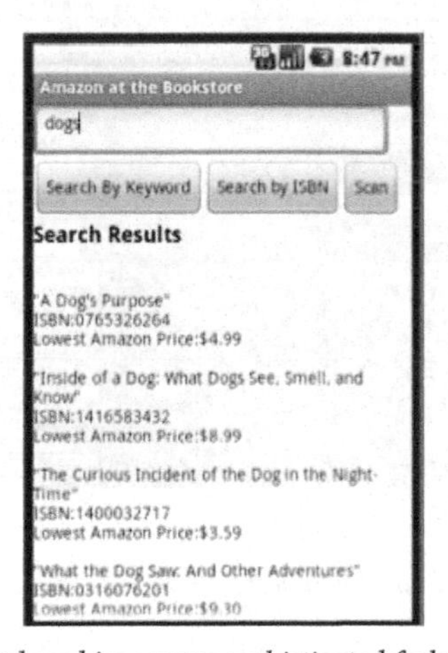

Figure 13-12. The search listing displayed in a more sophisticated fashion

The Complete App: Amazon at the Bookstore

Figure 13-13 shows the final block configuration for Amazon at the Bookstore.

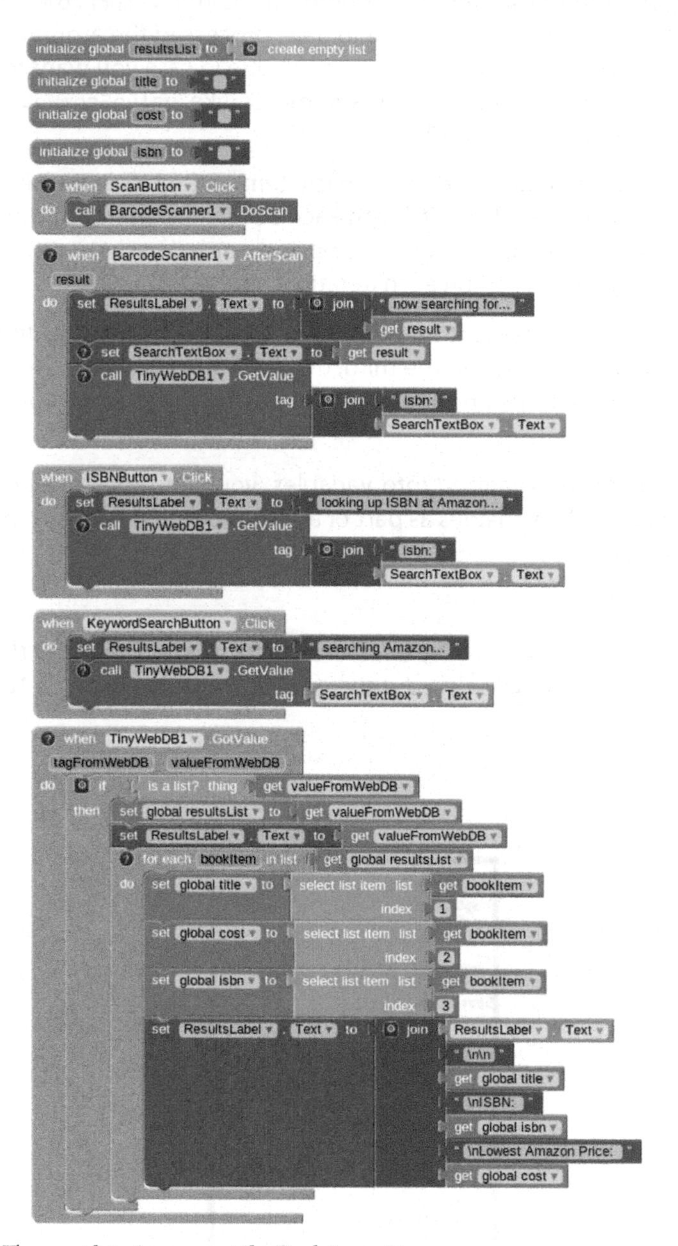

Figure 13-13. The complete Amazon at the Bookstore app

Customizing the API

The API you connected to, *http://aiamazonapi.appspot.com*, was created with the programming language Python and Google's App Engine. App Engine lets you create and deploy websites and services (APIs) that live on Google's servers. You only pay for App Engine if your site or API becomes popular and attracts lots of hits.

The API service used in this tutorial provides only partial access to the full Amazon API and returns a maximum of five books for any search. If you'd like to provide more flexibility—for example, have it search for items other than books—you can download the source code for the service from *http://appinventorapi.com/amazon/* and customize it. Such customization does require knowledge of Python programming, so beware! But, if you've been completing the App Inventor apps in this book, you might just be ready for the challenge. To get started learning Python, check out the interactive version of the book *How to Think Like a Computer Scientist: Learning with Python* (*http://bit.ly/1uJ4Q2j*) and then check out the section on App Inventor API building in Chapter 24 of this book.

Variations

After you get the app working, you might want to explore some of the following variations:

- As is, the app hangs if the search doesn't return any books (for instance, when the user enters an invalid ISBN). Modify the blocks so that the app reports when there are no results.
- Modify the app so that it only displays books under $10.
- Modify the app so that after you scan a book, its lowest Amazon price is spoken aloud (use the `TextToSpeech` component discussed in the No Text While Driving app in Chapter 4).
- Download the *http://aiamazonapi.appspot.com* API code and modify it so that it returns more information. For example, you might have it return the Amazon URL of each book, display the URL along with each listed book, and let the user click the URL to open that page. As mentioned earlier, modifying the API requires Python programming and some knowledge of Google's App Engine. For more information, check out Chapter 24.

Summary

Here are some of the concepts we covered with this app:

- You can access the Web from an app by using `TinyWebDB` and specially constructed APIs. You set the `ServiceURL` of the `TinyWebDB` component to the API URL and then call `TinyWebDB.GetValue` to request the information. The data isn't immediately returned but can instead be accessed within the `TinyWebDB.GotValue` event handler.

- The `BarcodeScanner.DoScan` function launches the scan. When the user scans a barcode, the `BarcodeScanner.AfterScan` event is triggered and the scanned data is placed in the argument `result`.
- In App Inventor, complex data is represented with lists and lists of lists. If you know the format of the data returned from an API, you can use `for each` and `select list item` to extract the separate pieces of information into variables, and then perform whatever processing or set up the display however you'd like using those variables.

PART II
Inventor's Manual

CHAPTER 14

Understanding an App's Architecture

This chapter examines the structure of an app from a programmer's perspective. It begins with the traditional analogy that an app is like a recipe and then proceeds to reconceptualize an app as a set of components that respond to events. The chapter also examines how apps can ask questions, repeat, remember, and talk to the Web, all of which will be described in more detail in later chapters.

Many people can tell you what an app is from a user's perspective, but understanding what it is from a programmer's perspective is more complicated. Apps have an internal structure that you must understand in order to create them effectively.

One way to describe an app's internals is to break it into two parts, its *components* and its *behaviors*. Roughly, these correspond to the two main windows you use in App Inventor: you use the Component Designer to specify the objects (components) of the app, and you use the Blocks Editor to program how the app responds to the user and external events (the app's behavior).

Figure 14-1 provides an overview of this app architecture. In this chapter, we'll explore this architecture in detail.

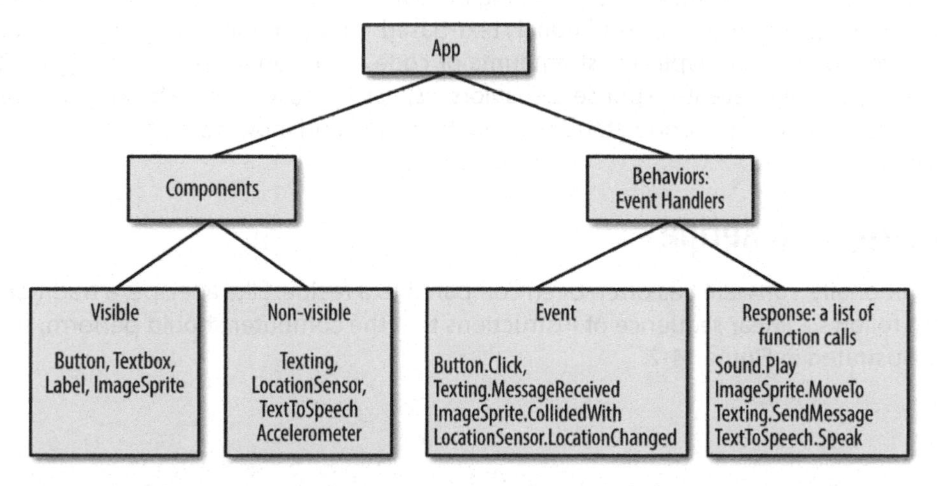

Figure 14-1. The internal architecture of an App Inventor app

Components

There are two main types of components in an app: visible and non-visible. The app's visible components are those that you can see when the app is launched—buttons, text boxes, and labels. These are often referred to as the app's *user interface*.

Non-visible components are those that you can't see, so they're not part of the user interface. Instead, they provide access to the built-in functionality of the device; for example, the `Texting` component sends and processes SMS texts, the `LocationSensor` component determines the device's location, and the `TextToSpeech` component talks. The non-visible components are the technology within the device—little worker bees that do jobs for your app.

Both visible and non-visible components are defined by a set of *properties*. Properties are memory slots for storing information about the component. Visible components like buttons and labels have properties such as `Width`, `Height`, and `Alignment`, which together define how the component looks.

Component properties are like spreadsheet cells: you modify them in the Component Designer to define the *initial* appearance of a component. You can also change the values with blocks.

Behavior

App components are generally straightforward and easy to understand: a text box is for entering information, a button is for clicking, and so on. An app's behavior, on the other hand, is conceptually difficult and often complex. The behavior defines how the app should respond to events, both user initiated (e.g., a button click) and external (e.g., an SMS text arriving to the phone). The difficulty of specifying such interactive behavior is why programming is so challenging.

Fortunately, App Inventor provides a high-level blocks-based language for specifying behaviors. The blocks make programming behaviors more like plugging puzzle pieces together, as opposed to traditional text-based programming languages, which involve learning and typing vast amounts of code. And App Inventor is designed to make specifying event-response behaviors especially easy. The following sections provide a model for understanding app behavior and how to specify it in App Inventor.

An App as a Recipe

Traditionally, software has often been compared to a recipe. Like a recipe, a traditional app follows a linear sequence of instructions that the computer should perform, such as illustrated in Figure 14-2.

A typical app might start a bank transaction (A), perform some computations and modify a customer's account (B), and then print out the new balance on the screen (C).

Figure 14-2. Traditional software follows a linear sequence of instructions

An App as a Set of Event Handlers

The *app as a recipe* paradigm fit the early number-crunching computer well, but its not a great fit for mobile phones, the Web, and in general most of the computing done today. Most modern software doesn't perform a bunch of instructions in a predetermined order; instead, it *reacts* to *events*—most commonly, events initiated by the app's end user. For example, if the user taps a button, the app responds by performing some operation (e.g., sending a text message). For touchscreen phones and devices, the act of dragging your finger across the screen is another event. The app might respond to that event by drawing a line from the point at which your finger first contacts the screen to the point where you lifted it.

Modern apps are better conceptualized as event-response machines. The apps do include recipes—sequences of instructions—but each recipe is only performed in response to some event, as shown in Figure 14-3.

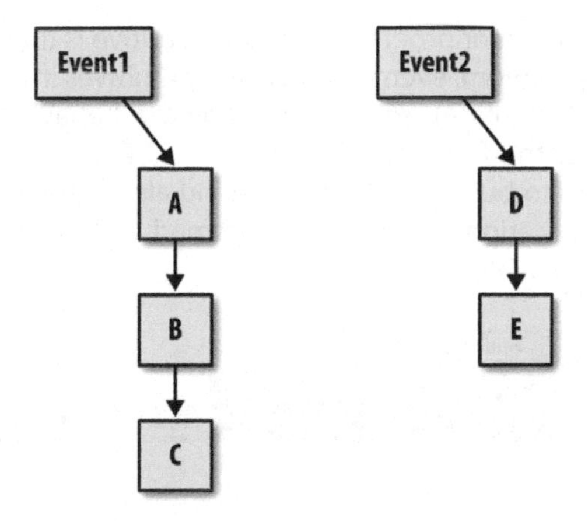

Figure 14-3. An app as multiple recipes hooked to events

As events occur, the app reacts by calling a sequence of *functions*. Functions are things you can do to, or with, a component; these can be operations such as sending an SMS text, or property-changing operations such as changing the text in a label of the user interface. To *call* or *invoke* a function means to carry out the function—to make it happen. We call an event and the set of functions performed in response to it an *event handler*.

Many events are initiated by the end user, but some are not. An app can react to events that happen within the phone, such as changes to its orientation sensor and the clock (i.e., the passing of time), or it can respond to events that originate outside the phone, such as an incoming text or call from another phone, or data arriving from the Web (see Figure 14-4).

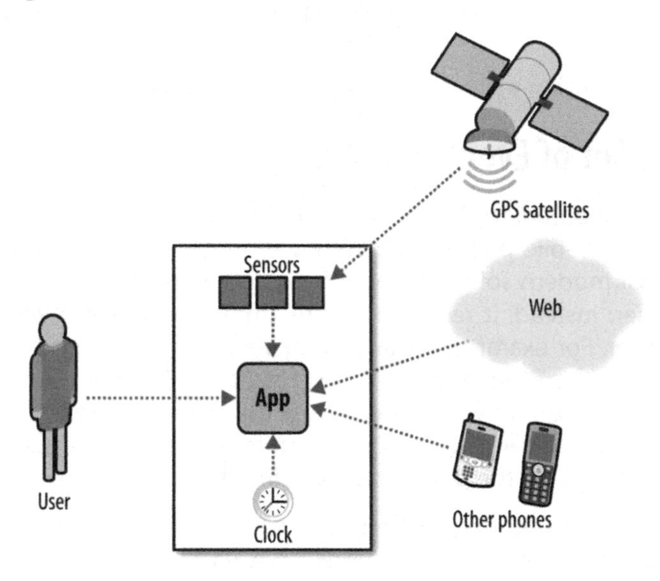

Figure 14-4. An app can respond to both internal and external events

One reason why App Inventor programming is so intuitive is that it's based directly on this event-response paradigm; event handlers are primitives in the language (in many languages, this is not the case). You begin defining a behavior by dragging out an *event block*, which has the form, "When *<event>* do." For example, consider an app, SpeakIt, that responds to button clicks by speaking aloud the text the user has typed in a textbox. This application could be programmed with a single event handler, as demonstrated in Figure 14-5.

```
when SpeakItButton .Click
do  call TextToSpeech1 .Speak
                  message  TextBox1 . Text
```

Figure 14-5. An event handler for a SpeakIt app

These blocks specify that when the user clicks the button named `SpeakItButton`, the `TextToSpeech` component should speak the words the user typed in the text box named `TextBox1`. The response is the call to the function `TextToSpeech1.Speak`. The event is `SpeakItButton.Click`. The event handler includes all the blocks in Figure 14-5.

With App Inventor, all activity occurs in response to an event. Your app shouldn't contain blocks outside of an event's `when do` block. For instance, the blocks in Figure 14-6 accomplish nothing when floating alone.

Figure 14-6. Floating blocks won't do anything outside an event handler

Event Types

The events that can trigger activity fall into the categories listed in Table 14-1.

Table 14-1. Events that can trigger activity

Event type	Example
User-initiated event	*When* the user clicks `button1`, *do*...
Initialization event	*When* the app launches, *do*...
Timer event	*When* 20 milliseconds passes, *do*...
Animation event	When two objects collide, *do*...
External event	*When* the phone receives a text, *do*...

User-Initiated Events

User-initiated events are the most common type of event. With input forms, it is typically the user tapping a button that triggers a response from the app. More graphical apps respond to touches and drags.

Initialization Events

Sometimes, your app needs to perform certain functions immediately upon startup, not in response to any end-user activity or other event. How does this fit into the event-handling paradigm?

Event-handling languages such as App Inventor consider the app's launch as an event. If you want specific functions to be performed as the app opens, you drag out a `Screen1.Initialize` event block and place the pertinent function call blocks within it.

For instance, in the game MoleMash (Chapter 3), the `MoveMole` procedure is called upon app startup (see Figure 14-7) to randomly place the mole.

Figure 14-7. Using a Screen1.Initialize event block to move the mole when the app launches

Timer Events

Some activity in an app is triggered by the passing of time. You can think of an animation as an object that moves when triggered by a *timer event*. App Inventor has a `Clock` component that you can use to trigger timer events. For instance, if you wanted a ball on the screen to move 10 pixels horizontally at a set time interval, your blocks would look like Figure 14-8.

Figure 14-8. Using a timer event block to move a ball whenever Clock1.Timer fires

Animation Events

Activity involving graphical objects (sprites) within canvases will trigger events. So you can program games and other interactive animations by specifying what should occur on events such as an object reaching the edge of the canvas or two objects colliding, as depicted in Figure 14-9. For more information, see Chapter 17.

Figure 14-9. When the FlyingSaucer sprite hits another object, play a sound

External Events

When your phone receives location information from GPS satellites, an event is triggered. Likewise, when your phone receives a text, an event is triggered (Figure 14-10).

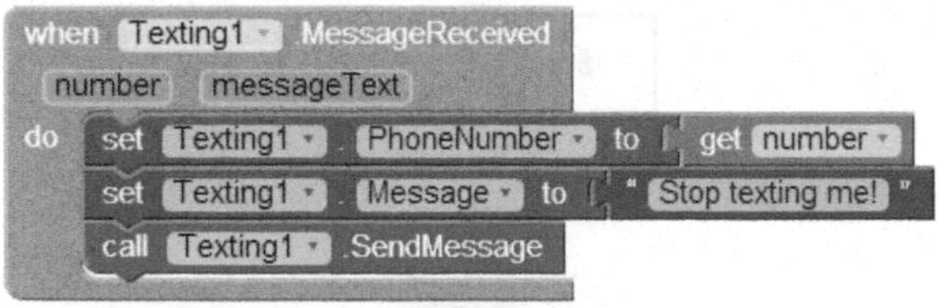

Figure 14-10. The Texting1.MessageReceived event is triggered whenever a text is received

Such external inputs to the device are considered events, no different than the user clicking a button.

Thus, every app you create will be a set of event handlers: one to initialize things, some to respond to the end user's input, some triggered by time, and some triggered by external events. Your job is to conceptualize your app in this way and then design the response to each event handler.

Event Handlers Can Ask Questions

The responses to events are not always linear recipes; they can ask questions and repeat operations. "Asking questions" means to query the data the app has stored and determine its course (branch) based on the answers. We say that such apps have *conditional branches*. Figure 14-11 illustrates just such a branch.

In the diagram, when the event occurs, the app performs operation A and then checks a condition. Function B1 is performed if the condition is true. If the condition is false, the app instead performs B2. In either case, the app continues on to perform function C.

Conditional tests are questions such as "Has the score reached 100?" or "Did the text I just received come from Joe?" Tests can also be more complex formulas including multiple relational operators (less than, greater than, equal to) and logical operators (and, or, not).

You specify conditional behaviors in App Inventor by using the `if` and `if else` blocks. For instance, the block in Figure 14-12 would report "You Win!" if the player scored 100 points.

Conditional blocks are discussed in detail in Chapter 18.

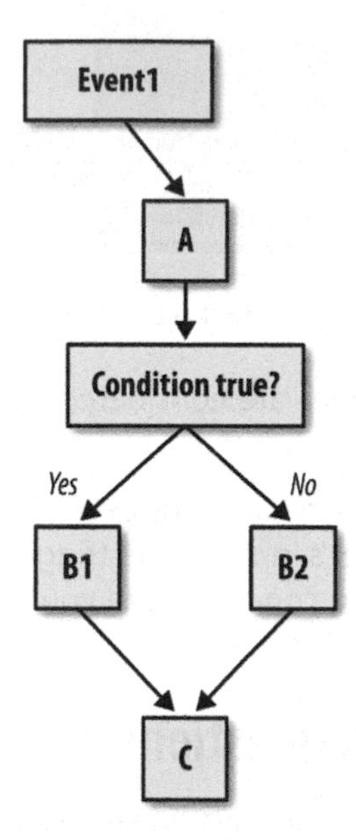

Figure 14-11. An event handler can "branch" based on the answer to a question

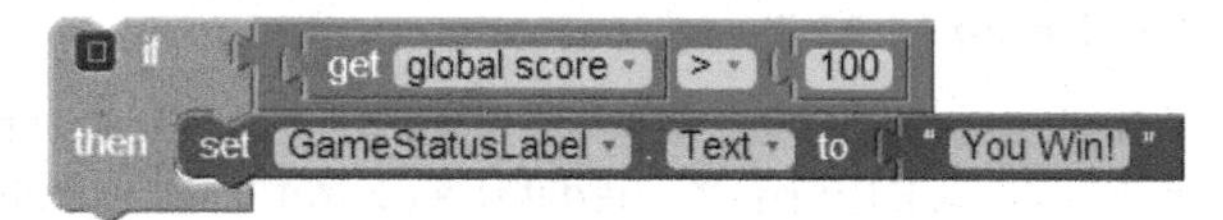

Figure 14-12. Using an if block to report a win when the player reaches 100 points

Event Handlers Can Repeat Blocks

In addition to asking questions and branching based on the answer, a response to an event can also repeat operations multiple times. App Inventor provides a number of blocks for repeating, including the `for each` and the `while do`. Both enclose other blocks. All the blocks within `for each` are performed once for each item in a list. For instance, if you wanted to text the same message to a list of phone numbers, you could use the blocks in Figure 14-13.

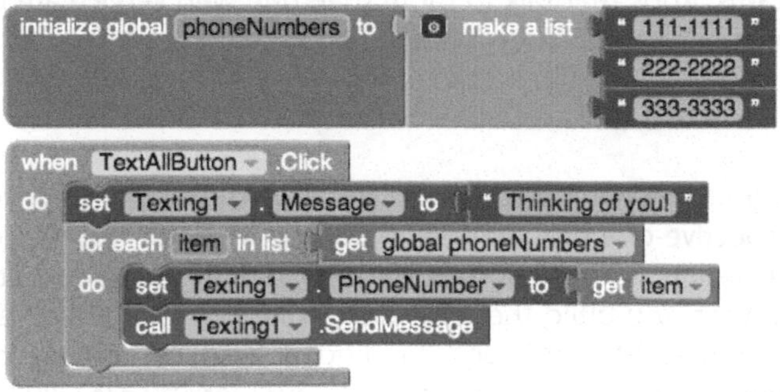

Figure 14-13. The blocks within the for each block are repeated for each item in the list PhoneNumbers

The blocks within the `for each` block are repeated—in this case, three times, because the list `PhoneNumbers` has three items. In this example, the message "Thinking of you..." is sent to all three numbers. Repeating blocks are discussed in detail in Chapter 20.

Event Handlers Can Remember Things

Because an event handler executes blocks, it often needs to keep track of information. Information can be stored in memory slots called *variables*, which you define in the Blocks Editor. Variables are like component properties, but they're not associated with any particular component. In a game app, for example, you can define a variable called *score*, and your event handlers would modify its value when the user does something accordingly. Variables store data temporarily while an app is running; when you close the app, the data is lost and no longer available.

Sometimes, your app needs to remember things not just while it runs, but when it is closed and then reopened. If you tracked a high score for the history of a game, for example, you'd need to store this data so that it is available the next time someone plays the game. Data that is retained even after an app is closed Is called *persistent data*, and it's stored in some type of a database.

We'll explore the use of both short-term memory (variables) and long-term memory (database data) in Chapter 16 and Chapter 22, respectively.

Event Handlers Can Interact with the Web

Some apps use only the information within the phone or device. But many apps communicate with the Web, either by displaying a web page within the app, or by sending requests to *web service APIs* (application programming interfaces). Such apps are said to be "web-enabled."

Twitter is an example of a web service with which an App Inventor app can talk. You can write apps that request and display your friends' previous tweets and also update your Twitter status. Apps that talk to more than one web service are called *mashups*. We'll explore web-enabled apps in Chapter 24.

Summary

An app creator must view his app both from an end-user perspective and from the inside-out perspective of a programmer. With App Inventor, you design how an app looks and you design its behavior—the set of event handlers that make an app behave as you want. You build these event handlers by assembling and configuring blocks representing events, functions, conditional branches, repeat loops, web calls, database operations, and more, and then test your work by actually running the app on your phone. After you write a few programs, the mapping between the internal structure of an app and its physical manifestation becomes clear. When that happens, you're a programmer!

CHAPTER 15

Engineering and Debugging an App

HelloPurr, MoleMash, and the other apps covered in this book's early chapters are relatively small software projects and don't really require a significant amount of software engineering. As soon as you take on a more complicated project, you'll realize that the difficulty of building software increases rapidly for each bit of complexity you add—it is not anywhere close to a linear relationship. You'll quickly learn that to build even moderately complex software, you need forethought, planning, blueprints, user and system testing, and in general, techniques and skills that are more engineering than programming. For most of us, it takes a few hard knocks before we realize this fact. At that point, you'll be ready to learn some software engineering principles and debugging techniques. If you're already at that point, or if you're one of those few people who want to learn a few techniques in the hope of avoiding some of those growing pains, this chapter is for you.

Software Engineering Principles

Here are some basic principles that we'll cover in this chapter:

- Involve your prospective users in the process as early and as often as possible.
- Build an initial, simple prototype and then add to it incrementally.
- Code and test in small increments, never more than a few blocks at a time.
- Design the logic for your app before beginning to code.
- Divide, layer, and conquer.
- Comment your blocks so that others (and you) can understand them.
- Learn to trace blocks with pencil and paper so that you understand their mechanics.

If you follow this advice, you will save yourself time and frustration and build better software. But, you probably won't follow it every time! Some of this advice might seem counterintuitive. Your natural inclination is to think of an idea, assume you know what your users want, and then start piecing together blocks until you think you've finished the app. Let's go back to the first principle and look at how to understand what your users want before you start building anything.

Solve Real Problems

In the movie *Field of Dreams*, the character Ray hears a voice whisper, "If you build it, [they] will come." Ray listens to the whisper, builds a baseball field in the middle of his Iowa corn patch, and indeed, the 1919 White Sox and thousands of fans show up.

You should know right now that the whisperer's advice does not apply to software. In fact, it's the opposite of what you should do. The history of software is littered with *great solutions for which there is no problem*. Solving a *real* problem is what makes for an amazing app and a successful and perhaps lucrative project. And to know what the problem is, you've got to talk to the people who have it. This is often referred to as *user-centered* design, and it will help you build better apps.

If you meet some programmers, ask them what percentage of the programs they have written have actually been deployed with real users. You'll be surprised at how low the percentage is, even for great programmers. Most software projects run into so many issues that they don't ever see the light of day.

User-centered design means thinking and talking to prospective users early and often. Really, this should start even before you decide what to build. Most successful software was built to solve a particular person's pain point, and then—and only then—generalized into the next big thing.

Build a Prototype and Show Users

Most prospective users won't provide useful feedback if you ask them to read a document that specifies what the app will do and give their feedback based on that. What *does* work is to show them an interactive model for the app you're going to create—a *prototype*. A prototype is an incomplete, unrefined version of the app. When you build it, don't worry about details or completeness or having a beautiful graphical interface; build it so that it does just enough to illustrate the core value of the app. Then, show it to your prospective users, be quiet, and listen.

Incremental Development

When you begin your first significantly sized app, your natural inclination might be to add all of the components and blocks you'll need in one grand effort and then download the app to your phone to see if it works. Take, for instance, a quiz app. Without guidance, most novice programmers will add blocks with a long list of the questions and answers, blocks to handle the quiz navigation, blocks to handle checking the user's answer, and blocks for every detail of the app's logic, all before testing to see if any of it works. In software engineering, this is called the *Big Bang approach*.

Just about every new programmer uses this approach. In my (author Wolber) classes at the University of San Francisco, I will often ask a student, "How's it going?" as the student is working on an app.

"I think I'm done," the student will reply.

"Splendid. Can I see it?"

"Ummm, not yet; I don't have my phone with me."

"So you haven't run the app at all?" I ask.

"No."

I'll look over the student's shoulder at an amazing, colorful configuration of 30 or so blocks, none of them tested. The problem is that when you test all at once, it is much more difficult to diagnose the bugs, and there will be bugs—big hairy ones!

Probably the best advice I can give my students—and aspiring programmers everywhere—is this:

> *Code a little, test a little, repeat.*

Build your app one piece at a time, testing as you go. You'll find bugs, alright, but tiny ones that you can easily swat away. And the process will become surprisingly satisfying, because you'll see results sooner when you follow it.

Hundreds of books and theses have been written on incremental software development. If you're interested in the process of building software (and other things), check out the *agile development* methodology.[1]

Design Before Coding

There are two parts to programming: understanding the logic of the app, and then translating that logic into code in some programming language. Before you tackle the translation, spend some time on the logic. Specify what should happen both for the user and internally in the app. Nail down the logic of each event handler before moving on to translating that logic into blocks.

Entire books have been written on various program design methodologies. Some people use diagrams such as flowcharts or structure charts for design, whereas others prefer handwritten text and sketches. Some people believe that all "design" should end up directly alongside your code as annotation (comments), not in a separate document. The key for beginners is to understand that there is a logic to all programs that has nothing to do with a particular programming language. Simultaneously tackling both that logic and its translation into a language, no matter how intuitive the language, can be overwhelming. So, throughout the process, get away from the

1 Beck, Kent; et al. (2001). "Manifesto for Agile Software Development". Agile Alliance, Retrieved June 5, 2014

computer and think about your app, be sure that you're clear on what you want it to do, and document what you come up with in some way. Then, be sure to hook that design documentation to your app so that others can benefit from it.

Comment Your Code

If you've completed a few of the tutorials in this book, you've probably seen the small yellow boxes within the blocks (see Figure 15-1). These are called *comments*. In App Inventor, you can add comments to any block by right-clicking it and choosing Add Comment. Comments are just annotations; they don't affect the app's execution at all.

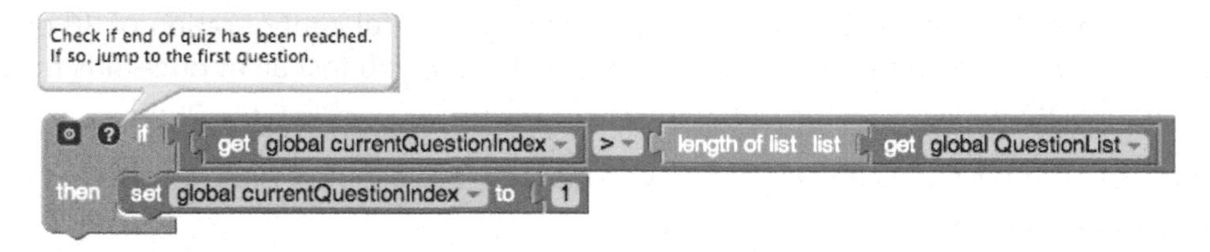

Figure 15-1. Using a comment on the if block to describe what it does in plain English

Why comment, then? Well, if your app is successful, it will live a long life. Even after spending only a week away from your app, you will forget what you were thinking at the time and not have a clue what some of the blocks are for. For this reason, even if nobody else will ever see your blocks, you should provide comments for them.

And if your app is successful, it will undoubtedly pass through many hands. People will want to understand it, customize it, and extend it. As soon as you encounter the wonderful experience of starting a project with someone's uncommented code, you'll understand completely why comments are essential.

Annotating a program is not intuitive, and I've never met a novice programmer who thought it was important. Conversely, I've also never met an experienced programmer who didn't do it.

Divide, Layer, and Conquer

Problems become overwhelming when they're too big. The key is to break a problem down. There are two main ways to do this. The one we're most familiar with is to break a problem down into parts (A, B, C) and tackle each one individually. A second, less common way is to break a problem into layers from simple to complex. Add a few blocks for some simple behavior, test the software to verify that it behaves as you want, and then add another layer of complexity, and so on.

Using the President's Quiz app in Chapter 10 as an example, let's evaluate these two methods. Recall that the President's Quiz app lets the user navigate through the questions by clicking a Next button. It also checks the user's answers to determine if she's correct. So, in designing this app, you might break it into two parts—question navigation and answer checking, and program each separately.

However, within each of those two parts, you could also break down the process from simple to complex. So, for question navigation, start by creating the code to display only the first question in the list of questions, and test it to ensure that it works. Then, build the code for getting to the next question, but ignore the issue of what happens when you get to the last question. After you've confirmed that the quiz will take you to the end, add the blocks to handle the "special case" of the user reaching the last question.

It's not an either/or case of whether you should break a problem down into parts or into layers of complexity: you should do both. Those who can do this well—software architects—are in extremely high demand.

Understand Your Language: Tracking with Pen and Paper

When an app is in action, it is only partially visible. The end user of an app sees only its outward face, the images and data that are displayed in the user interface. The inner workings of software are hidden to the outside world, just like the internal mechanisms of the human brain (thankfully!). As an app executes, we don't see the instructions (blocks), we don't see the program counter that tracks which instruction is currently being executed, and we don't see the software's internal memory cells (its variables and properties). In the end, this is how we want it: the end user should see only what the program explicitly displays. However, while you are developing and testing software, you want to see *everything* that is happening.

You, the programmer, see the code during development, but only a static view of it. Thus, you must *imagine* the software in action: events occurring, the program counter moving to and executing the next block, the values in the memory cells changing, and so on.

Programming requires a shift between two different views. You begin with the static model—the code blocks—and try to envision how the program will actually behave. When you are ready, you shift to testing mode: playing the role of the end user and testing the software to see if it behaves as you expect. If it does not, you must shift back to the static view, tweak your model, and test again. Through this back and forth process, you move toward an acceptable solution.

When you begin programming, you have only a partial model of how a computer program works—the entire process seems almost magical. You begin with some simple apps: clicking a button causes a cat to meow! You then move on to more complex apps, step through some tutorials, and maybe make a few changes to customize them. The beginner partially understands the inner workings of the apps, but certainly does not feel in control of the process. The beginner will often say, "*It's* not working," or, "*It's* not doing what it's supposed to do." The key is to learn how things work to the point that you think more subjectively about the program and say things such as, "*My* program is doing this," and, "*My* logic is causing the program to...."

One way to learn how programs work is to trace the execution of some simple app, representing on *paper* exactly what happens inside the device when each block is performed. Envision the user triggering some event handler and then step through and show the effect of each block: how do the variables and properties in the app change? How do the components in the user interface change? Like a close reading in a literature class, this step-by-step *tracing* forces you to examine the elements of the language—in this case, App Inventor blocks.

The complexity of the sample you trace is almost immaterial; the key is that you slow down your thought process and examine the cause and effect of each block. You'll gradually begin to understand that the rules governing the entire process are not as overwhelming as you originally thought.

For example, consider the blocks depicted in Figure 15-2, which are slight alterations of those from the President's Quiz app (Chapter 8).

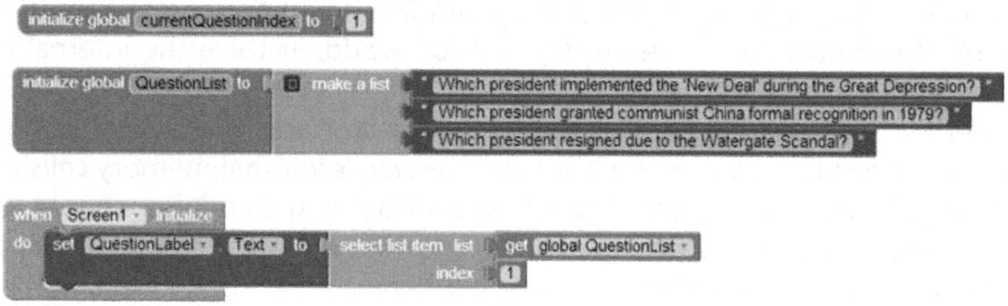

Figure 15-2. Setting the Text in QuestionLabel to the first item in QuestionList when the app begins

Do you understand this code? Can you trace it and show exactly what happens in each step?

You start tracing by first drawing memory cell boxes for all pertinent variables and properties. In this case, you need boxes for the `currentQuestionIndex` and the `QuestionLabel.Text`, as shown in Table 15-1.

Table 15-1. Memory cell boxes for tracing

QuestionLabel.Text	currentQuestionIndex

Next, think about what happens when an app begins—not from a user's perspective, but internally, within the app when it initializes. If you've completed some of the tutorials, you probably know this, but perhaps you haven't thought about it in mechanical terms. When an app begins:

1. All the component properties are set based on their initial values in the Component Designer.
2. All variable definitions and initializations are performed.
3. The blocks in the `Screen.Initialize` event handler are performed.

Tracing a program helps you understand these mechanics. So, what should go in the boxes after the initialization phase?

As shown in Table 15-2, the 1 is in `currentQuestionIndex` because the variable definition is executed when the app begins, and it initializes it to 1. The first question is in `QuestionLabel.Text` because `Screen.Initialize` selects the first item from `QuestionList` and puts it there.

Table 15-2. The values after the President's Quiz app initializes

QuestionLabel.Text	currentQuestionIndex
Which president implemented the "New Deal" during the Great Depression?	1

Next, trace what happens when the user clicks the Next button, using the blocks shown in Figure 15-3.

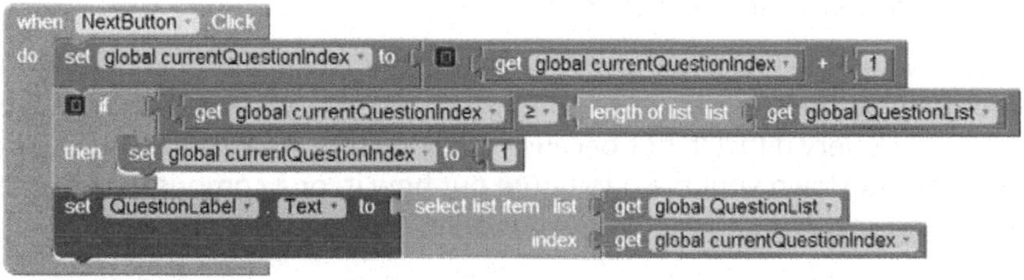

Figure 15-3. This block is executed when the user clicks NextButton

Examine each block, one by one. First, the `currentQuestionIndex` is incremented. At an even more detailed level, the current value of the variable (1) is added to 1, and the result (2) is placed in `currentQuestionIndex`. The `if` statement is false because the value of `currentQuestionIndex` (2) is less than the length of `QuestionList` (3). Therefore, the second item is selected and put into `QuestionLabel.Text`, as illustrated in Table 15-3.

Table 15-3. The values after NextButton is clicked

QuestionLabel.Text	currentQuestionIndex
Which president granted communist China formal recognition in 1979?	2

Trace what happens on the second click. Now, `currentQuestionIndex` is incremented and becomes 3. What happens with the `if`? Before reading ahead, examine it very closely and see if you can trace it correctly.

On the `if` test, the value of `currentQuestionIndex` (3) is indeed greater than or equal to the length of `QuestionList`. Consequently, the `currentQuestionIndex` is set to 1 and the first question is placed into the label, as shown in Table 15-4.

Table 15-4. The values after NextButton is clicked a second time

QuestionLabel.Text	currentQuestionIndex
Which president implemented the "New Deal" during the Great Depression?	1

The trace has uncovered a bug: the last question in the list never appears! Do you know how to fix it?

When you can trace an app to this level of detail, you become a programmer, an engineer. You begin to understand the mechanics of the programming language, absorbing sentences and words in the code instead of vaguely grasping paragraphs. Yes, the programming language is complex, but each "word" has a definite and straightforward interpretation by the machine. If you understand how each block maps to some variable or property changing, you can figure out how to write or fix your app. You realize that *you* are in complete control.

Now, if you were to tell your friends, "I'm learning how to let a user click a Next button to get to the next question; it's really tough," they'd think you were crazy. In fact, such programming *is* very difficult, not because the concepts are so complex, but because you have to slow down your brain to figure out how it, or a computer, processes each and every step, including those things your brain does subconsciously.

Debugging an App

Tracing an app step by step, on paper, is one way to understand programming; it's also a time-tested method of debugging an app when it has problems.

Programming environments, including App Inventor, also provide the high-tech version of pen-and-paper tracing through debugging tools that automate some of the process. Such tools improve the app development process by providing an illuminated view of an app *in action*. These tools allow the programmer to do the following:

- Pause an app at any point and examine its variables and properties
- Perform individual instructions (blocks) to examine their effects

Watching Variables

The values of component properties and variables are not visible when you test an app in App Inventor. One common debugging technique is to add blocks to display these values in labels of the user interface during testing, then remove the labels and display code after the app is debugged.

The earlier version of App Inventor (App Inventor Classic) had a mechanism for watching variable and property values in the Blocks Editor while testing, without using labels in the user interface. The plan is for such a mechanism to be added to App Inventor 2 as well, so keep a lookout for it because it's very helpful in debugging and understanding code.

Testing Individual Blocks

While you can use the Watch mechanism to examine variables during an app's execution, another tool called Do It makes it possible for you to try out individual blocks *outside* the ordinary execution sequence. Right-click any block and choose Do It; the block will be performed. If the block is an expression that returns a value, App Inventor will show that value in a box above the block.

Do It is very useful for debugging logic problems in your blocks. Consider the quiz's `NextButton.Click` event handler again, and suppose that it has a logic problem in which you don't navigate through all the questions. You could test the program by clicking Next in the user interface and checking to see if the appropriate question appears each time. You might even watch the `currentQuestionIndex` to see how each click changes it.

Unfortunately, this type of testing only allows you to examine the effect of entire event handlers. The app will perform all the blocks in the event handler for the button click before allowing you to examine your Watch variables or the user interface.

With the Do It tool, you can slow down the testing process and examine the state of the app after any block. The general scheme is to initiate user interface events until you get to the problem point in the app. After discovering that the third question wasn't appearing in the quiz app, you might click the `NextButton` once to get to the second question. Then, instead of clicking the `NextButton` again and having the entire event handler performed in one swoop, you could use Do It to perform the blocks within the `NextButton.Click` event handler, one at a time. You'd start by right-clicking the top row of blocks (the increment of `currentQuestionIndex`) and choosing Do It, as illustrated in Figure 15-4.

This would change the index to 3. App execution would then stop—Do It causes only the chosen block and any subordinate blocks to be performed. This affords you, the tester, the ability to examine the watched variables and the user interface. When you're ready, you can choose the next row of blocks (the `if` test) and select Do It so that it's performed. At every step of the way, you can see the effect of each block.

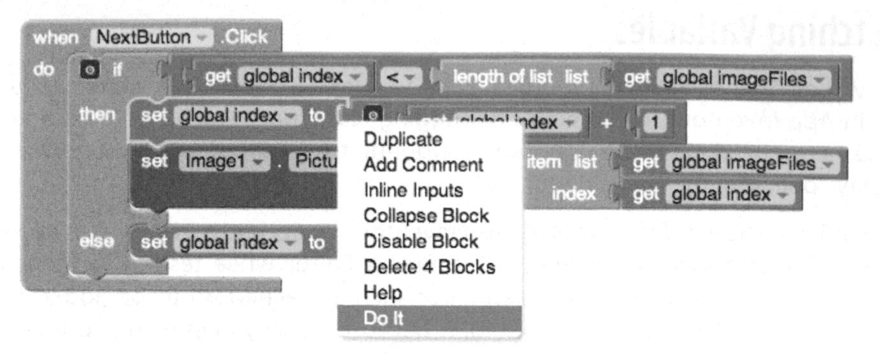

Figure 15-4. Using the Do It tool to execute the blocks one at a time

Incremental Development with Do It

It 's important to note that performing individual blocks is not just for debugging. You can also use it during development to test blocks as you go. For instance, if you were creating a long formula to compute the distance in miles between two GPS coordinates, you might test the formula at each step to verify that the blocks make sense.

Disabling Blocks

Another way to help you debug and test your app incrementally is to disable blocks. By doing this, you can leave problematic or untested blocks in an app but direct the system to ignore them temporarily as the app runs. You can then test the active blocks and get them to work fully without worrying about the problematic ones. You can disable any block by right-clicking it and choosing Disable Block. The block will be grayed out, and when you run the app, it will be ignored. When you're ready, you can activate the block by right-clicking it again and choosing Enable Block.

Summary

The great thing about App Inventor is how easy it is. Its visual nature gets you started building an app right away, and you don't have to worry about a lot of low-level details. But, the reality is that App Inventor can't figure out what your app should do for you, much less exactly *how* to do it. Even though it's tempting to just jump right into the Designer and Blocks Editor and start building an app, it's important to spend some time thinking about and planning in detail exactly what your app will do. It sounds a bit painful, but if you listen to your users, prototype, test, and trace the logic of your app, you'll be building better apps in no time.

CHAPTER 16

Programming Your App's Memory

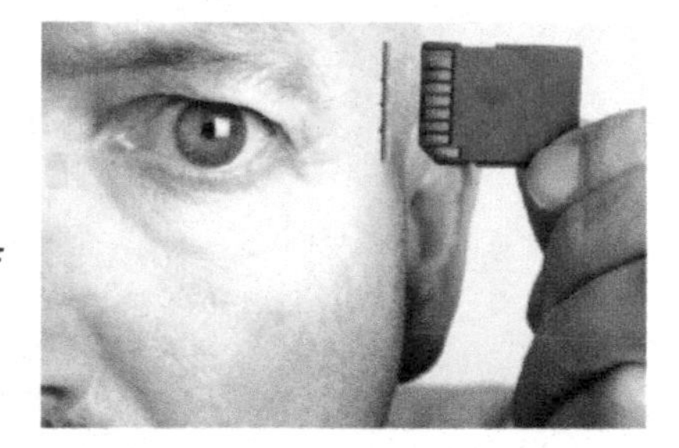

Just as people need to remember things, so do apps. This chapter examines how you can program an app to remember information.

When someone tells you the phone number of a pizza place, your brain stores it in a memory slot. If someone calls out some numbers for you to add, you store the numbers and intermediate results in memory slots. In such cases, you are not fully conscious of how your brain stores information or recalls it.

An app has a memory, as well, but its inner workings are far less mysterious than those of your brain. In this chapter, you'll learn how to set up an app's memory, how to store information in it, and how to retrieve that information at a later time.

Named Memory Slots

An app's memory consists of a set of *named memory slots*. Some of these memory slots are created when you drag a component into your app; these slots are called *properties*. You can also define named memory slots that are not associated with a particular component; these are called *variables*. Whereas properties are typically associated with what is visible in an app, variables can be thought of as the app's hidden "scratch" memory.

Properties

The user of an app can see visible components such as buttons, textboxes, and labels. Internally, however, each component is completely defined by a set of properties. The values stored in the memory slots of each property determine how the component appears.

You set the values of properties directly in the Component Designer. For instance, Figure 16-1 shows the panel for modifying the properties of a `Canvas` component.

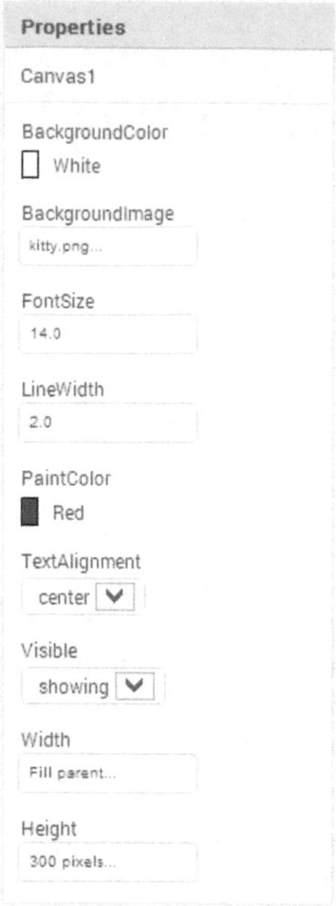

Figure 16-1. You can set component properties in the Designer; you are setting the initial values of the properties (they don't show the current values as an app runs)

The `Canvas` component has numerous properties of various types. For instance, the `BackgroundColor` and `PaintColor` are memory slots that hold a color. The `Background Image` holds a filename *(kitty.png)*. The `Visible` property holds a *Boolean* value (true or false, depending on whether the box is checked). The `Width` and `Height` slots hold a number or a special designation (e.g., "Fill parent").

When you set a property in the Component Designer, you are specifying the initial value of the property—its value when the app first begins. Property values also can be changed as the app runs, with blocks. Yet, the values shown in the Component Designer, such as those in Figure 16-1, don't change; these always show only the initial values. This can be confusing when you test an app—the current value of the app's properties are not visible.

Defining Variables

Like properties, variables are named memory slots, but they are not associated with a particular component. You define a variable when your app needs to remember something that is not being stored within a component property. For example, a game app might need to remember what level the user has attained. If the level number were going to appear in a `Label` component, you might not need a variable, because you could just store the level in the `Text` property of the `Label` component. But if the level number is not something the user will see, you'd define a variable in which to store it.

The Presidents Quiz (Chapter 8) is another example of an app that needs a variable. In that app, only one question of the quiz should appear at a time in the user interface, yet the quiz has many questions (most of which are kept hidden from the user at anytime). Thus, you need to define a variable to store the list of questions.

Whereas properties are created automatically when you drag a component into the Designer, variables are defined explicitly in the Blocks Editor by dragging out an `initialize global` block. You can name the variable by clicking the text "name" within the block, and you can specify an initial value for it by dragging out a `number`, `text`, `color`, or `make a list` block and plugging it in. Here are the steps you'd follow to create a variable called `score` with an initial value of 0:

1. In Built-in blocks, open the Variables drawer and drag out the `initialize global` block.

   initialize global name to

2. Change the name of the variable by clicking the text "name" and typing "score".

   initialize global score to

3. From the Math drawer, drag out a number block and plug it into the open socket of the variable definition to set the initial value.

   initialize global score to 0

When you define a variable, you instruct the app to set up a named memory slot for storing a value. These memory slots, as with properties, are not visible to the user when the app runs.

The number block you plug in specifies the value that should be placed in the slot when the app begins. Besides initializing with numbers or text, you can also initialize the variable with a `make a list` or `create empty list` block. This informs the app that the variable will store a list of memory slots instead of a single value. To learn more about lists, see Chapter 19.

Setting and Getting a Variable

When you define a variable, App Inventor creates two blocks for it: `set` and `get`. You can access these blocks by hovering over the variable name in the initialization block, as shown in Figure 16-2.

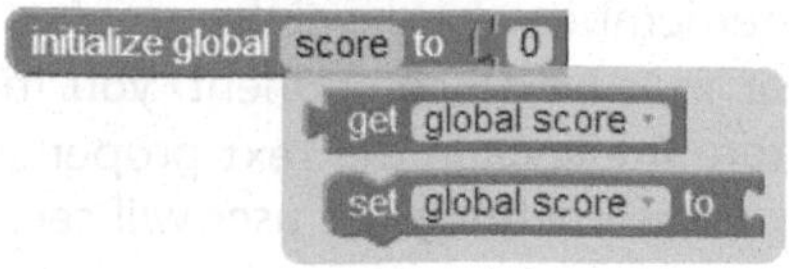

Figure 16-2. The initialization block contains set and get blocks for that variable

The `set global to` block lets you modify the value stored in the variable. For instance, the number block in Figure 16-3 places the value 5 in the variable `score`. The term "global" in the `set global score to` block refers to the fact that the variable can be used in all of the program's event handlers and procedures. With the newest version of App Inventor, you can also define variables that are "local" to a particular procedure or event handler—that is, local variables can be used only by the procedure or event with which they're associated (more on this a little later in the chapter).

Figure 16-3. Placing a number 5 into the variable score

You use the block labeled `get global score` to retrieve the value of a variable. For instance, if you wanted to check if the value inside the memory slot was greater than 100, you'd plug the `get global score` block into an `if` test, as demonstrated in Figure 16-4.

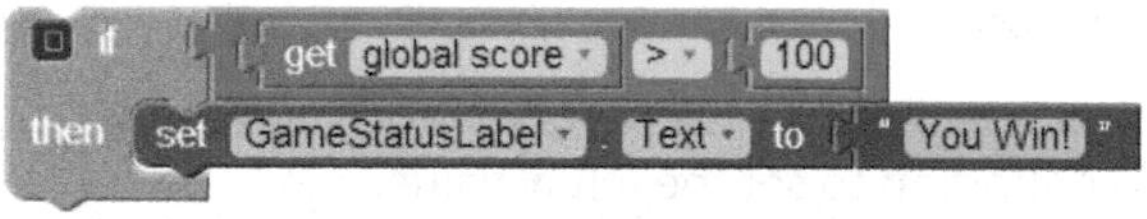

Figure 16-4. Using the global score block to get the value stored in the variable

Setting a Variable to an Expression

As you've seen, you can put simple values such as 5 into a variable, but often you'll set the variable to a more complex *expression* (expression is the computer-science term for a formula). For example, when the user clicks Next to get to the next question in a quiz app, you'll need to set the `currentQuestion` variable to *one more than its current value*. When someone loses ten points in a game app, you need to modify the `score` variable to *10 less than its current value*. In a game like MoleMash (Chapter 3), you change the horizontal *(x)* location of the mole to *a random position within a canvas*. You'll build such expressions with a set of blocks that plug into a `set global to` block.

Incrementing a Variable

Perhaps the most common expression is for *incrementing* a variable, or setting a variable based on its own current value. For instance, in a game, when a player scores a point, the variable score can be incremented by 5. Figure 16-5 shows the blocks to implement this behavior.

Figure 16-5. Incrementing the variable score by 5

If you can understand these kinds of blocks, you're well on your way to becoming a programmer. You read these blocks as "set the score to five more than it already is," which is another way to say *increment* your variable. The way it works is that the blocks are interpreted inside out, not left to right. Thus, the innermost blocks—the `get global score` and the `number 5` block—are evaluated first. Then, the + block is performed and the result is "set" into the variable `score`.

Suppose that there were a 10 in the memory slot for `score` before these blocks; the app would perform the following steps:

1. Retrieve the 10 from `score`'s memory slot (evaluate the `get` block).
2. Add 5 to it to get 15.
3. Place the result, 15, into `score`'s memory slot (performing the `set`).

Building Complex Expressions

In the Math drawer, App Inventor provides a wide range of mathematical functions similar to those you'd find in a spreadsheet or calculator. There are arithmetic operators (e.g., +,–,*,/), blocks for generating random values, and operators such as sqrt, cosine, and sine.

You can use these blocks to build a complex expression and then plug them in as the *righthand-side expression* of a `set global to` block. For example, to move an image sprite to a random column within the bounds of a canvas, you'd configure an expression consisting of a multiply (*) block, a subtract (–) block, a `Canvas1.Width` property, an `ImageSprite1.Width` property, and a `random fraction` block, as illustrated in Figure 16-6.

Figure 16-6. You can use Math blocks to build complex expressions like this one

As with the increment example in the previous section, the blocks are interpreted by the app in an inside-out fashion. Suppose that the `Canvas` has a `Width` of 300 and the `ImageSprite` has a `Width` of 50, the app would perform the following steps:

1. Retrieve the 300 and the 50 from the memory slots for `Canvas1.Width` and `Image Sprite.Width`, respectively.

2. Subtract: 300 – 50 = 250.
3. Call the random fraction function to get a number between 0 and 1 (say, .5).
4. Multiply: 250 * .5 = 125.
5. Place the 125 into the memory slot for the `ImageSprite1.X` property.

Displaying Variables

When you modify a component property, as in the preceding example, the user interface is directly affected. This is not true for variables; changing a variable has no direct effect on the app's appearance. If you just incremented a variable score but didn't modify the user interface in some other way, the user would never know there was a change. It's like the proverbial tree falling in the forest: if nobody was there to hear it, did it really happen?

Sometimes, you do not want to immediately manifest a change to the user interface when a variable changes. For instance, in a game you might track statistics (e.g., missed shots) that will only appear when the game ends.

This is one of the advantages of storing data in a variable as opposed to a component property: you can show just the data you want when you want to show it. You can also separate the computational part of your app from the user interface, making it easier to change that user interface later.

For example, with a game, you could store the score directly in a `Label` or in a variable. If you store it in a `Label`, you'd increment the `Label`'s `Text` property when points were scored, and the user would see the change directly. If you stored the score in a variable and incremented the variable when points were scored, you'd need to include blocks to also move the value of the variable into a label.

However, if you decided to change the app to display the score in a different manner, perhaps with a slider, the variable solution would be easier to change. You wouldn't need to modify all the places that change the score; you'd only need to modify the blocks that display the score.

Local Variables

The variables described in this chapter thus far are *global* variables and you define them with an `initialize global to` block. The "global" refers to the fact that the variable can be used in all event handlers and procedures. Such variables are said to have global *scope*.

With the latest version of App Inventor, you can now also define `local` variables, that is, variables whose use (scope) is restricted to a single event handler or procedure (see Figure 16-7).

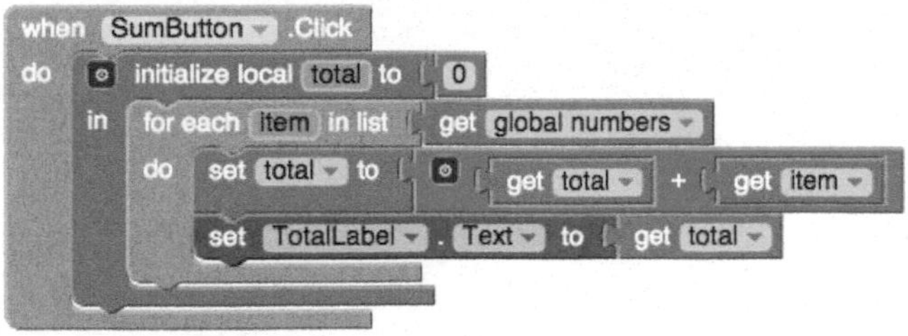

Figure 16-7. The variable "total" is local; it can only be used in the SumButton.Click event

If the variable is only needed in one place, it is a good idea to define it as a local, as the variable "total" is in Figure 16-7. By doing so, you limit the dependencies in your app and ensure that you won't mistakenly modify a variable. Think of a local variable like the private memory in your brain—you certainly don't want other brains to have access to it!

Summary

When an app is launched, it begins executing its operations and responding to events that occur. When responding to events, the app sometimes needs to remember things. For a game, this might be each player's score or the direction in which an object is moving.

Your app remembers things within component properties, but when you need additional memory slots not associated with a component, you can define variables. You can store values into a variable and retrieve the current value, just like you do with properties.

As with property values, variable values are not visible to the end user. If you want the end user to see the information stored in a variable, you add blocks that display that information in a label or another user interface component.

CHAPTER 17

Creating Animated Apps

This chapter discusses methods for creating apps with simple animations (objects that move). You'll learn the basics of creating two-dimensional games with App Inventor and become comfortable with image sprites and handling events such as two objects colliding.

When you see an object moving smoothly along the computer screen, what you're really seeing is a quick succession of images with the object in a slightly different place each time. It's an illusion not much different from flipbooks, in which you see a moving picture by flipping quickly through the pages. It's the concept behind how animated films are made!

With App Inventor, you'll program animation by placing `Ball` and `ImageSprite` components within a `Canvas` component and then moving and transforming those objects every successive fraction of a second. In this chapter, you'll learn how the `Canvas` coordinate system works, how you can use the `Clock.Timer` event to trigger movement, how to control the speed of objects, and how to respond to events such as two objects crashing into each other.

Adding a Canvas Component to Your App

From the Drawing and Animation palette, drag a `Canvas` component into your app. After you place it, specify its `Width` and `Height`. Often, you'll want the `Canvas` to span the width of the device screen. To do this, choose "Fill parent" when specifying the `Width`.

You can do the same for the `Height`, but generally you'll set this to some number (e.g., 300 pixels) to leave room for other components above and below the `Canvas`.

The Canvas Coordinate System

A drawing on a `Canvas` is really a grid of *pixels*, where a pixel is the tiniest possible dot of color that can appear on the screen. Each pixel's location is defined by x-y coordinates on a grid system, as illustrated in Figure 17-1. In this coordinate system, x defines a location on the horizontal plane (starting at 0 on the far left and increasing as you move to the right across the screen), and y defines a location on the vertical plane (starting at 0 at the top and increasing as you move down the screen).

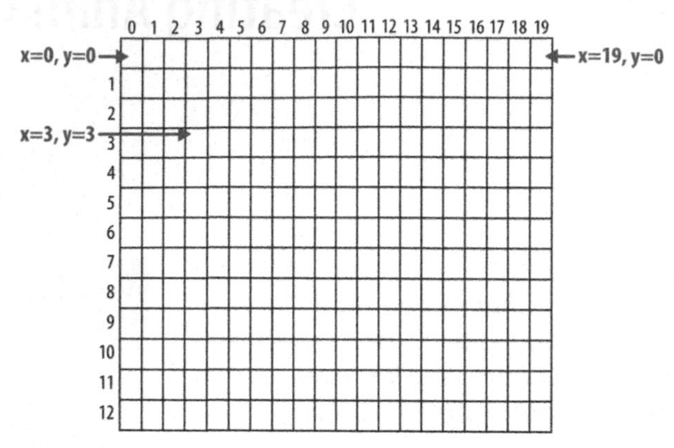

Figure 17-1. The Canvas coordinate system

The top-left cell in a `Canvas` starts with 0 for both coordinates, so this position is represented as (x=0,y=0). As you move right, the x coordinate increases; as you move down, the y coordinate increases. The cell to the immediate right of the top-left corner is (x=1,y=0). The upper-right corner has an x coordinate equal to the width of the `Canvas` minus 1. Most phone screens have a width around 300 pixels, but for the sample shown here, the `Width` is 20, so the upper-right corner is the coordinate (x=19,y=0).

You can change the appearance of the canvas in two ways: by painting on it, or by placing and moving objects within it. This chapter focuses primarily on the latter, but let's first discuss how you "paint" and how to create animation by painting (this is also the topic of the PaintPot app in Chapter 2).

Each cell of the `Canvas` holds a pixel defining the color that should appear there. The `Canvas` component provides the `Canvas.DrawLine` and `Canvas.DrawCircle` blocks for painting pixels. You first set the `Canvas.PaintColor` property to the color you want and then call one of the Draw blocks to draw in that color. With `DrawCircle`, you can paint circles of any radius, but if you set the radius to 1, as shown in Figure 17-2, you'll paint an individual pixel.

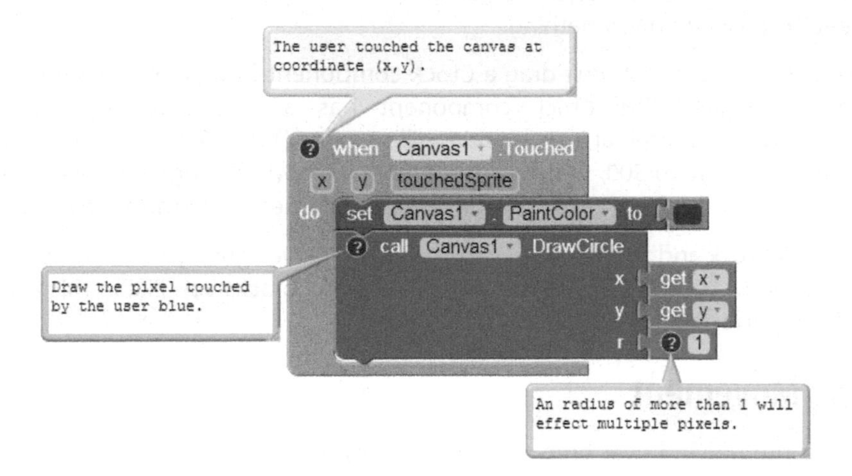

Figure 17-2. DrawCircle with a radius of 1 paints an individual pixel with each touch

App Inventor provides a palette of basic colors that you can use to paint pixels (or other user interface components). You can access a wider range of colors by using the color numbering scheme explained in the App Inventor documentation at *http://appinventor.mit.edu/explore/ai2/support/blocks/colors.html*.

Besides painting individual pixels, you can also place `Ball` and `ImageSprite` components on a `Canvas`. A *sprite* is a graphical object placed within a larger scene (in App Inventor, the "scene" is a `Canvas` component). Both the `Ball` and `ImageSprite` components are sprites; they are different only in appearance. A `Ball` is a circle that has an appearance that can only be modified by changing its color or radius, whereas an `ImageSprite` can take on any appearance, as defined by an image file. `Balls` and `ImageSprites` can only be added within a `Canvas`; you can't drag them into the user interface outside of one.

Animating Objects with Timer Events

One way to specify animation in App Inventor is to change an object in response to a timer event. Most commonly, you'll move sprites to different locations on the canvas at set time intervals. Using timer events is the most common method of defining those set time intervals. Later, we'll also discuss an alternative method of programming animation using the `Speed` and `Heading` properties of the `ImageSprite` and `Ball` components.

Button clicks and other user-initiated events are simple to understand: the user does something, and the app responds by performing some operations. Timer events are different, though, because they aren't triggered by the end user but instead by the passing of time. You need to conceptualize the phone's clock triggering events in the app instead of a user doing something.

To define a timer event, you first drag a `Clock` component into your app within the Component Designer. The `Clock` component has a `TimerInterval` property associated with it. The interval is defined in milliseconds (1/1,000 of a second). If you set the `TimerInterval` to 500, that means a timer event will be triggered every half-second. The smaller the `TimerInterval`, the faster the frame-rate of the animation.

After adding a `Clock` and setting a `TimerInterval` in the Designer, you can drag out a `Clock.Timer` event in the Blocks Editor. You can put any blocks you like in this event, and they'll be performed every interval.

Creating Movement

To show a sprite moving over time, you'll use the `MoveTo` function found in both the `ImageSprite` and `Ball` components. For example, to move a ball horizontally across the screen, you'd use blocks like those in Figure 17-3.

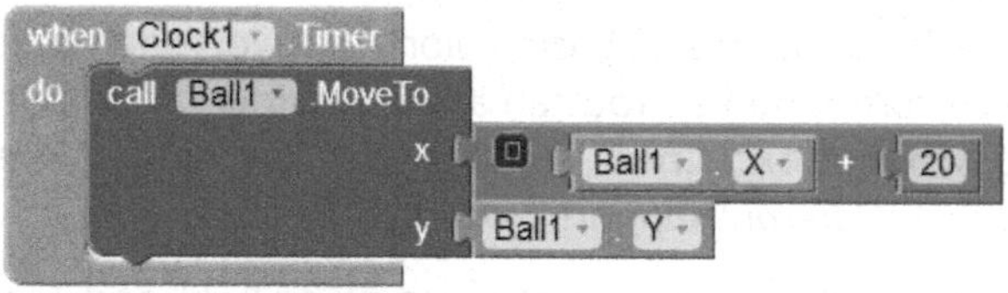

Figure 17-3. Moving the ball horizontally across the screen

`MoveTo` moves an object to an *absolute* location on the canvas, not a relative amount. So, to move an object some amount, you set the `MoveTo` arguments to the object's current location plus an offset. Because we're moving horizontally, the x argument is set to the current x location (`Ball1.X`) plus the offset 20, whereas the y argument is set to stay at its current setting (`Ball1.Y`).

To move an object down, you'd modify just the `Ball1.Y` coordinate and leave `Ball1.X` the same. If you wanted to move the ball diagonally, you'd add an offset to both the x and y coordinates, as shown in Figure 17-4.

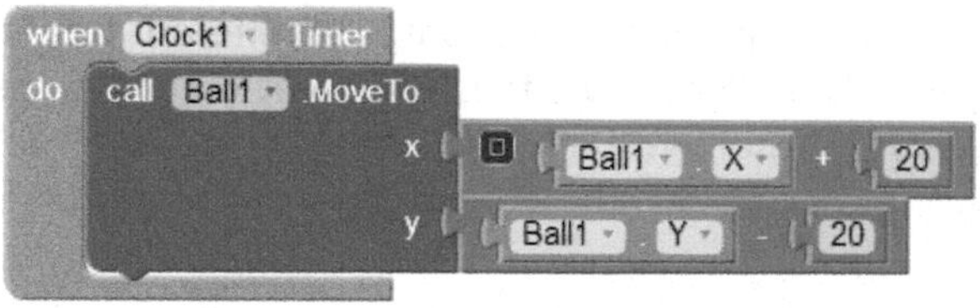

Figure 17-4. Offsetting both the x and y coordinates to move the ball diagonally

Speed

How fast is the ball moving in the preceding example? The speed depends on both the settings you provide for the `TimerInterval` property of `Clock1` and the parameters you specify in the `MoveTo` function. If the `Clock.TimerInterval` is set to 1,000 milliseconds, this means that a `Clock1.Timer` event will be triggered every second. For the horizontal example shown in Figure 17-3, the ball will move 20 pixels per second.

But a `TimerInterval` of 1,000 milliseconds doesn't provide very smooth animation; the ball will only move once per second, which will appear jerky. To achieve smoother movement, you need a shorter interval. If the `TimerInterval` were instead set to 100 milliseconds, the ball would move 20 pixels every tenth of a second, or 200 pixels per second—a rate that will appear much smoother.

Collision Detection

To create games and other animated apps, you need more complex functionality than just movement. Fortunately, App Inventor provides some high-level blocks for dealing with animation events such as an object reaching the screen's edge or two objects colliding.

In this context, *high-level block* means that App Inventor takes care of the *lower-level* details of determining when an event such as a collision occurs. You could check for these occurrences manually by checking sprite and canvas properties within `Clock.Timer` events. This level of programming requires some fairly complex logic, however. Fortunately, App Inventor provides them for you, and it's a good thing that it does because these events are common to many games and other apps.

EdgeReached

Consider again the animation in Figure 17-4, in which the object is moving diagonally from the upper left to the lower right of the canvas. As programmed, the ball would move diagonally and then stop when it reached the right or bottom edge of the canvas (the system won't move an object past the canvas boundaries).

If you instead wanted the object to reappear at the upper-left corner each time it reached the bottom or right edge, you could define a response to the `Ball.EdgeReached` event similar to that shown in Figure 17-5.

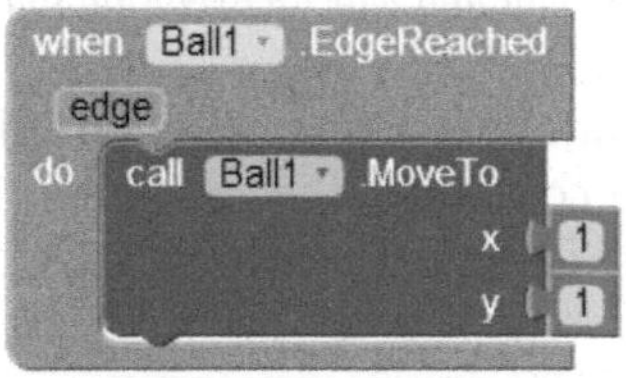

```
when Ball1 .EdgeReached
  edge
do  call Ball1 .MoveTo
              x  1
              y  1
```

Figure 17-5. Making the ball reappear in the upper-left corner when it reaches an edge

EdgeReached is triggered when a ball or image sprite hits any edge of a canvas. This event handler, combined with the diagonal movement specified with the previously described timer event (Figure 17-4), causes the ball to move diagonally from upper left to lower right, pop back up to the upper left when it reaches an edge, and then do it all over again, forever (or until the app tells it otherwise).

For this example, we didn't distinguish between which edge was hit. The EdgeReached event does have a parameter, edge, which specifies the particular edge by using the following code:

- North = 1
- Northeast = 2
- East = 3
- Southeast = 4
- South = –1
- Southwest = –2
- West = –3
- Northwest = –4

CollidingWith and NoLongerCollidingWith

Games and other animated apps often rely on activity occurring when two or more objects collide (e.g., a bat hitting a ball).

Consider a game, for instance, in which an object changes colors and plays an explosion sound when it hits another object. Figure 17-6 shows the blocks for such an event handler.

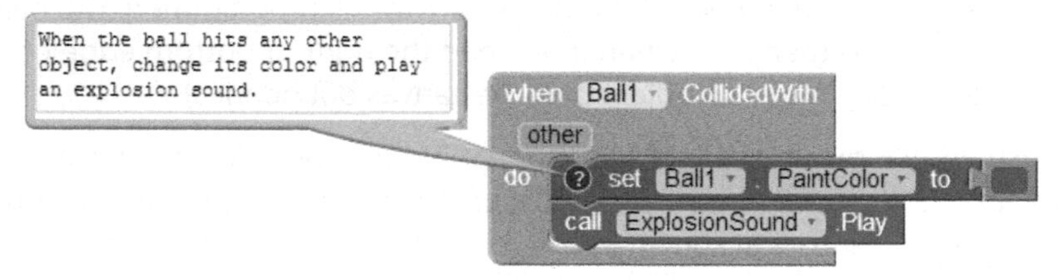

Figure 17-6. Making the ball change color and play an explosion sound when it hits another object

NoLongerCollidingWith provides the opposite event of CollidedWith. It is triggered only when two objects have come together and then separated. So, for your game, you might include the blocks depicted in Figure 17-7.

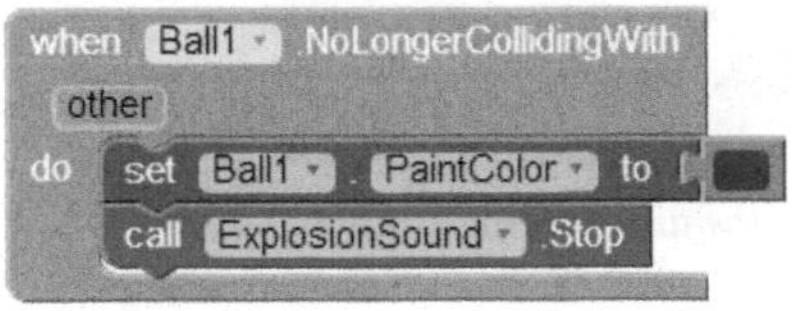

Figure 17-7. Changing the color back and stopping the explosion noise when the objects separate

Note that both `CollidedWith` and `NoLongerCollidingWith` have an argument, `other`, which specifies the particular object with which you collided (or from which you separated). This allows you to perform operations only when the object (e.g., `Ball1`) interacts with a particular other object, as shown in Figure 17-8.

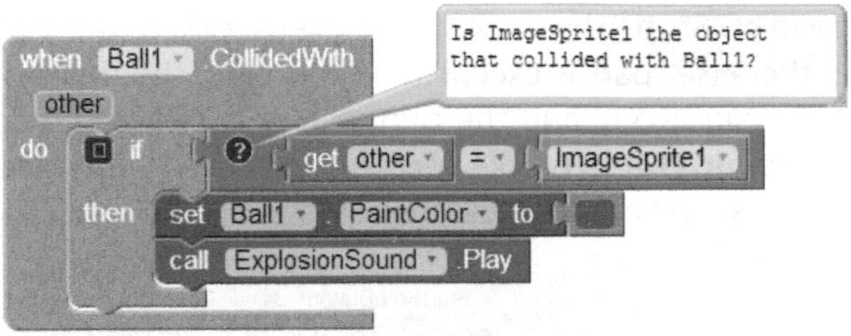

Figure 17-8. Only perform the response if Ball1 hit ImageSprite1

The `ImageSprite1` block is one we haven't yet discussed. This block refers to the component as a whole, not a particular property of the component. When you need to compare components (e.g., to know which ones have collided), you use this block. Each component has such a block in its drawer, and the block has the same name as the component.

Interactive Animation

In the animated behaviors we've discussed so far, the end user isn't involved. Games are interactive, of course, with the end user playing a central role. Often, the end user controls the speed or direction of an object with buttons or other user interface objects.

As an example, let's update the diagonal animation by giving the user the ability to stop and start the diagonal movement. You can do this by programming a `Button.Click` event handler to disable and re-enable the timer event of the clock component.

By default, the `Clock` component's `timerEnabled` property is checked. You can disable it dynamically by setting it to false in an event handler. The event handler in Figure 17-9, for example, would stop the activity of a `Clock` timer on the first click.

Figure 17-9. Stopping the timer the first time the button is clicked

After the Clock1.TimerEnabled property is set to false, the Clock1.Timer event will no longer trigger, and the ball will stop moving.

Of course, stopping the movement on the first click isn't too interesting. Instead, you could "toggle" the movement of the ball by adding an if else in the event handler that either enables or disables the timer, as demonstrated in Figure 17-10.

This event handler stops the timer on first click and resets the button so that it displays "Start" instead of "Stop." The second time the user clicks the button, the TimerEnabled is false, so the "else" part is executed. In this case, the timer is enabled, which gets the object moving again, and the button text is switched back to "Stop." For more information about ifelse blocks, see Chapter 18, and for examples of interactive animations that use the orientation sensor, see Chapter 5 and Chapter 23.

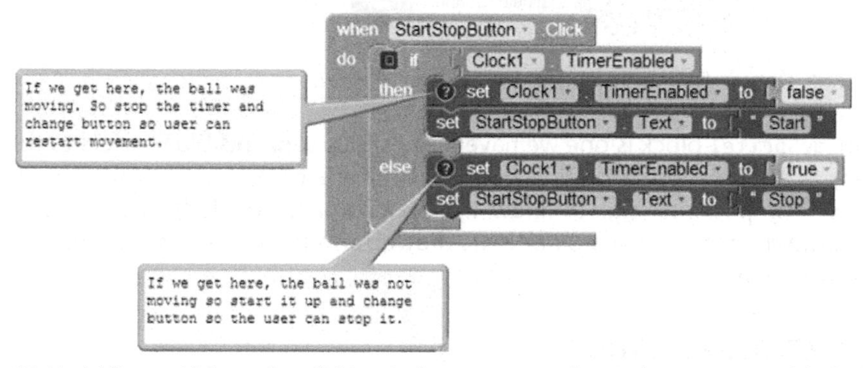

Figure 17-10. Adding an if else so that clicking the button starts and stops the movement of the ball

Specifying Sprite Animation Without a Clock Timer

The animation samples described so far use a Clock component and specify that an object should move each time the Clock.Timer event is triggered. The Clock.Timer event scheme is the most general method of specifying animation. Beyond simply moving an object, you could also have it change an object's color over time, change some text (to appear as though the app is typing), or have the app speak words at a certain pace.

If you only want to move objects, App Inventor provides an alternative that doesn't require the use of a Clock component. As you might have noticed, the ImageSprite and Ball components have properties for Heading, Speed, and Interval. Instead of defining a Clock.Timer event handler, you can set these properties in the Component Designer or Blocks Editor to control how a sprite moves.

To illustrate, let's reconsider the example that moved a ball diagonally. The `Heading` property of a sprite or ball has a range of 360 degrees, as illustrated in Figure 17-11.

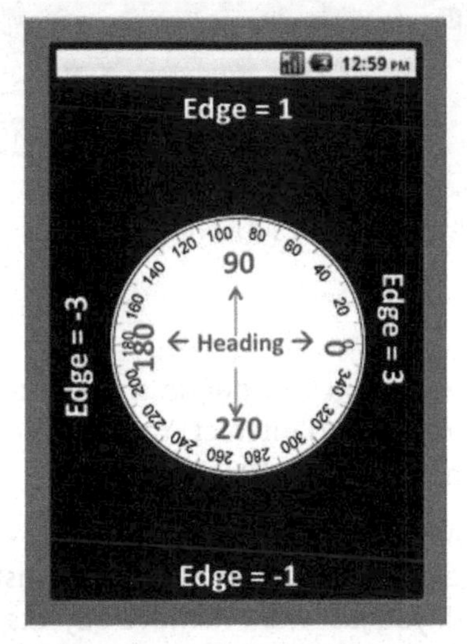

Figure 17-11. The Heading property has a range of 360 degrees

If you set the `Heading` to 0, the ball will move left to right. If you set it to 90, it will move bottom to top. If you set it to 180, it will move right to left. If you set it to 270, it will move top to bottom. And if you set it to 315, the ball will move from upper left to lower right.

To cause an object to move, you also need to set the `Speed` property to a value other than 0. The speed the object moves is actually determined by the `Speed` and `Interval` properties together. The `Speed` property is the distance, in pixels, that the object will move each `Interval`.

To try out these properties, create a test app with a `Canvas` and `Ball` and connect your device or emulator for live testing. Then, modify the `Heading`, `Speed`, and `Interval` properties of the ball to see how they work.

For instance, suppose that you wanted to move a ball back and forth from the upper left to the lower right of the canvas. In the Designer, you might initialize the ball's `Speed` to 5 and `Interval` to 100, and then set the `Heading` property to 315. You'd then add the `Ball1.EdgeReached` event handler, which you can see in Figure 17-12, to change the ball's direction when it reaches either edge.

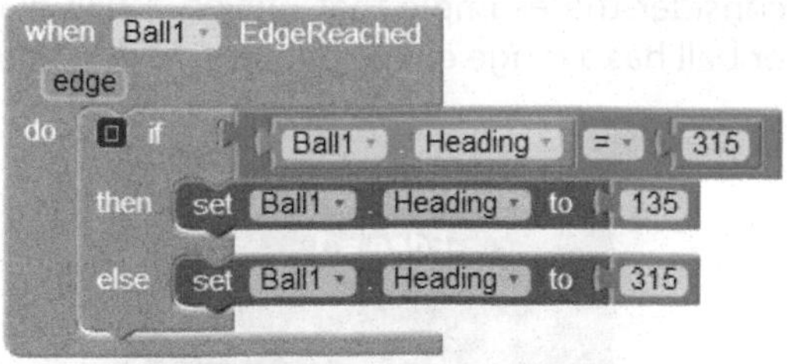

Figure 17-12. Changing the ball's direction when it reaches either edge

Summary

Using the Canvas component, you can define a sub-area of the device's screen in which objects can move around and interact. You can put only two types of components within a Canvas: ImageSprites and Balls.

Animation is an object moving or otherwise transforming over time. You can program animation, including movement and other graphical transformations, with the Clock component's Timer event. If you just want to move objects, you can use an alternative method based on the Heading, Speed, and Interval properties internal to Image Sprite and Ball components.

With either method, you can also take advantage of high-level functionality for handling events that handle collisions.

CHAPTER 18

Programming Your App to Make Decisions: Conditional Blocks

Computers, even small ones like the phone in your pocket, are good at performing millions of operations in a single second. Even more impressively, they can also make decisions based on the data in their memory banks and logic specified by the programmer. This decision-making capability is probably the key ingredient of what people think of as artificial intelligence, and it's definitely a very important part of creating smart, interesting apps! In this chapter, we'll explore how to build this decision-making logic into your apps.

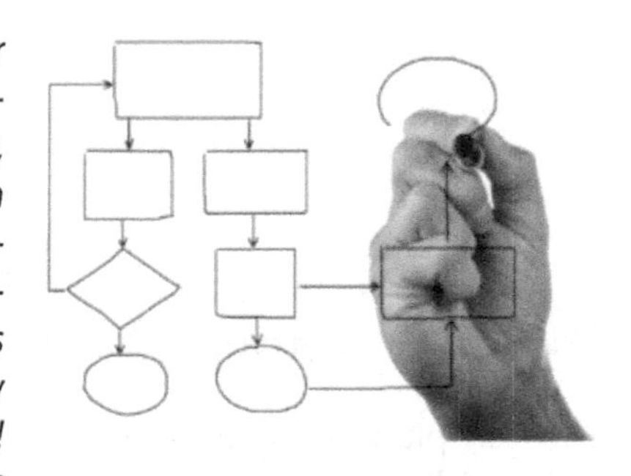

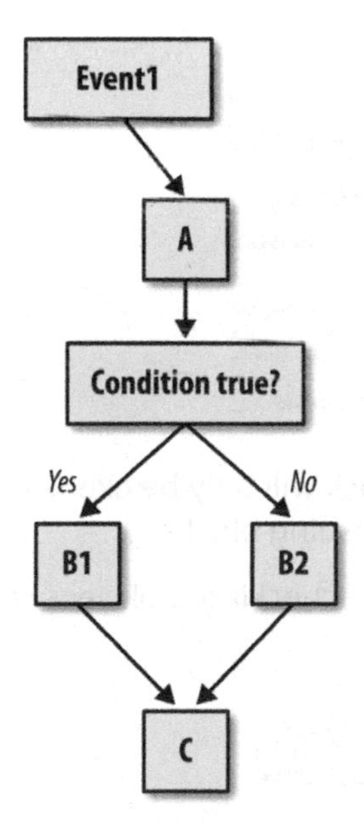

Figure 18-1. An event handler that tests for a condition and branches accordingly

Chapter 14 discusses how an app's behavior is defined by a set of event handlers. Each event handler executes specific functions in response to a particular event. The response need not be a linear sequence of functions, however; you can specify that some functions be performed only under certain conditions. For example, a game app might check if a player's score has reached 100, or a location-aware app might ask if the phone is within the boundaries of some building. Your app can ask such questions and, depending on the answer, proceed accordingly.

Consider the diagram in Figure 18-1. When the event occurs, function (block) A is performed. Then, a decision test is performed. If the test is true, B1 is performed. If it is false, B2 is performed. In either case, the rest of the event handler (C) is completed.

Because app decision diagrams like this one look something like trees, we say that the app "branches" one way or the other depending on the test result. So, in this instance, you'd say, "If the test is true, the branch containing B1 is performed."

Testing Conditions with if and else if Blocks

To allow conditional branching, App Inventor provides an `if-then` conditional block in the Control drawer. You can extend the block with as many `else` and `else if` branches as you'd like by clicking the blue icon, as shown in Figure 18-2.

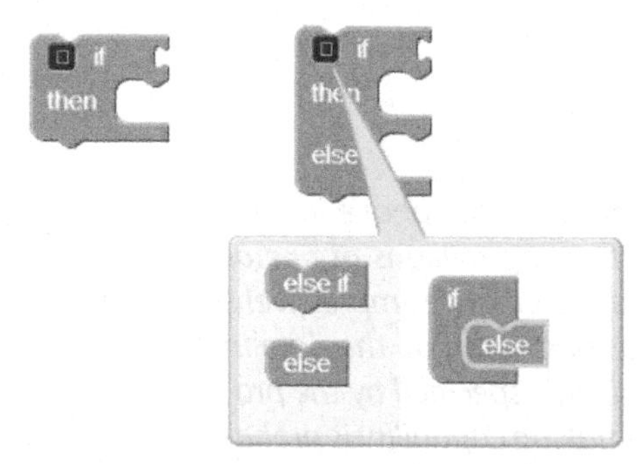

Figure 18-2. The if and else if conditional blocks

You can plug any *Boolean expression* into the *test* sockets of the `if` and `else if` blocks. A Boolean expression is a mathematical equation that returns a result of either true or false. The expression tests the value of properties and variables by using relational and logical operators such as those shown in Figure 18-3.

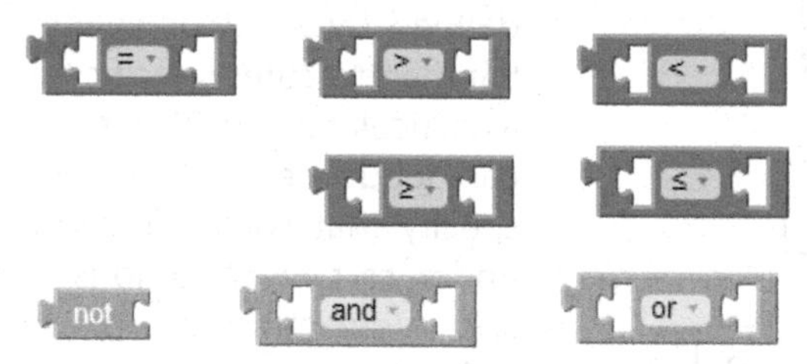

Figure 18-3. Relational and logical operator blocks used in conditional tests

The blocks you put within the "then" socket of an `if` block will only be executed if the test is true. If the test is false, the app moves on to the ensuing blocks.

For a game, you might plug in a Boolean expression for checking a player's score, as shown in Figure 18-4.

Figure 18-4. A Boolean expression used to test the value of the variable score

In this example, a sound file is played if the score is greater than 100. In this example, if the test is false, the sound isn't played and the app jumps below the entire `if-then` block and moves on to the next block in your app. If you want a false test to trigger an action, you can use an `else` or `else if` block.

Programming an Either/Or Decision

Consider an app that you could use when you're bored: you press a button on your phone, and it calls a random friend. In Figure 18-5, a `random integer` block is used to generate a random number and then an `if else` block calls a particular phone number based on that random number.

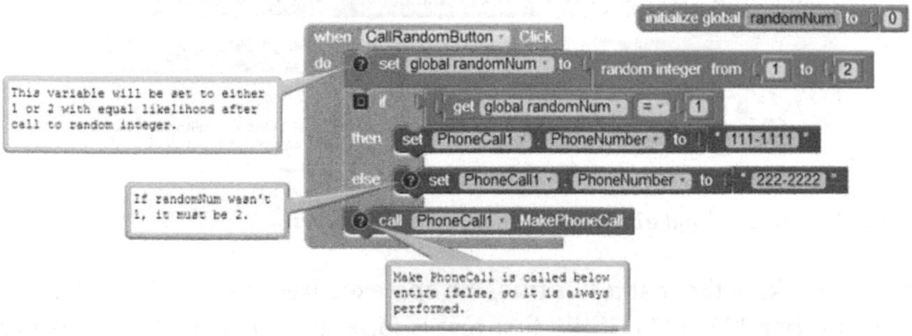

Figure 18-5. This else if block calls one of two numbers based on the randomly generated integer

In this example, `random integer` is called with arguments 1 and 2, meaning that the returned random number will be 1 or 2 with equal likelihood. The variable `RandomNum` stores the random number returned.

After setting `RandomNum`, the blocks compare it to the number 1 in the `if` test. If the value of `RandomNum` is 1, the app takes the first branch (`then`), and the phone number is set to 111–1111. If the value is not 1, then the test is false, in which case the app takes the second branch (`else`), and the phone number is set to 222–2222. The app makes the phone call either way because the call to `MakePhoneCall` is below the entire `if else` block.

Programming Conditions Within Conditions

Many decision situations have more than just two outcomes from which to choose. For example, you might want to choose between more than two friends in your Random Call program. To do this, you could place an `else if` prior to the original `else` branch, as demonstrated in Figure 18-6.

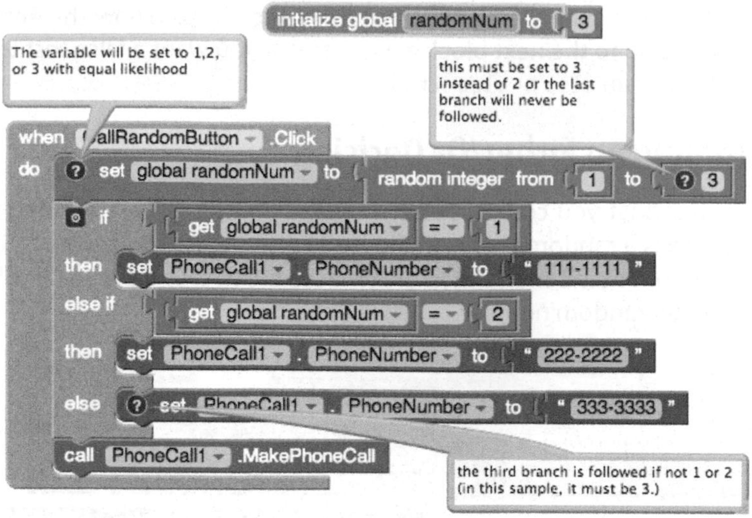

Figure 18-6. `if`, `else if` *and* `else` *provide three possible branches*

With these blocks, if the first test is true, the app executes the first then-do branch and calls the number 111–1111. If the first test is false, the `else if` branch is executed, which immediately runs another test. So, if the first test (`RandomNum=1`) is false and the second (`RandomNum=2`) is true, the second branch is executed and 222–2222 is called. If both tests are false, `else` branch at the bottom is executed and the third number (333–3333) is called.

Note that this modification only works because the to parameter of the `random integer` call was changed to 3 so that 1, 2, or 3 is generated with equal likelihood.

You can add as many `else if` branches as you'd like. You can also nest conditionals within conditionals. When conditional tests are placed within branches of another conditional test, we say they are *nested*. You can nest conditionals and other *control constructs* such as `for each` loops to arbitrary levels in order to add complexity to your app.

Programming Complex Conditions

Besides nesting conditionals, you can also specify single conditional tests that are more complex than a simple equality test. For example, consider an app that vibrates when your phone (and presumably you!) leave a building or some boundary. Such an app might be used by a person on probation to warn him when he strays too far from his legal boundaries. Parents might use it to monitor their children's whereabouts. A teacher might use it to automatically take roll (if all her students have an Android phone!).

For this example, let's ask this question: is the phone within the boundary of Harney Science Center at the University of San Francisco? Such an app would require a complex test consisting of four different questions:

- Is the phone's latitude less than the maximum latitude (37.78034) of the boundary?
- Is the phone's longitude less than the maximum longitude (–122.45027) of the boundary?
- Is the phone's latitude more than the minimum latitude (37.78016) of the boundary?
- Is the phone's longitude more than the minimum longitude (–122.45059) of the boundary?

You need the `LocationSensor` component for this example. You should be able to follow along here even if you haven't been exposed to `LocationSensor`, but you can learn more about it in Chapter 23.

You can build complex tests by using the logical operators and, or, and not, which you can find in the Logic drawer. In this case, you drag out an `if` block and some and blocks, place one of the and blocks within the "test" socket of the `if`, and the others within the first and block, as illustrated in Figure 18-7.

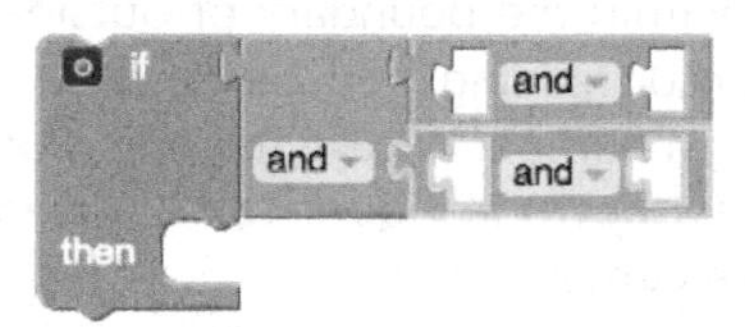

Figure 18-7. An `if` test can test many conditions using and, or, and other relational blocks

You'd then drag out blocks for the first question and place them into the first block's "test" socket, as shown in Figure 18-8.

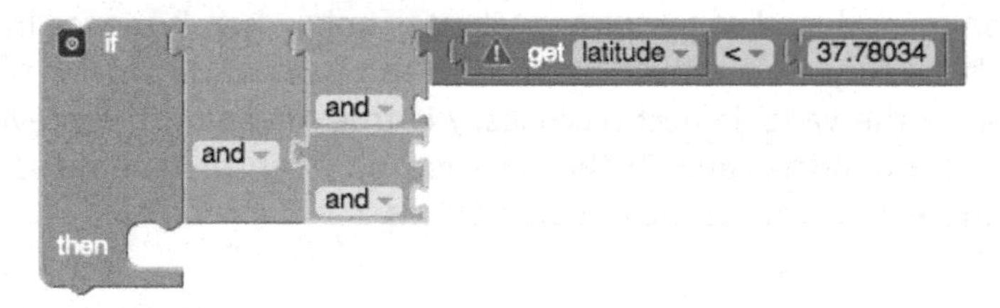

Figure 18-8. Blocks for the first test are placed into the and block

You can then fill the other sockets with the other tests and place the entire `if` within a `LocationSensor.LocationChanged` event. You now have an event handler that checks the boundary, as illustrated in Figure 18-9.

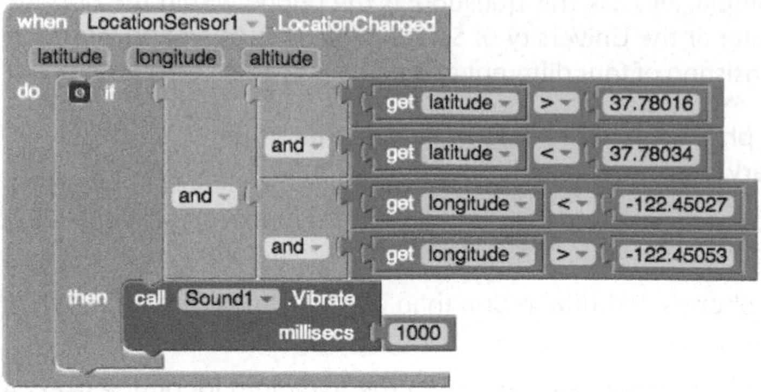

Figure 18-9. This event handler checks the boundary each time the location changes

With these blocks, each time the `LocationSensor` gets a new reading and its location is within the boundary, the phone vibrates.

OK, so far this is pretty cool, but now let's try something even more complicated to give you an idea of the full extent of the app's decision-making powers. What if you wanted the phone to vibrate only when the boundary was crossed from inside to outside? Before moving ahead, think about how you might program such a condition.

Our solution is to define a variable `withinBoundary` that remembers whether the *previous* sensor reading was within the boundary or outside of it, and then compares that to each successive sensor reading. `withinBoundary` is an example of a *Boolean variable*—instead of storing a number or text, it stores true or false. For this example, you'd initialize it to false, as shown in Figure 18-10, meaning that the device is not within USF's Harney Science Center.

Figure 18-10. withinBoundary is initialized to false

The blocks can now be modified so that the `withinBoundary` variable is set on each location change, and so that the phone vibrates only when it moves from inside to outside the boundary. To put that in terms we can use for blocks, the phone should vibrate when 1) the variable `withinBoundary` is true, meaning the previous reading was inside the boundary, and 2) the new location sensor reading is outside the boundary. Figure 18-11 shows the updated blocks.

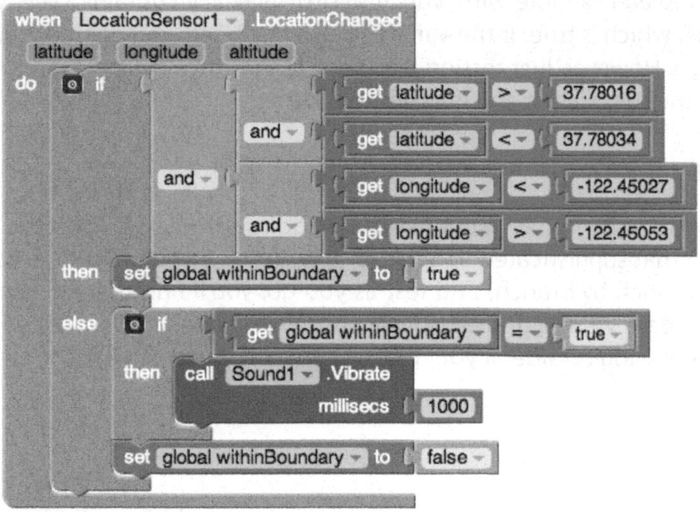

Figure 18-11. These blocks cause the phone to vibrate only when it moves from within the boundary to outside the boundary

Let's examine these blocks more closely. When the `LocationSensor` gets a reading, it first checks if the new reading is within the boundary. If it is, `LocationSensor` sets the `withinBoundary` variable to true. Because we want the phone to vibrate only when we are outside the boundary, no vibration takes place in this first branch.

If we get to the `else`, we know that the new reading is outside the boundary. At that point, we need to check the previous reading: if we're outside the boundary, we want the phone to vibrate only if the previous reading was *inside* the boundary. `withinBoundary` gives us the previous reading, so we can check that. If it is true, we vibrate the phone.

There's one more thing we need to do after we've confirmed that the phone has moved from inside to outside the boundary—can you think of what it is? We also need to reset `withinBoundary` to false so that the phone won't vibrate again on the next sensor reading.

One last note on Boolean variables: check out the two `if` tests in Figure 18-12. Are they equivalent?

Figure 18-12. Can you tell whether these two `if` tests are equivalent?

The answer is "yes!" The only difference is that the test on the right is actually the more sophisticated way of asking the question. The test on the left compares the value of a Boolean variable with true. If `withinBoundary` contains `true`, you compare `true` to `true`, which is true. If the variable contains `false`, you compare `false` to `true`, which is false. However, just testing the value of `withinBoundary`, as in the test on the right, gives the same result and is easier to code.

Summary

Is your head spinning? That last behavior was quite complex! But, it's the type of decision making that sophisticated apps need to perform. If you build such behaviors part by part (or branch by branch) and test as you go, you'll find that specifying complex logic—even, dare we say, *artificial intelligence*—is doable. It will make your head hurt and exercise the logical side of your brain quite a bit, but it can also be lots of fun.

CHAPTER 19

Programming Lists of Data

As you've already seen, apps handle events and make decisions; such processing is fundamental to computing. But, the other fundamental part of an app is its data—the information it processes. An app's data is rarely restricted to single memory slots such as the score of a game. More often, it consists of lists of information and complex, interrelated items that must be organized just as carefully as the app's functionality.

In this chapter, we'll examine the way App Inventor handles data. You'll learn the fundamentals of programming both static information, in which the data doesn't change, and dynamic information, in which data is entered by the end user. You'll learn how to work with lists, and then you'll explore a more complex data structure involving lists of lists and a multiple-choice quiz app.

Many apps process lists of data. For example, Facebook processes your list of friends and lists of status reports. A quiz app works with a list of questions and answers. A game might have a list of characters or all-time high scores.

You specify list data in App Inventor with a variable, but instead of naming a single memory cell with the variable, you name a set of related memory cells. You specify that a variable is multi-item by using either the `make a list` or `create empty list` blocks. For instance, the variable `phoneNumbers` in Figure 19-1 defines a list of three items.

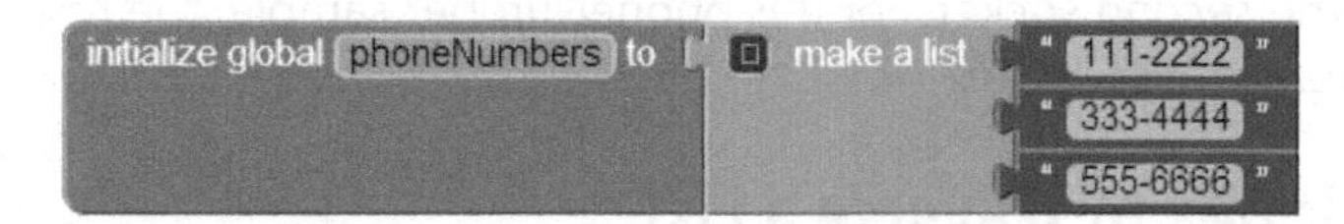

Figure 19-1. phoneNumbers names three memory cells initialized with the numbers shown

Creating a List Variable

You create a list variable in the Blocks Editor by using an `initialize global variable` block and then plugging in a `make a list` block. You can find the `make a list` block in the Lists drawer, and it has only two sockets. But you can specify the number of sockets you want in the list by clicking on the blue icon and adding items, as depicted in Figure 19-2.

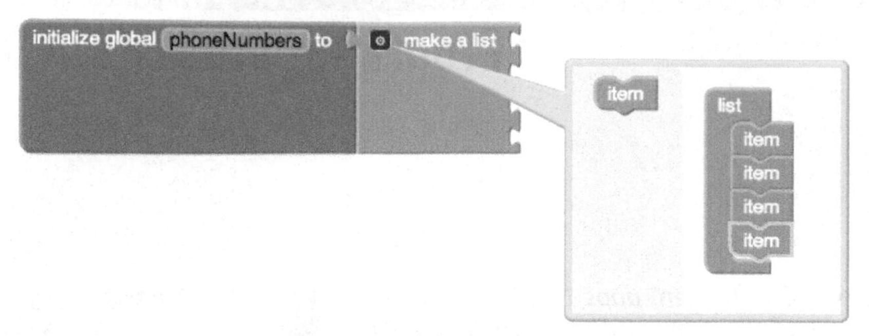

Figure 19-2. Click the blue icon on `make a list` to change the number of items

You can plug any type of data into the "item" sockets of `make a list`. For the phoneNumbers example, the items should be text objects, not numbers, because phone numbers have dashes and other formatting symbols that you can't put in a number object, and you won't be performing any calculations on the numbers (in which case, you would want number objects, instead).

Selecting an Item in a List

As your app runs, you'll need to select items from the list; for example, a particular question as the user traverses a quiz or a particular phone number chosen from a list. You access items within a list by using an index; that is, by specifying a position in the list. If a list has three items, you can access the items by using indices 1, 2, and 3. You can use the `select list item` block to grab a particular item, as shown in Figure 19-3.

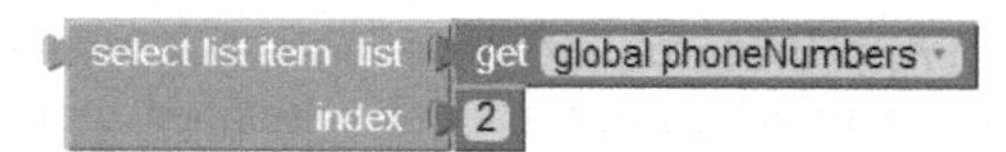

Figure 19-3. Selecting the second item of a list

With `select list item`, you plug in the list you want in the first socket, and the index you want in the second socket. For this phoneNumber sample, the result of selecting the second item is "333–4444."

Using an Index to Traverse a List

In many apps, you'll define a list of data and then allow the user to step through (or *traverse*) it. The Presidents Quiz in Chapter 8 provides a good example of this: in that app, when the user clicks a Next button, the next item is selected from a list of questions and displayed.

The previous section showed how to select the second item of a list, but how do you select the *next* item? When you traverse a list, the item number you're selecting changes each time; it's your *current* position in the list. Therefore, you need to define a variable to represent that current position. "index" is the common name for such a variable, and it is usually initialized to 1 (the first position in the list), as demonstrated in Figure 19-4.

initialize global index to 1

Figure 19-4. Initializing the variable index to 1

When the user does something to move to the next item, you *increment* the index variable by adding a value of 1 to it, and then select from the list by using that incremented value. Figure 19-5 shows the blocks for doing this.

set global index to get global index + 1
set SomeLabel . Text to select list item list get global phoneNumbers
index get global index

Figure 19-5. Incrementing the index value and using the incremented value to select the next list item

Example: Traversing a List of Paint Colors

Let's consider an example app with which the user can peruse each potential paint color for his house by tapping a "ColorButton." Each time the user taps, the button's color changes. When the user makes it through all of the possible colors, the app goes back to the first one.

For this example, we'll use some basic colors. However, you could customize the code blocks to iterate through any set of colors.

Your first step is to define a list variable for the `colors` list and initialize it with some paint colors as items, as depicted in Figure 19-6.

Figure 19-6. Initializing the list colors with a list of paint colors

Next, define an index variable that tracks the current position in the list. It should start at 1. You could give the variable a descriptive name such as `currentColorIndex`, but if you aren't dealing with multiple indexes in your app, you can just name it "index", as in Figure 19-4.

The user traverses to the next color in the list by clicking the `ColorButton`. Upon each tap, the index should be incremented and the `BackgroundColor` of the button should change to the currently selected item, as shown in Figure 19-7.

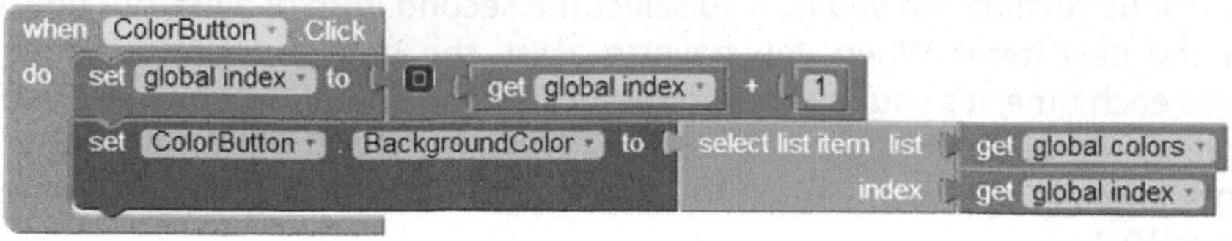

Figure 19-7. Each tap of the button changes its color

Let's assume the button's background is initially set to Red in the Component Designer. The first time the user taps the button, `index` changes from its initial value of 1 to 2, and the button's background color changes to the second item in the list, green. The second time the user taps it, the `index` changes from 2 to 3, and the background color switches to Blue.

But what do you think will happen the next time the user taps it?

If you said there would be an error, you're right! `index` will become 4 and the app will try to select the fourth item in the list, but the list only has three items. The app will *force close*, or quit, and the user will see an error message like the one in Figure 19-8.

Figure 19-8. The error message displayed when the app tries to select a fourth item from a three-item list

Obviously, that message is not something you want your app's users to see. To avoid that problem, add an `if` block to check whether the last color in the list has been reached. If it has, the `index` can be changed back to 1 so that the first color is again displayed, as illustrated in Figure 19-9.

Figure 19-9. Using an if to check whether the index value is larger than the length of the list

When the user taps the button, the `index` is incremented and then checked to see if its value is too large. The `index` is compared to `length of list`, not 3; this way your app will work even if you add items to the list. By checking if the index is greater than your list length (versus checking if it is greater than the specific number 3), you've eliminated a code dependency in your app. A *code dependency* is a programming term that describes code that is defined *too* specifically and lacks flexibility. Thus, if you change something in one place—in our example here, you add items to your list—you'll need to search for every instance where you use that list and change it explicitly.

As you can imagine, these kinds of dependencies can get messy very quickly, and they generally lead to many more bugs for you to chase down, as well. In fact, the design for our Color app contains another code dependency as it is currently programmed. Can you figure out what it is?

If you changed the first color in your list from red to some other color, the app won't work correctly unless you also remembered to change the initial `Button.BackgroundColor` you set in the Component Designer. The way to eliminate this code dependency is to set the initial `ColorButton.BackgroundColor` to *the first color in the list* rather than to a specific color. Because this change involves behavior that happens when your app first opens, you do this in the `Screen.Initialize` event handler that is invoked when an app is launched, as illustrated in Figure 19-10.

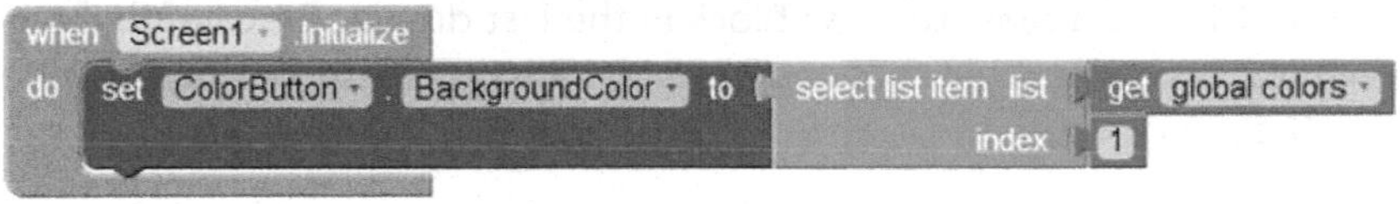

```
when Screen1 .Initialize
do  set ColorButton . BackgroundColor to  select list item list  get global colors
                                                          index  1
```

Figure 19-10. Setting the BackgroundColor of the button to the first color in the list when the app launches

Creating Input Forms and Dynamic Data

The previous Color app involved a *static* list: one whose elements are defined by the programmer (you) and whose items don't change unless you change the blocks themselves. More often, however, apps deal with *dynamic* data: information that changes based on the end user entering new items, or new items being loaded in from a database or web information source. In this section, we discuss an example Note Taker app, in which the user enters notes in a form and can view all of her previous notes.

Defining a Dynamic List

Apps such as a Note Taker begin with an empty list. When you want a list that begins empty, you define it with the `create empty list` block, as depicted in Figure 19-11.

```
initialize global notes to  create empty list
```

Figure 19-11. The blocks to define a dynamic list don't contain any predefined items

Adding an Item

The first time someone launches the app, the `notes` list is empty. But when the user types some data in a form and taps Submit, new notes will be added to the list. The form might be as simple as the one shown in Figure 19-12.

Figure 19-12. Using a form to add new items to the notes list

When the user types a note and taps the Submit button, the app calls the `add items to list` function to append the new item to the list, as illustrated in Figure 19-13.

```
when SubmitButton .Click
do  add items to list  list  get global notes
                       item  NoteTextBox . Text
```

Figure 19-13. Calling add items to list to add the new note when the user taps the SubmitButton

You can find the `add items to list` block in the List drawer. Be careful: there is also an `append to list` block, but that one is a fairly rare block used to append one entire list to another.

Displaying a List

The contents of list variables, like all variables, are not visible to the user. The blocks in Figure 19-13 add items to the list each time `SubmitButton.Click` is invoked, but the user will not receive feedback that the list is growing until you program more blocks to actually display the content of the list.

The simplest way to display a list in your app's user interface is to use the same method you use for displaying numbers and text: put the list in the `Text` property of a `Label` component, as illustrated in Figure 19-14.

```
when SubmitButton .Click
do  add items to list  list  get global notes
                       item  NoteTextBox . Text
    set NoteListLabel . Text to  get global notes
```

Figure 19-14. Displaying the list to the user by placing it in a label.

Unfortunately, this simple method of displaying a list isn't very elegant; it puts the list within parentheses, with each item separated by a space and not necessarily on the same line. For instance, if the user were to type, "Will I ever finish this book?" as the first note, and "I forget what my son looks like!" as the second, the app would display the notes list similar to what we see in Figure 19-15.

Figure 19-15. These entries are listed using default formatting

In Chapter 20, you can see a more sophisticated way to display a list.

Removing an Item from a List

You can remove an item from a list by using the `remove list item` block, as shown in Figure 19-16.

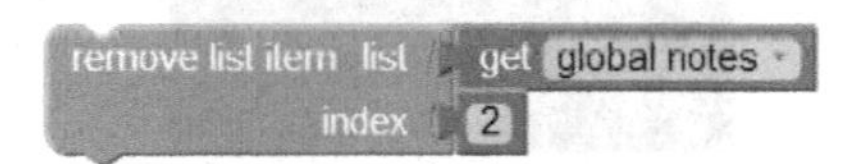

Figure 19-16. Removing an item from a list

The blocks in Figure 19-16 remove the second item from the list named `notes`. Generally, however, you won't want to remove a fixed item (e.g., 2), but instead will provide a mechanism for the user to choose the item to remove.

You can use the `ListPicker` component to provide the user with a way to select an item. `ListPicker` comes with an associated button. When the button is tapped, the `ListPicker` displays the items of a list from which the user can choose one. When the user chooses an item, the app can remove it.

`ListPicker` is easy to program if you understand its key events, `BeforePicking` and `AfterPicking`, and its key properties, `Elements`, `Selection`, and `SelectionIndex` (see Table 19-1).

Table 19-1. The key events and properties of the ListPicker component

Event	Property
`BeforePicking`: Triggered when button is clicked.	`Elements`: The list of choices.
`AfterPicking`: Triggered when user makes a choice.	`Selection`: The user's choice.
	`SelectionIndex`: Position of choice.

The user triggers the `ListPicker.BeforePicking` event by tapping the `ListPicker`'s associated button. In the `ListPicker.BeforePicking` event handler, you'll set the `ListPicker.Elements` property to a list variable so that the data in the list displays. For the Note Taker app, you'd set `Elements` to the `notes` variable that contains your list of notes, as shown in Figure 19-17.

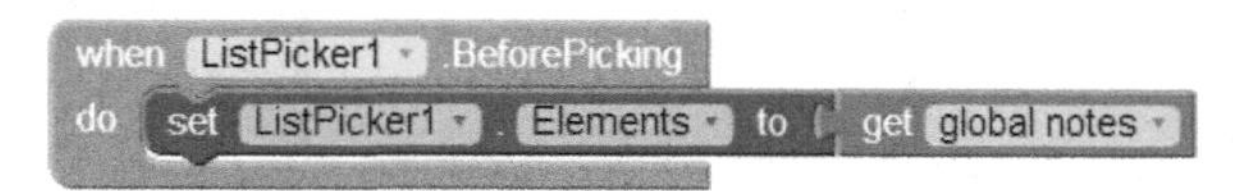

Figure 19-17. The Elements property of ListPicker1 is set to the notes list

With these blocks, the items of the list notes will appear in the `ListPicker`. If there were two notes, it would appear as shown in Figure 19-18.

Figure 19-18. The list of notes appears in the ListPicker

When the user chooses an item in the list, it triggers the `ListPicker.AfterPicking` event. In this event handler, you can access the user's selection in the `ListPicker.Selection` property.

However, your goal in this example is to remove an item from the list, and the `remove item from list` block expects an index, not an item. The `Selection` property of the `ListPicker` is the actual data (the note), not the index. Therefore, you need to use the `SelectionIndex` property instead because it provides you with the index of the chosen item. It should be set as the index of the `remove list item` block, as demonstrated in Figure 19-19.

Figure 19-19. Removing an item by using ListPicker.SelectionIndex

Lists of Lists

The items of a list can be of any type, including numbers, text, colors, or Boolean values (true/false). But, the items of a list can also, themselves, be lists. Such complex data structures are common. For example, a list of lists could be used to convert the Presidents Quiz (Chapter 8) into a multiple-choice quiz. Let's look again at the basic structure of the Presidents Quiz, which is a list of questions and a list of answers, as shown in Figure 19-20.

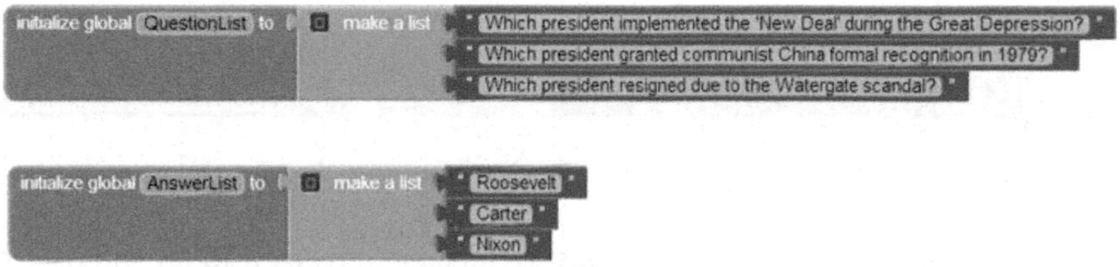

Figure 19-20. A list of questions and a list of answers

Each time the user answers a question, the app checks to see if it is correct by comparing the answer to the current item in the `AnswerList`.

To make the quiz multiple choice, you need to keep an additional list, one which stores the choices for each answer to each question. You specify such data by placing three `make a list` blocks within an inner `make a list` block, as demonstrated in Figure 19-21.

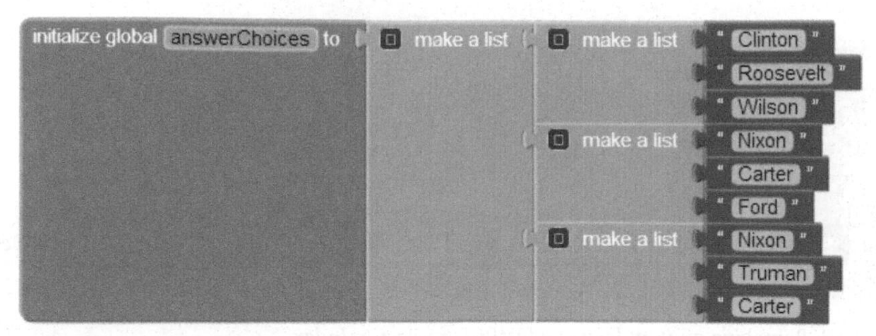

Figure 19-21. A list of lists is formed by inserting `make a list` blocks as items within an inner `make a list` block

Each item in the variable `answerChoices` is itself a list containing three items. If you select an item from `answerChoices`, the result is a list. Now that you've populated your multiple-choice answers, how would you display that to the user?

As with the Note Taker app, you could use a `ListPicker` to present the choices to the user. If the index were named `currentQuestionIndex`, the `ListPicker.BeforePicking` event would appear as shown in Figure 19-22.

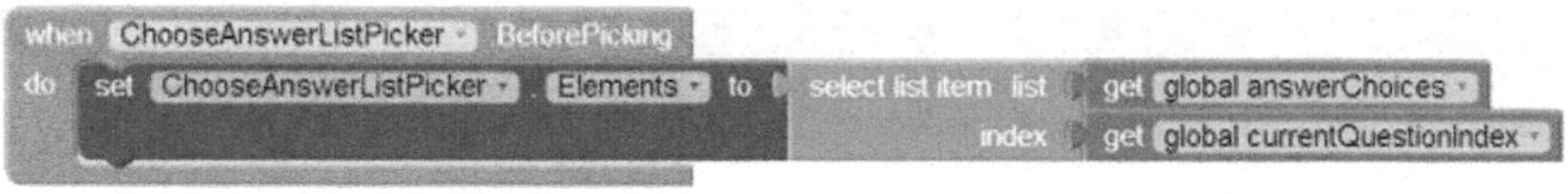

Figure 19-22. Using the List Picker to present one of the list of answer choices to the user

These blocks would take the current sublist of `answerChoices` and let the user choose from it. So, if `currentQuestionIndex` were 1, the `ListPicker` would show a list like the one in Figure 19-23.

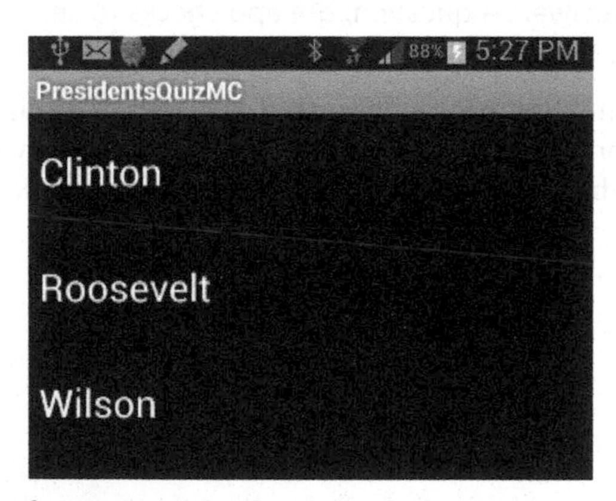

Figure 19-23. The answer choices presented to the user for the first question

When the user chooses, you check the answer with the blocks shown in Figure 19-24.

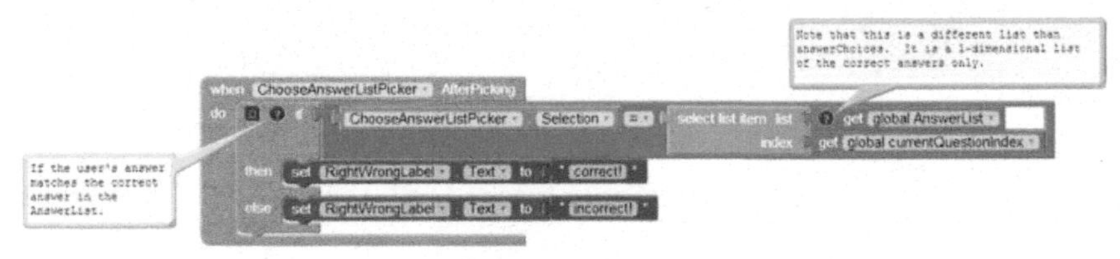

Figure 19-24. Checking whether the user chose the correct answer

In these blocks, the user's selection from the `ListPicker` is compared to the correct answer, which is stored in a different list, `AnswerList` (because `answerChoices` provides only the choices and does not denote the correct answer).

Summary

Lists are used in almost every app you can think of. Understanding how they work is fundamental to programming. In this chapter, we explored one of the most common programming patterns: using an index variable that starts at the beginning of the list and is incremented until each list item is processed. If you can understand and customize this pattern, you are indeed a programmer!

We then covered some of the other mechanisms for list manipulation, including typical forms for letting the user add and remove items. Such programming requires yet another level of abstraction, as you have to envision the dynamic data before it really exists. After all, your lists are empty until the user puts something in them. If you can understand this, you might even think of quitting your day job.

We concluded the chapter by introducing a complex data structure, a list of lists. This is definitely a difficult concept, but we explored it by using fixed data: the answer choices for a multiple-choice quiz. If you mastered that and the rest of the chapter, your final test is this: create an app that uses a list of lists but with dynamic data. One example would be an app with which people can create their own multiple-choice quizzes, extending even further the MakeQuiz app in Chapter 10. Good luck!

While you think about how you'll tackle that, understand that our exploration of lists isn't done. In the next chapter, we continue the discussion and focus on list iteration with a twist: applying functions to each item in a list.

CHAPTER 20

Repeating Blocks

If there's one thing that computers are good at, it's repeating things—like little children, they never tire of repetition. They are also very fast and can do things such as process your entire list of Facebook friends in a microsecond.

In this chapter, you'll learn how to program repetition with special repeat blocks instead of copying and pasting the same blocks over and over. You'll learn how to send an SMS text to every phone number in a list and how to add up a list of numbers. You'll also learn that repeat blocks can significantly simplify an app.

Controlling an App's Execution: Branching and Looping

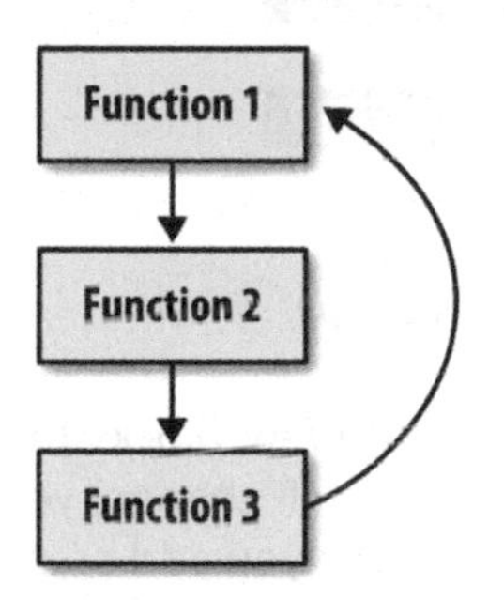

Figure 20-1. Repeat blocks cause a program to loop

In previous chapters, you learned that you define an app's behavior with a set of event handlers—events and the functions that should be executed in response. You also learned that the response to an event is often not a linear sequence of functions and can contain blocks that are performed only under certain conditions.

Repeat blocks are the other way in which an app behaves in a nonlinear fashion. Just as `if` and `else if` blocks allow a program to branch, repeat blocks allow a program to loop; that is, to perform a set of functions and then jump back up in the code and do it again, as illustrated in Figure 20-1. When an app executes, a program counter working beneath the hood of the app keeps track of the next operation to be performed. So far, you've examined apps in which the program counter starts at the top of an event handler and (conditionally) performs operations top to bottom. With repeat blocks, the program counter loops back up in the blocks, continuously performing the same operations.

App Inventor provides a number of repeat blocks, including the `for each` and `while`, which we'll focus on in this chapter. `foreach` is used to specify functions that should be performed on each item of a list. So if you have a list of phone numbers, you can specify that a text should be sent to each number in the list

The `while` block is more general than the `for each`. With it, you can program blocks that continually repeat until some arbitrary condition changes. You can use `while` blocks to compute mathematical formulas such as adding the first *n* numbers or computing the factorial of *n*. You can also use `while` when you need to process two lists simultaneously; `for each` processes only a single list at a time.

Iterating Functions on a List with for each

Chapter 18 demonstrates an app that randomly calls one phone number in a list. Randomly calling one friend might work out sometimes, but if you have friends like mine, they don't always answer. A different strategy would be to send a "Thinking of you!" text to *all* of your friends and see who responds first (or most charmingly!).

One way to implement such an app is to simply copy the blocks for texting a single number and then paste them for each friend who you want to text, as shown in Figure 20-2.

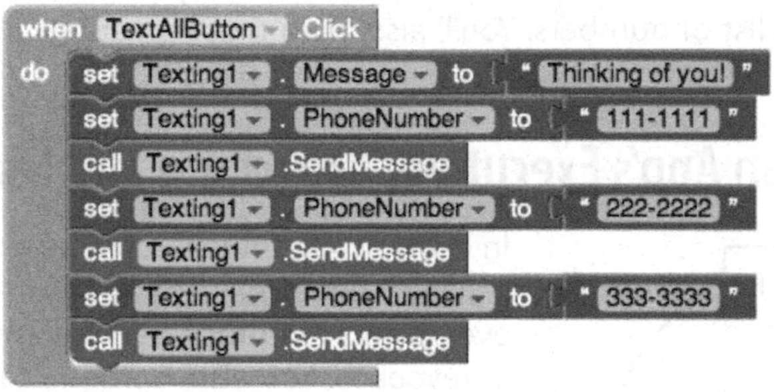

Figure 20-2. Copying and pasting the blocks for each phone number to be texted

This "brute force" copy-paste method is fine if you have just a few blocks to repeat. But, if you're dealing with large amounts of data or data that will change, you won't want to modify your app with the copy-paste method each time you add or remove a phone number from your list.

The `for each` block provides a better solution. You define a `phoneNumbers` variable with all the numbers and then wrap a `for each` block around a single copy of the blocks that you want to perform. Figure 20-3 shows the `for each` solution for texting a group.

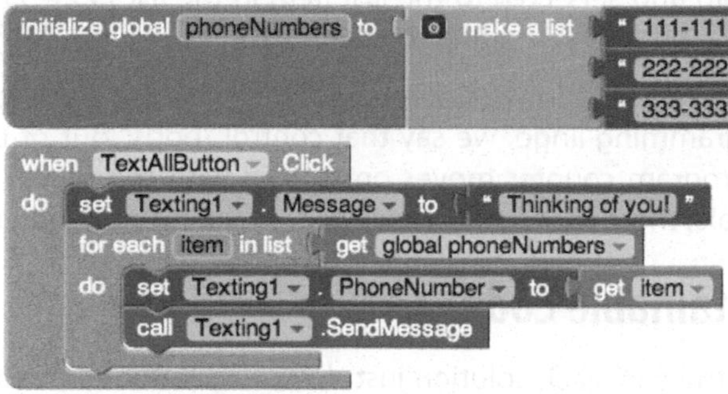

Figure 20-3. Using the for each block to perform the same blocks for each item in the list

You can read this code as, "For each item (phone number) in the list `phoneNumbers`, set the `Texting` object's phone number to the item and send out the text message."

At the top of the `for each` block, you specify the list that will be processed. The block also has a *placeholder* variable that comes with the `for each`. By default, this placeholder is named "item." You can leave it that way or rename it. This variable represents the *current item* being processed in the list.

If a list has three items, the inner blocks will be executed three times. The inner blocks are said to be subordinate to, or nested within, the `for each` block. We say that the program counter "loops" back up when it reaches the bottom block within the `for each`.

A Closer Look at Looping

Let's examine the mechanics of the `for each` blocks in detail, because understanding loops is fundamental to programming. When the user taps `TextAllButton` and the event handler is invoked, the first operation executed is the `set Texting1.Message to` block, which sets the message to "Thinking of You!" This block is executed only once.

The `for each` block then begins. Before the nested blocks of a `for each` are executed, the placeholder variable `item` is set to the first number in the `phoneNumbers` list (111–1111). This happens automatically; the `for each` relieves you of having to manually call `select list item`. After the first `item` is selected into the variable item, the blocks within the `for each` are executed for the first time. The `Texting1.PhoneNumber` property is set to the value of `item` (111–1111) and the message is sent.

After reaching the last block within a `for each` (the `Texting.SendMessage` block), the app "loops" back up to the top of the `for each` and automatically puts the next item in the list (222–2222) into the variable `item`. The two operations within the `for each` are then repeated, sending the "Thinking of You!" text to 222–2222. The app then loops back up again and sets `item` to the last item in the list (333–3333). The operations are repeated a third time, sending the third text.

Because the final item in the list has been processed, the `for each` looping stops at this point. In programming lingo, we say that control "pops" out of the loop, which means that the program counter moves on to deal with the blocks below the `for each`. In this example, there are no blocks below it, so the event handler ends.

Writing Maintainable Code

To the app's user, the `for each` solution just described behaves exactly the same as the "brute force" method of copying and then pasting the texting blocks. From a programmer's perspective, however, the `for each` solution is more *maintainable* and can be used even if the data (the phone list) is entered dynamically.

Maintainable software is software that can be changed easily without introducing bugs. With the `for each` solution, you can change the list of friends who are sent texts by modifying *only* the list variable—you don't need to change the logic of your program (the event handler) at all. Contrast this with the brute-force method, which requires you to add new blocks in the event handler when a new friend is added. Anytime you modify a program's logic, you risk introducing bugs.

Equally important, the `for each` solution would work even if the phone list was dynamic; that is, one in which the end user can add numbers to the list. Unlike our sample, which has three particular phone numbers listed in the code, most apps work with dynamic data that comes from the end user or some other source. If you redesigned this app so that the end user could enter the phone numbers, you would *have* to use a `for each` solution, because when you write the program, you don't know what numbers to put in the brute-force solution.

Using for each to Display a List

When you want to display the items of a list on the phone, you can plug the list into the `Text` property of a `Label`, as shown in Figure 20-4.

set PhoneNumbersLabel . Text to get global phoneNumbers

Figure 20-4. The simple way to display a list is to plug it directly into a label

When you plug a list directly into a `Text` property of a `Label`, the list items are displayed in the label as a single row of text, separated by spaces and contained in parentheses:

(111–1111 222–2222 333–3333)

The numbers might or might not span more than one line, depending on how many there are. The user can see the data and perhaps comprehend that it's a list of phone numbers, but it's not very elegant. List items are more commonly displayed on separate lines or with commas separating them.

To display a list properly, you need blocks that transform each list item into a single text value with the formatting you want. Text objects generally consist of letters, digits, and punctuation marks. However, text can also store special *control* characters, which don't map to a character you can see. A tab, for instance, is denoted by \t. (To learn more about control characters, check out the Unicode standard for text representation at *http://www.unicode.org/standard/standard.html*.)

In our phone number list, we want a newline character, which is denoted by \n. When \n appears in a text block, it means "go to the next line before you display the next item." Thus, the text object "111–1111\n222–2222\n333–3333" would appear as:

111–1111
222–2222
333–3333

To build such a text object, we use a `for each` block and "process" each item by adding it along with a newline character to the `PhoneNumberLabel.Text` property, as shown in Figure 20-5.

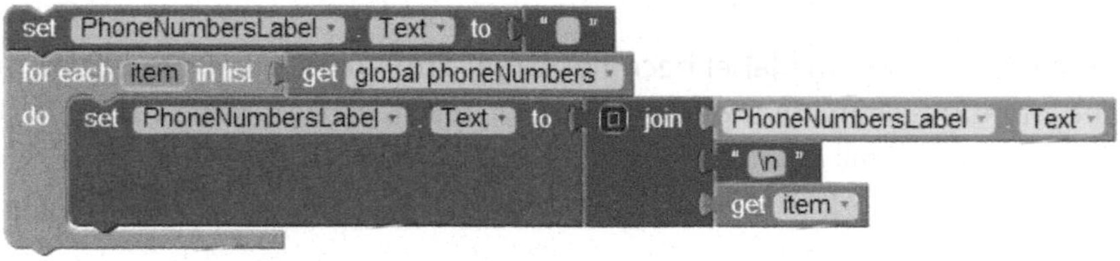

Figure 20-5. A for each block used to display a list with items on separate lines

Let's trace the blocks to see how they work. As discussed in Chapter 15, tracing shows how each variable or property changes as the blocks are executed. With a `for each`, we consider the values after each *iteration*; that is, each time the program goes through the `for each` loop.

Before the `for each`, the `PhoneNumbersLabel`, is initialized to the empty text. When the `for each` begins, the app automatically places the first item of the list (111–1111) into the placeholder variable `item`. The blocks in the `for each` then make `join` with `PhoneNumbersLabel.Text` (the empty text), \n, and the item, and set the result into `PhoneNumbersLabel.Text`. Thus, after the first iteration of the `for each`, the pertinent variables store the values shown in Table 20-1.

Table 20-1. The values after the first iteration

item	PhoneNumbersLabel.Text
111–1111	\n111–1111

Because the bottom of the for each has been reached, control loops back up, and the next item on the list (222–2222) is put into the variable item. When the inner blocks are repeated, text concatenates the value of PhoneNumbersLabel.Text (\n111-1111) with \n, and then with item, which is now 222–2222. After this second iteration, the variables store the values shown in Table 20-2.

Table 20-2. The values after the second iteration

item	PhoneNumbersLabel.Text
222–2222	\n111–1111\n222–2222

The third item of the list is then placed in item, and the inner block is repeated a third time. The final value of the variables, after this last iteration, is shown in Table 20-3.

Table 20-3. The variable values after the final iteration

item	PhoneNumbersLabel.Text
333–3333	\n111–1111\n222–2222\n333–3333

So, after each iteration, the label becomes larger and holds one more phone number (and one more newline). By the end of the for each, PhoneNumbersLabel.Text is set so that the numbers will appear as follows:

```
111-1111
222-2222
333-3333
```

The while-do Block

The while-do block is a bit more complicated to use than for each. The advantage of the while-do block lies in its generality: for each repeats over a list, but while can repeat *so long as any arbitrary condition is true.*

As you learned in Chapter 18, a condition tests something and returns a value of either true or false. while-do blocks include a conditional test, just like if blocks. If the test of a while evaluates to true, the app executes the inner blocks, and then loops back up and rechecks the test. As long as the test evaluates to true, the inner blocks are repeated. When the test evaluates to false, the app pops out of the loop (like we saw with the for each block) and continues with the blocks below the while-do.

Using while-do to Compute a Formula

Here's an example of a `while-do` block that repeats operations. What do you think the blocks in Figure 20-6 do? One way to figure this out is to trace each block (see Chapter 15 for more on tracing), tracking the value of each variable as you go.

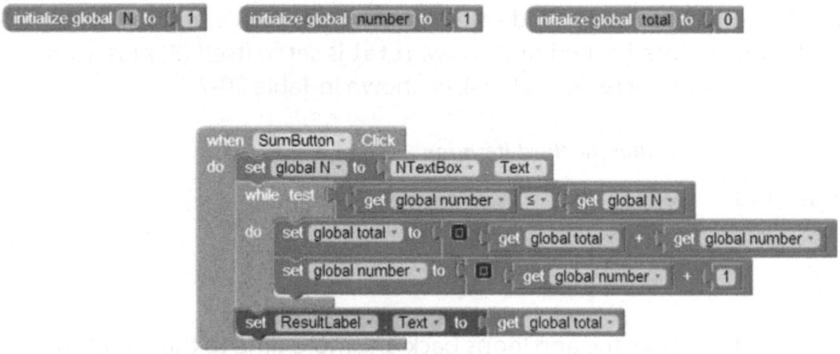

Figure 20-6. Can you figure out what these blocks are doing?

The blocks within the `while-do` loop will be repeated *while the variable number is less than or equal to the variable N.* For this app, `N` is set to a number that the end user types in a text box (`NTextBox`). Suppose that the user types a 3. The variables of the app would look like Table 20-4 when the `while-do` block is first reached.

Table 20-4. Variable values when while-do is first reached

N	number	total
3	1	0

The `while-do` block first tests the condition: is `number` less than or equal to (≤) N? The first time this question is asked, the test is true, so the blocks nested within the `while-do` block are executed. `total` is set to itself (0) plus `number` (1), and `number` is incremented. After the first iteration of the blocks within the `while-do`, the variable values are as listed in Table 20-5.

Table 20-5. The variable values after the first iteration of the blocks within the while block

N	number	total
3	2	1

On the second iteration, the test "number≤N" is still true (2≤3), so the inner blocks are executed again. `total` is set to itself (1) plus `number` (2). `number` is incremented. When this second iteration completes, the variables hold the values listed in Table 20-6.

Table 20-6. The variable values after the second iteration

N	number	total
3	3	3

The app loops back up again and tests the condition. Once again, it is true (3≤3), so the blocks are executed a third time. Now, `total` is set to itself (3) plus `number` (3), so it becomes 6. `number` is incremented to 4, as shown in Table 20-7.

Table 20-7. The values after the third iteration

N	number	total
3	4	6

After this third iteration, the app loops back one more time to the top of the `while-do`. When the test "number≤N" runs this time, it tests 4≤3, which evaluates to false. Thus, the nested blocks of the `while-do` are not executed again, and the event handler completes.

So what did these blocks do? They performed one of the most fundamental mathematical operations: counting numbers. Whatever number the user types, the app will report the sum of the numbers 1..*N*, where *N* is the number entered. In this example, N is 3, so the app came up with a total of 1+2+3=6. If the user had typed 4, the app would have calculated 10.

Summary

Computers are good at repeating the same function over and over. Think of all the bank accounts that are processed to accrue interest, all the grades processed to compute students' grade point averages, and countless other everyday examples for which computers use repetition to perform a task.

This chapter explored two of App Inventor's repeat blocks. The `for each` block applies a set of functions to each element of a list. By using it, you can design processing code that works on an abstract list instead of concrete data. Such code is more maintainable; and if the data to be processed is dynamic, it's required.

Compared to `for each`, `while-do` is more general: you can use it to process a list, but you can also use it to synchronously process two lists or compute a formula. With `while-do`, the inner blocks are performed continuously for as long as a certain condition is true. After the blocks within the `while` are executed, control loops back up and the test condition is tried again. Only when the test evaluates to false does the `while-do` block complete.

CHAPTER 21

Defining Procedures and Reusing Blocks

Programming languages such as App Inventor provide a base set of built-in functionality—in App Inventor's case, a base set of blocks. Programming languages also provide a way to extend that functionality by adding new functions (blocks) to the language. In App Inventor, you do this by defining procedures—named sequences of blocks—that your app can call just as it calls App Inventor's predefined blocks. As you'll see in this chapter, being able to create such abstractions is very important for solving complex problems, which is the cornerstone of building truly compelling apps.

When parents tell their child, "Go brush your teeth before bed," they really mean, "Take your toothbrush and toothpaste from the cabinet, squeeze out some toothpaste onto the brush, swivel the brush on each tooth for 10 seconds (ha!)," and so on. "Brush your teeth" is an abstraction: a recognizable name for a sequence of lower-level instructions. In this case, the parents are asking the child to perform the instructions that they've all agreed mean "brush your teeth."

In programming, you can create such named sequences of instructions. Some programming languages call them *functions* or *subprograms*. In App Inventor, they're called *procedures*. A procedure is a named sequence of blocks that you can call from any place in an app.

Figure 21-1[1] is an example of a procedure that estimates the distance, in miles, between two GPS coordinates you send to it.

1 These blocks are shown with Inline inputs, which reduces the width of the blocks. You can right-click blocks to toggle between "Inline" and "External" inputs.

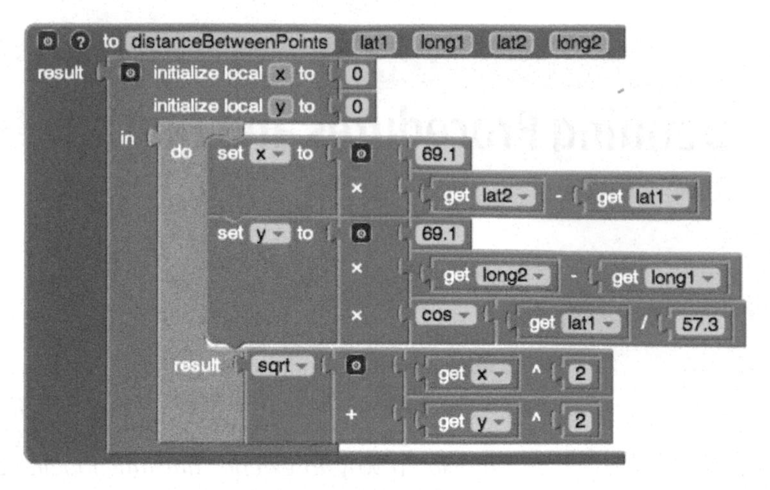

Figure 21-1. Procedure for computing the distance between points

Don't worry too much about the internals of this procedure just yet; all you need to realize at the moment is that procedures like this let you extend the language by which you design and build programs. If every parent had to explain the steps of "brush your teeth" to his or her child each night, that kid might not make it to the fifth grade. It's much more efficient to just say, "Brush your teeth," and everyone can move on with getting to bed at a reasonable hour.

Similarly, after you define the procedure `distanceBetweenPoints`, you can ignore the details of how it works and simply refer to (call) the procedure's name when designing or coding a larger app. This type of *abstraction* is key to solving large problems and lets us break down a large software project into more manageable chunks of code.

Procedures also help reduce errors because they eliminate *redundancy* in your code. With procedures, you can put a chunk of code in one place and then call it from various places throughout your app. So, if you're building an app that needs to know the minimum distance between your current location and 10 other spots, you don't need to have 10 copies of the blocks shown in Figure 21-1. Instead, you just define the `distanceBetweenPoints` procedure and then call it whenever you need it. The alternative —copying and pasting blocks—is much more code-dependent (recall the discussion from Chapter 19) and, consequently, error-prone because when you make a change, you have to find all the other copies of those blocks and change each one in the same way. Imagine trying to find the 5 to 10 places where you pasted a particular chunk of code in an app with 1,000 lines or blocks! A procedure lets you instead *encapsulate* blocks in one place, and then call it many times.

Procedures also help you build up a library of code that can be reused in many apps. Even when building an app for a very specific purpose, experienced programmers are always thinking of ways to create the code in such a way that you can reuse it in other apps. Some programmers never even create apps, but instead focus solely on building reusable code libraries for other programmers to use in their apps!

Eliminating Redundancy

The blocks in Figure 21-2 are from a Note Taker app. Take a look at the blocks and see if you can you identify the redundant ones.

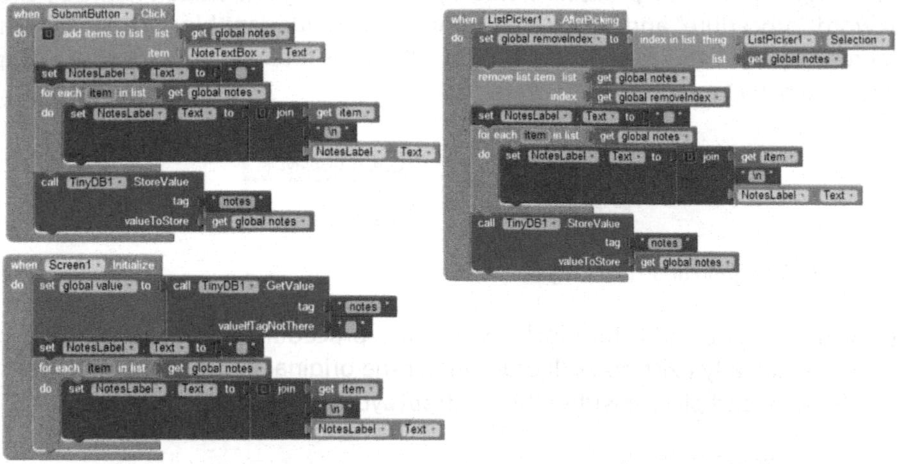

Figure 21-2. A Note Taker app with redundant code

The redundant blocks are the ones involving a `for each` block (actually the `for each` and its nested blocks and the `set NotesLabel.Text to` above it). In all three `for each` instances, the block's job is to display the list of notes. In this app, this behavior needs to take place in three event handlers: when a new item is added, when an item is removed, and when the list is loaded from the database upon application launch.

When experienced programmers see such redundancy, a bell goes off in their heads, probably even before they've copied and pasted the blocks in the first place. They know that it's best to encapsulate such redundancy into a procedure, both to make the program more understandable and so that changes will be much easier to make later.

Accordingly, an experienced programmer would create a procedure, move a copy of the redundant blocks into it, and then call the procedure from the three places containing the redundant blocks. The app will not behave any differently, but it will be easier to maintain and easier for other programmers to work with. Such code (block) reorganization is called *refactoring*.

Defining a Procedure

Let's build a procedure to do the job of the redundant code blocks from Figure 21-2. In App Inventor, you define a procedure in a manner similar to how you define variables. From the Procedures drawer, drag out either a `to procedure` block or a `to procedure result` block. Use the latter if your procedure should calculate some value and return it (we'll discuss this approach a bit later in the chapter).

After dragging out a `to procedure` block, you can change its default name by clicking the word "procedure" and typing a new name. The redundant blocks that you want to refactor carry out the job of displaying a list, so we'll name the procedure `displayList`, shown in Figure 21-3.

Figure 21-3. Click "procedure" to name your procedure

The next step is to add the blocks within the procedure. In this case, we're using blocks that already exist, so we'll drag one of the original redundant blocks out of its event handler and place it within the `to displayList` block, as shown in Figure 21-4.

Figure 21-4. The displayList procedure encapsulates the redundant code

Calling a Procedure

Procedures, like `displayList` and "brush your teeth," are entities with the *potential* to perform a task. However, they'll only perform that task if they are called upon to do so. Thus far, we've created a procedure but haven't *called* it. To call a procedure means to *invoke* it, or to make it happen.

In App Inventor, when you define a procedure, a call block is automatically added to the Procedures drawer as shown in Figure 21-5.

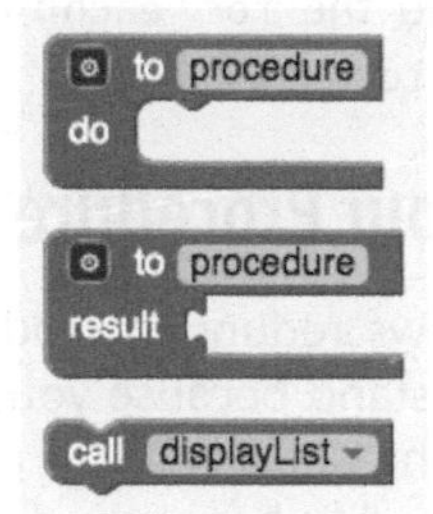

Figure 21-5. A call block appears in the Procedures drawer when you define a procedure

You've been using `call` blocks already to call App Inventor's predefined functions, such as `Ball.MoveTo` and `Texting.SendMessage`. When you define a procedure, you have in essence created your own block; you've extended the App Inventor language. Using the new `call` block, you can invoke your creation.

For the Note Taker app example, you'd drag out three `call displayList` blocks and use them to replace the redundant code in the three event handlers. For instance, the `ListPicker1.AfterPicking` event handler (for deleting a note) should be modified as illustrated in Figure 21-6.

Figure 21-6. Using the displayList call to invoke the blocks now in the procedure

The Program Counter

To understand how the `call` block works, think of an app as having a pointer that steps through the blocks that are performing functions. In computer science, this pointer is called the *program counter*.

When the program counter is performing the blocks within an event handler and it reaches a `call` block, it jumps over to the procedure and executes the blocks in it. When the procedure completes, the program counter jumps back to its previous location (the `call` block) and proceeds from there. So, for the Note Taker example, the `remove list item` block is executed; then the program counter jumps to the `display List` procedure and performs the blocks in that procedure (setting the `NotesLa` bel.Text to the empty text, and the for each); and finally the program counter returns to perform the TinyDB1.StoreValue block.

Adding Parameters to Your Procedure

The displayList procedure allows redundant code to be refactored into a single place. The app is easier to understand because you can read the event handlers at a high level and generally ignore the details of how a list is displayed. It is also helpful because you might decide to modify how you display the list, and the procedure makes it possible for you to make such a modification in a single place (instead of three).

The displayList procedure has limits in terms of its *general* usefulness, however. The procedure only works for a specific list (notes) and displays that list in a specific label (NotesLabel). You couldn't use it to display a different data list—for example, a list of the app's users—because it is defined too specifically.

App Inventor and other languages provide a mechanism called parameters for making procedures more general-purpose. Parameters comprise the information a procedure needs to do its job. They provide the specifics of how the procedure should be performed. In our bedtime tooth-brushing example, you might define "toothpaste type" and "brushing time" as parameters of the procedure "brush your teeth."

You define parameters for a procedure by clicking the blue icon at the upper-left of the procedure definition. For the displayList procedure, we would define a parameter named "list," as shown in Figure 21-7.

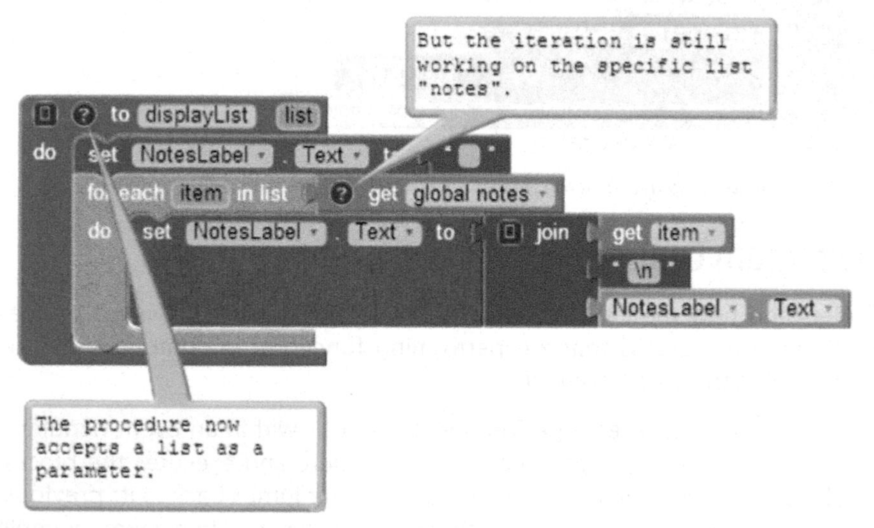

Figure 21-7. The procedure now accepts a list as a parameter

Even with the parameter defined, the blocks still refer directly to the specific list notes (it's plugged into the "in list" slot of the for each). Because we want the procedure to use the list we send in as a parameter, we replace the reference to `global notes` with a reference to `get list`, as demonstrated in Figure 21-8.

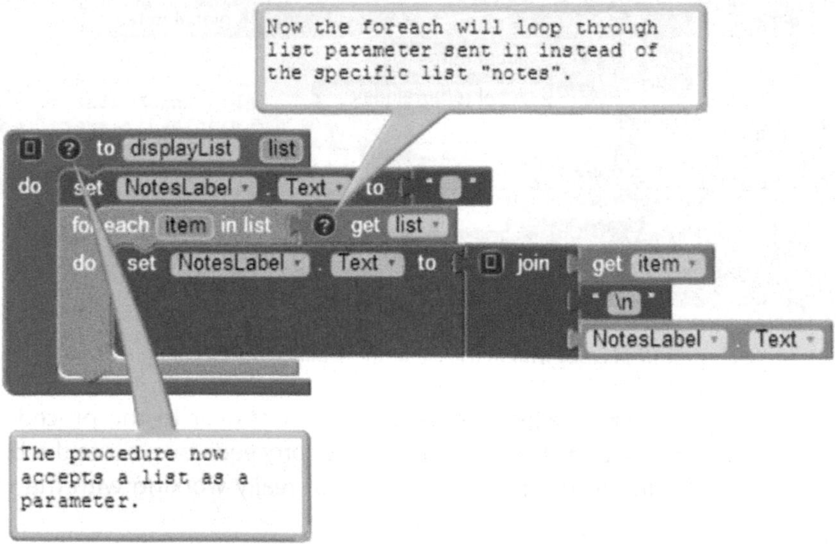

Figure 21-8. Now the for each will use the list sent in

The new version of the procedure is more generic: calls to `displayList` can now send it any list, and `displayList` will display it. When you add a parameter to a procedure, App Inventor automatically puts a corresponding socket in the `call` block. So, when the parameter list is added to `displayList`, the call blocks to `displayList` look like Figure 21-9.

Figure 21-9. Calling displayList now requires you to specify which list to display

The parameter `list` within the procedure definition is called a *formal parameter*. The corresponding socket within the call block is called an *actual parameter*. When you call a procedure from somewhere in the app, you must supply an actual parameter for each formal parameter of the procedure. You do this by filling in all the sockets in the call.

For the Note Taker app, you add a reference `get global notes` as the actual parameter. Figure 21-10 shows how `ListPicker.AfterSelection` should be modified.

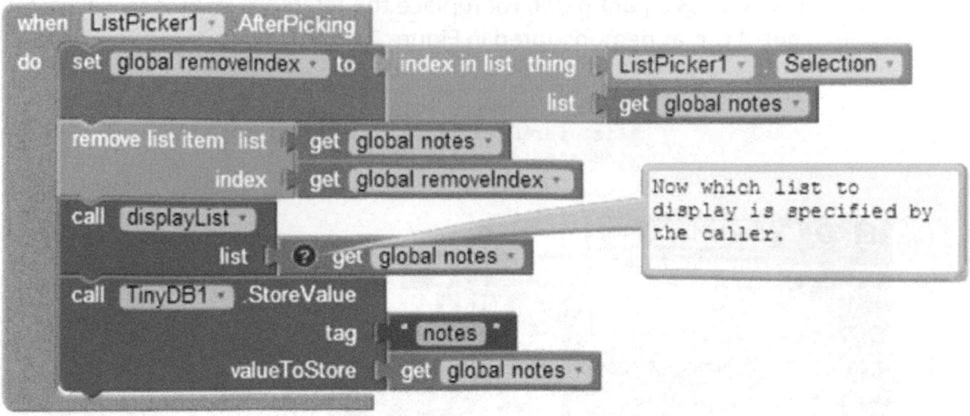

Figure 21-10. Calling the displayList with notes sent as the actual parameter

Now, when `displayList` is called, the list `notes` is sent over to the procedure and placed in the parameter `list`. The program counter proceeds to execute the blocks in the procedure, referring to the parameter `list` but really working with the variable `notes`.

Because of the parameter, you can now use the procedure `displayList` with any list, not just `notes`. For example, if the Note Taker app were shared among a list of users and you wanted to display the list of users, you could call `displayList` and send it the `userList`, as demonstrated in Figure 21-11.

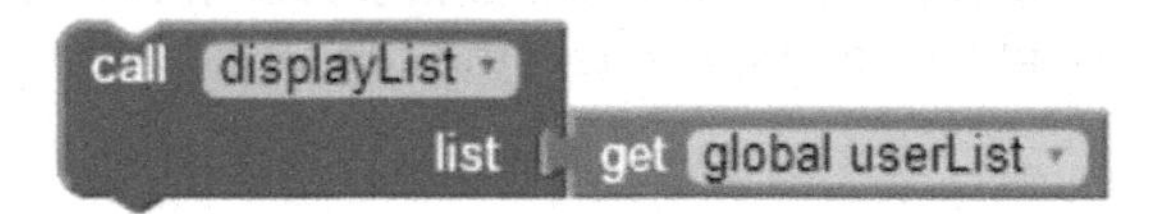

Figure 21-11. The displayList procedure can now be used to display any list, not just notes

Returning Values from a Procedure

There is still one issue with the `displayList` procedure in terms of its general usefulness—can you figure out what it is? As it's currently written, it can display any list of data, but it will always display that data in the label `NotesLabel`. What if you wanted the list to be displayed in a different user interface object (e.g., you had a different label for displaying the `userList`)?

One solution is to reconceptualize the procedure and change its job from displaying a list in a particular label to simply returning a text object that you can display anywhere. To do this, you use a `procedure result` block, depicted in Figure 21-12, instead of the `procedure` block.

Figure 21-12. The procedure result block

You'll notice that, when compared to the `procedure` block, the `procedure result` block has an extra socket at the bottom. You place a variable in this slot and it's returned to the caller. So, just as the caller can send data to a procedure with a parameter, a procedure can send data back with a return value.

Figure 21-13 shows the reworked version of the preceding procedure, this time using a `procedure result` block. Observe that because the procedure is now doing a different job, its name is changed from `displayList` to `listToText`.

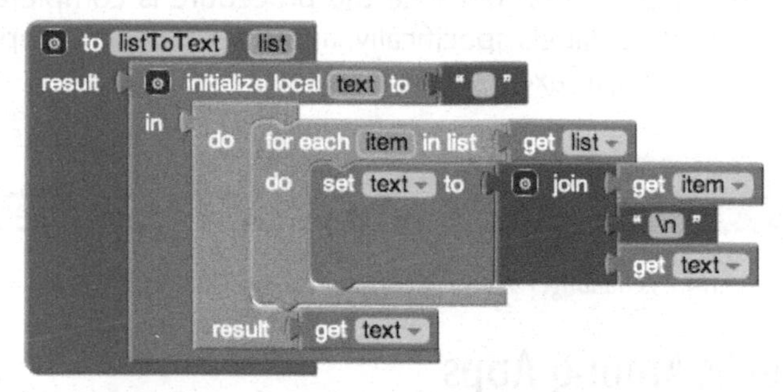

Figure 21-13. listToText returns a text object that the caller can place in any label

In the blocks shown in Figure 21-13, a *local variable* `text` is defined to hold the data as the procedure iterates through each item on the list. `text` is initialized as a local variable, instead of a global one, because it is used only in this procedure.

This `text` variable replaces the overly specific `NotesLabel` component that was being used in the `displayList` version of this procedure. When the `for each` completes, the variable `text` contains the list items, with each item separated by a newline character, \n (e.g., "item1\nitem2\item3"). This `text` variable is then plugged into the return value socket.

When a `procedure result` is defined, its corresponding call blocks look different than those for a procedure. Compare the call to `listToText` with the call to the `display List` in Figure 21-14.

Figure 21-14. The call on the right returns a value and so must be plugged into something

The difference is that the `call listToText` has a plug on its left side. This is because when the call is executed, the procedure will run through its task and then return a value to the `call` block. That return value must be plugged into something.

In this case, the callers to `displayList` can plug that return value into any label they want. For the Note Taker example, the three event handlers that need to display a list will call the procedure, as shown in Figure 21-15.

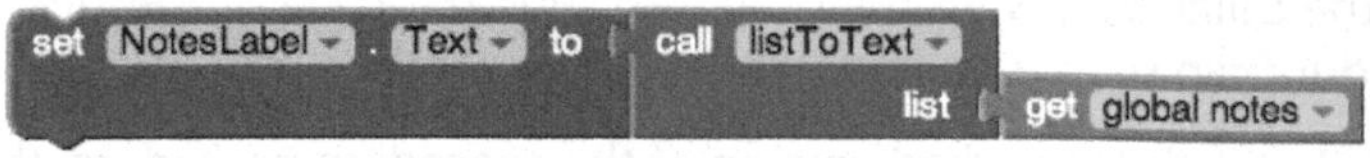

Figure 21-15. Converting the list notes into text and displaying it in NotesLabel

The important point here is that because the procedure is completely generic and doesn't refer to any lists or labels specifically, another part of the app could use it to display any list in any label, as exemplified in Figure 21-16.

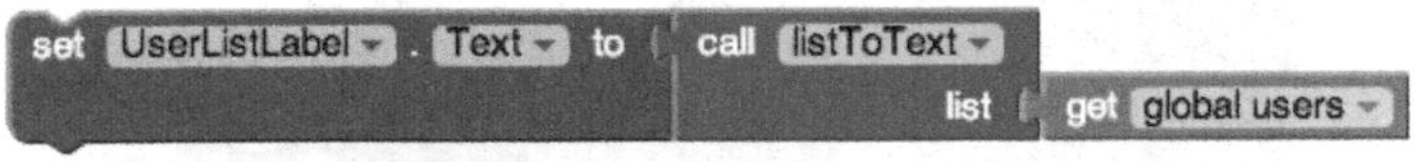

Figure 21-16. The procedure is no longer tied to a particular Label component

Reusing Blocks Among Apps

Reusing code blocks through procedures need not be restricted to a single app. There are many procedures, such as `listToText`, that you could use in just about any app you create. In practice, organizations and programming communities build up code libraries of procedures for their domains of interest.

Typically, programming languages provide an *import* utility through which you can include library code in any app. App Inventor doesn't yet have such a utility. The only way to share procedures is to create a special *library app* and begin new app development by saving a new copy of that app and working from it.

The distanceBetweenPoints Procedure

With the `displayList` (`listToText`) example, we characterized procedure definition as a way to eliminate redundant code: you start writing code, find redundancies as you go along, and refactor your code to eliminate them. Generally, however, a software developer or team will design an app from the beginning with procedures and reusable parts in mind. This sort of planning can save you significant time as the project progresses.

Consider an app to determine the closest local hospital to the user's current location —something that would come in very handy in case of an emergency. Here's a high-level design description of the app:

When the app launches, find the distance, in miles, between the current location and the first hospital. Then find it for the second hospital, and so on. When you have the distances, determine the minimum distance and display the address (and/or a map) to that location.

From this description, can you determine the procedures this app needs?

Often, the verbs in such a description hint at the procedures you'll need. Repetition in your description, as indicated with the "so on," is another clue. In this case, *finding the distance between two points* and *determining the minimum of some distances* are two necessary procedures.

Let's think about the design of the procedure for finding the *distance between two points,* which we'll name `distanceBetweenPoints` (fine, so originality is not my strong suit). When designing a procedure, you need to determine its inputs and outputs: the parameters the caller will send to the procedure for it to do its job, and the result value the procedure will send back to the caller. In this case, the caller needs to send the latitude and longitude of both points to the procedure, as shown in Figure 21-17. The procedure's job is to return the distance, in miles.

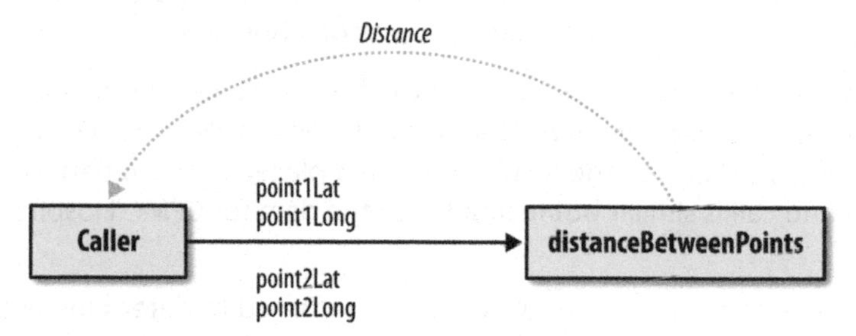

Figure 21-17. The caller sends four input parameters and receives a distance

Figure 21-18 shows the procedure we encountered at the beginning of the chapter, using a formula for approximating the mileage between two GPS coordinates.

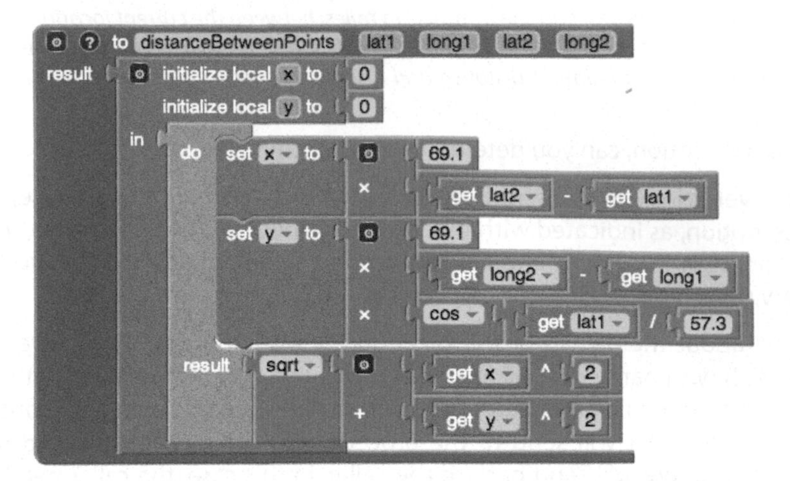

Figure 21-18. distanceBetweenPoints procedure

Figure 21-19 shows blocks that make two calls to the procedure, each of which finds the distance from the current location to a particular hospital.

For the first call, the actual parameters for the first point are the the current readings from the `LocationSensor`, whereas the second point is defined by the GPS coordinates for St. Mary's Hospital. The resulting value is placed in the variable `distanceStMarys`. The second call is similar but instead uses the data for CPMC Hospital for the second point.

The app goes on to compare the two distances returned to determine which hospital is closest. But, if there were more hospitals involved, you'd really need to compare a list of distances to find the shortest. From what you've learned, can you create a procedure called `findMinimum` that accepts a list of numbers as a parameter and returns the index of the minimum?

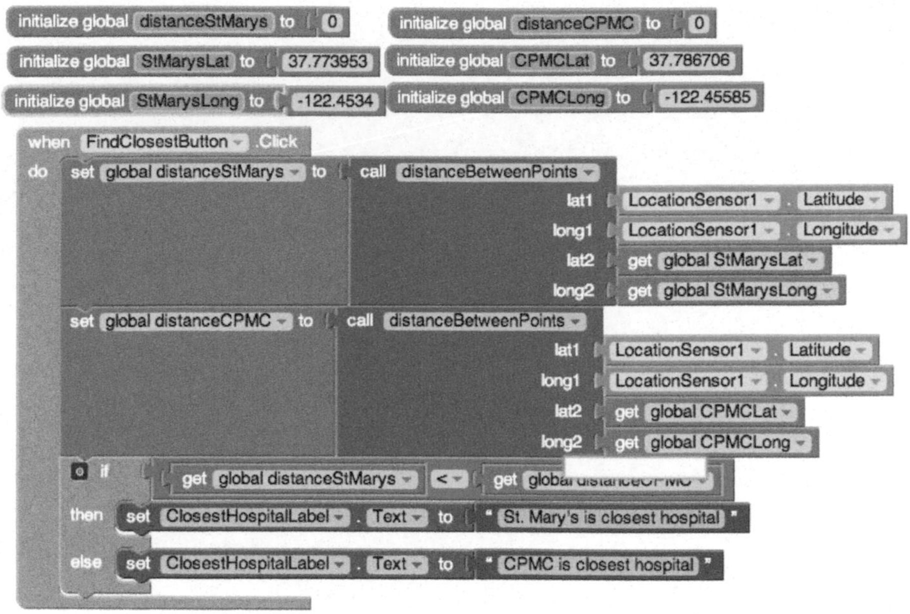

Figure 21-19. Two calls to the distanceBetweenPoints procedure

Summary

Programming languages such as App Inventor provide a base set of built-in functionality. Through the use of procedures, app inventors can extend that language with new abstractions. App Inventor doesn't provide a block for displaying a list, so you build one. Need a block for computing the distance between GPS coordinates? You can create your own.

The ability to define higher-level procedure blocks is the key to engineering large, maintainable software and solving complex problems without being constantly overwhelmed by all of the details. Procedures let you encapsulate code blocks and give those blocks a name. While you program the procedure, you focus solely on the details of those blocks. However, in programming the rest of the app, you now have an abstraction—a name—that you can refer to at a high level.

CHAPTER 22

Working with Databases

Facebook has a database of every member's account information, friends list, and posts. Amazon has a database of just about everything you can buy. Google has a database of information about every page in the World Wide Web. Though not to such a scale, almost every nontrivial app you can create will interact with a database.

In most programming environments, building an app that communicates with a database is an advanced programming technique: you have to set up a server with database software such as Oracle or MySQL and then write code that interfaces with that database. In many universities, such database programming isn't taught until an upper-level software engineering or database course.

When it comes to databases, App Inventor does the heavy lifting for you (and lots of other useful things!). The language provides components that reduce database communication to simple store and get operations. You can create apps that store data directly on the Android device, and with some setup, you can create apps that share data with other devices and people by storing it in a centralized database on the Web.

The data stored in variables and component properties is short-term: if the user types some information in a form and then closes the app before that information has been stored in a database, the information will be gone when the app is reopened. To store information *persistently*, you must store it in a database. The information in databases is said to be *persistent* because even when you close the app and reopen it, the data is still available.

As an example, consider Chapter 4's No Texting While Driving app, which sends an auto-response to incoming SMS text messages. The app has a default response that is sent, but it lets the user enter a custom message to be sent, instead. If the user changes the custom message to "I'm sleeping; stop bugging me" and then closes the app, the message should still be "I'm sleeping; stop bugging me," and not the original default, when the app is reopened. Thus, the custom message must be stored in a database, and every time the app is opened, that message must be retrieved from the database back into the app.

Storing Persistent Data in TinyDB

App Inventor provides two components to facilitate database activity: `TinyDB` and `TinyWebDB`. You use `TinyDB` to store persistent data directly on the Android device; this is useful for personal apps for which the user won't need to share data with another device or person, as in No Texting While Driving. On the other hand, you use `TinyWebDB` to store data in a web database that can be shared among devices. Being able to access data from a web database is essential for multiuser games and apps with which users can enter and share information (like the "MakeQuiz" app in Chapter 10).

The database components are similar, but `TinyDB` is a bit simpler, so we'll explore it first. With `TinyDB`, you don't need to set up the database at all; the data is stored in a database directly on the device and associated with your app.

You transfer data to long-term memory with the `TinyDB.StoreValue` block, as shown in Figure 22-1, which comes from the No Texting While Driving app.

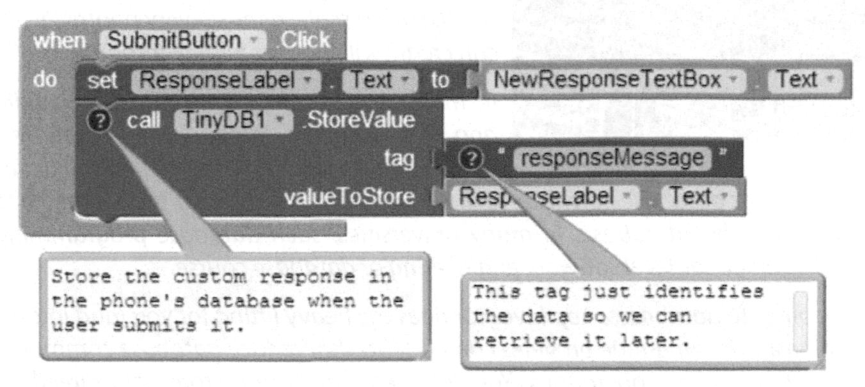

Figure 22-1. The TinyDB.StoreValue block stores data to the device's long-term memory

A tag-value scheme is used for database storage. In Figure 22-1, the data is tagged with the text "responseMessage." The value is some text that the user has typed in a text box for the new custom response—something like, "I'm sleeping; stop bugging me."

The `tag` parameter gives the data you're storing in the database a name, a way to reference the information. The `value` is the data itself. You can think of the tag as a key that you'll use later when you want to retrieve the data from the database.

Likewise, you can think of an App Inventor `TinyDB` database as a table of tag-value pairs. After the `TinyDB1.StoreValue` in Figure 22-1 is executed, the device's database will have the value listed in Table 22-1.

Table 22-1. The value stored in the databases

Tag	Value
responseMessage	I'm sleeping; stop bugging me

An app might store many tag-value pairs for the various data items that you want to be persistent. The tag is always text, whereas the value can be either a single piece of information (a text or number) or a list. Each tag has only one value; every time you store to a tag, it overwrites the existing value.

Retrieving Data from TinyDB

You retrieve data from the database by using the `TinyDB.GetValue` block. When you call `GetValue`, you request particular data by providing a tag. For the No Texting While Driving app, you can request the custom response by using the same tag as you used in the `StoreValue`, "responseMessage." The call to `GetValue` returns the data, so you must plug it into a variable.

Often, you'll retrieve data from the database when the app opens. App Inventor provides a special event handler, `Screen.Initialize`, which is triggered when the app launches. You need to be careful to consider the case when there is no data yet in the database (e.g., the first time app is launched). When you call `GetValue`, you specify a `valueIfTagNotThere` parameter. If there is no data, that value will be returned from the call.

The blocks in Figure 22-2, for the `Screen.Initialize` of No Texting While Driving app, are indicative of the way many apps load database data on initialization.

The blocks put the data returned from `GetValue` into the label `ResponseLabel`. If there is data already in the database, it is placed in `ResponseLabel`. If there is no data for the given tag, the `valueIfTagNotThere` value, "I'm driving right now, I'll text you later" in this case, is placed in `ResponseLabel`.

Figure 22-2. When the app launches, you'll often retrieve database information

Shared Data and TinyWebDB

The `TinyDB` component stores data in a database located directly on the Android device. This is appropriate for personal-use apps that don't need to share data among users. For instance, many people might install the No Texting While Driving app, but there's no need for the various people using the app to share their custom responses with others.

Of course, many apps do share data: think of Facebook, Twitter, and multiuser games. For such data-sharing apps, the database must reside on the Web, not the device, so that different app users can communicate with it and access its information.

`TinyWebDB` is the web counterpart to `TinyDB`. With it, you can write apps that store data on the Web, using a StoreValue/GetValue protocol similar to that of `TinyDB`.

By default, the `TinyWebDB` component stores data by using a web database set up by the App Inventor team and accessible at *http://appinvtinywebdb.appspot.com*. That website contains a database and serves (responds to) web requests for storing and retrieving data. The site also provides a human-readable web interface that a database administrator (you) can use to examine the data stored there.

This default database is for development only; it is limited in size and accessible to all App Inventor programmers. Because any App Inventor app can store data there, you have no assurance that another app won't overwrite your data!

If you're just exploring App Inventor or in early the stages of a project, the default web database is fine. But, if you're creating an app for real-world deployment, at some point you'll need to set up your own web database. Because we're just exploring right now, we'll use the default web database. Later in the chapter, you'll learn how to create your own web database and configure `TinyWebDB` to use that instead.

In this section, we'll build a voting app (depicted in Figure 22-3) to illustrate how `TinyWebDB` works. The app will have the following features:

- Users are prompted to enter their email address each time the app loads. That account name will be used to tag the user's vote in the database.
- Users can submit a new vote at any time. In this case, their old vote will be overwritten.
- Users can view the votes from everyone in the group.
- For the sake of simplicity, the issue being voted on is determined outside the app, such as in a classroom setting in which the teacher announces the issue and asks everyone to vote electronically. (Note that this example could be extended to allow users to prompt votes by posting issues to vote on from within the app.)

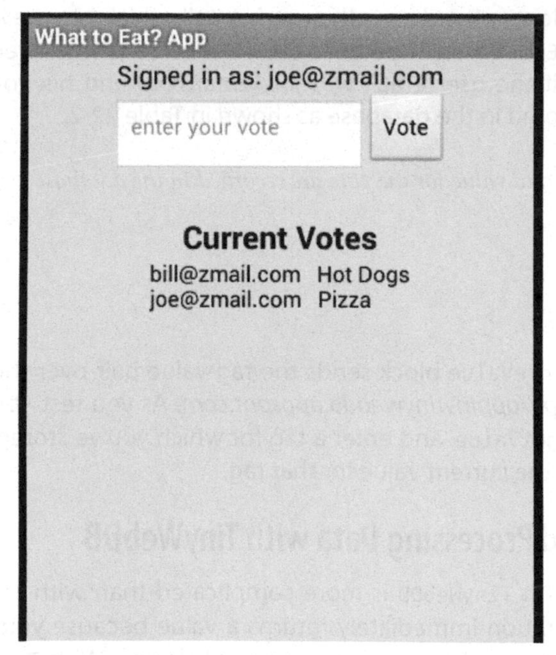

Figure 22-3. A Voting app that stores votes to TinyWebDB

Storing Data by Using TinyWebDB

The `TinyWebDB.StoreValue` block works in the same manner as `TinyDB.StoreValue`, except that the data is stored on the Web. For our voting sample, assume that the user can enter a vote in a text box named `VoteTextBox` and tap a button named `VoteButton` to submit the vote. To store the vote to the web database so that others can see it, we'll code the `VoteButton.Click` event handler like the example in Figure 22-4.

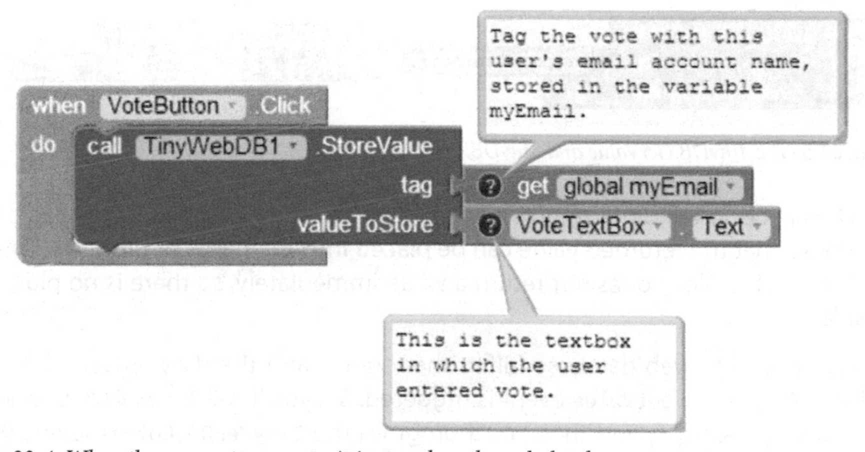

Figure 22-4. When the user enters a vote, it is stored on the web database

The tag used to identify the data is the user's email, which has previously been stored in the variable `myEmail` (you'll see this later). The value is whatever the user typed in VoteTextBox. So, if the user email was *joe@zmail.com* and his vote was "Pizza," the entry would be stored in the database as shown in Table 22-2.

Table 22-2. The tag and value for the vote are recorded in the database

tag	value
joe@zmail.com	Pizza

The `TinyWebDB.StoreValue` block sends the tag-value pair over the Web to the database server at *http://appinvtinywebdb.appspot.com*. As you test your app, you can go to that URL, click `getValue`, and enter a tag for which you've stored a value. The website will show you the current value for that tag.

Requesting and Processing Data with TinyWebDB

Retrieving data with `TinyWebDB` is more complicated than with `TinyDB`. With `TinyDB`, the `GetValue` operation immediately returns a value because your app is communicating with a database directly on the Android device. With `TinyWebDB`, the app is requesting data over the Web, which can take time, so Android requires a two-step scheme for handling it.

With `TinyWebDB`, a call to `GetValue` only *requests* the data; it should really be called "RequestValue" because it just makes the request to the web database and doesn't actually get a value from it right away. To see this more clearly, check out the difference between the `TinyDB.GetValue` block and the `TinyWebDB.GetValue` block shown in Figure 22-5.

Figure 22-5. The TinyDB.GetValue and TinyDB.GotValue blocks

The `TinyDB.GetValue` block returns a value right away, and thus a plug appears on its left side so that the returned value can be placed into a variable or property. The `TinyWebDB.GetValue` block does not return a value immediately, so there is no plug on its left side.

Instead, when the web database fulfills the request and the data arrives back at the device, a `TinyWebDB.GotValue` event is triggered. So, you'll call `TinyWebDB.GetValue` in one place of your app, and then you'll program the `TinyWebDB.GotValue` event handler to specify how to handle the data when it actually arrives. An event handler such as `TinyWebDB.GotValue` is sometimes called a *callback procedure*, because some external entity (the web database) is in effect calling your app back after processing your request. It's similar to ordering at a busy coffee shop: you place your order and then wait for the barista to call your name to actually go pick up your drink. In the meantime, she's been taking orders from everyone else in line, too (and those people are all waiting for their names to be called, as well).

GetValue-GotValue in Action

For our sample app, we need to store and retrieve a list of the voters who have the app, as the app needs to show the votes of all users.

The simplest scheme for retrieving list data is to request the data when the app launches, in the `Screen.Initialize` event, as shown in Figure 22-6. (In this example, we'll just call the database with the tag for "voterlist.")

```
when Screen1.Initialize
do  call TinyWebDB1.GetValue
         tag  "voterlist"
```

Figure 22-6. Requesting data in the Screen1.Initialize event

When the list of voters arrives from the web database, the `TinyWebDB1.GotValue` event handler is triggered. Figure 22-7 shows some blocks for processing the returned list.

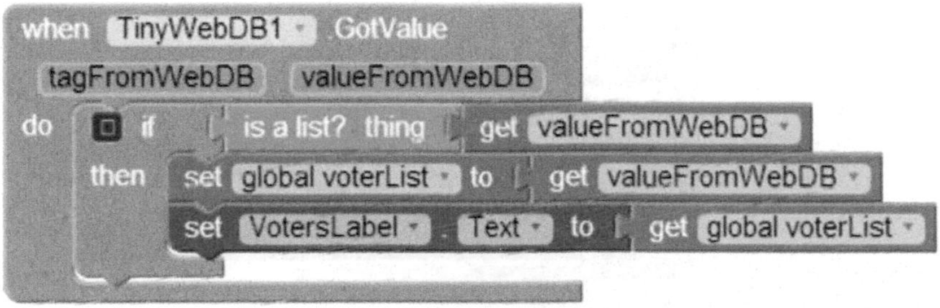

```
when TinyWebDB1.GotValue
 tagFromWebDB  valueFromWebDB
do  if  is a list? thing  get valueFromWebDB
    then  set global voterList to  get valueFromWebDB
          set VotersLabel.Text to  get global voterList
```

Figure 22-7. Using the GotValue event handler to process the returned list

The `valueFromWebDB` *argument* of `GotValue` holds the data returned from the database request. Event arguments such as `valueFromWebDB` have meaning only within the event handler that invokes them. They are considered *local* to the event handler, as you can't reference them in other event handlers.

Because arguments such as `valueFromWebDB` aren't globally accessible, if you need the information throughout your app, you need to transfer it to a global variable. In the example, `GotValue`'s primary job is to transfer the data returned in `valueFromWebDB` into the variable `voterList`, which you'll use in another event handler.

The `if` block in the event handler is also often used in conjunction with `GotValue`, the reason being that the database returns an empty text ("") in `valueFromWebDB` if there is no data for the requested tag. This empty return value occurs most commonly when it's the first time the app has been used. By asking if the `valueFromWebDB` is a list, you're making sure that there is some data actually returned. If the `valueFromWebDB` is the empty text (the `if` test is false), you don't put it into `voterList`.

A More Complex GetValue/GotValue Example

The blocks in Figure 22-7 are a good model for retrieving data in a fairly simplistic app. In our voting example, however, we need more complicated logic. Specifically:

- The app should prompt the user to type an email address when the program starts. We can use a `Notifier` component for this, which pops up a window. (You can find the `Notifier` in the "User Interface" palette in the Designer.) When the user types an email, we'll store it in a variable.
- Only after determining the user's email should you call `GetValue` to retrieve the voter list. Can you figure out why?

Figure 22-8 shows the blocks for this more complicated scheme for requesting the database data.

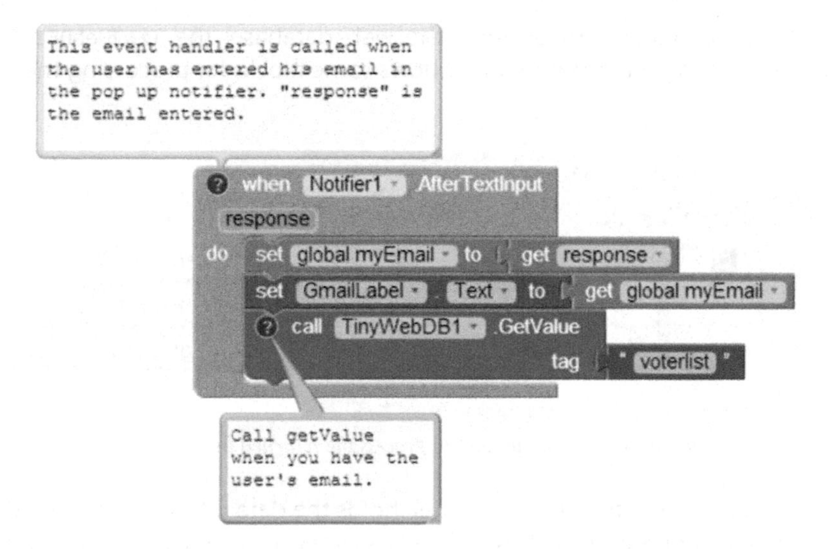

Figure 22-8. In this more complex scheme, GetValue is called after getting the user's email instead of in Screen.Initialize

Upon startup (`Screen1.Initialize`), a `Notifier` component prompts the user to type an email address. When the user does so, and the `Notifier.AfterTextInput` event handler is triggered, the entry is put into a variable and label, and then `GetValue` is called to get the list of voters. Note that `GetValue` isn't called directly in `Screen.Initialize`, because we need the user's email address to be set first.

So, with these blocks, when the app initializes, it prompts the user to type an email address and then calls `GetValue` with a tag of "voterlist." When the list arrives from the Web, `GotValue` is triggered. Here's what should happen:

- `GotValue` should check if the data that arrives is non-empty (someone has used the app and initiated the voter list). If there is data (a voter list), `GotValue` should check if our particular user's email address is already in the voter list. If it's not, it should be added to the list, and the updated list should be stored back to the database.
- If there isn't yet a voter list in the database, we should create one with the user's email address as the only item.

Figure 22-9 shows the blocks for this behavior.

The blocks first ask if a non-empty voter list came back from the database by calling `is a list?` If so, the data is put into the variable `voterList`. Remember, `voterList` will have email addresses for everyone who has used this app. However, we don't know if this particular user is in the list yet, so we need to check. If the user is not yet in the list, the user's email address is added with `add item to list`, and the updated list is stored to the web database.

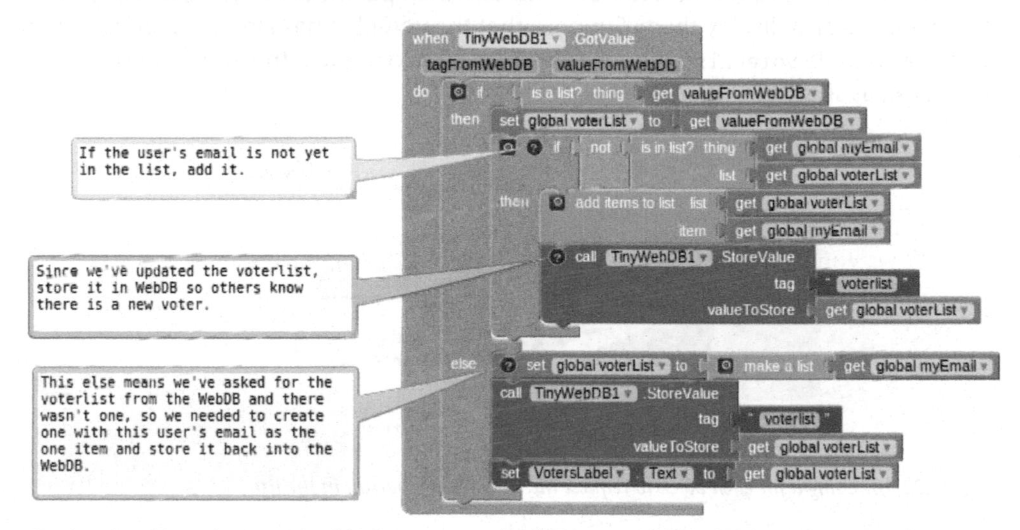

Figure 22-9. Using the GotValue blocks to process the data returned from the database and perform different actions based on what is returned

The `else` of the `if else` block is invoked if a list wasn't returned from the web database; this happens if nobody has used the app yet. In this case, a new `voterList` is created with the current user's email address as the first item. This one-item voter list is then stored to the web database (with the hope that others will join, as well!).

Requesting Data with Various Tags

The voting app thus far manages a list of an app's users. Each person can see the email addresses of all the other users, but we haven't yet created blocks for retrieving and displaying each user's vote.

Recall that the `VoteButton.Click` event submited a vote with a tag-value pair of the form "email: vote." If two people had used the app and voted, the pertinent database entries would look something like Table 22-3.

Table 22-3. The tag-value pairs stored in the database

tag	value
voterlist	[*bill@zmail.com*, *joe@zmail.com*]
bill@zmail.com	Hot dogs
joe@zmail.com	Pizza

When the user clicks on the `ViewVotes` button, the app should retrieve all votes from the database and display them. Suppose that the voter list has already been retrieved into the variable `voterList`; we can use a `for each` to request the vote of each person in the list, as shown in Figure 22-10.

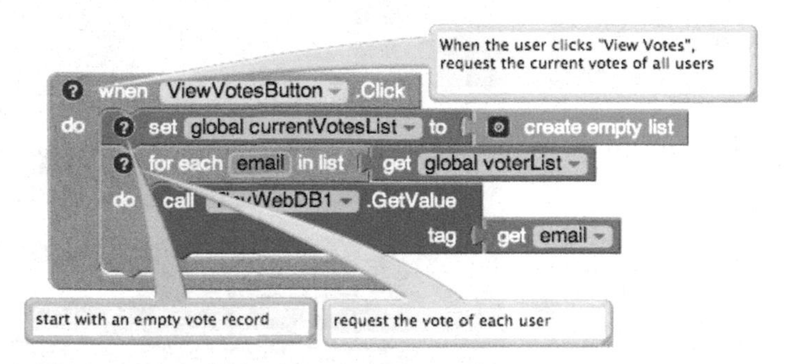

Figure 22-10. Using a for each block to request the vote of each person in the list

Here we initialize a variable, `currentVotesList`, to an empty list, because our goal is to add the up-to-date votes from the database into this list. We then use `for each` to call `TinyWebDB1.GetValue` for every email address in the list, sending the current item of the `for each`, renamed "email," as the tag in the request. Note that the votes won't actually be added to `currentVotesList` until they arrive via a series of `GotValue` events.

Now that we want to display the votes in our app, things get a bit more complicated yet again. With the requests from `ViewVotesButton`, `TinyWebDB.GotValue` will now be returning data related to all the email tags, as well as the "voterlist" tag used to retrieve the list of user email addresses. When your app requests more than one item from the database with different tags, you need to code `TinyWebDB.GotValue` to handle all possible requests. (You might think that you could try to code multiple `Got Value` event handlers, one for each database request—can you figure out why this won't work?)

To handle this complexity, the `GotValue` event handler has a `tagFromWebDB` argument that informs you as to which request has just arrived. In this case, if the tag is "voterlist," we should continue to process the request as we did previously. If the tag is something else, we can assume it's the email of someone in the user list, stemming from the requests triggered in the `ViewVotesButton.Click` event handler. When those requests come in, we want to add the incoming data—the voter and vote—to the `currentVotesList` so that we can display it to the user.

Figure 22-11 shows the entire `TinyWebDB.GotValue` event handler.

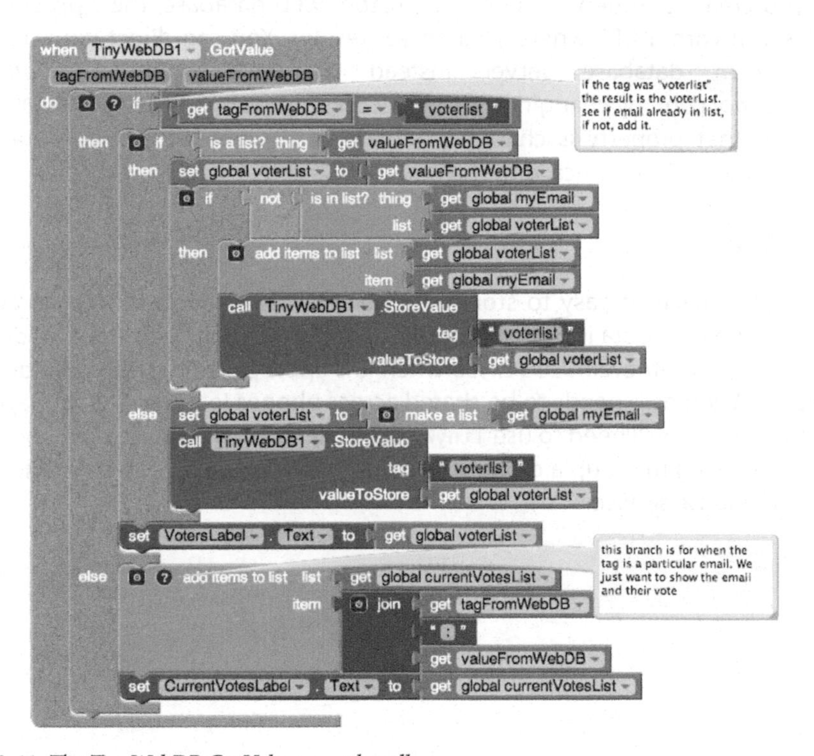

Figure 22-11. The TinyWebDB.GotValue event handler

Setting Up a Web Database

As we mentioned earlier in the chapter, the default web database at *http://appinvtiny-webdb.appspot.com* is intended for prototyping and testing purposes only. Before you deploy an app with real users, you need to create a database specifically for your app.

You can create a web database by using the instructions at *http://appinventorapi.com/create-a-web-database-python-2-7*. This site was set up by one of the authors (Wolber) and contains sample code and instructions for setting up App Inventor web databases and APIs. The instructions point you to some code that you can download and use with only a minor modification to a configuration file. The code download is the same as that used for the default web database set up by App Inventor. It runs on Google's App Engine, a cloud-computing service that will host your web database on Google's servers for free (well, at least until the site receives a certain number of hits). By following the instructions, you can have your own private web database that is compliant with App Inventor's protocols up and running within minutes and begin creating web-enabled mobile apps that use it.

When you create and deploy your own custom web database, the App Engine tool provides you with a URL where your server resides. You can direct your app to use your custom database server instead of the default *http://appinvtiny-webdb.appspot.com*, by changing the `ServiceURL` property in the `TinyWebDB` component. After that property is changed, all calls to `TinyWebDB.StoreValue` and `TinyWebDB.GetValue` will interface with the new web service.

Summary

App Inventor makes it easy to store data persistently through its `TinyDB` and `TinyWebDB` components. Data is always stored as a tag-value pair, with the tag identifying the data for later retrieval. Use `TinyDB` when it is appropriate to store data directly on the device. When data needs to be shared across phones (e.g., for a multiplayer game or a voting app), you'll need to use `TinyWebDB`, instead. `TinyWebDB` is more complicated because you need to set up a callback procedure (the `GotValue` event handler) as well as a web database service.

CHAPTER 23

Reading and Responding to Sensors

Point your phone at the sky, and Google Sky Map tells you which stars you're looking at. Tilt your phone, and you can control the game you're playing. Take your phone on your daily run, and an app records your route. All of these apps are possible because the mobile devices we carry have high-tech sensors for detecting our location, orientation, and acceleration.

In this chapter, you'll explore the App Inventor components `LocationSensor`, `OrientationSensor`, *and* `AccelerometerSensor`. *Along the way, you'll learn about the global positioning system (GPS); orientation measures such as pitch, roll, and azimuth; and some math for processing accelerometer readings.*

Creating Location-Aware Apps

Until the popularization of the smartphone, computing was on desktop lockdown. Yes, laptops are mobile, but not in the same sense as the tiny devices we now carry around in our pockets. Computing has left the lab and the office, and is now taking place out in the world, beyond the constraints of four walls.

One significant effect of carrying our computing with us is a new, very interesting piece of data for every app: a current location. Knowing where people are as they move about the world has far-reaching implications and the potential to help us greatly in our lives. It also has the potential to invade our privacy and be a detriment to humanity.

The Android, Where's My Car? app (Chapter 7) is an example of a *location-aware* app that provides a personal benefit. It lets you remember a previous location so that you can get back to it at a later time. That app is private, meaning that your location information is stored only in your device's database.

Groups can also use location sensing. For instance, a group of hikers might want to keep track of one another's whereabouts in the wilderness, or a group of business associates might want to find one another at a large conference (or a bar). Some people use such "check-in" apps everyday.

Another type of location-aware app uses *augmented-reality* tools. These apps use your location and the phone's orientation to provide overlay information that augments the natural setting. So, you might point a phone at a building and see its price on the real-estate market, or you might walk near an exotic plant in a botanical garden and an app can tell you its species.

The Global Positioning System

To create a location-aware app, you first need to understand how the *global positioning system* (GPS) works. GPS data is generated via a series of geosynchronous satellites maintained by the United States government. As long as you have an unobstructed sight line to at least three satellites in the system, your phone can get a reading. A GPS reading consists of your latitude, longitude, and altitude. Latitude is how far north or south you are relative to the equator, with values for north being positive and south being negative. The range is –90 to 90. Figure 23-1 shows a Google map of a spot near Quito, Ecuador. The latitude shown on the map is –0.01, just barely south of the equator!

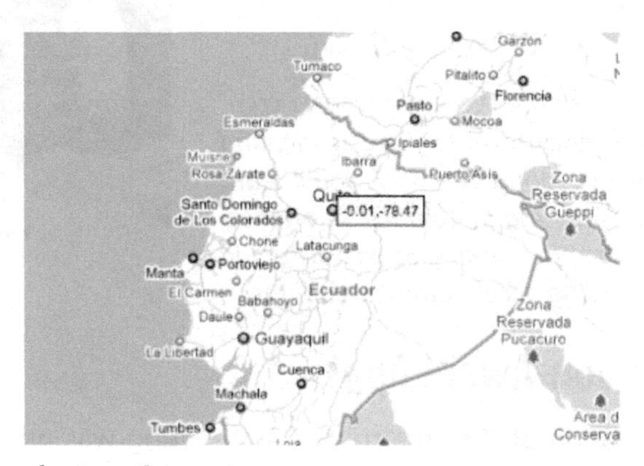

Figure 23-1. Quito, Ecuador, is on the equator

Longitude is how far east or west you are of the Prime Meridian; east coordinates have positive values and west coordinates are negative. The Prime Meridian, which stretches north-south, is located in Greenwich, a town near London that is the home of the Royal Observatory, the organization that originally established the Prime Meridian as a basis for measurement for astronomers and navigators alike. The map in Figure 23-2 shows Greenwich and its longitude of 0.0.

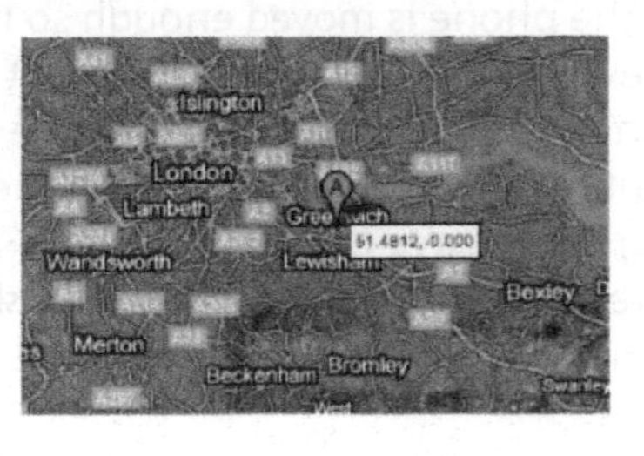

Figure 23-2. The Royal Observatory in Greenwich shoots a beam of light along the Prime Meridian

Longitude values range from –180 to 180. Figure 23-3 shows a spot in Russia, very close to Alaska, that has a 180.0 longitude. You might say that a location like this is halfway around the world from Greenwich (0.0 longitude).

Figure 23-3. A point near the Russian–Alaskan border has longitude 180

Sensing Location with App Inventor

App Inventor provides the `LocationSensor` component for accessing GPS information. The component has properties for `Latitude`, `Longitude`, and `Altitude`. It also communicates with Google Maps, so you can get a reading for your current street address.

`LocationSensor.LocationChanged`, pictured in Figure 23-4, is the key event handler for the `LocationSensor`.

Figure 23-4. The LocationSensor1.LocationChanged event handler

This event is triggered the first time the sensor establishes a reading and each subsequent time the phone is moved enough so that new data is read. There's often a delay of quite a few seconds before an app's first reading, and sometimes the device can't get a reading at all. For instance, if you're indoors and not connected to WiFi, the device might not get a reading. Your phone also has settings by which you can turn GPS reading off to save battery life; this is another potential reason the component can't get a reading. For these reasons, you shouldn't assume that the `LocationSensor` properties have a valid setting until the `LocationSensor.LocationChanged` event occurs.

One way to deal with the unknowns in location sensing is to create a variable `lastKnownLocation`, initialize it to "unknown," and then have the `LocationSensor.LocationChanged` event handler change the value of that variable, as shown in Figure 23-5.

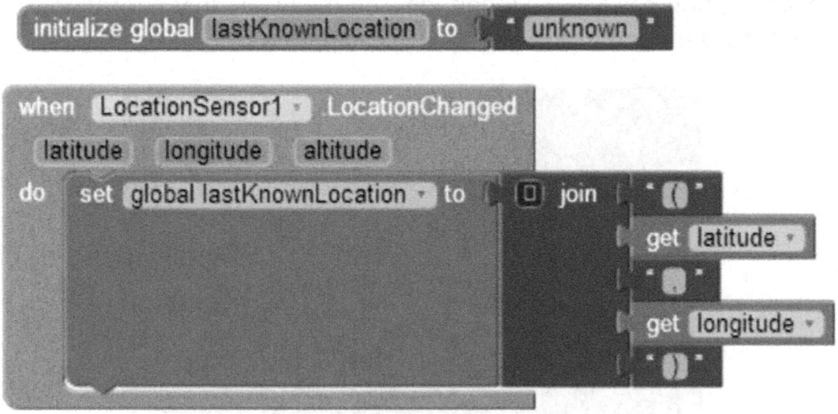

Figure 23-5. The value of the lastKnownLocation variable changes whenever the location changes

By programming the `LocationSensor.LocationChanged` event handler in this way, you can always display the current location or record it in a database, with "unknown" appearing until the first reading. This strategy is used in the No Texting While Driving! app (Chapter 4); that app auto-responds to SMS texts and includes either "unknown" or the last reading taken in the response.

You can also ask explicitly whether the sensor has a reading by using the `LocationSensor.HasLongitudeLatitude` block illustrated in Figure 23-6.

Figure 23-6. Testing whether the sensor has a reading by using the HasLongitudeLatitude block

Checking Boundaries

One common use of the `LocationChanged` event is to check whether the device is within a *boundary*, or a set area. For example, consider the code in Figure 23-7, which vibrates the phone each time a new reading shows that a person has moved farther than 0.1 degree longitude from the Prime Meridian.

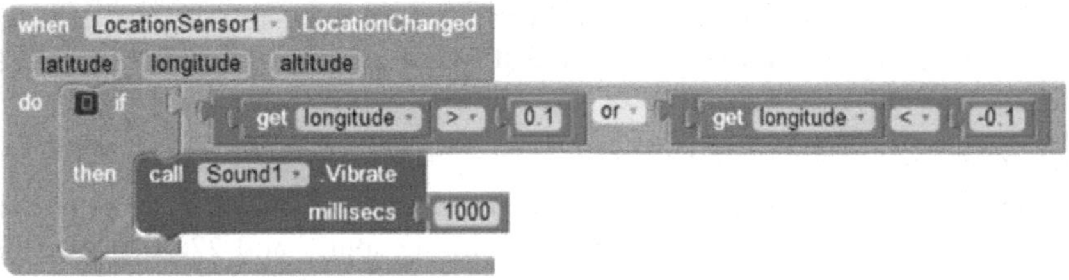

Figure 23-7. If a reading isn't close to the Prime Meridian, the phone vibrates

Such boundary checking has numerous applications; for example, warning parolees if they're nearing a legally specified distance from their home, or alerting parents or teachers if a child leaves the playground area. If you'd like to see a slightly more complex example, see the discussion in Chapter 18 on conditional blocks.

Location Information Providers: GPS, WiFi, and Cell ID

An Android device can determine its own location in a number of ways. The most accurate method—within a few meters—is through the GPS satellites. You won't get a reading, however, if you're inside or there are skyscrapers or other obstructions around you; you need a clear path to at least three satellites in the system.

If GPS isn't available or the user has disabled it, the device can obtain its position through a wireless network. You must be near a WiFi router, of course, and the position reading you'll get is the latitude/longitude of that WiFi station

A third way a device can determine positioning is through *Cell ID*. Cell ID provides a location for the phone based on the strength of signals from nearby cell phone towers. It is generally not very accurate unless you have numerous cell towers near you. However, it does use the least amount of battery power compared to GPS or WiFi connectivity.

Using the Orientation Sensor

You can use the `OrientationSensor` for game-like apps in which the user controls the action by tilting the device. It can also be used as a compass to find out which direction (north/south, east/west) the phone is pointing.

The `OrientationSensor` has five properties, all of which are unfamiliar to most people other than aeronautical engineers:

`Roll` *(Left–Right)*
: Roll is 0 degrees when the device is level, increases to 90 degrees as the device is tilted toward its left side, and decreases to -90 degrees when the device is tilted toward its right side.

`Pitch` *(Up–Back)*
: Pitch is 0 degrees when the device is level, increases to 90 degrees as the device is tilted so that its top is pointing down, and increases further to 180 degrees as it is turned over. Similarly, as the device is tilted so that its bottom points down, Pitch decreases to -90 degrees and then down to –180 degrees as it is turned all the way over.

`Azimuth` *(Compass)*
: Azimuth is 0 degrees when the top of the device is pointing north, 90 degrees when it is pointing east, 180 degrees when it is pointing south, and 270 degrees when it is pointing west.

`Magnitude` *(Speed of a rolling ball)*
: Magnitude returns a number between 0 and 1 that indicates how much the device is tilted. Its value indicates the force exerted by a ball rolling on the surface of the device.

`Angle` *(Angle of a rolling ball)*
: Angle returns the direction in which the device is tiled. That is, it indicates the direction of the force that would be exerted by a ball rolling on the surface of the device.

The `OrientationSensor` provides the `OrientationChanged` event, which is triggered every time the orientation changes. To explore these properties further, let's write an app that illustrates how the properties change as the user tilts the device. Just add five heading labels, and five other labels to show the current values of the properties in the preceding list. Then, add the blocks shown in Figure 23-8.

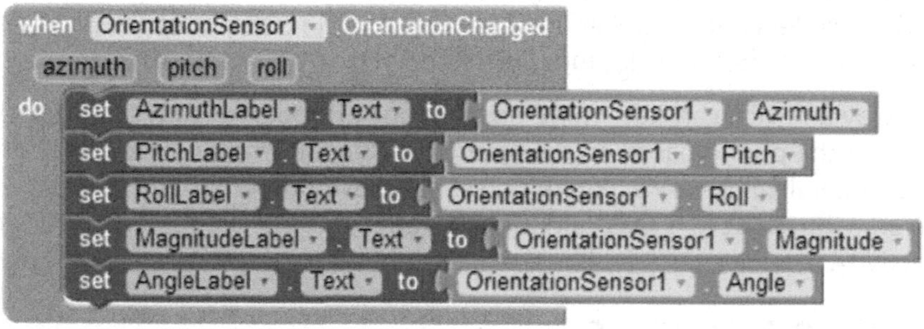

Figure 23-8. Blocks to display the OrientationSensor data

Using the Roll Parameter to Move an Object

This time, let's try to move an image left or right on the screen based on the user tilting the device, as you might do in a shooting or driving game. Drag out a `Canvas` and set the `Width` to "Fill parent" and the `Height` to 200 pixels. Then, add an `ImageSprite` or `Ball` within the `Canvas`, and add a `Label` named `RollLabel` under it to display a property value, as shown in Figure 23-9.

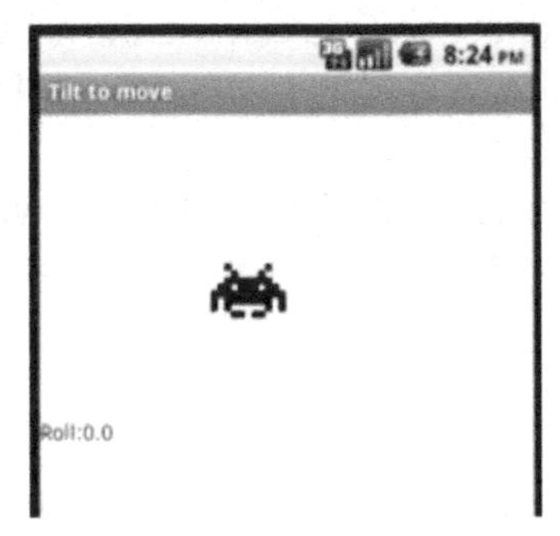

Figure 23-9. A user interface for exploring how you can use roll to move an image

The `Roll` property of `OrientationSensor` will indicate if the phone is tilted left or right —if you hold the phone upright and tilt it slightly to the left, you'll get a positive reading for the roll; if you tilt it slightly right, you'll get a negative reading. Therefore, you can let the user move an object with an event handler such as the one shown in Figure 23-10.

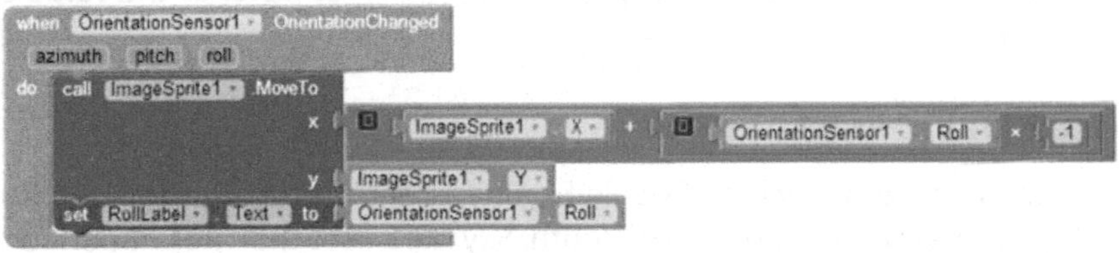

Figure 23-10. Responding to changes in the Roll property with the OrientationChanged event

The blocks multiply the roll by –1, because tilting left gives a positive roll and should move the object left (thereby making the x coordinate smaller). For a review of how the coordinate system works in animated apps, see Chapter 17.

Notice that this app works only when the device is in Portrait mode (upright), not in Landscape mode. As is, if you tilt the phone too far, the screen will change into Landscape mode and the image will stay marooned on the left side of the screen. The reason is that if the device is on its side, it is tilted left and thus will always get a positive reading for the roll. A positive roll reading, as shown in the blocks in Figure 23-10, will always make the x coordinate smaller.

Note that App Inventor does provide the `Screen.ScreenOrientation` property, which you can use to lock the orientation if you don't want it to switch between modes.

Moving in Any Direction by Using Heading and Magnitude

The example in the previous section moves the image left or right. If you want to allow for movement in any direction, you can use the `Angle` and `Magnitude` properties of the `OrientationSensor`. These are the properties used to move the ladybug in the game described in Chapter 5.

In Figure 23-11, you can see the blocks for a test app in which the user tilts the device to move a character in any direction (you need two labels and an image sprite for this example).

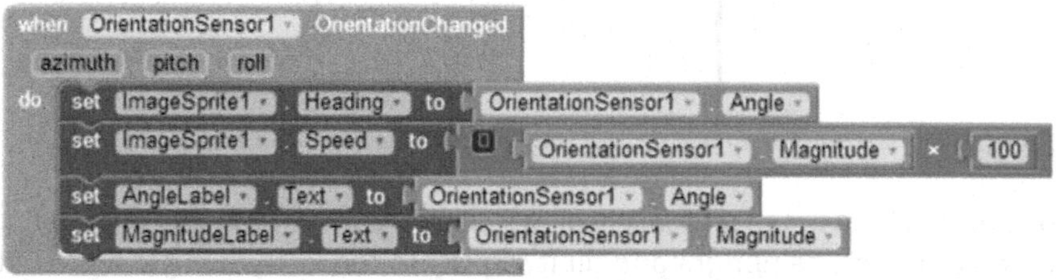

Figure 23-11. Moving a character by using angle and magnitude

Try this one out. The `Magnitude` property, a value between 0 and 1, indicates how much the device is tilted. In this test app, the image moves faster as the value of magnitude increases.

Using the Phone As a Compass

Compass apps and apps such as Google Sky Map need to know the phone's orientation in the world, east/west and north/south. Sky Map uses the information to overlay information about the constellations at which the phone is pointing.

The `Azimuth` reading is useful for this type of orientation. `Azimuth` is always between 0 and 360 degrees, with 0 being north; 90, east; 180, south; and 270, west. Thus, a reading of 45 means the phone is pointing northeast, 135 means southeast, 225 means southwest, and 315 means northwest.

The blocks in Figure 23-12 are for a simple compass that displays in text which direction the phone is pointing (e.g., northwest).

As you might have noticed, the blocks show only one of four possibilities: northwest, northeast, southwest, and southeast. As a challenge, see if you can modify it to show just a single direction (north, south, east, or west) if the reading specifies that you are pointing within a few degrees of it.

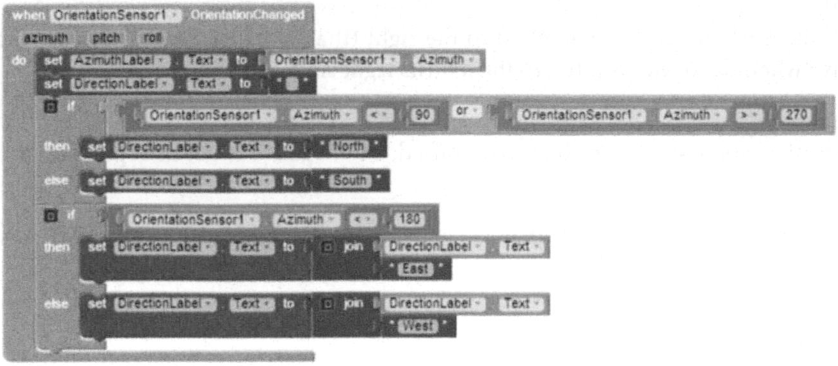

Figure 23-12. Programming a simple compass

Using the Accelerometer

Acceleration is the rate of change of velocity over time. If you press your foot to the gas pedal of your car, the car accelerates—its velocity increases at a particular rate.

An accelerometer like the one in your Android device measures acceleration, but its frame of reference is not the device at rest, but rather the device in free fall: if you drop the phone, it will register an acceleration reading of 0. Simply put, the readings take gravity into account.

If you want to know more about the physics of the matter, you'll need to consult your Einstein-related books. But in this section, we'll explore the accelerometer enough to get you started. We'll even examine an app that could help save lives!

Responding to the Device Shaking

If you've completed the Hello Purr app in Chapter 1, you've already used the `AccelerometerSensor`. In that app, you used the `Accelerometer.Shaking` event to make the kitty meow when the phone was shaken, as shown in Figure 23-13.

Figure 23-13. Playing a sound when the phone is shaken

Using the AccelerometerSensor's Readings

Like the other sensors, the accelerometer has an event for when the readings change, `AccelerometerSensor.AccelerationChanged`. That event has three arguments corresponding to the acceleration in three dimensions:

`xAccel`
: Positive when the device is tilted to the right (that is, its left side is raised), and negative when the device is tilted to the left (its right side is raised).

`yAccel`
: Positive when the device's bottom is raised, and negative when its top is raised.

`zAccel`
: Positive when the device display is facing up, and negative when the display is facing down.

Detecting Free Fall

We know that if all the acceleration readings are near 0, the device is free-falling to the ground. With this in mind, we can detect a free-fall event by checking the readings in the `AccelerometerSensor.AccelerationChanged` event. You could use such blocks, with lots of testing, to detect when an elderly person has fallen and automatically send an SMS message out in response.

Figure 23-14 shows the blocks for an app that simply reports that a free-fall has occurred (and lets the user click a Reset button to check again).[1]

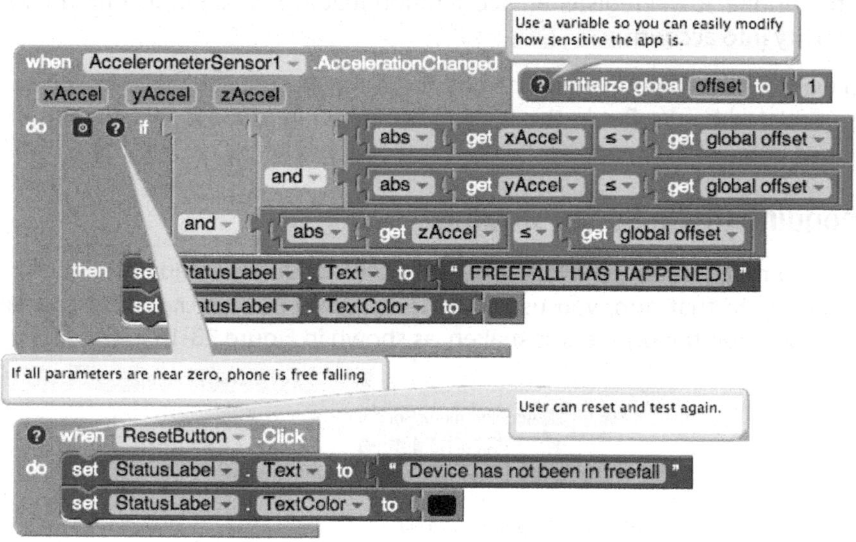

Figure 23-14. Reporting when a free-fall has occurred

1 You can right-click a block and choose "Inline inputs" to change the way blocks appear. This was done for the blocks in this example to reduce the width of the event handler.

Each time the sensor gets a reading, the blocks check the x, y, and z dimensions to see if they're near 0 (if their absolute value is less than 1). If all three are near 0, the app changes a status label to denote that the phone is in free-fall. When the user taps the `ResetButton`, the status label is reset to its original state ("Device has NOT been in free fall").

Summary

Sensors are of great interest in mobile apps because they make it possible for your users to truly interact with their environments. By taking computing mobile, you are opening up a whole world of opportunities in user experiences and app development. However, you'll need to think carefully about how, where, and when you use sensors in your apps. Many people have privacy concerns, and they might not use your app if they're worried about what you're doing with their sensor data. Still, with all the options in games, social networking, travel, and more, the possibilities for positive implementations are nearly endless.

CHAPTER 24

Communicating with the Web

Mobile technology and the ubiquitous nature of the Web have changed the world we live in. You can now sit in the park and do your banking, search Amazon.com to find reviews of the book you're reading, and check Twitter to see what people in every other park in the world are thinking about. Mobile phones have moved well past just calling and texting—now, you have instant access to the world's data, too.

You can use your phone's browser to reach the Web, but often the small screen and limited speed of a mobile device can make this problematic. Custom apps, specially designed to pull in small chunks of particularly suitable information from the Web, can provide a more attractive alternative to the mobile browser.

In this chapter, we'll take a look at App Inventor components that access information from the Web. You'll learn how to show a web page within the user interface of your app, and you'll learn about APIs and how to access information from a web service.

Creativity is about remixing the world, combining (*mashing*) existing ideas and content in interesting new ways. Eminem is among many artists over the past few decades who popularized the music mashup when he set his Slim Shady vocal over AC/DC and Vanilla Ice tracks. This kind of "sampling" is now common, and numerous artists, including Girl Talk and Negativland, focus primarily on creating new tracks from mashing together old content.

The web and mobile world are no different: websites and apps remix content from various data sources, and most sites are now designed with such interoperability in mind. An illustrative example of a web mashup is Housing Maps (*http://www.housingmaps.com*), pictured in Figure 24-1, which takes apartment rental information from Craigslist (*http://www.craigslist.org*) and mashes it with the Google Maps API.

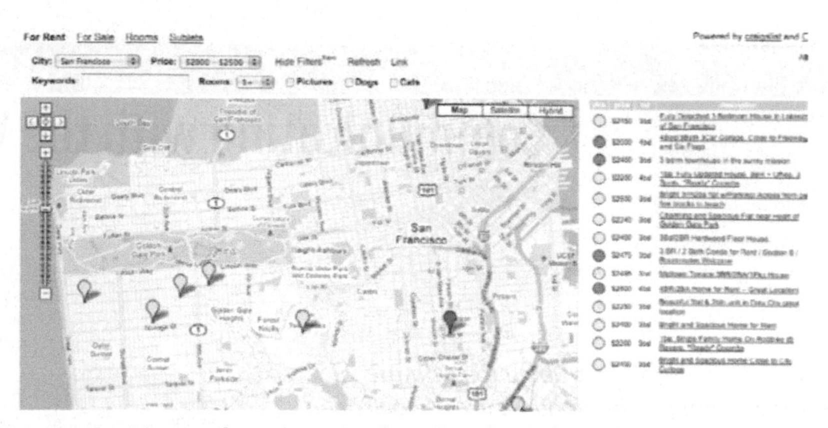

Figure 24-1. Housing Maps mashes information from Craigslist and Google Maps

Mashups akin to Housing Maps are possible because services such as Google Maps provide both a website and a corresponding *web service API*. We humans visit *http://maps.google.com/* in a browser, but apps such as Housing Maps communicate *machine to machine* with the Google Maps API. Mashups process the data, combine it with data from other sites (e.g., Craigslist), and then present it in new and interesting ways.

Just about every popular website now provides this alternative, machine-to-machine access. The program providing the data is called a *web service*, and the protocol for how a *client* app should communicate with the service is called an *application programmer interface*, or API. In practice, the term *API* is used to refer to the web service, as well.

The Amazon Web Service (AWS) was one of the first web services, as Amazon realized that opening its data for use by third-party entities would eventually lead to more books being sold. When Facebook launched its API in 2007, many people raised their eyebrows. Facebook's data isn't book advertisements, so why should it let other apps "steal" that data and potentially draw many users away from the Facebook site (and its advertisements!)? Yet, its openness led Facebook toward becoming a *platform* instead of just a site—meaning that other programs could build on and tap into Facebook's functionality, and no one can argue with its success today. By the time Twitter launched in 2009, API access was an expectation, not a novelty, and Twitter acted accordingly. Now, as shown in Figure 24-2, most websites offer both an API and a human interface.

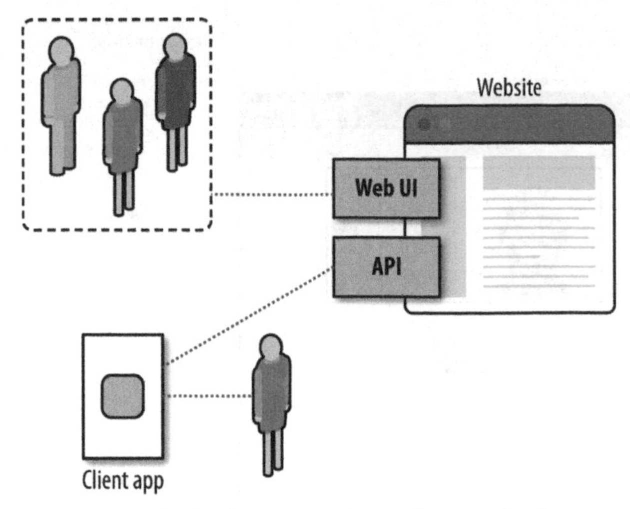

Figure 24-2. Most websites provide both a human interface and an API for client apps

Thus, the Web is one thing to us average humans (a collection of sites to visit). To programmers, it is the world's largest and most diverse database of information.

The WebViewer Component

The `WebViewer` component lets you show a web page within your app. You can show a Google Maps page showing the user's current location, a twitter page showing the most recent trending topics related to your app, or a page from nba.com showing the statistics for your favorite players.

`WebViewer` (see Figure 24-3) is like the `Canvas` component in that it defines a subpanel of the screen. But whereas `Canvas` is used for drawings and animations, `WebViewer` shows a web page.

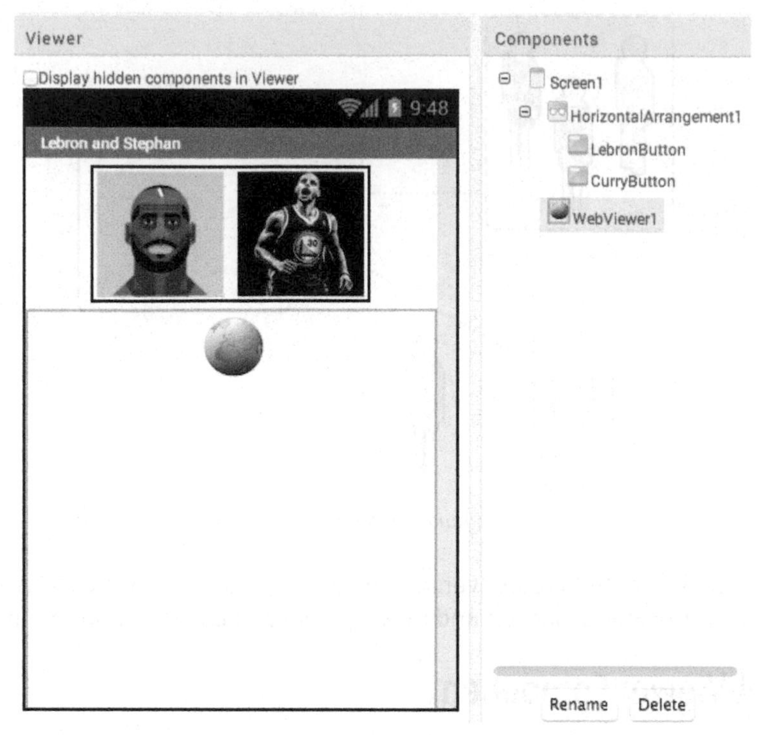

Figure 24-3. The WebViewer as it appears in Designer.

You can drag in a WebViewer from the User Interface drawer. You can then dynamically change the URL that appears, as in Figure 24-4, which depicts blocks from an app that shows the stats of NBA players Lebron James and Stephen Curry:

when LebronButton .Click
do call WebViewer1 .GoToUrl
url " http://www.nba.com/playerfile/lebron_james/ "

when CurryButton .Click
do call WebViewer1 .GoToUrl
url " http://www.nba.com/playerfile/stephen_curry/ "

Figure 24-4. Blocks to show the web page for the chosen players

If the user taps the picture of Stephen Curry, the app would show his page from *nba.com* in the `WebViewer`, as in Figure 24-5.

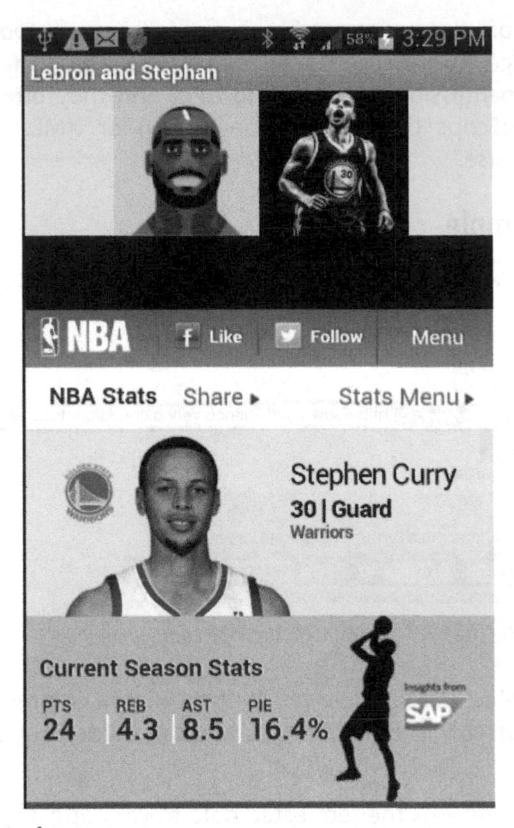

Figure 24-5. WebViewer in the app

The Web Component

Whereas `WebViewer` displays a web page, the `Web` component, a relatively new component in App Inventor, facilitates an app communicating with a web service via the standard Hypertext Transfer Protocol (HTTP). That protocol provides `Get`, `Put`, and `Post` methods for bringing information into your app. The information arrives not as a displayable page, but as data that you can display or process as you like.

The component is fairly low level, and using it requires some programming expertise. You typically set the `Web.URL` property to specify which web service you will communicate with, and then you call one of the HTTP methods to request some action. It's complicated because you need to understand the API of the web service (the protocol for communication), and you need to understand how to process the information that the web service returns to your app. This processing is known as parsing, and it is an advanced programming technique.

In this chapter, you'll be introduced to the `Web` component through a relatively simple example that accesses financial stock price information from a public API made available by Yahoo Finance. The protocol for talking to this API is fairly simple, and the data returned is in a list of values separated by commas (*comma-separated values*, or CSV), so it serves as a nice introduction to API communication. Unfortunately, most APIs have complicated permission schemes and APIs, and they often return data in formats such as JavaScript Object Notation (JSON) or XML, which require some advanced code to parse.

Stock Market Sample

Figure 24-6 shows the blocks for an app that displays Google stock information when the app launches.

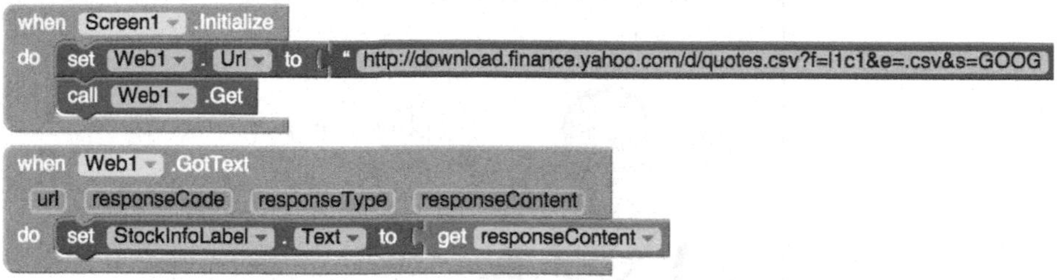

Figure 24-6. Accessing live stock information via the Web component

On `Screen.Initialize`, `Web1.Url` is set to the URL for communicating with Yahoo Finance. When `Web1.Get` is called, the request is made, but no data is returned immediately.

Instead, when Yahoo returns the requested data to your app, the `Web1.GotText` event is triggered, and this is where you can process the returned data. The event parameter `responseContent` holds the data. As just mentioned, the Yahoo Finance API returns data in CSV format. If you build this app and run it, you'll see that the current Google stock price and the change in the price for the day are displayed in `StockInfoLabel`, separated by commas.

You can customize the Web.Url to get the information for a different company (or companies), and to get various types of stock market information. The Yahoo Finance API, at *https://code.google.com/p/yahoo-finance-managed/wiki/CSVAPI*, specifies how you can change the URL to customize your request, as well as the format of the data it returns.

TinyWebDB and TinyWebDB-Compliant APIs

The `Web` component provides a method for accessing APIs. If an API is fairly simple, such as Yahoo Finance, novice programmers can use the `Web` component to directly access it. But other APIs, like the Amazon API introduced in Chapter 13, are more complicated.

For complicated APIs, an experienced programmer can set up a TinyWebDB-compliant web service that can then be used by less experienced App Inventor programmers to access the API. When such a service is set up, other programmers can access the web service with the simple tag-value protocol inherent in the `TinyWebDB.GetValue` function. You send a particular tag as the parameter, and a list or text object is returned as the value. In this way, the App Inventor programmer is shielded from the difficult programming required to *parse* (understand and extract data) standard data formats such as XML or JSON.

"TinyWebDB-compliant" just means a web service that follows `TinyWebDB`'s expected protocol: it expects a specific request, and returns data that TinyWebDB can understand. The Amazon API web service used in Chapter 13 is an example of such a web service, and can be used as a sample for programmers who would like to set up such a service (e.g., if you're a teacher and want to provide access to some API for your students).

In the past, building APIs was difficult because you not only needed to understand the programming and web protocols, but you also needed to set up a server to host your web service, and a database to store the data. Now, it's much easier because you can leverage cloud-computing tools such as Google's App Engine and Amazon's Elastic Compute Cloud to immediately deploy the service you create. These platforms will not only host your web service, but they'll also let hundreds of users access it before charging you a single dime. As you can imagine, these sites are a great boon to innovation.

The details of creating a TinyWebDB-compliant web service are beyond the scope of this book. But if you're interested, check out the documentation and samples at *http://appinventorapi.com/*.

Summary

Most websites and many mobile apps are not standalone entities; to do their jobs, they rely on the interoperability of other sites. With App Inventor, you can build games, quizzes, and other standalone apps, but soon enough, you'll encounter issues related to web access. Can I write an app that tells me when the next bus will arrive at my usual stop? Can I write an app that texts a special subset of my Facebook friends? Can I write an app that sends tweets? App Inventor provides three components that can talk to the Web: the `WebViewer` for showing a live web page; the `Web` component, for accessing information from an API; and the `TinyWebDB` component to access data in a specially designed web API.

Accessing an API can be complicated; you need to know the protocol for requesting information, and you need to process (parse) the often complex data returned. But the reward for learning how to do this is great; your apps can interact with the world!

Index

A

B

S

T

U

About the Authors

David Wolber is a leader in App Inventor education and teaching beginners how to program their phones and tablets. His focus is empowering artists, designers, kids, women, men, humanity majors, business students—makers of all types—to add coding to their creative arsenals. His teaching materials, video screencasts, and course-in-a-box are available at *appinventor.org*, and his students have been chronicled in articles of the *New York Times*, *San Francisco Chronicle*, and *Wired Magazine*.

David is a professor at the University of San Francisco. He taught one of the first App Inventor courses in 2009 as part of a Google pilot and has been teaching and working with the App Inventor teaching community ever since. His teaching materials on the Google and MIT sites, and on *appinventor.org*, have provided the first introduction to coding for thousands of new app builders, and his course-in-a-box materials have served as a template for many App Inventor courses at the K–12 and university levels. David recently took a sabbatical at MIT to work with coauthor Hal Abelson and contribute to the development of App Inventor 2. He is also contributing to the Mobile Computer Science Principles (*http://mobile-csp.org*) course for the new Advanced Placement (AP) course in US high schools.

Hal Abelson, a professor of Electrical Engineering and Computer Science at MIT, has a longstanding interest in using computation as a conceptual framework in teaching. He has played a key role in fostering MIT institutional educational technology initiatives, and is a founding director of Creative Commons and Public Knowledge. Hal's book, *Turtle Geometry*, written with Andrea diSessa in 1981, presented a computational approach to geometry that has been cited as "the first step in a revolutionary change in the entire teaching/learning process."

Ellen Spertus is an Associate Professor of Computer Science at Mills College, where she has taught with App Inventor, and a Senior Research Scientist at Google, where she was one of the App Inventor developers. She and her work have been written about In *Wired*, *USA Today* (which described her as "a geek with principles"), and in The *New York Times* (as one of three "women who might change the face of the computer industry"). In addition to her many technical publications, her writings have appeared in the book *She's Such a Geek: Women Write about Science, Technology, and Other Nerdy Stuff* and in the magazines *Technology Review*, *Chronicle of Higher Education*, *Odyssey: Adventures in Science*, and *Glamour*.

Liz Looney is a senior software engineer at Google, where she helped develop App Inventor. She started coding in high school and now has over 35 years of programming experience. She holds a bachelor's degree in Computer Science from the University of New Hampshire.

Colophon

The cover font is Gravur Condensed Black. The text font is Adobe Myriad Pro; the heading font is Adobe Myriad Pro Semibold Condensed; and the code font is Dalton Maag's Ubuntu Mono.

Lightning Source UK Ltd.
Milton Keynes UK
UKOW07f2343181117
312934UK00001B/2/P

9 781491 906842